CAPITALISM V. DEMOCRACY

MONEY IN POLITICS
AND THE
FREE MARKET CONSTITUTION

Timothy K. Kuhner

STANFORD LAW BOOKS
An Imprint of Stanford University Press
Stanford, California

Stanford University Press
Stanford, California

Printed in the United States of America on acid-free, archival-quality paper

Library of Congress Cataloging-in-Publication Data

Kuhner, Timothy K., author.
Capitalism v. democracy : money in politics and the free market constitution /
Timothy K. Kuhner.
pages cm
Includes bibliographical references and index.
ISBN 978-0-8047-8066-7 (cloth : alk. paper) --
ISBN 978-0-8047-9156-4 (pbk. : alk. paper)
1. Campaign funds--Law and legislation--United States. 2. Constitutional
law--United States. 3. United States--Politics and government. 4. United States.
Supreme Court. 5. Capitalism--United States. 6. Democracy--United States.
I. Title. II. Title: Capitalism versus democracy.
KF4920.K84 2014

324.7'80973--dc23   201.4004712

ISBN 978-0-8047-9158-8 (electronic)

Typeset by Bruce Lundquist in 10/15 Sabon

To Ana, Cindy, and Tom

Contents

Preface   ix

1   The Question Raised by America's Design   1

2   Free Market Democracy   33

3   Corporations Speak   65

4   Consumer Sovereignty   90

5   Why Capitalism Governs Democracy   141

6   Plutocracy   189

7   Capitalism and Democracy Reconciled   237

Notes   289

Bibliography   341

Index   351

Preface

AMERICAN DEMOCRACY RAISES THE STRANGEST QUESTIONS. Why does it cost nearly a billion dollars to mount a successful presidential election campaign? Why are corporations considered citizens and entitled to unlimited political spending? Will unaccountable organizations such as superPACs and dark money groups become more influential than political parties? How have citizens been forced into the role of consumers in a political marketplace? Indeed, how did democracy become a market?

For those who fought throughout our nation's history for political equality and popular sovereignty, these questions would prove fantastical or maddening. Civil rights movements occupied the better part of the last two centuries, as white males without property, women, and African Americans struggled to become equal citizens. It took several constitutional amendments to prevent political power from being officially conditioned upon property ownership, sex, and race. Today, however, political power is increasingly conditioned upon wealth—not exactly a satisfactory conclusion to centuries of progressive political reforms.[1] Foreign observers reinforce the point, marveling at how American democracy decides all manner of political issues through commerce, not civics, and wondering if commerce will someday become the new civics everywhere. After all, it would not be the first time that an American innovation spread across the globe.

These questions and concerns arise from money in politics. Political parties, political campaigns, and elections must be financed by one source or another. And in today's world, interest groups, lobbyists, and political ads in the mass media also receive tremendous financial backing. The sources, amounts, and implications of all those funds are addressed by an area of law called political finance or, more commonly, campaign finance. In the exercise of this responsibility, campaign finance law acquires profound power over the character of American democracy, shaping its opportunities for popular participation, modes of collaboration and competition, levers of control, and, ultimately, its loyalties.

Most Americans have heard of campaign finance reform, a social movement and grouping of laws that have attempted to diminish the role of money in politics. Despite its popularity among the general public and legislators, anyone observing U.S. politics and elections knows that campaign finance reform has been largely defeated. And so Americans have reluctantly become familiar with questions about the rising cost of elections, the political power of corporations and interest groups, and the diminishing role of ordinary citizens. Some are even developing a fatalistic sense that the problem of money in politics is too big to solve and that it is now pointless to ask principled questions about democratic integrity.

This book is based on the belief that such questions are essential, not pointless, and that a particular set of answers will motivate change. The following chapters discuss why money in politics is the defining issue of our time, how campaign finance reform has been defeated, how wealth has become a means of political exclusion, why this state of affairs corrupts capitalism just as much as democracy, and what sorts of principles could solve the problem. Of course there are many perspectives on each of these fronts. The tremendous number of relevant historical events, political practices, journalistic reports, legislative provisions, judicial decisions, academic studies, and political theories ensure an endless supply of arguments. Still, one current runs through all these components. I have followed this current long enough to conclude that it reveals the essence of the problem. Along the way, a possibility has etched itself into my mind. Perhaps the problem of money in politics has proved insurmountable only because it has yet to be seen for what it is: a series of conflicts between capitalism and democracy for control of the political sphere. To be clear, those who use financial means to control politics do not always seek to reduce the role of government and increase the role of the market; they often seek to reshape (or even increase the role of) government for their own purposes. Either way, however, money in politics co-opts the political sphere by substituting economic forms of empowerment and accountability for democratic ones.

This book exposes the problem's essence, lays out its implications, and offers it up for contemplation by a critical mass of citizens. This task could encompass many different areas of campaign finance law, including legislative debate, legislation, and judicial opinions. Each is bustling at local, state, and federal levels, where elections pose familiar concerns over money in politics. The problem is not even limited to the election of politicians, whether city council members, state legislators, governors, members of Congress, or the president. It extends to the election of judges as well, a common practice in the states. Although all of these areas deserve attention, they are not equally important for purposes of revealing the problem's essence and ultimate cause. This book makes a more focused inquiry, one shaped by the power dynamics in play.

The U.S. Constitution trumps inconsistent federal and state laws.[2] This legal hierarchy has determined the fate of campaign finance provisions at all levels. It even shapes the possibility of future reform, as lawmakers are hesitant to put the legislative process in motion only to see its creations dismembered on the constitutional chopping block. The judiciary wields an axe forged by the authority to invalidate legislation on the grounds of its unconstitutionality. As the nation's highest court, the U.S. Supreme Court has the last word in this process of judicial review. The Court has used its power to "say what the law is" viciously enough to refute the Federalist Papers' view: the judiciary is not "the least dangerous" branch.[3]

Initially just a concession to the facts of political life, this focus on constitutional interpretation soon rewards us with a view of the justifications for a democracy ruled by the market. Those of us with burning questions about democratic integrity will find a great many answers, but we will also discover unforeseen challenges. The situation is not merely one of expensive campaigns, officeholders beholden to big donors and spenders, interest-group competition, corporate political power, and a diminishing role for ordinary citizens. It is one in which such threats to democratic integrity are supported and even amplified by constitutional rights. Therefore, the question is not so simple as how to restore democratic integrity (and of course that question is hardly simple). The question, first and foremost, is how democratic corruption was sewn into the Constitution and how to unstitch those threads. Until this part of the problem has been addressed, democratic integrity will remain an unlawful endeavor. At present, those of us concerned with money in politics do not part from the desirable position of those seeking to correct a recognized problem. We begin instead from the position of constitutional dissidents, members of a legal counterculture.

Because democratic integrity is in a position far worse than commonly acknowledged, its prospects are immeasurably greater. As Chapter 1 describes the problem of money in politics and Chapters 2 to 4 locate its cause in the Supreme Court, we will experience a well-known paradox: sometimes things have to get worse before they can get better. The present level of money in politics and the violence done to the Constitution's values are bad enough to provoke the sort of clarity generally reserved for moments of crisis. Chapters 5 and 6 reinforce the point, exposing the theoretical weaknesses of the Court's approach to campaign finance reform and the practical effect of that approach—the creation of a market for political goods. Chapter 7 rounds out the book's deep, conceptual approach by explaining how the corruption of democracy leads to the corruption of capitalism and offering a path to restoring the integrity of both systems.

While the great majority of this material is new, some of it has been repurposed from articles I have published in law journals. These sources provide additional information on the cases I discuss and the implications of my approach for concerns as varied as constitutional law, democratic theory, human rights, and international law: "The Separation of Business and State," *California Law Review* 95 (2007): 2353; "Citizens United as Neoliberal Jurisprudence: The Resurgence of Economic Theory," *Virginia Journal of Social Policy and the Law* 18 (2011): 395; "The Democracy to Which We Are Entitled: Human Rights and the Problem of Money in Politics," *Harvard Human Rights Journal* 26 (2013): 39; and "Consumer Sovereignty Trumps Popular Sovereignty: The Economic Explanation for Arizona Free Enterprise v. Bennett," *Indiana Law Review* 46 (2013): 603. I wish to recognize these journals and their capable staffs.

Sincere thanks are due to Stanford University Press, in particular Kate Wahl, who first saw value in this book and motivated me to complete it, and Michelle Lipinski, whose patience and insight capably guided it through rounds of peer review and editing.

For comments on drafts, conversations about the issues, and support along the way, I thank Allison Averbuch, Kent Bicknell, Pablo Gómez

Blanes, Carl Bogus, James Boyle, María Jesús Taboada Calvar, Asunción de la Iglesia Chamarro, Sarah Dadush, Charles Derber, Megan Farkas, Alberto Muñoz Fernández, Sean Golan, Jared Goldstein, Kent Greenfield, Mary Alice Jasperse, Steven Kaminshine, Patricia Palomino León, David Logan, Michael Lonergan, Daniel Villar López, Gonzalo Gil López, Craig McEwen, Angel José Gómez Montoro, Rafael Domingo Oslé, Rafael García Pérez, Carmen Sevilla Pérez, H. Jefferson Powell, William Rooks, Phyllis Saarinen, Celeste Beck Sagi, Eric Segall, Nicolás Zambrana Tévar, Matthew Titolo, Anne Tucker, and Scott Wishart.

I also wish to thank the following institutions for supporting my research and hosting workshops to discuss my approach to money in politics: Georgia State University College of Law, The University of Navarra (especially its School of Law and La Fundación de Amigos de la Universidad de Navarra), Roger Williams University School of Law, and Duke University School of Law.

CAPITALISM V. DEMOCRACY

The Question Raised by America's Design

THE PRESENT MOMENT HAS ACQUIRED A RARE CONSTITUTIONAL quality, as though the essence of the country has become unstable and is on the verge of being redefined. Some say this is eternally the case—that citizens in a democracy can always exercise their political rights to bring about the changes they desire, and that a degree of instability is in the nature of a system of elected lawmakers. This view fails to admit that these fundamental ingredients—"citizens," "political rights," and "political representation"—are vulnerable to radical shifts, their meanings dependent upon the ideologies of those in power. Democracy is heading towards new meanings whose contours run deep in the waters ahead.

Sensational threats to democracy spring up to the surface and clamor for attention, but a different focus is now required. This is not the time to marvel at the faces of the FBI agents who found $90,000 in Congressman William Jefferson's freezer.[1] Nor is it the time to compare Jack Abramoff's boyish, admiring grin as he shook hands with President Reagan with his disdainful scowl years later as he strode into federal court, prepared to plead guilty to the corruption of public officials.[2] It would be useless to inspect the private wine lockers at the Capitol Hill Club where an engraved plaque once read, "Brent Wilkes"—Wilkes, the defense contractor who contributed to the more than $2.4 million in bribes that Representative Randy Cunningham accepted.[3] Focusing on bribery and other obvious forms of corruption—the rule breakers—recalls the bromide "rearranging the deck chairs on the *Titanic*."

The gravity of the moment is a function of what is legal, not what is illegal. In order to perceive democracy's vulnerability, we must leave the criminals aside, as colorful as they are, and train our eyes on the nation's present course. What sorts of citizens are becoming most influential and how do they exercise their political rights? Just one couple, the Adelsons, single-handedly prolonged Newt Gingrich's 2012 presidential primary run through $20 million in donations to a pro-Gingrich superPAC.[4] The Adelsons went on to donate an additional $130 million to other political organizations,[5] roughly the same amount that each presidential campaign spent in the 2000 election. One hundred and fifty-nine other individuals, corporations, and interest groups have followed the Adelson playbook, giving $1 million or more.[6] Other, more creative spenders, such as the Koch brothers, have propelled their preferred causes and candidates to prominence through funneling hundreds of millions of dollars into a variety of organizations and candidates. Meanwhile, one nonprofit association, ALEC, has succeeded in having thousands of bills based on its model legislation introduced in state legislatures.[7] Noting that approximately 17 percent of its bills get passed, ALEC bragged to its members that their donations were "a good investment," adding that "nowhere else can you get a return that high."[8] In 2010, AT&T, Pfizer, and Reynolds American agreed, contributing between $130,000 and $398,000 each to ALEC's treasury.[9]

And what about the course that lawmakers are setting for political representation? During the 2009 debate on health care legislation in the House of Representatives, more than a dozen officeholders gave speeches ghostwritten by lobbyists who bundle contributions for their reelection campaigns.[10] In a time of tornados, record-setting heat, and melting icecaps, lawmakers postpone emissions regulations and weaken environmental protections at the behest of entrenched companies.[11] As with natural disasters, so too with financial ones. On the same day they voted on the financial overhaul bill, legislators collected campaign money from the financial firms with the strongest interest in the outcome.[12] The same pattern occurs in other policy areas, as members of important congressional committees tend to take in 10 percent to 30 percent more donations during their tenure, "rais[ing] money from many of the same industries affected by their work."[13]

All of this is perfectly normal, predictable even. Everyone is doing exactly what the system encourages them to do, propelled forward by its momentum and incentives. Because political parties, campaigns, and political speech are almost exclusively privately financed, politicians and parties compete for funds, and the private sources contributing those funds exploit the situation in order to press their interests. As of the 2012 elections, it costs approximately $1 billion to become president,[14] $10 million to become a senator, and \$1 million to become a member of the House.[15] Candidates and officeholders depend on friendly donations and outside spending; and to the same severe extent, they fear unfriendly donations and spending. So long as such dependency and fear are operative, the political power of wealthy donors and spenders, corporations, superPACs, lobbyists, and special-interest groups is secure.

Beyond casting donors and spenders in the role of political master, however, candidates and officeholders' tremendous demand for political funds casts donors and spenders in the role of slave. A growing body of evidence shows that limits on donations and expenditures are, in essence, limits on the amount of money that politicians will extort from citizens and businesses.[16] Even former senators have confessed that "donors . . . feel shaken down" and that some dynamics behind money in politics are "more like extortion than . . . bribery."[17] The discovery that donors and spenders are both political predators and political victims strengthens the cause of campaign finance reform.

Whether they are spending money to pressure officeholders to enact favorable policies or spending money to appease officeholders who might otherwise punish them with unfavorable policies, donors and spenders feel tremendously insecure. What is to stop their competitors from outspending them? How do they know when they have employed sufficient funds to successfully press or protect their interests? Candidates face similar insecurity. How can they be sure that their cash reserves and campaign spending are sufficient to beat out their opponents? Because there is no limit to the total amount of money that campaigns or outside groups can raise and spend, an arms race ensues.

Spending on U.S. congressional and presidential campaigns topped \$6 billion in 2012, up from \$5.3 billion in 2008, and \$4.2 billion in 2004.[18] While each presidential campaign raised over \$1 billion in 2012, Obama and McCain raised little more than \$1 billion together in 2008. And yet that amount set a record in its time, outstripping the \$646.7 million raised by Bush and Kerry in 2004, and more than tripling the \$325 million raised by Bush and Gore in 2000.[19] A similar dynamic attends congressional elections. The \$448 million spent in House and Senate races in 1988, for example, was six times greater than the amount spent in 1976. And still, this number had tripled by 2006 and quadrupled by 2012, reaching $1.8 billion.[20] For candidates, these trends signal a rising financial bar for obtaining elected office. Interested individuals and groups, on the other hand, face a rising financial bar for obtaining political influence.

The price tags attached to political power have never been so daunting. For the first time ever, both presidential candidates rejected the public financing system passed in the wake of Watergate. Neither candidate was willing to limit himself to public funds in the final stage of the election and risk being surpassed by the other candidate's private funds. When all is said and done, campaigning seems better defined by private fundraisers than public rallies. Consider that President Obama appeared at 221 fundraisers in 24 states in the 2012 election season, a financial regimen that dwarfed his civic regimen of 101 rallies in 10 states during that same period.[21] Romney's fundraising routine was similarly rigorous and notably more informative than his public appearances. Audiences of donors, who commonly paid $30,000–$40,000 each, enjoyed detailed policy descriptions and long question-and-answer sessions. Public audiences, in contrast, were generally privy to nothing more than vague twenty-minute speeches with little or no time for questions.[22]

Various types of financial competition fuel the fundraising imperative. It has long been the case that political actors have to guard against being outspent by opponents within their same grouping—candidates versus candidates, parties versus parties, lobbyists versus lobbyists, and spending groups versus other spending groups. Lately, however, another dynamic has begun to fuel the money race as well: candidates and their parties scramble to avoid being outgunned by superPACs and dark money groups. This risk revealed itself to be formidable in the 2012 election as outside spending reached $1.3 billion,[23] a number equal to or greater than what both presidential candidates had raised in any prior election. Although each candidate aided the formation of one or more friendly superPACs to do battle against his superPAC foes, this only exacerbated the larger trend of candidates and parties being marginalized by unaccountable, private organizations.

By the end of the 2012 election, superPACs and dark money groups had raised more than the national party committees themselves. While the size of individual donations to candidates and parties is limited by law, the majority of superPAC funds came in the form of seven-figure checks.[24] And while parties, candidates, and even superPACs must disclose the identities of their donors, dark money groups, such as Karl Rove's Crossroads GPS, do not have to do so. As one dark money group told potential donors, "[N]o politician, no bureaucrat, and no radical environmentalist will ever know you helped . . . the only thing we plan on reporting is our success to contributors like you."[25] As a result of this strategy, the people and interests behind $400 million in 2012 election spending will never be known.[26] This even holds true for spending by the U.S. Chamber of Commerce, a nonprofit that serves as a political front for unlimited corporate cash.[27] In recent years, for example, Prudential Financial donated $2 million to the Chamber as part of its efforts against stricter financial regulations, and Dow Chemical donated $1.7 million to oppose the push for greater security at chemical facilities.[28]

The need to raise private funds did not end with the general election. Bruised and battered by the money race, President Obama solicited unlimited corporate and individual donations to fund his 2013 inauguration.[29] The invitation sent to campaign donors spelled out categories of donations between $10,000 and $1 million. As the amount increases, so do the perks, which include varying degrees of access to exclusive receptions and meetings, and varying numbers of tickets to the inaugural ball.[30] While the administration expected some donors to keep on giving after the election, other donors lined up to demand a reward—most notably, bundlers of significant campaign funds who now stand at the front of the line for diplomatic appointments as ambassadors to choice foreign nations.[31] The same occurred after the 2008 election when "[n]early 80 percent of those who collected more than $500,000 for Obama took 'key administration posts,' as defined by the White House."[32]

I. WARNINGS HEEDED IN VAIN

Power, exclusiveness, and distortion are among the themes common to these diverse examples of money in politics. In terms of power, nobody goes so far as to claim that money alone is *sufficient* for political success. Many well-funded candidates lose elections, and many wealthy spenders and interest groups have failed to get their way in elections and lawmaking.[33] Money is *necessary* for political success, however, and in increasingly high sums at that. Officeholders spend roughly half their time raising funds for their reelection campaigns, and the feasibility of candidacies, meanwhile, is judged by fundraising ability.[34] No candidate or politician can afford to alienate his or her donor base. Moreover, money has extraordinary power in certain contexts, such as lifting unpopular candidates to prominence, prolonging campaigns, influencing the legislative agenda, and saturating media markets with whatever political messages are favored by wealthy spenders—or even by just one wealthy spender.[35]

After power comes exclusiveness. Even in the context of donations to political campaigns and parties, where legal limits on money in politics are strongest, only one-third of one percent of citizens contributes over $200.[36] And yet those donations constitute the vast majority of all the money raised by candidates and parties in federal elections.[37] In the case of superPACs and dark money groups, where limits are weakest, 200 millionaires and billionaires (0.000063 percent of the population) stand behind roughly 80 percent of all the money spent.[38] In the end, 0.37 percent of the population supplies approximately 70 percent of all the money in politics.[39] It is little wonder that most Americans feel disenfranchised. Political freedoms appear trivial unless buoyed by significant cash; and when raised up in this way, political freedoms become a means of dominating those who lack financial resources.

Exclusion and domination at the individual level give way to distortion at the level of the system itself. The experience of self-governance and the outputs of the policymaking process cannot help being colored by the money race. Although they contain many shades of gray and do not always fall neatly within the lines, the hues and the basic forms they compose are evident. Candidates who are successful at fundraising go further; outside spending groups shape the debate; interest groups with deep pockets enjoy greater access, if not sway; organizations with a larger lobbying budget receive more attention than their competitors; congressional activity reflects the priorities of donors and spenders . . . and so on. When systematized and repeated in countless contexts, the conversion of financial power into political power distorts self-governance. What does democratic integrity mean in the system as we know it today? How do popular sovereignty and political accountability work in such a system? What is the present-day status of political equality?

To begin to answer such questions is to realize that American democracy is charting a precarious course, its regard for ordinary citizens dubious, its values open to question, its purposes uncertain, its nature shifting, and, ultimately, its legitimacy jeopardized. The problem is much less a function of individual instances of acute corruption than it is a widespread system of corruption, broadly understood. The question is not who cheats democracy, but who lawfully owns it. After all, the $90,000 in a particular officeholder's freezer matters less than the billions of dollars invested in officeholders' campaigns and their associated superPACs. The few lobbyists who con their clients are less significant than the thousands who bring their clients excellent returns on their political investments. Could the occasional legislative provision produced in conjunction with a bribe possibly matter more than the hundreds of thousands of provisions produced through an opaque interest-group process? Attention should be focused on the market for political power, the privileged position of the wealthy and corporations therein, and the laws produced thereby.

That focus matured quickly on American soil. Seventy-five years prior to the Declaration of Independence, the New World's first popular legislative body outlawed the bribing of voters.[40] And in the way of foreshadowing the problem in the United States proper, George Washington himself came under scrutiny for "treating" voters to refreshments, spending an amount worth more than the average voter's real assets.[41] Concerns over bribery and candidate spending soon gave way to our broader focus, spurred on by the words of democracy's and capitalism's icons. For example, note the fear expressed by the author of the Declaration of Independence. "I wish," Thomas Jefferson wrote, "never to see all offices transferred to Washington, where, further withdrawn from the eyes of the people, they may more secretly be bought and sold as a market."[42] On another occasion, he put it even more bluntly:

This country is headed toward a single and splendid government of an aristocracy founded on banking institutions and moneyed incorporations and if this tendency continues it will be the end of freedom and democracy, the few will be ruling and riding over the plundered plowman and the beggar.[43]

He suggested that his countrymen "take warning [from the case of England] and crush in its birth the aristocracy of our monied corporations which dare already to challenge our government to a trial of strength and bid defiance to the laws of our country."[44]

Decades later, Abraham Lincoln voiced a similar concern. Referencing the rise of corporate power during the Civil War, Lincoln predicted that "an era of corruption in high places will follow, and the money power of the country will endeavor to prolong its reign by working upon the prejudices of the people until all wealth is aggregated in a few hands and the Republic is destroyed."[45] Though he was witnessing the dismemberment of the United States, he assessed the danger of concentrated wealth in these terms: "I feel at this moment more anxious for the safety of my country than ever before, even in the midst of war."[46]

How did the father of capitalism feel about these concerns? In his revolutionary book, *The Wealth of Nations*, Adam Smith wrote that "[o]ur merchants and master-manufacturers complain much of the bad effects of high wages . . . [but t]hey are silent with regard to the pernicious effects of their own gains."[47] He described those who "employ the largest capitals" and "dealers in any particular branch of trade or manufacturers" as "an order of men whose interest is never exactly the same with that of the public, who have generally an interest to deceive and even to oppress the public, and who accordingly have, upon many occasions, both deceived and oppressed it."[48] Considering that these classes use their wealth to "draw[] to themselves the greatest share of public attention" and that they desire restraints upon competition and an increase in profits at the public's expense, Smith recommended that proposed laws be "long and carefully examined, not only with the most scrupulous, but with the most suspicious attention."[49]

It is as though Smith had traveled in time to read the latest exposés on ALEC. It would seem that Jefferson and Lincoln had joined him and made it their first priority to examine the cost of today's campaigns, the power of lobbyists in the legislative process, and the billions of dollars in corporate funds spent on political advertising. Their ancient warnings echo today: if economic power translates into political power, then democracy is threatened—its core values of political equality and popular sovereignty cannot survive.

Over and over again, citizens and their representatives have agreed, proclaiming that money unduly influences politics, that it is unfair for wealthy individuals and corporations to freely employ their economic power for political gain, that this displaces the role of the ordinary citizen, skews debate, corrupts the law-making process, and undermines the political accountability of lawmakers. Various packages of campaign finance reform have been enacted in the states and at the federal level, and numerous laws limiting the power of corporations in the political process have been passed. Those who catalog such reforms at the federal level alone cite 1883, 1907, 1910, 1911, 1925, 1940, 1946, several years in the 1970s, and 2001 as dates that Congress took action.[50] Reforms enacted at the state level are even more numerous.[51] All included, these political finance reforms have addressed many topics, including campaign contributions, campaign expenditures, political party funding, public financing for political campaigns, disclosure and transparency, individual expenditures, political action committee spending, and corporate political spending. Our moment in history becomes increasingly suspenseful as these laws are erased, one by one, from the books.[52]

II. THOSE WHO INSIST, "FULL SPEED AHEAD"

For anyone wondering why reforms are being eliminated and why the problem is being allowed to spiral out of control, it is a waste of time to pay much attention to the Congress, the president, state governments, or the public. Forget that the role of money in politics has long been contested in legislatures, state and lower federal courts, specialized agencies, boardrooms, political campaigns, the media, university classrooms, and even the street. Attention must be directed instead to those who have had the final say. The power of judicial review continues, time after time, to bring campaign finance reform efforts within the reach of the Supreme Court.

The pattern is clear: state and federal lawmakers restrict the role of money in politics, lawsuits are filed, and the Supreme Court ultimately declares some portion of the legislation unconstitutional. Comprehensive reforms are rendered ineffective, and meaningful future reforms are not attempted because their fate is a foregone conclusion. In short, we can count on the Court to riddle campaign finance laws with holes, if not to strike them down entirely, and we can count on resourceful lawyers and lobbyists to find their way through those tattered parchments. Taking in its considerable power, the Court once remarked, "[m]oney, like water, will always find an outlet."[53] Perhaps so. But this inevitability does not explain why the Court has created so many of these outlets itself. Indeed, the historical dynamic of Supreme Court reversals amounts to outlets of considerable width opened on purpose. Here lies the mysterious heart of the problem.

Limitations on political finance constrain freedom, economic freedom: citizens cannot bestow their wealth (or as much of it as they might like) upon political candidates and political parties. Corporations encounter additional limits—they are not treated as equal citizens in democracy. When lawmakers restrain political spending, they separate economic power from political power, and move away from economic conceptions of core values. They announce that speech, freedom, equality, and citizenship mean one thing in democracy and another thing in capitalism. This course decouples speech from money, equality from non-discrimination in political spending, and citizenship from incorporation. Those harmed by political finance reform, by these distinctions between the political system and the economy, have asked the Court to define speech as financial donations and expenditures competing for market share, freedom as freedom to spend, equality as no more than a formal condition in which nobody's money is turned down, citizenship as inclusive of corporations, and democracy as a free market. The Court has acquiesced to each request.

After striking down limits on how much candidates and campaigns could spend, a core component of the nation's first comprehensive law on political finance, the Court proceeded to free corporations to spend unlimited sums to influence state ballot questions. It accomplished this much between 1976 and 1978. Even Chief Justice Rehnquist's long and more critical leadership of the Court did not reverse these nation-defining holdings. The additions of Chief Justice Roberts and Justice Alito have moved the Court even further to the side of financial power. Joined by Justices Scalia, Thomas, and Kennedy, these fledgling Justices wasted no time in striking down many election laws, including the strictest campaign finance rules at the state level, the most promising form of public financing

for elections, and long-standing federal restrictions on corporate political·
activity. *Citizens United*, handed down in 2010, is the most infamous of
these cases, granting corporations a First Amendment right to unlimited
political expenditures.[54]

It is only natural for private interests to seek political influence. But
instead of permitting the states and the federal government to moderate
that natural tendency and provide for a principled democratic framework,
the Court has liberated big spenders and corporations. This would not be
such a bad thing if officeholders and parties were in a position to critically
evaluate the claims of the private parties and interest groups that clamor
for their attention. By striking down Arizona's public financing system,
one of the most effective nationwide, the Court has helped to ensure that
officeholders will not obtain such a position.[55] This precedent has frustrated
state and national efforts to prevent candidates from becoming dependent
upon (and ultimately indebted to) a narrow class of donors and spenders.

After issuing passionate dissenting opinions in *Citizens United* and
other related cases, Justices Stevens and Souter retired. Justices Kagan
and Sotomayor have taken up their predecessors' cause, but it is of little
use. Once Rehnquist and O'Connor were replaced by Roberts and Alito,
concern over money in politics became a minority position. Chief Justice
Roberts and Justices Scalia, Kennedy, Thomas, and Alito constitute a majority of the Court. These five men can rule however they like, a power they
have steadily directed against campaign finance reform since 2006. Their
rulings stand behind today's ever-increasing heights of money in politics.

III. PROPOSED SOLUTIONS

Responses to the problem vary more than one might expect. Some reforms
would eliminate all existing limits on money in politics so that candidates
and parties could better compete against superPACs and dark money
groups. Others would leave money in politics alone and focus instead
on changing corporations so that corporate political activity would seek
more progressive ends. And still others would strengthen limits on money
in politics, through either new legislation or a constitutional amendment.
Citizens face a choice between conflicting solutions, each promising to
lead democracy in a better direction.

It is too soon to choose, however, although not for the reasons one might think. True, the ink has barely dried on the Supreme Court's latest opinion on money in politics. And yes, new facts and figures on political spending will continue to arise, election after election. Still, the problem in choosing between reforms is not that there are new things we do not yet know; it is, rather, that there are old things we have not yet understood.

All reforms are crafted with reference, whether explicit or implicit, to Supreme Court rulings. Often enough, such proposals put forth a view of democracy that the Court has already contradicted. Other times, they build on the Court's view, but seek to extend it further than the Court intended. How can such proposals be evaluated if the Court's rulings have not been fully understood? How can we decide where democracy *should* go if we have yet to understand the reasons for its present course? Upon discovering those reasons, one can make an informed choice between reforms. The types of proposals on the table today initially demand attention, not judgment. In return, they offer to serve as a guide, focusing and grounding the inquiry into the Supreme Court's design for democracy.

A. Anti-Reform

To opponents of campaign finance reform, the rising tide of money in politics represents a movement towards a better democracy, a democracy with fewer limits on financial power. A popular initiative among Republican politicians and ultra-conservative policy groups is to relax or eliminate the limits on contributions directly to candidates and parties.[56]

The Supreme Court heard arguments along these lines on October 8, 2013, in *McCutcheon v. FEC*. A Republican activist and the Republican National Committee brought the case in order to challenge the aggregate limits on political contributions enacted shortly after the Watergate scandal. If the Court rules for the plaintiffs, the biennial contribution limits of $74,600 to non-candidate committees and $48,600 to candidate organizations will be struck down, ushering in a new era of multi-million dollar contributors.[57] Donors would still have to respect limits on contributions to each individual candidate and committee,[58] but without an aggregate limit, donors could spend up to $3.5 million each,[59] thus becoming a vastly more powerful force in federal campaigns and political parties. The next logical step (and subsequent item on the anti-reform agenda) is to abolish those individual contribution limits, enabling wealthy financiers to donate unlimited amounts to particular candidates and committees.

One notable libertarian organization, the Center for Competitive Politics, would abolish other rules as well, including the ban on corporate contributions directly to political campaigns and parties, and the disclosure rules that require the identification of individual and corporate donors and spenders.[60] The center describes campaign finance reform as "an assault on the First Amendment" and positions its agenda within its overall mission "to promote and defend citizens' First Amendment political rights of speech, assembly, and petition."[61]

James Bopp, a lawyer who has persuaded the Court to adopt this line of thought in several cases, believes that we have reached "the tipping point." Noting the ability of superPACs to rival candidate spending so rapidly after their creation, Bopp predicts that "they'll [soon] exceed candidate spending by 50 percent [and] [o]nce the Democrats realize there ain't any going back on this, then their contributors will start realizing the only thing they can do is participate." Bopp's prediction for superPAC spending in 2016? "[I]t'll be three times candidate spending."[62] Aside from its own importance as a major achievement of the anti-reform agenda, unlimited outside spending is a catalyst for the elimination of contribution limits. Illinois recently proved the point, suspending contribution limits once outside groups spend over $250,000 in a statewide race.[63] The new law seeks to allow candidates and parties to more effectively compete with superPACs. Commenting on the law, Bopp proudly announced, "We're in the endgame."[64]

Even if the Court were to defy Bopp and end its streak of holdings striking down campaign finance laws, the surviving laws would not necessarily be on safe footing. Although the Court long ago upheld the constitutionality of limits on individual contributions to parties and candidates, and bans on direct corporate contributions, it has not deemed such measures constitutionally required.[65] Nobody doubts that the Court would allow the Congress and the states to weaken or even repeal them.[66] The same goes for a bill, passed by the House of Representatives, to eliminate the limited presidential public financing system, another measure that the Court long ago upheld as constitutional.[67]

Anti-reformers pursue such legislative means, but they also go further, urging the Court itself to strike down the last remaining campaign finance laws. This end run around the Congress and state legislatures alike is entirely predictable. The Court's view of the First Amendment presently drifts towards "unlimited campaign freedom." Given this judicial mood, many cases are being primed and finessed with a view to finishing, once and for all, the messy judicial execution of campaign finance reform.

In order to explain why anti-reform is a plausible agenda despite the present extremes of money in politics, and in order to evaluate the terms of that agenda, we too must look to the Court. Why does the Constitution (as interpreted by the Court) protect the free flow of political funds? What aspects of the Court's vision of democracy demand further violence to campaign finance reform? Can this vision be justified or must it be corrected?

B. Corporate Reform

An influential group of scholars suggests that the best way to save democracy is to reform corporations, not campaign finance. Larry Ribstein summarized the new trend: "*Citizens United* shifted the debate over corporate speech from corporations' power to distort political debate to the corporate governance processes that authorize this speech."[68] Anne Tucker explains that this shift "from government legislation to the private sector . . . plac[es] the burden on the corporations and the shareholders . . . that have the resources to monitor corporate political contributions and the sway to influence corporate policies."[69] Unlike the anti-reformers discussed above, corporate reformers believe that money in politics, especially corporate money, is a cause for concern.[70] But rather than addressing campaign finance law, they would change corporate law in order to ensure that corporate political power be exercised in different ways and possibly for different ends.

For example, Kent Greenfield urges us "to focus on changing corporations themselves so that overturning *Citizens United* would be unnecessary."[71] Consider his assessment:

The reason why corporate political speech is so corrosive to democracy is that the benefits and prerogatives of the corporate form are marshaled to bolster the speech of a tiny sliver of the financial and managerial elite. The fact that corporations speak is not itself a problem; whom they speak for is.[72]

Adam Winkler confirms that "[m]anagement, not shareholders, makes the determination of what to say, where to say it, and how much to spend," concluding that "corporate speech is really corporate management's speech."[73] This could change, however. As Lisa Fairfax notes, "shareholders have launched an aggressive campaign to increase their voting power with the corporation[,] seeking to make the corporation more 'democratic.'"[74]

Part of the push for increased shareholder rights addresses political spending directly. The proposed Shareholder Protection Act "gives shareholders of public companies the right to vote on the company's annual budget for political expenditures."[75] Others would take corporate law in the same direction, providing "shareholders with a veto over the overall amount of corporate resources spent on political speech" and permitting them "to adopt binding resolutions concerning corporate political spending."[76] Shareholders across the country have increasingly demanded similar measures, and a popular petition urges the Securities and Exchange Commission to "force publicly traded corporations to reveal their political giving to shareholders."[77] Whether championed by Congress, law professors, shareholders, or the SEC, such reforms would respond to an age-old concern. Corporate speech was long seen as "amount[ing] to a misuse of 'other people's money': company executives were opportunistically misappropriating the company owners' money to purchase legislation benefitting the executives themselves."[78] Justice Stevens recently called it "coerced speech," noting that "shareholders who disagree with the corporation's electoral message may find their financial investments being used to undermine their political convictions."[79]

Greenfield and other corporate reformers have something more inclusive in mind than shareholder rights, however. They would make corporations accountable to corporate *stakeholders*, a group broad enough to include "employees, consumers, communities, and bondholders."[80] If the fiduciary duties of corporate managers and the composition of corporate boards of directors were altered to include stakeholders, corporate political power might be leveraged by and for a larger set of interests. Inspired by the possibility of robust corporate democracy, Greenfield offers a curious thought: "There is nothing inherently undemocratic in corporate speech, unless corporations themselves are undemocratic."[81]

Michael Siebecker helps to explain the realization that underlies Greenfield's remark.

[T]o the extent corporations increasingly dominate the political sphere itself, a new blend of political and business theory seems necessary to ensure the basic legitimacy of decisionmaking within the corporate setting . . . As decisions traditionally left to . . . standard political processes now get made—or controlled—by corporations, giving shareholders some of the traditional rights of citizens within a polity does not seem all that radical. In many respects, the corporation has become the new public forum in which political decisions get made.[82]

The tremendous power of corporations over the people they employ, the goods and services we all rely upon, the global flow of capital, and the health of any given economy is significant enough (and still growing); but, as corporate reformers recognize, corporations also exercise significant power over political advertising, the legislative agenda, and the information that informs decisions on that agenda.[83] Reformers' focus on how corporations make decisions must be understood in light of corporate dominance of the economy *and* the political sphere. If we concede that corporate power is and will remain so all-encompassing, then perhaps the best progressive strategy is to promote deliberative and more broadly accountable decision making within corporations. And so Siebecker imports political theory into the context of corporate governance, advocating "rules and incentives [in corporate law] to promote autonomous expression of ideas, fair and equal participation in the deliberative process, respectful consideration of expressed viewpoints, and the ability to alter previously accepted positions through continued discourse."[84]

If corporate spending is democratized to the point of shareholder accountability or even further to the point of stakeholder accountability, and if corporate decision making takes on more participatory and deliberative forms, the implication is clear: corporate governance is being converted into an acceptable form of political governance. Perhaps an inclusive, deliberative form of corporate governance would make the ever-expanding role of corporations in society a more benevolent and legitimate force.

We might concede, as Greenfield states, that "in the United States, the law of corporate governance is among the most conservative and least democratic in the developed world"[85] and that changes are due. But this is a separate issue from whether corporate governance, however inclusive and deliberative, should be allowed to become a proxy for political governance in the first place.

Even the broadest conception of stakeholder accountability would not encompass anything like accountability to all citizens; and even if this were imaginable, it would still be unimaginable for corporations to become units of representative democracy. Why do progressive scholars accept the challenge of legitimizing a polity of corporate citizens to begin with? What versions of popular sovereignty and political equality welcome corporate political participation as a democratic vehicle?

Again, we must look to the Supreme Court. Its interpretation of core political values has guaranteed corporations a sizable role in politics. Indeed, the Court's construction of democracy, speech, equality, and freedom has transformed political power into a corporate, capitalist, and, above all, economic phenomenon. Accordingly, progressive reformers have undertaken the challenge of democratizing capitalism for democracy's sake. This is not to deny the importance of corporate law reform in its own right or the possibility that it could function as an adjunct to political finance reforms. It is only to say that a logical order ought not be ignored: before deciding whether the political market should be more democratic, people ought to decide whether politics should be a market to begin with; before deciding how to make corporations better citizens within democracy, it is necessary to decide whether corporations should be citizens; before focusing attention on how to make corporate political spending a more representative force, attention is due to the question of whether corporations should have a right to political spending. The Court's work should be the first order of concern.

C. Partial Reform

Moving away from anti-reformers and corporate reformers, we come upon a number of proposals to regulate money in politics more strictly. Beginning with the most cautious, the DISCLOSE Act mainly pursued the humble goal suggested by its name.[86] Under the 2012 version of the act, dark money groups (principally 501(c)(4) organizations) would have to disclose their donors, and superPACs, already required to disclose, would have more frequent reporting obligations.[87] Meanwhile, corporations would have to disclose their political spending to shareholders via periodic reports and to the general public via their websites.[88] The 2010 version of the act went further. For instance, it barred expenditures by government contractors and by corporations with a specified degree of foreign control, including corporations with at least 20% foreign shareholders or a majority foreign presence on their boards of directors.[89]

Despite the variation in terms between 2010 and 2012, Senate Republicans mustered unanimous opposition to the DISCLOSE Act both times its proponents attempted to overcome a filibuster. Leading the opposition to the act, Mitch McConnell skillfully maligned its purpose: "advocacy groups ranging from the NAACP to the Sierra Club to the Chamber of Commerce . . . would now be forced to subject their members to public intimidation and harassment." He accused Democrats of trying to "shut up their critics" and "scare off the funders."[90] Although the Court continues to uphold basic disclosure rules,[91] Republican resistance to rigorous disclosure rules builds from a view of democracy that the Court has helped to construct. That view holds that political spending is a highly protected enterprise, one involving the exercise of sacred rights. As a *Wall Street Journal* article put it, the act "is a blatant attempt by its sponsors to do indirectly, through excessively onerous regulatory requirements, what the Supreme Court told Congress it cannot do directly—restrict political speech."[92]

Although Republicans have a material interest in shielding large donors and spenders from public scrutiny and opposing legislative terms that might favor political spending by unions over corporations, a principled view of the Constitution accompanies their pragmatism. They believe that core political rights protect economic investments in campaigns, parties, and independent committees. Some even view political spending as a form of speech so sacrosanct as to entitle its authors to remain anonymous. Meanwhile, some people on the other side of the aisle believe disclosure to be one of the last remaining ways to address money in politics without violating the Constitution. All of these beliefs suggest that we ought to get used to high levels of money in politics; and all of them are rooted in the Court's decisions.

The 2012 DISCLOSE Act falls on the opposite side of the spectrum from two separate sets of reforms that would test the limits of the Court's tolerance. The first is contained within the Presidential Funding Act and the Empowering Citizens Act, both introduced in Congress in 2012. These acts would strengthen the position of small donors and weaken the role of outside spending and special interests.[93] They provide for a voluntary system under which participating presidential and congressional candidates would accept lower contribution limits and swear off bundled contributions from lobbyists and political action committees in exchange for public matching funds.[94] The incentive is simple: the government would match small contributions (defined as $250 or less) five to one. Reformers believe this would encourage "candidates to rely on small, non-corrupting donations from regular voters, instead of contributions from mega donors seeking influence, access, and legislative favors."[95] Other parts of the legislation seek greater disclosure of donations to political committees, including superPACs and dark money groups, and attempt to prevent these same groups from unofficially coordinating their activities with candidates and party officials.[96]

The second set of reforms is contained in the American Anti-Corruption Act proposed by the Represent Us coalition, which includes such notable reformers as Trevor Potter and Lawrence Lessig. The Anti-Corruption Act aims to accomplish a series of remarkable tasks, including the following:

Prohibit members of Congress from soliciting and receiving contributions from entities, special interests, and lobbyists from industries they regulate. Limit the amount that lobbyists and their clients can contribute to federal candidates, political parties, and political committees to $500 per year. Mandate full transparency of all political money. Empower voters by creating an annual $100 Tax Rebate that can be used for qualified contributions to one or more federal candidates, political parties, and political committees.[97]

Beyond this, the act would also strengthen enforcement of existing campaign finance laws, impose contribution limits on SuperPACs, make it more difficult for superPACs to coordinate their messages with candidates and parties, and prevent elected representatives and their senior staff from accepting employment as lobbyists shortly after leaving their posts.[98]

These reforms raise a host of questions. Why not simply cap super-PAC spending? Although a five-to-one match is a generous public financing equation, might not privately funded candidates still outspend their publicly funded rivals? Instead of a matching system, why not establish a trigger-mechanism system in which public funds are distributed in step with private funds routed to other candidates? This would ensure that publicly financed candidates could compete with privately financed ones. Or why not establish limits on spending by candidates and parties, ensuring in this way that public candidates would not be outgunned? Indeed, why not simply mandate public financing for federal campaigns? This is, after all, the reform measure requested by a wide-ranging group of corporate executives seeking to free themselves and their companies from the competitive pressure to spend on politics.[99] And finally, why not simply abolish contributions and bundling by lobbyists, limiting the role of lobbying to the provision of information?

The narrow, technical nature of the measures proposed by reformers provides the necessary clue. Their authors are walking on eggshells and tinkering around the edges of a larger problem. Any other course of action would open them up to censure by the Supreme Court. Indeed, even the limited reforms they propose would contradict the spirit and direction of the caselaw by reducing the power of donors and spenders. As the Court takes new appeals and continues to extend its views, these reforms might be struck down despite their cautious and incremental nature. Their ability to withstand constitutional challenge cannot be appraised without reference to the caselaw. The same holds for their desirability. Alternatives to the status quo cannot be assessed without first examining the reasons for the status quo.

D. Constitutional Reform

A final group of reformers wants to confront the Court and address the problem head-on. They maintain that money in politics requires fundamental changes of the sort anticipated by Article V of the Constitution.[100]

The Constitution's admission that amendments might be necessary reflects a certain humility and foresight. Consider George Washington's view, expressed while the thirteen states were busy deciding whether or not to ratify it: "The People (for it is with them to Judge) can, as they will have the advantage of experience on their Side, decide with as much propriety on the alterations and amendments which are necessary . . . I do not think we are more inspired, have more wisdom, or possess more virtue, than those who will come after us."[101]

Nonetheless, those who have come after Washington and his fellows were not given an easy road. Even if their experience, inspiration, wisdom, and virtue counseled constitutional reform, Article V demands widespread agreement on the proposed solution.[102] James Madison wrote that its requirement of three-quarters of states, if not two-thirds of Congress as well, "guards equally against that extreme facility [of amendment], which would render the constitution too mutable; and that extreme difficulty [of amendment], which might perpetuate its discovered faults."[103] Reformers face a tremendous burden in terms of demonstrating the Constitution's faults and achieving a vast consensus on the proper solution.

One year after the *Citizens United* case, the nonprofit organization Public Citizen brought 750,000 signatures to Congress, proposing that the Constitution be made to reflect that "the First Amendment . . . was designed to protect the free speech rights of people, not corporations."[104] By late November 2012, approximately 350 municipalities, 12 states, numerous members of Congress, and even the president had joined the call for an amendment in one form or another.[105] Millions of voters registered their agreement on ballot questions to the same effect.[106] Attempting to gauge overall popular support, a small nationwide poll found that 87% of Democrats, 82% of Independents, and 68% of Republicans favor an amendment to reverse *Citizens United* specifically.[107]

Proposed amendments address much more than corporate speech rights, however. The Move to Amend coalition and Senator Bernie Sanders, for example, would revoke all corporate rights under the Constitution.[108] Such broad proposals derive from an expansive view of the problem. Consider that the Alliance for Democracy, a member of Move to Amend's steering committee, hopes to "free all people from corporate domination of politics, economics, the environment, culture and information."[109] The other portion of Move to Amend's proposal aims at a narrower target: "Federal, State and local government shall regulate, limit, or prohibit contributions and expenditures, including a candidate's own contributions and expenditures . . . The judiciary shall not construe the spending of money to influence elections to be speech under the First Amendment."[110]

This reformers' potpourri—ending corporate speech rights, ending corporate constitutional rights more generally, lowering contribution limits, establishing expenditure limits, and uncoupling political spending from free speech—almost rounds out the harvest of constitutional discontent. Other major proposals include mandatory public financing of campaigns,[111] a constitutional reinforcement of the existing ban on corporate contributions to candidates,[112] and the creation of a new body to enforce the terms of campaign finance law.[113] On balance, reform measures target the matter of money in politics above abstract questions of corporate power. To summarize, the fault discovered over the course of the nation's life is the undue influence of wealth in the political process.

To blame the Constitution for this is to allege a sin of omission. In striking down limits on money in politics, the Court has claimed to be doing the Constitution's command; but the Constitution does not mention the financing of elections or the financing of political speech, much less speech by corporations. How can a document that does not mention such issues prevent legislators from responding to them? As interpreted by the Justices, the Constitution has come to protect political spending as a right and strike down even conscientiously crafted reforms.

As in the cases of anti-reform, corporate reform, and partial reform, constitutional reform responds to the tangible realities of money in politics and to the Supreme Court holdings that make those realities possible. Awareness of the Court's holdings, however, its actions in the name of the Constitution, is nothing like a full sense of the Constitution's received faults. The entirety of those faults, the true and faithful quantity of political will aroused thereby, and the resulting consensus on the necessary alterations will not reveal themselves so easily.

Beyond protecting today's system of money in politics, the Court's rulings defend and legitimate it. When the Court speaks, it says what the law is and why the law is just. Its written opinions contain justifications addressed, curiously enough, to a political community that by and large never reads a word of them. Hiding amidst many pages of legal prose, those justifications speak to the way democracy should be, a way made authoritative by phrases such as "the Constitution requires." The missing actors, energies, and perspectives in the debate are those that would manifest if all citizens were exposed to the Court's ideas about democracy. These are the ideas, after all, that environ the Constitution with meanings it never had before, shaping our experience of self-government and providing the backdrop against which reforms must be judged. And still, even that formidable backdrop sits upon a larger stage.

IV. THE QUESTION RAISED BY AMERICA'S DESIGN

The Supreme Court, anti-reformers, corporate reformers, partial reformers, and constitutional reformers all agree on one thing. Money in politics is an inherently constitutional matter, "constitutional" in the broad sense of the makeup, essence, and structure of a thing. Those who defend money in politics defend a particular interpretation of democratic values, namely, the opposite interpretation advanced by partial and constitutional reformers. Meanwhile, corporate reformers attempt to maintain democratic baselines despite the changing vehicles of political power. All have their eyes fixed on American democracy, sensing that its essence fluctuates as the levers of political finance are set here or there. Before addressing the Court's placement and employment of those levers, it is important to recognize that those decisions represent constitutional judgments within law about a constitutional question within society. To what extent should economic power be allowed to translate into political power? The Court, together with all varieties of reformers, advances upon difficult terrain. The landscapes encountered here reveal deep, conceptual keys to the status quo, the caselaw that maintains it, and the reforms that would change it.

The United States was born of economic and political revolutions. The British Empire famously taxed and interfered in the colonies. The king prevented the colonists from deciding economic and political matters for themselves—prevented them, that is, from being a people free to fashion their own destiny. Blueprints for liberties so strongly desired were not long withheld. The Declaration of Independence and *The Wealth of Nations* were both published in the same year, enunciating new principles of justice and inspiring a contagious sense of untapped potential. Political and economic liberties were soon heaped upon a vast territorial expanse—new frontiers lavished upon new frontiers. It was suddenly for citizens to choose their own government and influence public policy, just as it was for them to decide their own trades and crafts and freely pursue them. Both sorts of choices were to be made within an environment of unprecedented opportunity, and their produce was not to be artificially lessened. A state set upon dictating one's course, capturing one's output, or aiding one's competitors was no longer tolerable. Politics and markets were on their way to becoming the people's domains.[114]

Democracy and capitalism claimed to answer the largest of questions. How was liberty to be guaranteed and wealth to be reliably produced? How could society be organized so as to provide opportunities for the bettering of one's person and one's fortune, while simultaneously bettering one's community? What economic and political principles were worthy of a free people's allegiance? Clues to the answers lay in the revolutionary rejection of noble birth and religious standing as criteria for political or economic power. By rejecting aristocracy and theocracy, the Framers emancipated the realms of economy and state. Indeed, these realms could be separated only by breaking up authoritarian systems. People and their produce had generally been dominated by the king, who saw little need to distinguish between the state and the economy.

As capitalist notions of economic freedom and democratic notions of political freedom were affirmed, a new question worked its way through the American landscape. Economic freedom (and productivity) had been linked to competition and the absence of state control. Political freedom (and legitimacy), on the other hand, had been grounded in debate, elections, and representative politics—that is, a state controlled by the people. The most profitable of arrangements is not necessarily the most legitimate, however. The tension goes the other way as well: there is no reason to suspect *ex ante* that the most politically legitimate outcome will produce the greatest profit, at least not in the self-interested calculations of each party.

This tension has been evident in struggles surrounding slavery, the labor movement, and environmental protection. On these and other fronts, the most essential of concerns—profit and legitimacy—have often counseled disparate courses of action.

The question is no longer whether democracy and capitalism are superior to their competitors; it is, rather, how to judge cases in which democracy and capitalism are competitors. The salient issues are thus relational, not absolute: How should democracy and capitalism interact? Which should prevail in the event of conflict? These general questions come up in countless contexts beyond money in politics. Consider, for example, the regulation of financial markets; state funding of education; government health care programs; prohibitions on drugs, the sale of body parts, and prostitution; and privately run jails. In each case, the question is whether (or to what extent) a given area of activity should be governed by the market or by the state.

In many cases, it is politically acceptable to argue that the market should govern. Today, health care reform is a paradigmatic case: Throughout the 2010 health care debate and election cycle, Republican opponents of the government plan regularly accused President Obama of being a socialist and proclaimed that the matter should be left to the market. Others maintained that it is necessary on ethical and pragmatic grounds for the state to intervene in the market and construct a safety net. Financial overhaul is also exemplary in that good arguments can be made for and against market control. Legislators rightly ask whether matters of financial products, such as derivatives, ought to be decided by the market or if the state should be allowed to preclude arrangements that lead to financial crisis. Matters are thus allocated to one system or another (or to both but in varying degrees).

Money in politics is also a paradigmatic case, but it represents the opposite paradigm. The belief that the market should govern politics is never publicly voiced. After all, candidates, political influence, and public policy are not supposed to be commodities or investments. Elections and political debate are located within democracy's territory. Because it would be too politically unpopular to argue that the market should govern, the argument takes an ideological form. One begins to hear claims that *market conceptions* should govern. Litigants and Justices speak the language of political legitimacy, but deeper meanings furtively play out in these terms.

For example, in cases on the prohibition of political expenditures from corporate treasuries, corporations claim that their speech is being censored and that this is politically illegitimate (per the Constitution). They do not claim that their profit margins are being harmed by the inability to influence legislation, or that regulations on political expenditures interfere with the market for political goods. The same distributive interest can be pursued, however, by contending that the Constitution protects "political free trade," a "political marketplace," or an "uninhibited marketplace of ideas."[115] If speech and democracy are construed in this way, then restrictions on the role of wealth amount to censorship. Political legitimacy is proving this malleable.

As the Constitution takes on a capitalist hue, an answer is given to the question raised by America's design: democracy must be privatized so that the market can govern the state. That answer is so categorical and frightful, however, as to require that the question be raised again and again until a better answer is given. Consider, for example, that the choices to pass only the weakest of financial reforms and to allocate matters of health care almost entirely to the market mean a great deal. Millions of Americans may not receive health care coverage, financial markets may remain turbulent waters of speculation, and millions of people's retirement funds will be more or less secure. But even so, these are individual portions of a larger contest, battles to be won or lost within a far greater war. Surely there will be more or less market control over particular portions of society, but if citizens find the ensuing state of health care and financial products objectionable, they can resort again to the political process. If the choice of health or financial regulations was made because lawmakers could not afford to alienate important financial donors, however, then the resulting choices mean something else entirely, something far more important.

Money in politics is unique among the conflicts between capitalism and democracy, because it concerns much more than the resolution of particular issues. It is the nature of money in politics to affect the process through which all issues before the government are resolved. If given enough leeway, it becomes the skeleton key that unlocks all doors, a privatization process through which political power is aligned with capital.

In matters of political inequality on the bases of race and sex, American history has borne witness to an evolving political community. Not so with political inequality on the basis of material wealth. The nation tolerated all three inequalities at its birth, and radically so, but only one has been praised and defended to this day. It is no longer acceptable for political power to be conditioned on race or sex, but socioeconomic status has proved to be a special case. Americans have learned to pursue, create, and spend wealth more vigorously than the people of any other nation. Should our national aptitude for trading, investing, producing, purchasing, and organizing in the corporate form be harnessed within democracy as well as capitalism? Doing so would give the wealthy a political advantage over the rest of society, but should that matter? Do not all people, natural and corporate alike, have a right to dispose of their own property—money included—as they please? Could not the *exchange* of ideas, political *consumers* and *entrepreneurs*, *incentives* for political action, and political *markets* all be invigorated by the same means as their economic equivalents?

There is something familiar about the Koch brothers, the Adelsons, George Soros, Foster Friess, and big corporate spenders. We know their names and faces from capitalism's hall of fame, but that does not explain the familiarity. An unbearable mix of collective emotions provides the clue: How can their lavish political spending be so repulsive and so attractive simultaneously? Rather than statesmen or robber barons, the big donors and spenders of the political class are an uncomfortable mixture of the two. And their produce can be similarly hard to judge. After candidates lower themselves to the status of the endorsement seeker or the beggar, they balloon up with funds and their messages explode across the land. At the same time when viewers are sickened by attack ads, media markets are invigorated by campaign spending. Certainly some of the pressure groups operate in the shadows and much legislation reeks of cigar smoke, but the interest-group process does bring a tremendous amount of energy and information to the capital—almost that same frenetic dynamism of the trading floor, that same relentless movement, that same purity of un-abashed self-interest.

Big donors and spenders are so familiar because they appeal to the consumer-investor-producer-seller inside each citizen, reminding the people that this land is not just a democracy. The political elite trigger a remembrance within all who observe politics, that of a question that must not be forgotten or set aside: to check financial power or to set it free? Rather than attempting time and time again to engineer a political community with democratic procedures, why not just let the market sort it out?

The perennial debate over money in politics provides a prime example of a polity fractured by incompatible allegiances, a polity that has not mastered the darkest and most conflictual aspect of its own character. This is not the recognition that the United States straddles the two most powerful systems in existence; it is, rather, the sobering confession that the nation has long been divided as to which system should prevail in the event of conflict.

Capitalism versus democracy—this is the underlying structure of money in politics controversies. It is their neglected essence and, perhaps, the analytical key to resolving this perennial conflict. American values and institutions derive from two different systems, each of incredible power, whose terms are sometimes irreconcilable. Each of these systems has long been focused on defeating its competitors. Capitalism faced off against mercantilism and was recently challenged globally by the central planning of communist regimes. Liberal democracy was a response to aristocracy and has since been challenged by authoritarian bureaucracies, dictatorships, and even theocratic elements. These conflicts were so intense and damaging that nobody is eager to do what the money-in-politics cases have long asked of us: to look inward, own up to the antagonistic potential of America's design, and confront the question it poses.

V. WHERE DOES THE FREE MARKET BELONG?

Consider what our constitutional architects set in motion. Political leadership would be accountable to the people, not a king, the church was walled off from the state, and the powers of the state were dispersed among different governmental institutions. It is fair to say that they sought to emancipate the sphere of politics. The same could be said for the economy, which was to become a place of free competition, open to all comers and relatively free of government control. Following through on this design, liberal democracy weakened, discredited, and defeated some of the greatest structural tyrannies of all time: theocracy, monarchy, dictatorship, and central economic planning.[116]

Still, one persistent source of tyranny remains. Communism allowed the state to dominate the market (and the rest of society). Should American democracy allow the market to dominate the state (and the rest of society)? Should it enthrone the wealthy as communism had enthroned the party, theocracy the pious, and aristocracy the wellborn?[117] While some democracies provide robust public funding for campaigns and parties, ensure public access to the media, limit the election period, and limit corporate expenditures,[118] the Court has indicated its hostility to such measures, striking many of them down. Its rulings enthrone those who possess or favor capital, a substance with no formal ties to party, lineage, or religion. Indeed, an anthropologist observing the United States might conclude that the robed architects of this particular society are in the process of adopting capitalism as a political system.

Given the Court's power to decide the constitutionality of legislation, the Constitution's short and often vague text produces a large quantum of judicial power. Election law scholars Samuel Issacharoff and Richard Pildes note that "[t]he Constitution is silent on virtually all the important issues regarding elections, from the method to be used for casting ballots, to the electoral system for all public offices save the President and Senate [and] issues of how elections are to be run and financed."[119] Constitutional scholar H. Jefferson Powell adds that "[t]he constitutional text itself presupposes that its interpreters will go outside the four corners of its language."[120] Powell's conclusion is central for us: "[J]udges . . . have always recognized (if implicitly) what the theorists are reluctant to admit, that there is no technological means of excluding politics from constitutional law."[121] Outcomes flow from a highly contested exercise in constitutional interpretation, which itself flows from the Justices' ideologies.

Although this might sound like an end to the question, it is actually the beginning. In his landmark survey of political-economic systems, Charles Lindblom put it this way: "[W]hen political science turns to institutions like legislatures . . . parties, and interest groups, it has been left with secondary questions."[122] According to Lindblom, the primary question upon which the operation of these institutions and actors depends is "the degree to which government replaces market or market replaces government."[123] It is one thing to invoke the market as an analogy to encourage competition between individual opinions on matters of political importance. It is quite another thing to do so in cases involving the proper role of money (market currency) or corporations (market actors) in the political process. The Court's application of market benchmarks to such cases opens the door to massive sums of money and strategic economic entities. Market then replaces (or controls) government to a greater degree.

This sort of broad-brush, ideological question often haunts society's architects when their structures come crashing down. Consider Alan Greenspan's monumental confession at the beginning of the latest economic crisis. As subprime lending and the housing bubble reaped disaster, Greenspan faced his congressional questioners. "You had a belief that 'free, competitive markets are by far the unrivaled way to organize economies,'" Representative Henry Waxman began.

You had the authority to prevent irresponsible lending practices that led to the subprime mortgage crisis [and] you were advised to do so by many others and now our whole economy is paying its price. Do you feel that your ideology pushed you to make decisions that you wish you had not made?

Greenspan responded:

An ideology is a conceptual framework with the way people deal with reality. Everyone has one. You have to—to exist, you need an ideology. The question is whether it is accurate or not. And what I'm saying to you is, yes, I found a flaw . . . [a] flaw in the model that I perceived as the critical functioning structure that defines how the world works, so to speak.[124]

Greenspan's ideology was instrumental in letting certain things be: derivatives markets, unconscionable mortgage products, skyrocketing CEO pay that encouraged excessive risk taking, the lack of capital requirements for firms "too big to fail," and, on the whole, a financial system with insufficient structural safeguards. And so, to explain why these are "uncomfortable times," the *Wall Street Journal* reported that "[t]he *laissez-faire* shibboleths of the last 30 years are in pieces on the ground."[125]

The question is whether democracy is falling victim to the same ideology—that is, whether Supreme Court Justices are dealing with reality in the same way Alan Greenspan did. It would be ironic if the ideology that Greenspan recently repudiated—a conceptual framework that assumes a perfect market and resists government efforts to ensure fair play—were discredited within economics but thriving within constitutional law. If this were the case, then it might not be coincidental that democracy is in a crisis comparable to the one that recently affected the economy. Low rates of popular participation, a cynical and disingenuous political debate, increasing price tags on elections, and a set of incentives that seems to prevent good-faith efforts to solve public problems are all widely observed.[126]

In order to understand the Justices' reasoning and the ideology beneath it, one must meet them on their own terms and their own turf. They offer official explanations for the choices they make in one place only. Although long and complex, the Court's written opinions brim with answers, which, if collected and pieced together, point to the ultimate explanation for money in politics today. A select few who teach and write in this field have glimpsed the heart of the matter but declined to provide a full demonstration. For example, Cass Sunstein concludes that the "goals of political equality and political deliberation"—the goals of campaign finance reform—"are related to the project of distinguishing between the appropriate spheres of economic markets and politics."[127] Richard Hasen concurs, noting the need to "recognize the differences between politics and economic markets."[128] Perhaps most tellingly, Owen Fiss has called the 1970s a time "when America wondered out loud whether capitalism and democracy were compatible."[129] He characterized a variety of cases as examining the "relationship between political and economic power,"[130] and concluded that "[c]apitalism almost always won."[131]

Nobody has yet shown what it means for capitalism to "win" within the pages of Supreme Court opinions on money in politics. What are the elements of the Court's ideology? How has the Court gone about making civic conceptions unconstitutional and market conceptions obligatory? How has this juxtaposition between capitalism and democracy played out in the cases that have determined the role of money in politics today? These questions direct our attention to the reasoning that colors the Constitution and controls its application to real-world controversies over political finance. Therein lies the key to the law as it stands and the law as it is becoming.

An examination of the most important Supreme Court cases leads to a deep understanding of the problem. Then comes the time to entertain today's burning questions: What has happened to democracy and capitalism as a result of the Court's approach? Can an alternative approach be found and the crisis alleviated?

CHAPTER 2

Free Market Democracy

PAUL KRUGMAN, A 2008 NOBEL LAUREATE IN ECONOMICS, characterizes the 160 years between the *Wealth of Nations* and the Great Depression as the time in which a new faith manifested: "[A]n extensive body of economic theory was developed whose central message was: Trust the market."[1] Krugman calls faith in the market the "basic presumption of 'neoclassical' economics."[2] The story of this faith is the story of many twists and turns—nothing less than the history of American capitalism.[3]

The Great Depression and John Maynard Keynes's calls for government intervention—including changes in fiscal policy and public works projects—diminished collective trust in the market. But shortly after the Keynesian revolution, Milton Friedman led a new push against government intervention under the guise of monetarism. Krugman describes the 1970s, Friedman's moment, as a time when "[d]iscussion of investor irrationality, of bubbles, or destructive speculation had virtually disappeared from academic discourse," replaced by "the 'efficient-market hypothesis.'"[4] That hypothesis "held that as more stocks, bonds, options, futures, and other financial instruments were created and traded, they would inevitably bring more rationality to economic activity."[5] There was an emerging consensus that prices in the market were a reflection of full information and that the market produced the right goods for the right people at the right prices— i.e., people could not beat the market and the market allocated resources without wasting them. The implication, as Justin Fox points out, is that "markets possessed a wisdom that individuals, companies, and governments did not."[6]

Although Friedman was a complex figure, it is fair to say that he was a leading proponent of the view that markets were "better, and far more accommodating of human liberty, than government."[7] He was, in his own words, "deeply concerned about the danger to freedom and prosperity from the growth of government." Friedman understood his own work as a response to the "readiness to rely primarily on the state rather than on private voluntary arrangements to achieve objectives regarded as desirable" and noted that his contrary position had for long been associated with a "small beleaguered minority regarded as eccentrics."[8] He labeled as a "flash of genius" Adam Smith's discovery that "the prices that emerged from voluntary transactions between buyers and sellers . . . could coordinate the activity of millions of people . . . in such a way as to make everyone better off." "The price system," concluded Friedman, "is the mechanism that fulfills this task without central direction."[9]

This faith in markets—-markets as wise, efficient, free, and in any case better than government—was bolstered in 1976 when Friedman was awarded the Nobel Prize. That same year, the Supreme Court converted the ongoing celebration of market wisdom into judicial reasoning in what would become one of the most important constitutional law opinions of all time.[10]

Buckley v. Valeo served as the Supreme Court's referendum on a new era of campaign finance reform.[11] From the colonial era through the New Deal era, limitations on money in politics were accomplished in a piecemeal fashion.[12] The Federal Election Campaign Act (FECA) of 1971 and a second bundle of reforms under the same name passed in 1974 contained a comprehensive approach to campaign finance, an unprecedented effort by Congress. Still, this comprehensive approach resulted from specific scandals, most notoriously Watergate. Although Nixon himself signed the first bundle of reforms into law, his "reelection committee then went on to funnel illegal corporate contributions into slush funds, pay for breakins and trade cash for favors."[13] It came to light, for instance, that the "Milk Producer[s'] Association pledged $2,000,000 to President Nixon's campaign for reelection . . . at the same time as the Nixon Administration granted an increase in the support price of milk."[14] Nixon followed through on his promise and "[d]airy farmers netted over $500 million due to this policy shift."[15] Such events led to an overhaul of the legislation that Nixon himself had signed. The amendments "attempted to give practical vent to the shame and guilt aroused by the whole sorry spectacle."[16]

With its various amendments included, FECA contained limits on how much money individuals and political action committees could give to campaigns (contribution limits), limits on how much money candidates and campaigns could spend (expenditure limits), public disclosure requirements, an administrative agency to enforce election law (the Federal Election Commission), and provisions for the voluntary public financing of presidential campaigns.[17] The Court was asked to invalidate all of these provisions.

To this day it is *Buckley*—not FECA and not Congress—that provides the essential constitutional baselines for state and federal legislation seeking to limit the role of money in politics. As the Roberts Court put it in 2006, "Over the last 30 years, in considering the constitutionality of a host of different campaign finance statutes, this Court has repeatedly adhered to *Buckley*'s constraints."[18] *Buckley* struck down FECA's limitations on expenditures by candidates and campaigns. Much of American democracy as we know it today can be explained by the fact that there is no limit to the total amount of money that candidates and parties can raise and spend, and that virtually all of that money comes from private sources, not the state. Even granting the monumental importance of *Buckley*'s holdings, however, *Buckley*'s ideological reasoning about what the Constitution means has proven equally significant. The value judgments featured in the opinion amount to an efficient-market hypothesis made binding. Inspiring subsequent holdings and constraining lower courts and legislatures, state and federal alike, those value judgments have been treated as sacred until the present day.

I. DEMOCRACY AND CAPITALISM ENTANGLED

The *Buckley* opinion gives no sign of authorship. It was signed "per curiam," by the Court as a whole. Central to its outcome are a series of instances in which the Court relied upon economic principles to discern the meaning of the Constitution. This adoption of economic values as binding political values stands as the deeper meaning of the Court's 2006 remark and the reason why anyone who wishes to understand the free market Constitution must get acquainted with *Buckley*'s theory of democracy.

A. Constitutional Alchemy

Buckley converts a heavy, coarse element into something precious. The process starts attractively and easily garners assent: "Discussion of public issues and debate on the qualifications of candidates are integral to the operation of the system of government established by our Constitution."[19]

Agreed. "In a republic where the people are sovereign, the ability of the citizenry to make informed choices among candidates for office is essential, for the identities of those who are elected will inevitably shape the course that we follow as a nation."[20] Yes. The First Amendment "has its fullest and most urgent application precisely to the conduct of campaigns for political office."[21] Indeed. "[D]ebate on public issues should be uninhibited, robust, and wide-open."[22] This string of statements resonates so strongly that the audience is unlikely to muster a critical thought. The Court has employed charged words; it is as though a magnetic field has developed.

Into this magnetic field, the Court then introduced a fundamental element. "[V]irtually every means of communicating ideas in today's mass society requires the expenditure of money."[23] To the "humblest handbill or leaflet," money grants printing and circulation; to "speeches and rallies," a venue and publicity; to the massive American "electorate," news and information via television, radio, and papers of record.[24] Now the implication is clear: the congressional limits placed on monetary expenditures reduce the "number of issues discussed, the depth of their exploration, and the size of the audience reached."[25]

The Court has set in motion a process of conversion. We might imagine economic currency flying through a circular track built on the progressions above. With each loop, its speed increases. First: political debate, informed choice, elected leaders, the fate of the nation, the humblest leaflet, the fullest expression of the First Amendment, political liberty, robust debate in our mass society. Next: money communicates ideas in our vast land, regulation impoverishes debate, information for the electorate, communication requires resources. Finally: money is expression, regulation is censorship, money . . . liberty, money . . . democracy, money . . . speech. Contained in these trajectories, charged by the weightiest of constitutional principles and enlisted in the service of the nation's political life, economic currency becomes democratic currency. The Court's act of constitutional alchemy is comparable to the work done by particle accelerators in the natural world.[26] It is only by crashing money at high speeds into the target object of American democracy that the Court transmutes it into speech.

Despite the significant power of this process, some still manage to see a difference between speech accessible to virtually everyone—such as speaking with people in a public square, handing out 1,000 leaflets, posting position papers on a website or blog, or organizing a protest in the town square—and speech acquired only through wealth. The latter might include a full-page ad in the *New York Times*, a political advertisement on ABC tested by focus groups and refined by psychologists, or the hiring of a major convention center for a rally with more provisions than Disney Land. The accessible sort of speech is really just speech, while the kind inaccessible to most Americans is less a matter of speech as such, and more a matter of making one's speech influential.[27]

But the opinion refuses to acknowledge any difference:

[T]his Court has never suggested that the dependence of a communication on the expenditure of money operates itself to introduce a nonspeech element or to reduce the exacting scrutiny required by the First Amendment.[28]

The transformation is complete. If money is used to purchase speech, the money itself becomes part of the public sphere of politics and its ties to the economic sphere are cast off, rendering it too pure for most any regulation. Regulators and campaign finance reformers could be forgiven for thinking that money was property and that the expenditure of money was conduct.

The *Buckley* appellees made this argument. They drew an analogy between limits on money in politics and prohibitions on burning draft cards, noting that "any effect on communication is incidental" and that "the harms result[ed] directly from unlimited money, not from unlimited speech."[29] Their brief provided another excellent argument destined for failure: "We are dealing here not so much with the right to personal expression or even association, but with dollars and decibels. And just as the volume of sound may be limited by law, so the volume of dollars may be limited, without violating the First Amendment."[30] Only after exchange in a market, the logical mind grasps, could speech issue from chattel.

The Court was unsympathetic: "Even if the categorization of the expenditure of money as conduct were accepted, the limitations challenged here would . . . involve 'suppressing communication' [and] include restricting the voices of people and interest groups who have money to spend."[31] The Court also held that the monetary limitations were not analogous to restrictions on the time, place, or manner of speech, which are often upheld by the Court. Unlike regulations on picketing, parading, and sound trucks, the Court noted, the "Act's contribution and expenditure limitations impose direct quantity restrictions on political communication and association by persons, groups, candidates, and political parties."[32]

Once the Court minimized the differences between money and speech, and consecrated money's enabling effect on speech, limits on money in politics became limits on political expression itself—censorship—and therefore deserving of strict scrutiny. In order to restrict spending that produces speech, the government interests justifying the regulations must be compelling (i.e., extremely weighty in the Court's view) and the means chosen to accomplish them must be narrowly tailored so as not to burden speech unnecessarily. While economic regulations are presumptively constitutional, speech regulations are presumptively unconstitutional.[33] If economic power wishes to continue translating into political power, it must avoid regulation. Avoiding regulation requires that economic power be transformed into something politically legitimate, and nothing is more legitimate in the political sphere than speech.

Something vulgar becomes something precious—this is the function of constitutional alchemy. Speaking of the "forms and phrases of classical democracy," the economist Joseph Schumpeter noted its design: "Any opposition to an established regime is likely to use these forms and phrases whatever its meaning and social roots may be. If it prevails and if subsequent developments prove satisfactory, then these forms will take root in the national ideology."[34] From the bench, Justice Potter Stewart heralded its victory: "[M]oney is speech and speech is money, whether it is buying television or radio time."[35]

Ultimately, *Buckley*'s alchemy ought to be understood in terms of property. The significance of money's newfound status as speech is that donors and spenders can leverage First Amendment protection in order to avoid regulation. This allows them to obtain a greater share of the market for political power. By making money into speech, the Court ensured that the rich can enjoy more speech than the poor; and by refusing to undo this burgeoning market, the Court allowed political influence to become a commodity. Commodities must be property in order to be salable, for one cannot buy what is not owned. Contracts are only the vehicle for transferring ownership and, as such, are less meaningful than the body of law that makes ownership possible. And thus Mill's remark on expansive property laws can be applied to *Buckley*, which by conflating property and speech has "made property of things which never ought to be property, and absolute property where only qualified property ought to exist."[36]

The Court did not take the prerogative of monetary speech as far as it could have, however. It validated the act's contribution limits on the basis that they burdened freedom of expression considerably less than expenditure limits: "The quantity of the communication by the contributor does not increase perceptibly with the size of his contribution [which a]t most . . . provides a very rough index of the intensity of the contributor's support for the candidate."[37] The contribution limits restricted donations to candidates and political committees only, not any other use of money for political purposes. So long as expenditures remained unregulated, contributors could turn their dollars into other forms of political expression.

The majority opinion noted that such "transformation of contributions into political debate involves speech by someone other than the contributor."[38] And yet contributions are essential to political debate within a system of privately funded campaigns. The Court could have invalidated the contribution limitations on the basis of this fact. Instead, it reached a compromise:

The overall effect of the Act's contribution ceilings is merely to require candidates and political committees to raise funds from a greater number of persons and to compel people who would otherwise contribute amounts greater than the statutory limits to expend such funds on direct political expression, rather than to reduce the total amount of money potentially available to promote political expression.[39]

The Court's tolerance of contribution limits preserved a central component of campaign finance reform. Still, the fact that the Court found no reason to limit the total amount of money spent reveals a great deal about its theory of democracy (and the news for campaign finance reformers would not be good). Congress had provided a number of reasons to limit both contributions and expenditures, but the majority of those reasons struck the Court as impermissible state intervention in the political market.

B. Dispensing with Corruption

Relying on the statements by the parties and *amici*, the Court discerned three governmental interests behind the act: (1) "the prevention of corruption and the appearance of corruption spawned by the real or imagined coercive influence of large financial contributions on candidates' positions and . . . actions"; (2) "mut[ing] the voices of affluent persons and groups in the election process and thereby equaliz[ing] the relative ability of all citizens to affect the outcome of elections"; and (3) slowing "the skyrocketing cost of political campaigns and thereby . . . open[ing] the political system more widely to candidates without access to sources of large amounts of money."[40]

Noting our private system of campaign finance and increasing reliance on expensive media and polling technologies, the Court highlighted the importance of private contributions to candidates.[41] Still, it considered the first government interest to be constitutionally sufficient in its relationship to democracy's design: "To the extent that large contributions are given to secure a political *quid pro quo* from current and potential office holders, the integrity of our system of representative democracy is undermined."[42] The Court then validated concerns over the appearance of corruption, considering such concerns "critical . . . if confidence in the system of representative Government is not to be eroded to a disastrous extent."[43] Amidst these noble words, this victory for reformers, we must retain our bearings, lest we miss the fact that the same breath that uttered these words defined corruption narrowly as a *quid pro quo*.

Observing that the expenditures limited by the act were not prearranged or coordinated with candidates or campaigns, the Court found it difficult to understand how they could produce corruption. Writing that the lack of ties between independent expenditures and candidates "alleviates the danger that expenditures will be given as a *quid pro quo* for improper commitments from the candidate,"[44] the Court revealed the significance of its narrow definition of corruption. Defined only as an improper exchange of favors for money, corruption is not implicated by citizens, independent of any campaign, using their money to speak their minds.

Surely politicians' favor could be earned just as easily by an uncoordinated media campaign that tipped an election their way as by direct contributions. But the Court's reference to "improper commitments" seems to also remove from corruption's definition that most natural of human phenomena—that we take care of those who have ingratiated themselves to us. Greater attentiveness to favorable donors and spenders would not be corruption in the Court's view and, in any case, it is very difficult to prove. Citizens may dedicate their money to political expenditures in order to promote points of view and candidates endorsing those points of view. It could just as easily be the case that politicians are successful when their views line up with the views of society's influential members, as it could that politicians provide legislative favors when those influential members advance, however indirectly, their campaigns.

Turning to limits on expenditures by candidates, the Court found a positive relationship between big spending and democratic integrity: "[T]he use of personal funds reduces the candidate's dependence on outside contributions and thereby counteracts the coercive pressures and attendant risks of abuse to which the Act's contribution limitations are directed."[45] This finding hinges on a view of corruption that sees no impropriety in the enjoyment of substantial advantages by wealthy candidates relative to poor candidates. Is there nothing corrupt about a system in which the great majority of congressmen and presidents are wealthy?[46] Is there no appearance of corruption when candidates with more money to spend enjoy a substantial advantage? If money is speech, then these questions are answered in the negative. Translating money into political activity renders it desirable, not a source of corruption but a source of information for the electorate.

Because the anti-corruption interest was held insufficient to justify expenditure limits, the opinion turned to the matters of equality and rising campaign costs at the heart of the remaining two government interests. The Court's conclusion that unlimited expenditures are more expressive of democracy than corruptive of it provides a clue as to what comes next. After converting money into speech, the Court plunged further into the free market vortex by declaring equality an unconstitutional goal.

C. Economic Alchemy

In an old-fashioned sense, the amount of speech one can produce depends on how many points one has to make, how much energy one has to talk, and whether one can stir up enough goodwill to convince others that it is worth their while to listen. In the *Buckley* sense, it depends only on how much money one has to spend. Although not everyone has points to make, everyone does have interests to further; money purchases others' time in the generation of expedient points. Not everyone has energy to make the points one has; money acquires the energy of others to do so. Certain actors and interests engender little goodwill; money buys the media time and packaging necessary to ensure an audience.

It is tempting to adopt *Buckley*'s reasoning on the basis of our mass-media culture alone. Owen Fiss writes: "[T]oday there are no street corners, and the doctrinal edifice that seems . . . so glorious when we have the street corner speaker in mind is largely unresponsive to the conditions of modern society."[47] And yet, there *are* still street corners and one still observes local rallies and neighborhood groups. Fiss's point must simply be that the conditions of modern society render humble political forms ineffectual. The noted philosopher Michael Walzer gets to the heart of the question:

It's often said that the exercise of these freedoms [of speech, press, religion, and assembly] costs money, but that's not strictly speaking the case: talk and worship are cheap; so is the meeting of citizens; so is publication in many of its forms. Quick access to large audiences is expensive, but that is another matter, not of freedom itself but of influence and power.[48]

Economic power, the gatekeeper of the most influential forms of political communication, is unequally distributed, and so we can surmise that political power itself will, absent strong regulations, tend to trace the outlines of economic inequality.[49] *Buckley*'s transmutation of money into speech feeds the source of political inequality that Congress sought to restrain.

For example, take Peter Buttenwieser, a particularly forthcoming member of the political class. "I am close to a number of senators and see them on a very consistent basis," he writes. "I understand that the unusual access I have correlates to the millions of dollars I have given to political party committees, and I do not delude myself into feeling otherwise."[50] The late Senator Paul Simon was also unusually candid: "[If] there were twenty phone calls waiting for me, nineteen of them names I did not recognize and the twentieth someone I recognized as a $1,000 donor to my campaigns, that is the one person I would call."[51] Nobody denies that contributions and expenditures can be instrumental in gaining access to officeholders. Moreover, as the *Buckley* Court knew, a disproportionate number of presidents and members of Congress have been wealthy. Justice Marshall spelled out a reason for this in his separate opinion:

[The] ability to generate contributions may itself depend upon a showing of a financial base for the campaign or some demonstration of pre-existing support, which in turn is facilitated by expenditures of substantial personal sums. The wealthy candidate's immediate access to a substantial personal fortune may give him an initial advantage that his less wealthy opponent can never overcome. And even if the advantage can be overcome, the perception that personal wealth wins elections may not only discourage potential candidates without significant personal wealth from entering the political arena, but also undermine public confidence in the integrity of the electoral process.[52]

Buckley's confrontation with these issues came at one of the many times when equality was a particularly unstable concept. Tocqueville called it "an irresistible revolution which has advanced for centuries in spite of every obstacle."[53] Just how far equality was advancing was a question deeply tied up with FECA. The underlying issue in *Buckley* was whether the Supreme Court would concur in the irresistibility of this ongoing revolution. Equality's forward march was particularly fruitful in the 1960s and early 1970s, to a degree uncommon perhaps since the passage of the Fourteenth Amendment. These were the years that immediately preceded *Buckley*, the years that had shaped the Justices' sense of social change, and that colored, for better or worse, their view of what *Buckley* was really about.

John Rawls's *A Theory of Justice* and the first installment of FECA were both published in 1971.[54] They were apparently being drafted at the same time, and both pursued a holistic vision of political values. It is no coincidence that vigorous efforts to enforce the Civil Rights and Voting Rights Acts were ongoing. This was the time when equality in matters of race, religion, gender, and national origin occupied the collective consciousness and legal landscape.[55] Why not equality in matters of socioeconomic status as well? Congress, Rawls, and, one could even say, America were coming to terms with the limits of formal equality: premising the right to vote on a literacy test was facially neutral but discriminatory in practice. Allowing enormous sums of money to influence the course of elections was also facially neutral, but discriminatory in practice. Was formal equality sufficient for American democracy, or should something closer to equality in outcomes be required? Rawls wrote:

The constitution must take steps to enhance the value of equal rights of participation for all members of society . . . those similarly endowed and motivated should have roughly the same chance of attaining positions of political authority irrespective of their economic and social class . . . The liberties protected by the principle of participation lose much of their value whenever those who have greater private means are permitted to use their advantages to control the course of public debate. For eventually these inequalities will enable those better situated to exercise a larger influence over the development of legislation.[56]

Rawls, who later became one of *Buckley*'s principal detractors, developed these principles into a more formal requirement designed to ensure the "fair value of political liberties." The mandate reads thus: "[T]he worth of the political liberties to all citizens, whatever their social or economic position, must be approximately equal, or at least sufficiently equal, in the sense that everyone has a fair opportunity to hold public office and to influence the outcome of political decisions."[57]

Following the observation that one's ability to influence the outcome of political decisions and to become a candidate for office varied largely on the basis of one's economic resources, reformers sought to narrow the gap.[58] Their goal was not to redistribute income, but to decouple income and political influence. In contrast to the "formal equality" of all being free to spend their money on politics, limits on the total amount that could be spent would increase "material equality," in that the *ability* of different groups to exercise the freedom to spend would become more equal. Formal equality is satisfied at the moment when all are free to spend. By the time the poor are spending $0–$50 and the rich $5,000–$1,000,000, it has already turned its back. Material equality, on the other hand, is staring, wide-eyed. Contribution limits, expenditure limits, and some public financing would all achieve greater parity in access to political power, not just parity in voting rights. FECA and Rawls had announced a new stage for the democratic currency of equality. The Court considered such projects to run against the Constitution itself.

In order to uproot the egalitarian agenda, the Court performed another act of alchemy. This time, instead of viewing a value in its highest form, it chose to view a value in its lowest form. Recall that if money was just money, mere property and economic currency, Congress could regulate it rather easily. But money spent for political ends was instead elevated to the status of political expression itself. Cast in a political light and viewed in its highest form, money became speech. Now, if limitations on spending were political equality in action, they would represent a strong purpose. But if limitations on spending were actually just government interference in a free market, if equality were seen not in a political light, but in an economic light, then such limitations would advance a weak goal. This is how equality was turned into scrap metal just as soon as gold was turned into speech. Or to vary the metaphor, after economic currency became the new democratic currency, the next step was to devalue the old democratic currency. This is done by evaluating it from a free market standpoint from which anything beyond formal equality is just a disfavored interference with freedom.

Equality as an Interference with the Free Market   Scrutinizing FECA's limits on express advocacy of the election or defeat of a candidate, the Court castigated Congress for its interest in "equalizing [the] relative ability of individuals and groups to influence the outcome of elections."[59] What exactly was wrong with a congressional plan, passed by the representative branches of government and signed by the president, to provide for a degree of equality among citizens to influence elections? The Court's answer took up all of one sentence, possibly the most influential sentence of any opinion since.

[T]he concept that government may restrict the speech of some elements of our society in order to enhance the relative voice of others is wholly foreign to the First Amendment, which was designed to secure the widest possible dissemination of information from diverse and antagonistic sources, and to assure unfettered interchange of ideas for the bringing about of political and social changes desired by the people.[60]

The Court rightly perceived that FECA limited the amount of speech that could be purchased, which would indeed enhance the relative voice of those who either did not wish to or could not afford to spend much on political speech. Thus the speech of "some elements" (the wealthy or those who had pooled resources effectively) was limited while the speech of others (the poor or disorganized) was enhanced.

Something, however, appears wrong or at least insincere in the reasoning above. The Court claimed to be interested in securing information from diverse and antagonistic sources—that is, in vindicating a First Amendment goal. Although supposedly requiring regulations to be struck down, this goal could just as easily require the regulation to be upheld. On distributive economic issues, the interests of the lower socioeconomic classes would logically be those most antagonistic to the interests expressed by the wealthy. It is easy for a court to condemn expenditure limits by focusing on how equality reduces freedom. It is just as easy, however, to validate such limits by focusing on how equality increases freedom.

For example, the Supreme Court of Canada, upholding independent expenditure limits, recently provided a strong counter to the *Buckley* quote above.

Equality in the political discourse promotes electoral fairness and is achieved, in part, by restricting the participation of those who have access to significant financial resources. The more voices that have access to the political discourse, the more voters will be empowered to exercise their right in a meaningful and informed manner.[61]

Although the Canadian Justices reached the opposite result from that of their U.S. counterparts, their reasoning partially overlapped in its preoccupation with the effect of equality on liberty.[62] More voices in the political discourse (equality) would lead to greater voter empowerment, which is to say a greater exercise of participatory rights (freedom). In this sense, regulations on speech can produce a greater quantity of speech, or at least speech from a greater number of sources. This is what *Buckley* acknowledged by warning that the speech of some cannot be restricted in order to enhance the speech of others. Both of these courts recognize that increasing the participatory freedoms of some (the poor) requires restricting the participatory freedoms of others (the rich). The courts disagreed over the propriety of such a plan.

Having to justify equality in terms of freedom gives pause. Why, after all, should equality be an inferior and codependent constitutional value? The Fourteenth Amendment's guarantee of equal protection has influenced many areas of law from voting to desegregation, establishing even in the field of election law that equality is a central constitutional value.[63] Why should the First Amendment trump the Fourteenth? Providing for a measure of equality in political speech is not necessarily an abridgement of speech—it might be seen as an enhancement of speech. And the "freedom of speech" that Congress cannot abridge is not necessarily the total, unqualified freedom to spend as much as one wants to the detriment of other, supposedly equal, citizens. How can the Court *know* that the First Amendment's free speech clause cannot tolerate (or be construed in light of) other constitutional values?

From within neoclassical economic ideology, one cannot fathom that regulations could actually increase the diversity of voices and foster the sort of antagonism, born of diverse interests and viewpoints, that the First Amendment desires. And yet the validation of economic transactions as political activity means that inexpensive or free forms of political activity will be overshadowed by expensive forms, and, as far as campaigns go, a minuscule percentage of Americans will provide the funding and shape the agenda.[64]

Certainly, Congress could not pass a law limiting people with an income above $X to a certain amount of speech, but FECA addressed only how much money could be spent. It said nothing about which classes of citizens could spend the money or about which viewpoints could be expressed. In a footnote, the Court did observe that no case held such a plan to be acceptable to the First Amendment.[65] But it strains credulity to consider this an obstacle. Most of what the Court says the Constitution means or does not mean is the product of creative interpretation.[66] And yet the Court, rejecting the government interest in "equalizing the relative financial resources of candidates competing for elective office," which stood behind the limits placed on candidates' own expenditures, said that "the First Amendment simply cannot tolerate [the] restriction upon the freedom of a candidate to speak without legislative limit on behalf of his own candidacy."[67] By equating money with speech, expenditure limits became censorship.

This construction depends on a particular view of rights. Bradley Smith, an influential opponent of campaign finance reform, understands the First Amendment to "keep government out of the business of deciding who may speak, why, how, and how much, on public issues."[68] Speech is, therefore, a purely negative right—it protects citizens (and entities) from government interference. Smith concludes that "[i]f that barrier is broken down, there is little between voters and outright censorship."[69] If speech were also a positive right, then the government could attempt to advance the speech of disadvantaged parties, or could at least attempt to limit conditions that tend to make only expensive speech audible. If we take the negative view, however, and if money is literally speech, then *Buckley*'s view on what the First Amendment can and cannot tolerate seems to follow from caselaw and even the Constitution's text.

Short of considering speech a positive right, however, the Court did find its protection warranted by more than just the negative rights of individuals. Recall its statement that "the First Amendment . . . was designed to secure the widest possible dissemination of information from diverse and antagonistic sources . . . for the bringing about of political and social changes desired by the people."[70] This justified construing money as speech, because money was necessary for disseminating the maximum quantity of information. The trouble then is not that the Court found a public, expressive function in these uses of monetary power, but rather that the Court did not follow through on its own discovery.

If the use of money is protected partly because of its public function of disseminating information for democratic decision making, then it is imperative to understand how equality, a fundamental public value, could not be invoked to temper the advantages of wealthy speakers. Speech is an individual right, but the Court was clear that its status as such derives from the public requirements of liberal democracy. Some of the requirements listed by the court—such as securing information from diverse sources apt for bringing about political changes desired by the people—cannot be met absent concern for poor or middle-class speakers who, even collectively, are at a disadvantage to wealthy speakers. But because the Court deemed equality an illicit rationale for campaign finance reform, we are forced to wonder whether it is really the public function of money in politics that is being protected. Either a public order that relies just on liberty is being constructed, or the private economic order that unconventionally does so is being imputed to govern. These possibilities are one and the same.

A director at the Cato Institute, whose mission is to advance "principles of limited government, free markets, individual liberty and peace,"[71] puts it this way:

Egalitarians claim that private financing of campaigns fosters an oligarchy where some citizens, the rich and powerful, have vastly more political power than others. A Madisonian would see a more constrained ambit for equality: votes would be allocated equally, but other forms of political participation would not have to meet the standard of equality in part because meeting that standard would impinge deeply on fundamental rights.[72]

This is true if by fundamental rights one means unrestricted liberty on the basis of power, which as a logical principle tolerates slavery. It is not true if by fundamental rights one means a balance between liberty and equality. If restricting the liberty of some to protect or promote the liberty of others is unconstitutional, then the abolition of slavery is unconstitutional. In a political order, liberties of all kinds must be balanced with other fundamental guarantees, including equality, others' rights of property and privacy, and community norms such as reciprocity. Markets, after all, can (and do today) tolerate slavery, the selling of body parts, prostitution, and so on.[73] Only political conceptions restrain such exchanges.

Liberty not susceptible to restrictions on the basis of equality is market liberty, not political liberty. FECA's egalitarian goals were not contrary to the public order; they were contrary, rather, to the notion that the public order should be part of the market sphere, governed by the norm of maximized freedom for individuals acting in their own self-interest. Attempting to correct the results of this system is, in the market view, inequitable. Robert Lekachman explains: "To its adherents, standard economics is a scoreboard on which people's unequal financial status appropriately reflects the wide range of their individual talents and energy. By implication, inequality of income and wealth is actually quite equitable."[74] The irony and the paradox, then, are that political equality itself becomes an inequitable project.

Labeling equality as an impermissible objective under the First Amendment was devastating for comprehensive forms of campaign finance reform.[75] It represented a judgment that the state could not intervene in society to ensure that the middle and lower classes would enjoy the fair value of their political liberties. The reason why equality is impermissible relates not just to the preservation of others' liberty to speak and spend as much as they want, but also to the maintenance of a particular system. The Court found the goal of equality intolerable because it contradicted a free market view of speech—indeed, a free market view of democracy.

D. Democracy as a Market

In order to understand why money was considered speech and why equality was considered illicit, we must look to the market. A crude, neoclassical view of capitalism controls *Buckley*'s reasoning.

Voting with Dollars: From Popular Sovereignty to Consumer Sovereignty
Rejecting the government interest in "equalizing the financial resources of candidates competing for federal office"[76] that stood behind the candidate expenditure limits, the Court invoked the principle of consumer sovereignty. With contribution limits in place, the Court surmised that the "financial resources available to a candidate's campaign . . . will normally vary with the size and intensity of the candidate's support."[77] This is very much like a company in the economic market: Companies whose goods or services are popular will, all other things equal, reap higher profits than less popular competitors. Consumers are sovereign not just because they have the freedom to purchase whatever they want, but also because their collective decisions determine which companies will rise and which will fall. In choosing one product over another within the same product line or between companies, consumers send signals that wise companies heed. Profits can then be sensibly invested in many ways, from product development to improved distribution, that produce increased satisfaction for consumers and, accordingly, an increasing revenue stream. Through its

incentives to gauge the market and satisfy consumers, capitalism proves a most responsive and popular system.

If campaign contributions are comparable to the purchasing behavior of consumers in this sense, then limits on campaign expenditures interfere with the system. Candidates who have succeeded in gauging the market and obtaining a large sum of contributions would be prevented from leveraging their hard work to obtain additional success. Referring to contributions raised by candidates, the Court flatly stated: "There is nothing invidious, improper, or unhealthy in permitting such funds to be spent to carry the candidate's message to the electorate."[78] Indeed, it would be horribly oppressive to regulate how much a firm could spend of its own money, money earned due to the popularity of its products. The goal of increasing the relative voice of a competing firm would distort consumer signals and strip a successful company of the advantages it had obtained through productive behavior.

The Court again invoked consumer sovereignty to vilify the state interest in limiting the skyrocketing cost of campaigns. After acknowledging that spending on federal campaigns had increased nearly 300 percent in just two decades, the Court summarily decided that this was "no basis for government restrictions on . . . campaign spending."[79] The Court channeled the First Amendment to explain why:

The First Amendment denies government the power to determine that spending to promote one's political views is wasteful, excessive, or unwise. In the *free society* ordained by our Constitution it is not the government, but the people individually as citizens and candidates and collectively as associations and political committees who must retain control over the quantity and range of debate on public issues in a political campaign.[80]

Did the Court mean the *free market society* ordained by our Constitution? It was as though the Court considered government limits on campaign spending to be price controls or the rescission of a popular product from the market without good reason. Such market interference would indeed stop citizen-purchasers from controlling, through demand, which products would be offered and which would be discontinued, and whether prices would decrease due to popularity. As Lekachman puts it, one of capitalism's merits is "the personal liberty that accompanies unfettered choice."[81]

Indeed, people are free to spend their entire savings on a fancy car and forgo college. They are free to spend as much as they can on any particular commodity. As a general rule, it is not for the state to dictate which consumer choices are wise and which are unwise. Regulating the expenditures of consumers or sellers constitutes an impermissible infringement on the free market ordained by capitalism. The government's posture toward the market for political speech must also be laissez-faire. This is what it means to live under a free market Constitution.

Laissez-faire Democracy   Another market principle at the heart of the opinion centers not on the rights of consumers but on the importance of free competition among producers and suppliers.[82] Adam Smith counseled that while respecting the "laws of justice," "[e]very man [be] left perfectly free to pursue his own interest his own way, and to bring both his industry and capital into competition with those of any other man."[83] This sums up the now familiar demand of government non-intervention, premised on a veritable faith that competition and self-interest will lead to optimal results. By seeking to generate the greatest possible value with his labor and capital, each man increases society's wealth, "led," in the words of Smith, "by an invisible hand to promote an end which was no part of his intention."[84]

Smith's theory about the collective function of self-interest leads to the removal of obstacles to each person's (and each firm's) quest for gains:

[T]he pure theory of competition, which furnished the main theoretical grounds for the desirability of unregulated capitalism, sought to demonstrate how the almost total autonomy of the firm and the near absence of all external controls were justified, provided only that each individual enterprise was small relative to the total market, hence unable to influence prices, hence completely responsive to the cues of the market, and so . . . exquisitely subject to the ultimate sovereignty of the consumer. The obligation of the state, then, was to ensure competition.[85]

This emphasis on competition heeds concerns about the abuse of private power. The inability to influence prices carries a concomitant inability to exploit consumers or laborers. Both could resort to any number of competing firms that were charging or paying the market rate.[86]

In *Buckley*'s assessment, FECA's limitation on expenditures interfered in an already competitive market. By encroaching on consumer sovereignty and disrupting the results of market competition that had thus far accrued, such interference constituted an inefficient and coercive path to eliminating corruption. In striking down the independent expenditure ceiling, the Court indicated that limitations on money spent on advocacy were restraints on competition.

Classical economics should be construed to support the opposite view, however, given that the political "firms" competing for market dominance were often quite large. Reducing expenditures could have been construed as breaking up the two-party duopoly that had cornered the market for political power and succeeded in undoing consumer (or popular) sovereignty. The leader of the law and economics movement, Judge Richard Posner, has noted that only a limited representation of viewpoints occurs in such a system.[87] As for anti-competitive effects, he notes the "erection of legal barriers to the competition of third parties."[88] The dictates of self-interest expose in the midst of the two major parties a "joint interest in killing any third party . . . unless one of the major parties is confident that the new party will draw more votes from the other major party than from itself."[89] Describing duopolistic collusion, he notes that "the two parties control every state's political system and can pass whatever laws are in their joint interest."[90]

Consider another reason that economics does not dictate an easy answer. FECA's personal expenditure limits targeted politicians who had accumulated great wealth in their private economic dealings and could then leverage that wealth as a competitive advantage within the political arena. That advantage had not accrued through competition within the political arena, and, therefore, does not correspond to political superiority or popularity. In short, FECA did not seek to interfere with an already competitive and responsive market; it sought instead to eliminate several of many causes of market failure. Despite this, the Court fixated upon the incidental reduction in political spending that might occur, reminding Congress that "[d]emocracy depends on a well-informed electorate, not a citizenry legislatively limited in its ability to discuss and debate candidates and issues."[91]

The Court praised FECA's disclosure requirements as the appropriate sort of government involvement, noting that "'informed public opinion is the most potent of all restraints upon misgovernment.'[92] The Court supported its view with Justice Brandeis's famous dictum "'Publicity is justly commended as a remedy for social and industrial diseases. Sunlight is said to be the best of disinfectants; electric light the most efficient policeman.'"[93] For bad speech, this view suggests the remedies of transparency and additional speech. Rather than being censored, bad speech should be opposed in the market. That way, the people can decide which view to support. Assuming that a product is not unreasonably dangerous, we allow the competition of the market to determine its fate.

This view of the First Amendment traces back to a dissenting opinion filed by Justice Holmes nearly one hundred years ago:

[T]he ultimate good desired is better reached by free trade in ideas . . . the best test of truth is the power of the thought to get itself accepted in the competition of the market . . . That at any rate is the theory of our Constitution.[94]

The implication is a familiar one. As Joseph Blocher describes it, speech is "worthy of constitutional protection precisely because—like the free flow of goods and services—it creates a competitive environment in which good ideas flourish and bad ideas fail."[95]

Holmes's theory of free speech is notable for its short treatment of the laissez-faire concept. Economists understand that "free trade" does not happen automatically. Free markets require that the state guarantee open access to the market by policing anti-competitive behavior. Any free market of any appreciable size is also a regulated market. Notwithstanding the fact that most people cannot afford to purchase anything in the already expensive market for media advertisements, and notwithstanding the tremendous inequality of wealth in America even before Reagan, the Court considered Congress's program to constitute an unjustified interference in the market instead of a much-needed restructuring of the market. In 1881, his intellectual journey just beginning its way to his 1919 dissent, Holmes famously wrote that "state interference is an evil where it cannot be shown to be a good."[96] Almost one hundred years later, the *Buckley* Court held that state interference in the market for political spending is an evil and that it is nearly impossible to show it to be a good.

Buckley's indifference to distributive concerns and its endorsement of a laissez-faire approach harkens back to the landmark case *Lochner v. New York*.[97] There, the Supreme Court invalidated a state law that prevented bakery employees from working more than 60 hours per week. The law sought to protect the health of bakers and prevent bakeries from exploiting them. The Court treated the law as a paternalistic affront to contractual freedoms, construing the Fourteenth Amendment as a contractarian guarantee: "The general right to make a contract in relation to his business is part of the liberty of the individual protected by the 14th Amendment of the Federal Constitution."[98]

Justice Holmes, writing fourteen years before his "speech as a free market" dissent, disagreed with the *Lochner* majority. Noting recent decisions upholding a similar limitation on miners' work schedules and a prohibition on sales of two different sorts of stock, Holmes reminded his brethren that their views on the larger issues underlying such laws are not the test of constitutionality.

[A] Constitution is not intended to embody a particular economic theory, whether of paternalism and the organic relation of the citizen to the state or of *laissez faire*. It is made for people of fundamentally differing views, and the accident of our finding certain opinions natural and familiar, or novel, and even shocking, ought not to conclude our judgment upon the question whether statutes embodying them conflict with the Constitution of the United States.[99]

Rawls echoed this sentiment in *Political Liberalism*, comparing *Buckley* to *Lochner*: "The First Amendment no more enjoins a system of representation according to influence effectively exerted in free political rivalry between unequals than the Fourteenth Amendment enjoins a system of liberty of contract and free competition between unequals in the economy."[100]

Now the essence of both cases is clear. Would the Court judge the contested question from the standpoint of the economic or the political sphere? Walzer calls the rights vindicated in *Lochner* "desperate exchanges" and "trades of last resort," labeling health and safety regulations the "basic standards, below which workers cannot bid against one another for employment."[101] Functionally speaking, these regulations constitute "[a] restraint of market liberty for the sake of some communal conception."[102] Once strong enough, a communal conception can redraw the borders between capitalism and democracy. This is why Margaret Jane Radin describes maximum-hour limitations and the prohibition on child labor as "reflect[ing] an incompletely commodified understanding of work."[103] If market control must be absolute, however, then human beings are entirely vulnerable to the forces of capitalism. The state cannot guarantee even a minimum degree of dignity.

The question, then, in *Buckley* was whether the Court would permit the Congress to decide an issue, validating a communal conception and requiring the market to cede ground to democracy, or whether the Court would invalidate such a plan as undue government interference in the market for political finance. The distributive consequences of this border conflict deserve our attention.

According to Cass Sunstein, "[a] principal problem with the pre–New Deal Court was that it treated existing distributions of resources as if they were prepolitical and just, and therefore invalidated democratic efforts at reform."[104] Indeed, the *Lochner* Court did not see injustice in formally consensual arrangements between bakeries and bakers. Nor did the *Buckley* Court consider a regime of freely donated and freely spent monies oppressive. Spending a great deal of money on politics was not an act of political control, but rather an act of freedom and political participation. Neither the *Lochner Court* nor the *Buckley* Court was capable of seeing exploitation and domination within the market domain, whether the market for political influence or the market for bakery labor. Sunstein's description of the pre–New Deal Court continues: "Regulatory adjustment of market arrangements was seen as interference with an otherwise law-free and unobjectionable status quo[,] a state-mandated transfer of funds from one group for another."[105] This description captures a key feature of neoclassical economic theory: Absent government coercion, "[c]ontrol, authority, power [are] concepts of no theoretical significance [and] all economic relationships dissolve[] into contracts freely and rationally consented to by autonomous individuals."[106]

The same precept is also evident in *Buckley*, where the Court considered irrelevant inequalities in political influence that favored the wealthy.[107] It was capable of recognizing quid pro quo corruption, however. A "dollars for votes" transaction would be akin to insider trading or price-fixing, which corrupt the system by forgoing the market mechanism. Even within a free market, some pieces of information and some services are not for sale. The proper way for wealth to influence political policy, *Buckley* reminds us, is through reasonably sized contributions and unlimited expenditures, which are thought to play out in the market for ideas and the market for representation.

The Court defined corruption broadly only in considering the mere appearance of corruption to be a veritable danger.[108] This is, however, a judgment about the requirement of popular confidence in democracy, not a realization that this confidence could be shaken by the sort of corruption inherent in vastly unequal degrees of political influence occurring as a function of wealth. Short of purchasing political favors or generating the appearance of such, the Court construed as constitutionally required the realities of control, authority, and power that obtain in a system of private financing of campaigns.

Parties as Firms, Contributors as Investors, Politicians as Salesmen, Voters as Consumers *Buckley*'s application of economic theory to decide issues of campaign finance validates an economic market for political power. Because Congress did not enact a regime of mandatory public financing, a regime of private financing for political campaigns could persist in all political contests at all stages. The only exception is the final stage of presidential contests where some candidates might opt to accept public funds, but even then such candidates may have to compete against privately financed competitors.

Without guaranteed funding, candidates and parties must raise enormous funds for their campaigns and other projects. As the Court put it, "The increasing importance of the communications media and sophisticated mass-mailing and polling operations to effective campaigning make the raising of large sums of money an ever more essential ingredient of an effective candidacy."[109] Under *Buckley*'s laissez-faire approach, the privatized media market sets the price for the effective exercise of First Amendment rights. The supply side of campaign finance is also elementary: people contribute to campaigns, and special interests spend heavily because politics decides the outcome of the contests that matter most. Whether material or ideological in nature, every issue of any importance is either decided through law or left alone by law. Legal action and inaction both have their price.

Judge Posner famously summed up where these conditions of supply and demand get us. The year before *Buckley* was decided, he and William Landes wrote that "legislation is supplied to groups or coalitions that outbid rival seekers of favorable legislation [and] [p]ayments take the form of campaign contributions, votes, implicit promises for future favors, and sometimes outright bribes."[110] On the basis of such observations, interest group pluralists conclude that "legislation is 'sold' by the legislature and 'bought' by the beneficiaries of the legislation."[111]

Some three decades before these remarks, Joseph Schumpeter noted similar conditions: "The incessant competitive struggle to get into office or to stay in it imparts to every consideration of policies and measures the bias so admirably expressed by the phrase about 'dealing in votes.'"[112] Schumpeter warned that manipulative tactics from consumer advertising were being employed in politics in order to sell policies and manufacture consent.[113] On the compatibility of ideal democracy with the capitalist order, he noted that economic resources secure legislative goods: "[T]here are some deviations from the principle of democracy which link up with the presence of organized capitalist interests . . . From the . . . standpoint [of classical democratic theory], the result reads that the means at the disposal of private interests are often used in order to thwart the will of the people."[114] What stops the supposedly competitive market for political speech, this place where all citizens may come to speak and to listen without censorship, from becoming an exclusive club in which organized interests accomplish their objectives?

Buckley's Lochnerian indifference to realities of control, power, and authority is most visible not at the moment of validating a market for political power, but rather at the moment of considering the market perfect despite its wealth-based inequalities and obvious failure to live up to the genuine dictates (or to produce the desired results) of classical economic theory. With regard to the inaccessibility of this market, many complaints about money in politics would cease if the Court and Congress agreed to a market for campaign contributions (and political power) in which each registered voter was given a $200 coupon to distribute to candidates of his or her choosing. One would begin to think of the market for breakfast cereal, in which everyone with a taste for this sort of thing can participate.

Such egalitarian or accessible markets are one thing. The reality of the market for political influence, however, is much more similar to the market for luxury vehicles. Ferraris and political power both cost a great deal. Like all commodities, they are allocated in accordance with one's ability and willingness to pay, and one's ability to pay is a function of one's income, property holdings, credit, and so on. If speech is viewed as a commodity, then speech that is more costly must be more valuable. Value in this case flows from the amount of power and influence that the speech can be expected to have. This "expressive value" would logically be a function of how many people the speech is projected to reach, the persuasiveness of the packaging surrounding it, and the gains expected to flow from persuading listeners. Once speech is commodified in this way, freedom requires that the government refrain from regulating individual choices as to buying and selling. The accessibility of speech in the political market becomes no more worrisome than the accessibility of Ferraris.

Once we understand the market concept—free speech as in a free market—the rest of these conundrums are resolved. In the free market view, it is impermissible to stop the rich from purchasing more of a certain product unless the product itself is illicit. Speech is not illicit of course—quite the contrary, it is actually desired that as many people as possible purchase it. But if many cannot afford it or as much of it as others, that is no more a problem than unequal distribution of powerful cars or designer watches. Equality enters into the equation only in the most basic of senses—dealers cannot exclude any purchaser on account of race or gender, for example. Short of discrimination, there is no role for equality. The market sets the price for fancy watches, powerful cars, and powerful speech. Each person is free to decide how best to dispose of whatever resources they can muster in the market; they have no just expectation for the state to address resource gaps or their secondary effects. These are the new values—freedom and equality now mean this in both the economy and politics.

All of this reminds us of a crucial fact: the free market is content to allow differences in wealth, whether earned or unearned, to translate into greater acquisitive power.[115] The question of whether this criterion for power should apply within democracy's sphere is raised poignantly by the system of private financing of campaigns and the homogeneity of those who contribute most of the money.

Numerous studies confirm that most campaign money comes from white males whose most distinguishing attributes are their wealth[116] and economic conservatism.[117] The prevalence of the wealthy among political donors was well known at the time of *Buckley*.[118] Wealth and economic conservatism are the calling cards of the group Spencer Overton has aptly called the "donor class."[119] Larry Bartels's conclusion from a longitudinal analysis of senators' votes on legislation on the minimum wage, civil rights, government spending, and abortion confirms the composition of the donor class: "[T]he views of constituents in the bottom third of the income distribution received no weight at all in the voting decisions of their senators."[120] Even on matters of wages, 33 percent of Americans are apparently of no account whatsoever. Bartels found this to be the case "regardless of how the data are sliced."[121] Overton reaches the same conclusion on the basis of the effect of political money emanating from such an exclusive and homogeneous group: "When less than 2% of voting-age Americans dominate a crucial element of political participation like funding campaigns, a narrow set of ideas and viewpoints obstruct fully-informed decision making."[122] In explaining how these political investors convey their points of view to parties and candidates, Overton cites "the special access [they] enjoy at fundraising events."[123]

Such events respond not just to the supply of funds from campaign contributors seeking to influence the course of government, but also (and perhaps primarily) to the demand for contributions caused by the fundraising arms race that *Buckley* perpetuated. The demand for money turns candidates, representatives, and parties into fundraisers, sellers, and merchandisers. Vincent Blasi considers the demands of fundraising a reason for campaign finance reform efforts within the Congress, noting the "frustration [Congressmen] feel concerning how much time they must devote to courting potential donors."[124] He characterizes fundraising efforts as employing "electoral merchandising" and "methods borrowed from the marketplace that can only be described as demeaning."[125] These contours of the post-industrial order are not well accounted for by the economic theory applied in *Buckley*.

Choosing Between Market Theories   The use of economic theory as a means of constitutional interpretation is perverse and damaging enough. To make matters worse, *Buckley* misapplied that theory to the benefit of the most powerful players. Competition was a genuine feature of the late-eighteenth-century world inhabited by the architects of classical economics. Galbraith called this moment in England "the time of free trade," maintaining that "[t]he kind of competition that was implicit in the pioneering designs of the classical economists of the nineteenth century was not unrealistic."[126] Even in the middle of the twentieth century in America, Galbraith notes, none of the wheat and cotton growers contributed an appreciable amount to the total supply. This related to the most important requirement of competition in the classical view: that "no buyer or seller [be] large enough to control or exercise an appreciable influence on the common price."[127]

Surely Justice Holmes, at the time of his 1919 "free speech as a market" dissent had come to labor under assumptions similar to those of classical economics. He wrote before the Great Depression at a time when those assumptions appeared reasonable and conducive to the humanitarian ends of efficiency.[128] Bartels, Overton, Blasi, media analysts, and numerous members of Congress have since reported, however, that a small class of buyers and sellers stands behind a large amount of speech, setting the price of political discourse and controlling access, agenda, and content. The assumptions that were reasonable enough at the time of Holmes's adoption of the market view no longer made sense as of 1976. Even by the 1940s, economists understood that competition required not just many sellers within any given market, but also "many sellers doing business with many buyers[, e]ach well informed as to the prices at which others are selling and buying."[129]

In the political sphere, this would mean, at the very least, reasonable pluralism and prices not artificially set by a duopolistic party structure or the oligopoly of mass media conglomerates. By the 1940s, economists also understood that corporate consolidation in numerous markets had rendered the classical theory of competition empirically and theoretically untenable.[130] The Supreme Court failed to achieve the robust and free debate it purportedly desired. It achieved a victory not for competition but for control, a victory for the centrality of two parties, several media corporations and their corporate advertisers, and a small class of donors and investors.

II. DISSENTING VOICES

Chief Justice Burger's dissenting opinion presented an even larger view of market freedom. Burger would have invalidated FECA's contribution limits and public financing system in addition to its expenditure limits: "The contribution limitations infringe on First Amendment liberties [and t]he system for public financing of Presidential campaigns is, in my judgment, an impermissible intrusion by the Government into the traditionally private political process."[131]

Although the nation had never attempted a public financing system for presidential races, Burger concluded that such a system would necessarily abuse governmental power; and he assumed that this abuse would be worse than the abuse of private power. "There are many prices we pay for the freedoms secured by the First Amendment," he wrote. "[T]he risk of undue influence is one of them, confirming what we have long known: Freedom is hazardous, but some restraints are worse."[132] This expresses the familiar conservative view that we have more to fear from the government than we do from private actors.

Justice Burger stood at one end of the spectrum on *Buckley*, while Justice White stood at the other. White would have upheld the expenditure limitations partly on the basis that FECA says nothing about the content of political speech. "What the Act regulates," he reminded the Court, "is giving and spending money, acts that have First Amendment significance not because they are themselves communicative with respect to the qualifications of the candidate, but because money may be used to defray the expenses of speaking."[133] In a strict sense, the act only required political actors to find less-expensive means of speaking.

White surmised that expenditure limitations might actually increase the depth of speech and its honesty, "free[ing] [the candidate] and his staff to communicate in more places and ways unconnected with the fundraising function."[134] Citing the "endless job of raising increasingly large sums of money," Justice White noted his "regret that the Court has returned [candidates] to the treadmill."[135] All of this stood behind White's most important point, one that would be a centerpiece of dissenting opinions yet to come. "[M]oney is not always equivalent to or used for speech," he wrote, "even in the context of political campaigns."[136]

Additionally, White emphasized the need to prevent politics from becoming or being perceived as a market: "The holding perhaps is not that federal candidates have the constitutional right to purchase their election, but many will so interpret the Court's conclusion in this case."[137] He notes "the impression that federal elections are purely and simply a function of money [and] that *federal offices are bought and sold* [emphasis mine],"[138] echoing Thomas Jefferson verbatim.

Viewed together, White's concerns refer to the incursion of markets into political terrain—money as speech, candidates as fundraisers, and offices for sale. He contextualized those dangers within the goal of protecting the "integrity of federal campaigns,"[139] that integrity being compromised when politics is conducted as a market. This is the opposite of Burger's view, which holds that the integrity of politics depends on its continuing presence within the private (economic) sphere, far away from the reach of the state.

These dissenting opinions reveal that *Buckley* is a compromise between a strict market view and a strict democratic view. *Buckley* errs on the side of markets, however. In its construction of money as speech, equality as an unconstitutional motivation, and democracy as a market, *Buckley* imported free market baselines into jurisprudence. And so Friedman's words and the efficient market hypothesis came to govern political finance—an area in which the government was now deemed to pose a "danger to freedom and prosperity," private transactions "would inevitably bring more rationality to economic activity," "markets possessed a wisdom that . . . governments did not," and the "prices that emerged from voluntary transactions be-tween buyers and sellers [would be allowed to] coordinate the activity of millions of people." This flourishing of capitalist dogma within the Court set a bold mood and signaled that a new ideology would retrace the lines of legal forms. Democracy was being remade in the image of capitalism, and additional renovations were scheduled immediately.

CHAPTER 3

Corporations Speak

RICHARD NIXON'S LEGACY FOR POLITICAL FINANCE REFORM did not stop with Watergate and the campaign finance legislation that issued in response. *Buckley* hollowed that legislation out, testifying to the Court's supremacy over Congress and even the presidents who signed the various pieces of legislation—*or almost so*. Well before oral argument in *Buckley*, Nixon had appointed Warren Burger, Harry Blackmun, Lewis Powell, and William Rehnquist to the Court. All four sided with *Buckley*'s hostility to expenditure limitations, and several would have gone so far as to strike down FECA's contribution limits and public financing provisions.[1] Nixon's judges undid a crucial part of the legislation that responded to his actions. The absence of expenditure limits and *Buckley*'s free market reasoning have had profound consequences, so much so that it was Nixon, not Congress or the outraged public, who prevailed in the political finance sagas of the 1970s. A subsequent case reinforced the point, preparing the way for *Citizens United*.

The Court confronted the question of corporate political power in *First National Bank of Boston v. Bellotti*,[2] decided just two years after *Buckley*. Because the Court had already determined that monetary expenditures were a form of speech, the next step was to declare that corporations are protected speakers under the First Amendment. Justice Powell eagerly assumed the task, as Nixon could have predicted he would. By the time Nixon nominated him, Powell had already enjoyed an illustrious career as a corporate lawyer and long-standing member of Philip Morris's board of directors. Just two months before his nomination to the Court, Powell wrote a memorandum to the U.S. Chamber of Commerce with a remarkable message: "Business must learn the lesson, long ago learned by labor and other self-interest groups[—]political power is necessary . . . such power must be assiduously cultivated [and] when necessary, it must be used aggressively and with determination."[3]

Although more delicately written, the Powell memo recalls a memo even closer to Nixon's hand, one written exactly seven days earlier by John Dean, White House counsel. Therein, Dean summarized the purpose of Nixon's Enemies List, a project being prepared by White House lawyers, as follows: to "maximize the fact of our incumbency in dealing with persons known to be active in their opposition to our Administration."[4] Dean noted the importance of exploring "how we can use the available federal machinery to screw our political enemies."[5] Nixon had a special talent for attracting this "politics as war" mentality. Indeed, Powell's and Dean's memos share a strategic sensibility—a self-conscious mustering of all available power to sink one's opponents—that appealed to Nixon, as the Watergate affair would later reveal.[6]

While Dean's advice led to a series of illegal acts, Powell's advice led to an invigorated Chamber of Commerce and motivated political engagement by corporations. In weighing Powell's remarks in his memo, bear in mind that he was not acting in the capacity of a legal representative bound to vehemently make his client's case within the bounds of the law. He was expressing his own views. Powell argued that the "American economic system is under broad attack"; he lamented that "in terms of political influence with respect to the course of legislation and government action, the American business executive is truly the 'forgotten man'"; and for chief executive officers he counseled "far more than an increased emphasis on 'public relations' or 'governmental affairs.'"[7] Addressing corporations and the Chamber that represented them, Powell located the necessary defense of free enterprise "in careful long-range planning and implementation, in consistency of action over an indefinite period of years, in the scale of financing available only through joint effort, and in the political power available only through united action and national organizations." Powell advised that "[t]here should not be the slightest hesitation to press vigorously in all political arenas for support of the enterprise system." "Nor," he continued, "should there be reluctance to penalize politically those who oppose it."[8]

To this Nixonian language, Powell added a legal twist: "Under our constitutional system, especially with an activist-minded Supreme Court, the judiciary may be the most important instrument for social, economic and political change."[9] Nixon gave Powell the chance to prove that assertion and to remedy the situation Powell perceived—that other groups "have been far more astute in exploiting judicial action than American business."[10] Six years after writing the memo, Powell removed an important obstacle to corporate political power.[11]

I. THE FIRST AMENDMENT DEMANDS
THAT THEY BE HEARD

Buckley lent constitutional protection to expenditures by individuals, candidates, and parties, and held that the government had no compelling reason to limit them. This left open the question of corporate political expenditures. In *Bellotti*, banks and other corporations challenged the constitutionality of a Massachusetts law prohibiting them from making contributions or expenditures "for the purpose of . . . influencing or affecting the vote on any question submitted to the voters, other than one materially affecting any of the property, business, or assets of the corporation."[12] In short, Massachusetts had decided to prevent corporations from intervening in ballot questions—that is, direct democracy.

The corporate plaintiffs wished to oppose a graduated income tax. The state legislature hoped to gain the power to impose that tax through a constitutional amendment, which was submitted to the people of Massachusetts as a ballot question.[13] The plaintiffs' goal was simple: to influence the public's choice. Naturally, such a tax would be unfavorable to business executives, including those employed by the plaintiffs, and would reduce the disposable income of the upper economic strata, potentially decreasing the sales of certain products offered by the plaintiffs.[14]

Besides advocating that corporations play a much more active role in politics and go on the offensive against those who threaten the free enterprise system, Powell's 1971 memo had also addressed taxation. "We in America already have moved very far indeed toward some aspects of state socialism," Powell had lamented. "In addition to the ideological attack on the system [of free enterprise] itself," he noted, the system is "also threatened by inequitable taxation."[15] "As the experience of the socialist and totalitarian states demonstrates," Powell continued, "the contraction and denial of economic freedom is followed inevitably by governmental restrictions on other cherished rights."[16] Just six years after Powell wrote these words, it was obvious where he would come out on a law that prevented corporations from spending money to oppose a graduated taxation scheme. Nobody knew how he would reach this foregone conclusion, however.

Powell's opinion struck down the law, four Justices dissented, and one concurred. Powell did not frame the issue as whether corporations possessed First Amendment rights. Focusing instead on the "societal interests" served by free speech, he re-described the issue as whether the Massachusetts law "abridges expression that the First Amendment was meant to protect."[17] This doctrinal refinement pays attention to content, not source, thereby rendering irrelevant all of the ways in which corporations differ from human beings. It distracts us from the central issue: whether entities from the economic sphere should be given rights possessed by human beings acting in their capacity as citizens.

Powell endorsed *Buckley*'s free market view of speech, aspiring to "the widest possible dissemination of information from diverse and antagonistic sources."[18] The ballot question did present a matter of public concern and nobody doubted that debate was vital, but Powell used that as a trump card. Here, wrote Powell, "is the type of speech indispensable to decisionmaking in a democracy, and this is no less true because the speech comes from a corporation rather than an individual."[19] Thus he prohibited government attention to the corporate status of the speaker. The implication is simple: if the government were to pick and choose who could participate in the market, then the market would cease to be free. Powell even suggested that attention to the corporate status of the speaker could only suggest a nefarious intention: "Freedom of expression has particular significance with respect to government because '[i]t is here that the state has a special incentive to repress opposition and often wields a more effective power of suppression.'"[20]

Those suspicions locate the government as an actor with a stake in the market, which is precisely the position of governments at the time of Adam Smith's writing of the *Wealth of Nations*. Smith observed that the function of the reigning economic system at the time, mercantilism, was to "increase the quantity of gold and silver in any country by turning the balance of trade in its favour."[21] The government did this by granting monopolies to favored persons, imposing tariffs to protect domestic manufacturers from foreign competitors, and acquiring colonies for purposes of extracting raw materials, cheap labor, and capturing new markets for goods.

That historical precedent elucidates how Powell conceived of state involvement in the market for speech. The law at issue in *Bellotti* effectively granted a monopoly on speech to individuals, and foreclosed entry into the market by banks and other corporations. Here, as in Burger's *Buckley* dissent, the government is conceived of as a threat, as a competitor seeking to prevent hostile forces from expressing themselves. Such a view does not admit the reply that the government is the guarantor of competition, much less the reply that the government expresses the people's will or protects democratic integrity.

With a simple shift of attention from speaker to speech, the market view renders the government's action censorship or odious market interference. But is it really so easy and persuasive to ignore the speaker? We might ask, for example, whether the Chinese government should be allowed to spend millions of dollars in order to publicize its views on ballot questions within the United States. A free market for political speech would include each and every viewpoint on matters of public concern, regardless of whether those viewpoints were instrumental for corporate or foreign domination. Powell wrote that "[i]f the speakers here were not corporations, no one would suggest that the State could silence their proposed speech."[22] We could say the same of the Chinese, after all. Powell explains that the "inherent worth of the speech in terms of its capacity for informing the public does not depend upon the identity of its source."[23]

Powell's philosophy of free speech would seem to consider the status of the Chinese as foreign nationals or a foreign government irrelevant to First Amendment protection. Federal law, however, bars foreign governments and foreign nationals from making political contributions.[24] Congress adopted a position contrary to Powell's in 1966 after foreign business and political interests funded several U.S. election campaigns. The prospect of Philippine sugar companies and Nicaraguan dictators influencing the success of U.S. federal candidates proved highly unpalatable. The congressional prohibition on foreign political contributions was widened in 1976 to include foreign donations, expenditures, and disbursements.[25] These prohibitions maintain national sovereignty within the political realm. Actors who make large expenditures, even independent expenditures, influence the public debate and the public's sense of the issues. Powell himself emphasized (albeit only in his memo) how "television . . . now plays such a predominant role in shaping the thinking, attitudes, and emotions of *our people.*"[26] Should the public's thinking, attitudes, and emotions be conditioned by foreign governments and corporations? If not the former, why the latter?

Powell must concede that every market has certain requirements for access. Notions of free competition cannot be taken literally, especially in the case of political markets where the political community defines itself and makes the rules by which it must abide. His plurality opinion did discuss corporate speech and corporate legal personhood, resting on the validation of economic entities as political citizens.[27] Powell, however, does not justify this choice. Some attention to the right holder would seem indispensable when considering what is, after all, a portion of the Bill of Rights enacted to protect individuals from oppression. Instead, Powell focused on the "societal interest" served by the First Amendment and "the type of speech indispensable to decisionmaking in a democracy."[28] He thus treated the First Amendment as a means to an end.

In this utilitarian view, the freedom of speech exists primarily to facilitate the greater good that arises through informed decision making, and only secondarily to secure rights.[29] Free speech protections create space for a free market of conflicting views. This connects up with the utilitarian justification for a free market: an overall increase in utility, wrought through the gains in efficiency, innovation, and incentives arising from free competition. It is not that self-interested speakers are necessarily well-intentioned, but rather that the forces of self-interest when exercised collectively would permit an increase in expression which would enable policies resulting from political debate to be based on the best views, as determined through competition.[30] As Powell put it, "The Court has declared . . . that 'speech concerning public affairs is more than self-expression; it is the essence of self-government.'"[31] The essence of self-government therefore is not the experience of expression or its benefits for self-realization; rather, it has to do with a collective function. Powell left little doubt, adding that "self-government suffers when those in power suppress competing views on public issues 'from diverse and antagonistic sources.'"[32] It was as though he was inspired by the technological innovation and gains in overall welfare that free market competition is supposed to produce.

Powell did recognize a rights-based rationale for free speech in passing. He stated that the "individual's interest in self-expression is a concern of the First Amendment separate from the concern for open and informed discussion."[33] On this "deontological" view, freedom of speech is guaranteed because the act of political expression is good in and of itself.[34] Liberal democracy, then, exists to secure rights for citizens, not to secure gains for the collective. Again, however, Powell did not explain how the deontological view makes sense in the context of corporate speech.

The ability of economic actors such as corporations to secure political rights depends upon the Court's acceptance of the utilitarian or systemic viewpoint. Viewing corporate speech on political matters as valuable for securing "'the widest possible dissemination of information from diverse and antagonistic sources,'"[35] Powell focused exclusively on the creation of a vibrant and competitive market for political discourse. *Buckley* accomplished the same thing by establishing the principle that "the dependence of a communication on the expenditure of money [does not] introduce a nonspeech element or . . . reduce the exacting scrutiny required by the First Amendment."[36] Thus it becomes irrelevant whether political speech emanates from a million-dollar ad campaign or a corporate person.[37]

All of this aside, the utilitarian, market-based view is in fact sympathetic to Massachusetts's rationale for limiting corporate participation. Powell recognized that preventing corruption, "sustaining the active role of the individual citizen in the electoral process[,] and . . . preventing diminution of the citizen's confidence in government"[38] were compelling State interests. If citizens ceased participating, the market would languish. If quid pro quo corruption occurred, the market would be distorted. Powell's plurality opinion, however, considered these dangers to be unsupported on the record.[39]

In response to Massachusetts's allegation of corporate influence on democracy, however, Powell was defiant. The State contended that corporate "participation would exert undue influence on the outcome of a referendum vote [given that] corporations are wealthy and powerful and their views may drown out other points of view."[40] Powell responded with a free market retort: "To be sure, corporate advertising may influence the outcome of the vote; this would be its purpose. But the fact that advocacy may persuade the electorate is hardly a reason to suppress it."[41] In support of this point, Powell quoted *Buckley*'s admonition against restricting the speech of some to enhance the relative voice of others. He then went on to assign to the electorate the "responsibility for judging and evaluating the relative merits of conflicting arguments," which might be facilitated through consideration of the "source and credibility of the advocate."[42]

Powell's argument is inspired by a simplistic free market theory: If a product proves dominant on the market, that is because the product is superior, at least in the eyes of consumers, who judge for themselves which products to purchase and which to ignore. The government should not interfere in this process by excluding certain firms or subsidizing others. It is up to consumers to determine the reputation, and, ultimately, the sales of different brands.

Schumpeter, writing twenty-eight years before Justice Powell, explains Powell's first mistake:

The ways in which issues and the popular will on any issue are being manufactured is exactly analogous to the ways of commercial advertising. We find the same attempts to contact the subconscious. We find the same technique of creating favorable and unfavorable associations which are the more effective the less rational they are. We find the same evasions and reticences and the same trick of producing opinion by reiterated assertion that is successful precisely to the extent to which it avoids rational argument and the danger of awakening the critical faculties of the people . . . Only, all these arts have infinitely more scope in the sphere of public affairs than they have in the sphere of private and professional life. The picture of the prettiest girl that ever lived will in the long run prove powerless to maintain the sales of a bad cigarette. There is no equally effective safeguard in the case of political decisions. Many decisions of fateful importance are of a nature that makes it impossible for the public to experiment with them at its leisure and at moderate cost. Even if that is possible, however, judgment is as a rule not so easy to arrive at as it is in the case of the cigarette, because effects are less easy to interpret.[43]

Speech designed to influence political policy is not like consumer products, and the process of selecting each varies in important ways. It is difficult for political consumers to determine the cause of an economic downturn, an electoral outcome, or most other events caused by public policies. The effects of such policies are debated endlessly by economists, political scientists, and political parties themselves. There is no truth here akin to that of whether a given car goes from 0 to 60 in ten seconds or less.

Because political consumers can hardly experiment with public policy at their leisure or very well discern its social effects ahead of time, political legitimacy is central. If the process through which society makes its choices lacks integrity, what vision of justice demands that the public abide by the laws or accept the trade-offs they impose? Democratic integrity justifies the uncertain outcomes of the policy-making process and furnishes a credible promise that unpopular policies will be revisited in due course. The Court demanded that corporations have an unlimited voice in moderating that process (at least within the referendum context), insisting, paradoxically, that any other outcome would undermine popular choice. The paradox fades slightly in the economic paradigm imposed by Powell, but a short inquiry restores it.

II. WELCOMING OLIGOPOLY

Even remaining within the economic paradigm and agreeing to its application, it is difficult to get around the second mistake in Powell's plurality opinion. He assumed that "the widest possible dissemination of information from diverse and antagonistic sources" would be achieved by invalidating the Massachusetts law and creating an unregulated market.[44] We will soon see that this assumption is unwarranted even on the basis of sources available to (and probably known to) the Justices on the *Bellotti* Court.

The government interest in preventing undue influence and maintaining the participation of the general public is analogous to an interest in maintaining a truly competitive market in which no player gets large enough to set prices. What are the implications of corporations launching expensive campaigns via television, radio, and print media, while the great majority of individuals have only enough funds to organize a gathering for twenty friends and only enough time to picket around a town square? This sort of radical inequality between political speakers is the same sort that one finds in the markets for motor vehicles and meat products. Just a few large firms carry on most of the activity, raising the problem of entry for new firms.[45] Without entry, one can hardly expect to have customers. One can always speak, but one cannot always produce cars. When it comes to political speech today, however, broad dissemination of views is necessary to have any impact. Automobile companies and political speakers compete in a large market. To say that without entry one cannot expect to have customers is to say that without finding reasonably effective venues for speech, one can hardly expect to be heard by any appreciable number of people.

Entry depends on raising capital. A market is accessible when capital requirements are low, and thus easy to obtain; when the industry itself is new and thus no firm yet has the advantages of experience and a number of entrants might entertain optimism; or when new firms might be expected to fare well against existing firms, and thus even large amounts of capital could be sensibly invested in them.[46] None of these conditions are found in the expensive media market for political speech: capital requirements are high at the outset (ads are expensive to make and to run); the industry is not new (existing firms are well established); and new entrants cannot be expected to fare well against existing firms due not just to existing firms' experience and expertise, but also to the particular structure of the market. Massive consolidation of firms has already occurred, a process through which firms realize economies of scale and generate credit and reputations that facilitate the raising of capital and a broad base of loyal consumers. Perhaps the government interests in preventing undue influence and maintaining citizen participation were astute even within the economic paradigm of speech adopted by the plurality.

In market terms, the ability of the individual to enter the market as anything but a consumer appears foreclosed by these conditions, and we have not even begun to discuss artificial barriers to entry. Because producing any of the goods located in a market occupied by corporate giants is not an individual right, complaints about such a market must be policy-oriented, not rights-based. There is an important connection, however, between the problems with an oligopolistic market (where only a limited number of large firms compete) and concern over individual liberty. It lies in the fact, as Adam Smith recognized, that the free market is about much more than social utility. Smith believed in "sacred and inviolable" rights, which included each person's property in his or her own labor.[47] The workman had the right to dispose of his labor as he pleased, and others had the right to offer him employment if they wished. Government interference with either, whether through preference or restraint, therefore constituted "a manifest encroachment upon . . . just liberty."[48] Absent such interference, Smith predicted that "the obvious and simple system of natural liberty [would] establish[] itself of its own accord."[49] He counseled that while respecting the "laws of justice," "[e]very man [be] left perfectly free to pursue his own interest his own way, and to bring both his industry and capital into competition with those of any other man."[50] What does this advice imply?

Smith assumed a relatively accessible market of more than several competitors of a normal size, the sort of market that could accommodate natural liberty and produce efficiency. He did not attempt to account for today's corporate consolidation. Competition had certain commonsense parameters in Smith's time, and as social and market conditions changed, so did the economic theory of competition. Originally, markets were thought of as either competitive or monopolistic. Then, following massive corporate growth into the beginning of the twentieth century, "a singularly important series of studies [showed] extensive concentration in American industry."[51]

Galbraith states the implications of corporate expansion and consolidation. Short of monopoly, this process produced situations of "few sellers or oligopoly."[52] In a competitive market of many producers, "some of them will certainly seize upon any known innovation."[53] In an imperfectly competitive market of just a few producers, "there is a chance that none will assume the initiative," opting instead for a "profitable and comfortable stagnation."[54] Within an oligopolistic market, the "producer now has measurable control over his prices."[55] Two important implications arise: "prices no longer reflect the ebb and flow of consumer demand,"[56] and "it no longer follows that any of the old goals of social efficiency are realized."[57]

Another major proposition Galbraith develops is that "a convention against price competition is inevitable under oligopoly."[58] Competition is routed into other forms and the implications are only too well known today:

[C]ompetitive energies are normally concentrated on persuasion and, especially in consumers' goods, on salesmanship and advertising. The cigarette manufacturer recruits customers, not by the self-defeating and dangerous device of cutting cigarette prices but, with the unreluctant aid of his advertising agency, by the recourse to the radio, billboards and television screens and through magazines and the press. This is competition but no longer the kind of competition that is eligible for the liberal's defense. On the contrary, the very instrument which once rewarded the community with lower prices and greater efficiency now turns up assailing its ear with rhymed commercials and soap opera . . . Competition becomes an exercise in uniquely ostentatious waste.[59]

These dynamics, even more accelerated in Powell's time, were obvious in the media, the same fora that the *Bellotti* plaintiffs would occupy.

By allowing economic entities of vastly superior resources and startling size to enter what would otherwise be a market of individual (or at least relatively small) "speech producers," Powell welcomed oligopoly. He acknowledged that corporate participation would likely be "highly visible" compared to other forms of political participation.[60] He proposed disclosure as a remedy, as though one could be consoled or the problem fixed by knowing which particular firms had subjected consumers and would-be producers to the domination of an imperfectly competitive and inefficient market.[61] In order to rationalize this injustice, Powell took recourse in the myth that popular responsibility can operate under all imaginable conditions. Assuming that most human beings are capable of teleporting above social structure and divining truth from mass propaganda, Powell concluded: "[P]eople in our democracy are entrusted with the responsibility for judging and evaluating the relative merits of conflicting arguments."[62]

This armchair approach to sovereignty is especially curious coming from Powell. His memo acknowledged the importance of the balance of information in affecting individual opinion. Noting that the "FBI publishes each year a list of speeches made on college campuses by avowed

Communists," Powell advised the Chamber of Commerce to "insist upon equal time on the college speaking circuit."[63] He predicted that "few invitations would be extended to Chamber speakers . . . unless the Chamber aggressively insisted upon the right to be heard—in effect, insisted upon 'equal time.'"[64] He advised the Chamber to "have attractive, articulate, and well-informed speakers" on hand and to "exert whatever degree of pressure—publicly and privately—[that] may be necessary to assure opportunities to speak."[65] Recognizing the difficulty of these tasks, Powell recommended that American business devote 10 percent of its total annual advertising budget as "part of a sustained, major effort to inform and enlighten the American people."[66] To ensure a higher quantity of favorable information, Powell stated that university faculties must be balanced out ideologically, and "national television networks should be monitored in the same way that textbooks should be kept under constant surveillance."[67]

Ultimately, as Justice Powell suggests, the responsibility for evaluating political arguments does lie with each citizen; however, Lewis Powell, Esquire, knew that individual responsibility was no answer to a situation in which the two sides are not able to make their arguments with equal force. Powell will have the better argument the day when the overall balance of information does not matter, human beings are capable of transcending the political environment itself, and cognitive errors are a rarity. He certainly understood that the law at issue in *Bellotti* did not prevent CEOs, business executives, employees, shareholders, or any other group of human beings from spending money to affect the ballot question (much less from engaging in non-economic political activity). He felt, however, that business executives were hesitant to engage politically and that corporate power was weak.

Powell's memo assessed that power at a very low level: "as every business executive knows, few elements of American society today have as little influence in government as the American businessman, the corporation, or even the millions of corporate stockholders."[68] "[I]n terms of political influence," continued Powell, "the American business executive is truly the 'forgotten man.'"[69] He contrasted the forgotten executive with "the single most effective antagonist of American business[,] Ralph Nader who—thanks largely to the media—has become a legend in his own time and an idol of millions of Americans."[70] He recounted the words of a media profile of Nader: "The passion that rules in him—and he is a passionate man—is aimed at smashing utterly the target of his hatred, which is corporate power. He thinks, and says so quite bluntly, that a great many corporate executives belong in prison—for defrauding the consumer with shoddy merchandise, poisoning the food supply with chemical additives, and willfully manufacturing unsafe products that will maim or kill the buyer."[71] Powell did not explain why jail time should be off the table when business executives do such things. He genuinely seemed to view Nader as an oppressive figure throttling that vulnerable class of forgotten men, business executives.

Powell's assessment of the political weakness of businesses deeply affected the *Bellotti* opinion and continues to present a mystery. The year before *Bellotti*, Charles Lindblom published his influential book *Politics and Markets*. Lindblom provided a tremendous amount of data from well before Powell's memo and much before Powell's plurality opinion. Discussing federal elections, Lindblom notes that in "1964 union committees made contributions of less than $4 million while a total of no more than 10,000 individuals, mostly from business, contributed $13.5 million."[72] "And in 1956," Lindblom continues, "it took the contributions of only 742 businessmen to match in amount the contribution of unions representing 17 million workers."[73] Citing the 40,000 American corporations large enough to have at least 100 employees, Lindblom notes that there is "nothing else like it in politics, no other category of organization so massively engaged in seeking to influence local, state, and national government."[74] Relying on U.S. Department of Commerce statistics from 1949, decades before Powell's writings, Lindblom noted how there were far more national associations devoted to business concerns than to any other issue.[75] And citing a more recent copy of the *Encyclopedia of Organizations in the United States*, Lindblom marvels at the 256 pages devoted to national business organizations, as compared with 17 pages to labor organizations and 60 to public affairs organizations. These data, together with the congressional drafting history of FECA and the Watergate record, suggest that Powell's portrayal of business and the businessman was far too humble.

III. OBJECTIONS TO CORPORATE
POLITICAL POWER

Dissenting in *Bellotti*, four Justices provided more accurate assessments of corporate power. Justice White wrote the first dissent, joined by Justices Brennan and Marshall, and Justice Rehnquist wrote the second. In reaching the conclusion that the Massachusetts act should have been upheld, the dissenters showed how the First Amendment could support democracy instead of dismantling it.

A. *Expression, Not Profit Maximization*

Justice White considered that a "free marketplace of ideas" would not be established by allowing corporate expenditures. In justifying his conclusion that corporate participation threatens the First Amendment's market function, White suggested that Powell had misapplied economic theory. According to Powell, the First Amendment's market function demanded open, unregulated access to speech. Natural persons and legal persons alike had to remain free to spend money in the production of speech. This supposedly guaranteed that diverse and antagonistic sources would not be excluded from the market, and that Massachusetts citizens could choose among all available opinions in deciding how to vote. In White's view, the market function depended not on unlimited "volume of expression," but rather on a strong, positive correlation between money spent and views held. He insisted that "[c]orporate political expression . . . bears no relation to the conviction with which the ideas expressed are held by the communicator."[76]

Motivating this insistence one finds a theoretical argument about how a free market is supposed to work, beginning with conviction. Consumers purchase what they desire, and the amount they spend, all other things being equal, is tied to the intensity of that desire. Collectively, these signals influence what is produced, at what price products are offered, and so on. White appears to be suggesting that in a market for speech those who consume airtime and newspaper space ought to behave like any other consumer. When they pay a great deal of money to make a certain point, we ought to be able to assume that they mean what they say and that their degree of conviction, their fervency of belief, is high. This, White intimates, is not the case with corporations, given the "ease with which [they] are permitted to accumulate capital."[77]

Anyone familiar with cost-benefit analysis and the duty of corporate directors to maximize revenue would beg to differ. Given corporate rationality, the level of corporate political spending should bear a rather precise relation to its level of conviction. One important caveat arises: In the case of a $250,000 ad campaign by a multimillion-dollar corporation and an opposing $250,000 expenditure by an individual who took out a second mortgage on his home to raise funds, we should not expect each expenditure to represent 250,000 units of conviction. Money has relative value—a person's last dollar is worth far more to her than the same amount to a solvent person. Given current patterns of income distribution, we might expect that a $100 contribution from a poor man will normally express a greater fervency of belief than even a $2,000 contribution from a rich person.

Several corporations might spend $250,000 to oppose a ballot initiative, the outcome of which is worth $500,000 to them. The rational amount to spend would depend on the odds that their political expenditures would produce the desired result, discounted by any negative unintended consequences that expenditure might have—such as producing resentment among consumers.[78] A political committee, representing citizens, might spend only $7,000 to support the initiative. This could be because the outcome was not worth very much to each citizen or because citizens believed that the expenditure itself would be marginally effective at best. Consumers in the market for speech surely bear in mind how much money the initiative would give or cost them and the odds that political expenditures would be outcome determinative. Corporate expenditures ought to be positively correlated with how much an issue is worth to each corporation and to the perceived odds that the expenditures would desirably affect the resolution of the issue. In this sense, conviction and willingness to spend align.

Still, White must have been aware of these points. Perhaps viewing market behavior through the lens of profit maximization leads us to misunderstand what he means by conviction and fervency. Genuine conviction or fervency differs from commercial interest. White maintained that "corporate expenditures . . . lack the connection with individual self-expression which is one of the principal justifications for the constitutional protection of speech."[79] The marketplace of ideas is not like other marketplaces. While money may be involved, it should represent genuine belief. Such a marketplace welcomes money in the service of expression, not profit maximization.

Through his civic sense of human flourishing, White disqualifies corporate speech.

[W]hat some have considered to be the principal function of the First Amendment, the use of communication as a means of self-expression, self-realization, and self-fulfillment, is not at all furthered by corporate speech. It is clear that the communications of profitmaking corporations are not "an integral part of the development of ideas, of mental exploration and of the affirmation of self."[80]

White is not prepared to endorse an instrumental economic market for speech, a place inhabited by those who will say whatever is necessary in order to accomplish commercial goals.[81] He seems to be headed instead towards a Deweyan idealism, an Emersonian perfectionism, or the sort of transformation praised by Whitman—democracy as a "mode of associated living, of conjoint communicated experience," an opportunity for self-improvement, a "formulator, general caller-forth . . . to become an enfranchised man."[82]

White's ultimate meaning lies in this direction, but he is faced with immediate obstacles along the way. Given the privatization of the mass media, communication is a good within a market. Those who purchase advertising time or space send signals within this market. If a large enough group of consumers is able and willing to pay big money for this good, media companies set prices high. They can maintain their revenues even while excluding those who cannot pay high rates. Wealthier speakers, both individuals and corporations, value this product highly, to be sure. Others, however, might value the advertising time even more highly, but lack the ability to pay for it.

In such a market, we hardly have a wide, vibrant, and representative distribution of viewpoints. It is not just that corporations are incapable of the self-realization that White has in mind; it is also that they are capable of making the self-realization of others a highly inaccessible process. This point relates to oligopoly once again, in that a small group has succeeded in influencing prices and in reducing competition to the uniquely ostentatious waste of political advertisements. What ought to be a market for expressive activity, efficient for the development of ideas, mental exploration, and so on, quickly becomes a war of sound bites efficient for manufacturing consent (or at least cynicism).

Just how White would create a market for sincere, expressive speech—speech as self-realization—is an elusive question. Even leaving corporate expenditures aside, we ought to assume that people generally speak in order to support their own interests, which are often unrelated to any civic sort of self-realization. Ideological speech itself may be a mere rationalization of material self-interest. But even if we were to find self-realization hopelessly entangled with the narrowest self-interest, there remains a chasmic difference between human nature and corporate nature. This, in combination with the material and organizational capabilities of the corporate form, makes White's view of the First Amendment something more than insincere idealism.

B. Corporate Nature

"Corporations are artificial entities created by law for the purpose of furthering certain economic goals," White reminded his colleagues.[83] It is only in the service of these goals that the state grants them the benefit of "special rules relating to such matters as limited liability, perpetual life, and the accumulation, distribution, and taxation of assets."[84] Or, as Rehnquist put it in his dissenting opinion, "[a] State grants to a business corporation the blessings of potentially perpetual life and limited liability to enhance its efficiency as an economic entity."[85]

Aside from the advantages of the corporate form, which were by no means easy to obtain, corporations naturally desire additional terms from the state. These include fewer regulations, lower taxes, and greater concessions, such as bailouts in times of crisis. Rational profit-maximizing entities do not want to pay for any of the following things unless the benefits—along the lines of publicity, productivity, or reduced liability, for example—exceed their costs: environmental cleanups, technological upgrades that reduce pollution, higher wages, injuries caused by dangerous products or injuries caused in the manufacturing of products generally, employee benefits, or safer workplaces.[86] In fulfilling their duty to maximize revenue for shareholders, corporations should spend money on political causes when variables such as these so dictate: the amount of money they (or a competitor) stand to lose should certain policies be enacted; the amount of money they (or a competitor) stand to gain should other policies be enacted; the odds that political expenditures will influence the outcome; and so on. Naturally, corporations wish to influence politics. So do human beings.

At least three sorts of differences between corporations and human beings swayed the dissenters: wealth, incentives, and nature. White wrote that "the special status of corporations has placed them in a position to control vast amounts of economic power."[87] He fixated upon their ability to amass wealth, again referencing the "special advantages extended [to them] by the State."[88] The concern over wealth owes to its potential conversion into political power. In justifying the Massachusetts law, Rehnquist said that "the States might reasonably fear that the corporation would use its economic power to obtain further benefits beyond those already bestowed."[89] Justice White cautioned that such economic power "may, if not regulated, dominate not only the economy but also the very heart of our democracy, the electoral process."[90]

It was not just the wealth of corporations that alarmed the *Bellotti* dissenters, however. In particular, it was their willingness to spend that wealth on political activity. This reveals something about the intensity of corporate interest in politics, which is a function of incentives. While an environmental ordinance might confer speculative and long-term benefits to each person's health, it would more obviously confer definitive and immediate costs on corporate persons whose business plans and technologies would need to be changed. Virtually any government policy aimed at clean air, clean water, or other public goods confers a small cost or benefit to many people, whose interest can be said to be diffuse. Virtually every such policy also inflicts a larger cost or benefit to a smaller set of people and businesses whose daily activities or primary interests are entwined with the policy. This latter set of people and businesses has concentrated, rather than diffuse, interests. It is on the basis of such differences in incentives, alongside factors relating to wealth, organizational capacity, and the mechanics of producing legislation, that some scholars explain unequal political outcomes.[91] Given such concentrated corporate interests in matters of public goods, interests made all the more concentrated by corporate consolidation, corporate speech is often quite fervent. Morally polarizing issues, such as abortion and gay marriage, are one of the great exceptions, and they lead us to the third difference between corporations and human beings.

The way White speaks of self-realization signals a difference assumed by most everyone familiar with corporate law. However avaricious one might believe human nature to be, it is unquestionable that our self-interest has unique human buffers. Consider why Rousseau did not believe human beings to be damned to narrowness by their strong self-love: "[T]here is another principle . . . which, having been given to man in order to mitigate, in certain circumstances, the ferocity of his egocentrism or the desire for self-preservation before this egocentrism of his came into being, tempers the ardor he has for his own well-being by an innate repugnance to seeing fellow man suffer . . . I am referring to pity."[92]

Even taking into account the corporate social responsibility movement, corporate nature is far simpler than human nature: organizational purpose and legal duty align in profit maximization.[93] As Joel Bakan puts it, the corporation "is compelled to cause harm when the benefits of doing so outweigh the costs[—]only pragmatic concern for its own interests and the laws of the land constrain the corporation's predatory instincts."[94] The meaning of this was clear to the *Bellotti* dissenters: nothing but law restrains the expansion of corporate power into the political sphere. Justice Rehnquist said it most clearly: "It might reasonably be concluded that [corporate advantages granted by the state], so beneficial in the economic sphere, pose special dangers in the political sphere."[95] He then added, "I would think that any particular form of organization upon which the State confers special privileges and immunities different from those of natural persons would be subject to regulation."[96] Justice White finally drove home the point in a way that would have appealed to Mary Shelley: "The State need not permit its own creation to consume it."[97]

Should the workings of corporate nature and concentrated interest be treated as optimal and deserving of deference from the state? Recall the notion from *Lochner* that bakers and bakery owners should be permitted to reach whatever deal they can. There can be no *injustice* in long hours or unsafe working conditions because such conditions are set by the market. Whether it be the surplus of bakers, the facility of making bread, or the relatively low effect of workplace injuries on their produce, the same conclusion arises: more reasonable hours and better conditions would be inefficient. And if bakers are unemployed it must be because they have chosen to hold out for *unjust* terms—namely, those terms that do not align with the conditions brought about by supply and demand. In relation to such a perfect, private ordering, government intervention would be harmful to overall social welfare. Consider the proposition, then, that if corporations and media companies have a propensity to reach mutually agreeable terms, this ought not be interrupted. Corporate political advertisements flow forth from interests generated by the market, and it is the market that must decide their worth.

Rehnquist and White sought to destroy this line of reasoning. "The State could say," White wrote, "that not to impose limits upon political activities of corporations would have placed it in a position of departing from neutrality and indirectly assisting the propagation of corporate views because of the advantages its laws give to the corporate acquisition of funds to finance such activities."[98] The propensity for corporations to come to terms with sellers of airtime results from laws that create and entrench corporate nature. The ability to come to such terms, potentially even cornering the market for speech, is also a state-created phenomenon: recall that the corporation's superior ability to amass capital is the product of state intervention— i.e., law. And therefore Rehnquist could argue with considerable acumen that "liberties of political expression are not at all necessary to effectuate the purposes for which States permit commercial corporations to exist."[99]

An uncritical market view in the context of corporate political speech contains tremendous weaknesses. As we have seen, the supposedly neutral state of affairs being defended is actually an unintended consequence of government intervention. Next, the better part of economic theory decries incredible imbalances of power and the domination they produce.

C. Democracy-Friendly Economics

Justices White and Rehnquist viewed the corporate vehicle's intrusion into the political sphere as an act of domination. White pointed out that the law did not personally restrict anyone aligned with a corporation:

"[E]ven complete curtailment of corporate communications on political/ideological questions would leave individuals, shareholders, and employees, and customers free to communicate their thoughts."[100] Moreover, the people would not be deprived of their right to hear and the systemic function of the First Amendment would not be impaired. White considered it "unlikely that any significant communication would be lost by such a prohibition."[101] Only power would be lost. Without the superior resources of a corporate treasury, the plaintiff's speech would have to compete with the speech of other human beings on a more equal playing field.

If speech is a facet of democratic governance, then the concern over corporate political power is recast in terms of political inequality and the sorts of actors that are appropriately taken into democracy's fold. Recall Rehnquist's warning about the "special dangers in the political sphere" created by corporate power.[102] White is clear on this point as well. He calls elections "the essence of our democracy[,] an arena in which the public interest in preventing corporate domination . . . is at its strongest."[103] Corporate domination of democracy flows from extreme inequality—the difference in economic power and organizational capabilities between average citizens and the corporations that seek to influence public policy. The source of that inequality is structural, even geographic: democracy (an arena or sphere, as White and Rehnquist described it) contains different sorts of actors than the economic market (a different arena). Blending the two domains together, economic actors will make short work of citizens, even on citizens' terrain.

But if we think of speech as a market, as all the Justices have done to an extent, then the concern over corporate control becomes a concern over monopoly or oligopoly. The classical economic emphasis on competition sought to prevent firms from exercising undue influence even within the market. This too evinces a concern about domination, albeit with regard to actors from within the same sphere. Contemplating how just a few large corporations control a great deal of many industries, Galbraith remarked that "[h]ere was power to control the prices the citizen paid, the wages he received, and which interposed the most formidable of obstacles of size and experience to the aspiring new firm."[104] Noting this sort of domination in the market, he asked, "What more might [such power] accomplish were it to turn its vast resources to corrupting politics and controlling access to public opinion."[105] Neoclassical theory tends not to entertain such questions.

White and Rehnquist sought the thicker thread of economic thought that remains tolerant of political society. To begin with, their desire to protect the political sphere from corporate domination has nothing to do with a progressive bias in favor of the powerless. Limits on wealth's conversion to political power need not be motivated by distributive considerations or social justice rationales. Two more plausible rationales for protecting the political sphere are in play: a liberal preference for a self-regulating economy and a liberal preference for a political order that is accessible and responsive to citizens.

Here, limitations on the translation of wealth into political power come into lasting focus. Walzer writes that "political power and wealth must check each other" and that "capitalists will be tyrants whenever their wealth is not balanced by a strong government."[106] Thus, Walzer meets Galbraith. Having concluded that corporate consolidation undermined the initial regulatory method of capitalism, competition, Galbraith looked around him, noticed that the system continued to function reasonably well, and asked whether another regulatory method was already in place. His theory of countervailing power describes a "new restraint[] on private power [that] replace[s] competition."[107] Galbraith explains that countervailing power is "nurtured by the same process of concentration which impaired or destroyed competition" and that it "appears not on the same side of the market but on the opposite side, not with competitors but with customers or suppliers."[108] Galbraith gives the examples of unions as a source of power that counters that of large corporations in the labor market, and large retailers who bargain with large manufacturers in order to keep prices low in the consumer goods market.[109] The design of this opposition is simple: "private economic power is held in check by the countervailing power of those who are subject to it[—t]he first begets the second."[110]

The power that seeks to hold concentrated wealth in check also emerges on the opposite side of the political market. On one side of the market are those who provide large sums of money in hopes of acquiring political influence, the leading donors and spenders. On the other side of the market are the objects of those attempts: candidates, officeholders, parties, and average voters. They represent, respectively, the demand for and supply of political influence—demand in the form of contributions and expenditures of all kinds; supply in the form of votes at the polls and on the floor, agenda setting, nominations, and myriad other ways of furthering or opposing political interests. To the extent that concentrated wealth has cornered the market for political influence, hopes for avoiding domination lie with a response from those most affected. This is the Congress enacting campaign finance reform and voters asking them to do so.[111]

Limitations on money in politics fit the mold of countervailing power for still another reason. As a response to oligopoly, such power is naturally asserted by a "numerous and disadvantaged group which seeks organization because it faces, in its market, a much smaller and more advantaged group."[112] The focus on corporate power in the *Bellotti* dissenting opinions matches this description perfectly.

Next, the necessary role of government in passing laws to restrict the role of money in politics and increase the relative power of average citizens is consistent with countervailing power. Galbraith notes that such power is not easy to organize and that government support is frequently required—to labor, the Wagner Act; to unorganized workers, minimum wage legislation; and so on.[113] He explains that "the provision of state assistance to the development of countervailing power has become a major function of government—perhaps *the* major domestic function of government."[114] He characterizes New Deal legislation generally as "designed to give a group a market power it did not have before."[115] The function of the government in facilitating the development of countervailing power is to "support[] or supplement[] a normal economic process," with the result of "strengthen[ing] competition."[116]

According to Galbraith, all of the functions listed above have a counterintuitive, market-friendly result:

Given the existence of private market power in the economy, the growth of countervailing power strengthens the capacity of the economy for autonomous self-regulation and thereby lessens the amount of over-all government control of planning that is required or sought.[117]

Whether at the state or national level, and whether through comprehensive campaign finance legislation or through piecemeal restrictions, the result is the same: A numerous, disadvantaged group on the other side of the political market from big donors and corporate spenders benefits from political finance reform. Limits on money in politics increase that group's relative power in the market, enabling it to serve as a check on concentrations of economic power, thus ensuring a degree of competition within the political market. This upholds the integrity of the system and, if cemented as a foundational structure, it may enable the system to regulate itself.

This sort of economic theory recognizes the role of the state in maintaining the integrity of the market. It is democracy's economic ally. With corporate domination at bay, the political order has less to fear from the economic order. Regulated capitalism is precisely that form of moderate capitalism that does not insist on commodifying every portion of society: it allows aspects of fundamental areas—such as health, product safety, education, and politics—to be regulated (or guaranteed) by the state.

. . .

These vying economic perspectives on the Constitution and corporate political participation ought to sound familiar. We have come across a strange setting for a constant controversy that many observe in American society. As economists George Akerlof and Robert Shiller put it, "The debate about which form of capitalism we should have goes far back in American history and is notable for its many sharp reversals."[118] The question is whether this debate has overstepped its bounds, expanding into a sphere that ought not be shaped by such terms.

Whether any given area of society should be viewed as a market is a case-sensitive inquiry, but the structure of the inquiry is the same in each case. Should the market, with its particular relationship to matters of freedom, equality, and accountability, be allowed to govern? With regard to the political sphere, Congress and many state legislatures have continued to say no. The Supreme Court continues to defy them, offering a defense of the free enterprise system in a most unusual place.

CHAPTER 4

Consumer Sovereignty

AN UNUSUAL CONFRONTATION PROVIDES CLUES TO WHERE
George W. Bush's appointees have taken the law. During his State of the
Union address on January 27, 2010, President Obama criticized the Jus-
tices sitting directly before him.

With all due deference to separation of powers, last week the Supreme Court
reversed a century of law that I believe will open the floodgates for special interests—including foreign corporations—to spend without limit in our elections.
(Applause.) I don't think American elections should be bankrolled by America's
most powerful interests, or worse, by foreign entities. (Applause.) They should
be decided by the American people. And I'd urge Democrats and Republicans to
pass a bill that helps to correct some of these problems.[1]

In the midst of this unprecedented reprimand, Justice Alito mouthed the
words "not true" back at the president.[2] Chief Justice Roberts, on the other
hand, remained motionless. A few days later, he complained that he had
felt trapped, as though by a mob.

The image of having the members of one branch of government standing up,
literally surrounding the Supreme Court, cheering and hollering, while the court,
according to the requirements of protocol, has to sit there, expressionless, I think
is very troubling . . . It does cause me to think whether or not it makes sense for
us to be there.[3]

The *Los Angeles Times* called Obama's words "a rare public rebuke that
left justices visibly upset."[4]

What had the Justices done to deserve this high-profile scolding? Just
six days before the president's address, the majority opinion in *Citizens
United* had officially bestowed upon corporations the right of free speech
and struck down a long-standing prohibition on corporate political advertising. Whereas Justice Powell's opinion in *Bellotti* had struck down

corporate prohibitions in the referenda context, *Citizens United* addressed the electoral context.[5] Powell had set corporations free to spend on ballot questions. Kennedy, who had been appointed to fill the vacancy left when Powell stepped down, expanded that freedom of influence to the context of elections. President Obama's reaction was nothing if not an indication of just how faithfully Kennedy had continued Powell's legacy, that quest to ensure that "businessmen . . . confront this [attack on free enterprise] as a primary responsibility of corporate management" and learn "the lesson that political power is necessary [and] must be used aggressively and with determination."[6]

Thanks to Kennedy's work in *Citizens United*, corporate speakers can now absorb (for some candidates) and increase (for others) without any limit one of the most expensive aspects of political campaigns: advertising. Former general counsel to the Federal Election Commission Lawrence Noble describes a familiar scenario. "Lobbyist to representative or candidate: 'We have got a million [dollars] we can spend advertising for you or against you—whichever one you want.'"[7] Maintaining a political platform contrary to the interests of this lobbyist's client costs roughly a million dollars, the money necessary to mount an opposing ad campaign. Hewing to the client's position, on the other hand, buys the politician a million dollars' worth of favorable ads. Candidates ignore corporate views at the peril of awakening to a media environment in which one's name and platform are constantly maligned (whether fairly or unfairly). Beyond affecting the balance of power between candidates, corporate money now has unlimited leeway to affect the overall political agenda, the salience of one issue over another, and the portrayal of each issue and candidate involved.

Anyone who paid attention to the 2012 election knows that President Obama's breach of decorum failed to convince lawmakers to take action. After the *SpeechNow* case, in which a federal appeals court built on *Citizens United*, the Federal Election Commission announced that corporations are free to donate unlimited funds to independent expenditure committees.[8] The attorney prevailing in the *SpeechNow* case described the holding: "The court affirmed that groups of passionate individuals, like billionaires—and corporations and unions . . . —have the right to spend without limit to independently advocate for or against federal candidates."[9] Such unlimited spending by corporations and billionaires has given birth to the new "superPACs," nominally independent committees that collect unlimited funds to influence the political debate. Noble's million-dollar hypothetical has already played out countless times.[10] Wealthy donors and corporations are now secure in their right to engineer and sound off the biggest voices in the nation's political debate.

Well before all of this began to play out, the legislative response called for by the president was tabled in the Senate. Even in its watered-down form, focusing mostly on disclosure of the source of political expenditures, and even six months after the *Citizens United* decision, not a single Republican was willing to sign it.[11] Republicans believe the ruling favors them. But their self-interest defies public opinion, even the opinion of Republican voters. A major poll conducted days after Obama's address found that 85 percent of Democrats, 81 percent of independents, and 76 percent of Republicans opposed the ruling. The findings showed "remarkably strong agreement . . . across all demographic groups [including] those with household incomes above and below $50,000."[12] President Obama's remarks had, at least, succeeded in drawing public attention to the Court's decision.

The president did not convey, however, what it was about the decision that most demanded public condemnation. The holding and the statistics above show the obvious importance of *Citizens United*, but the ruling also accomplished a more transcendent feat: it struck down the crowning accomplishments of the progressive evolution that had occurred since *Bellotti*. Over the final years of the Burger Court and the nearly twenty years of the Rehnquist Court, the caselaw yielded a rough balance of power between the competing approaches to democracy that we have seen. These years produced no victory for corporate or financial power akin to *Buckley* or *Bellotti*. Instead, the Court endorsed White's and Rehnquist's concerns over corporate political power and democratic integrity, gave greater deference to the political branches at state and federal levels, and validated many limits on money in politics. Although neither *Buckley* nor *Bellotti* was overturned, the majority of Justices backed away from the unregulated market view and began to embrace more civic conceptions of speech and democracy. Laissez-faire ideology began to seem like a relic from an earlier, uncivilized time.

Then in 2005, President George W. Bush replaced two Republican-appointed campaign finance moderates, Chief Justice Rehnquist and Justice O'Connor, with John Roberts and Samuel Alito. Upon seizing the helm, the new conservative majority wasted no time in reversing the Rehnquist Court's progressive evolution. Indeed, the radical shift evident in *Citizens United* was not the beginning. This is what seemed oddest about the president's otherwise audacious rebuke of the Court. He failed to mention that earlier Roberts Court opinions had already stood upon *Buckley*'s and *Bellotti*'s shoulders, seeing further into the neoliberal expanse than the Burger Court. What the president had described as a surprising affront to democracy—a foot kicking in the front door—was actually much closer to the proverbial final nail in a casket.

The free market theory now governing the law of democracy is so comprehensive and absolute that either a change in the Court's membership or a constitutional amendment would be required to support meaningful limits on money in politics. A great deal of popular will would be required to amend the Constitution or to elect presidents and senators who would make political finance the "make or break issue" in judicial appointments. The formation of popular will ought to take into account the progressive evolution that *Citizens United* crushed. Popular will, in whatever direction it points, must also take stock of how the Roberts Court has elaborated upon *Buckley* and *Bellotti*'s order that democracy conform to the market's design. This exercise will show how the various cases come together to form an entire blueprint, a comprehensive plan far more astounding than the single facet criticized by the president.

I. THE REHNQUIST COURT'S EVOLUTION
TOWARDS POPULAR SOVEREIGNTY

Recall Rehnquist's dissenting opinion in *Bellotti*, cautioning that state-conferred corporate advantages—such as "potentially perpetual life and limited liability"—"pose special dangers in the political sphere."[13] Four years later, but still before the start of his tenure as Chief Justice, Rehnquist had persuaded the entire Court to endorse his concern about corporate control of politics. His unanimous opinion in *FEC v. National Right to Work Committee* (NRWC) contained this warning:

Substantial aggregations of wealth amassed by the special advantages which go with the corporate form of organization should not be converted into political 'war chests' which could be used to incur political debts from legislators.[14]

The mere fact of unanimity in a campaign finance case is surprising, but unanimity with respect to this progressive sensibility to concentrated wealth is astounding. How could it be that every single Justice was alarmed by the prospect of legislators beholden to corporate interests?

The answer lies in the date of the opinion: 1982. Four years would pass before Rehnquist took over from Burger and Antonin Scalia occupied Rehnquist's former seat. Nine years would plod along before Clarence Thomas replaced Justice Marshall, and almost a quarter century would linger before John Roberts took over the chief justiceship from Rehnquist and Samuel Alito replaced Justice O'Connor. Notwithstanding their handiwork in *Buckley* and *Bellotti*, most of the conservatives on the Court in 1982 cannot be compared to the men selected to replace them—at least not on matters of money in politics. Indeed, as we shall soon see, the choice of Clarence Thomas for Thurgood Marshall's seat may well have been the most discourteous judicial substitution in the Court's history.

All Justices on the Court in 1982, including the four Justices from the *Bellotti* majority who had yet to retire, recognized that *Buckley* "specifically affirmed the importance of preventing . . . the eroding of public confidence in the electoral process" and protecting "the integrity of our electoral process."[15] Although *Buckley* framed these concerns only as rationales for contribution limits, the entire Court took their implications seriously. As for *Bellotti*, each Justice recognized that the case concerned corporate expenditures in the context of a referendum, where only individual citizens could be persuaded (or drowned out), not an election, where officeholders and candidates could become indebted to their corporate sponsors.

Having understood that no case provided a mandate for corporate electioneering and finding precedential grounds for preserving public confidence and democratic integrity, yesterday's conservatives proceeded to distinguish themselves in yet another way from their descendants in *Citizens United*.

They deferred to Congress. Surveying the (then) seventy-five-year-old history of congressional restrictions on corporate political activity, *NRWC* concluded that "this careful legislative adjustment of . . . electoral laws, in a 'cautious advance, step by step' . . . warrants considerable deference."[16]

While it may be correct to ascribe greater institutional comity and faithfulness to the separation of powers to yesterday's Court, deference to Congress tends to rest on more specific explanations. When it comes to restrictions on associational and expressive freedoms, the Court has long demanded proof of a compelling (or at least sufficiently important) state interest in play. Absent such a worthy motivation for political finance limitations, any curtailment of political rights is unjustified. Thus, deference derives from the subjective valuation of the government's motivation. Even if the Court demanded that only a valid state interest be established, it would still have to pass judgment on the validity of that interest. Whether deemed valid, important, or compelling, any state interest tolerated by the Court is also a state interest legitimated by the Court. Accordingly, the Court's concern over aggregated capital, indebted office-holders, democratic integrity, public confidence, and the responsibility of individual citizens deserves our attention.

That concern peaked twice during Chief Justice Rehnquist's long tenure. In illustrating the importance of personality and biography on the Court, these cases offer immediate intrigue. Greater value, however, lies in the general theories that these cases apply to determine the constitutionality of political finance reforms. These theories live on well beyond the tenure of their exponents, offering to each Court an inherited universe of conceptual approaches to democracy. The progressive evolution within the Rehnquist Court produced a civic, less market-oriented approach, which can be seen most clearly in *Austin* and *McConnell*. I refer, naturally, to the cases that the Roberts Court hastened to overturn.

A. Undue Influence:
Austin v. Michigan Chamber of Commerce (1990)

Passed in 1976, the Michigan Campaign Finance Act allowed corporations to make independent expenditures against or in favor of candidates for state office.[17] The Act did not allow corporations to use their treasury funds for this purpose, however. Instead, it required corporations wishing to be politically active to establish a segregated, political fund for which money could be drawn only from a limited group of people associated with the corporation. This requirement stood in the way of the Michigan Chamber of Commerce's plan to use general treasury funds to support a candidate for the Michigan House of Representatives. Accordingly, the Chamber sought an injunction against the act's enforcement.[18]

The reasons behind the Chamber's political activities are no mystery. Counting over 6,000 for-profit corporations among its list of 8,000 members, the Chamber's purposes included:

[T]o promote economic conditions favorable to private enterprise; to analyze, compile, and disseminate information about laws of interest to the business community and to publicize to the government the views of the business community on such matters; . . . to receive contributions and make expenditures for political purposes and to perform any other lawful political activity.[19]

These are the same purposes that Lewis Powell had encouraged the national Chamber of Commerce to pursue. Much corporate money seeks conditions desired by particular firms, not private enterprise as a whole. Still, the Michigan law against general treasury expenditures affects both types of corporate spending, making *Austin* a paradigmatic case.

Because the Chamber could accept unlimited corporate contributions directly into its general treasury funds, political expenditures from those funds would circumvent the act's limitations on political contributions and expenditures. The challenged provision of the act prevented the Chamber from "serv[ing] as a conduit for corporate political spending."[20] The Chamber's interest lay, obviously enough, in serving as such a conduit and thus evading limitations on corporate political power. The question was whether those limitations could withstand the First Amendment's freedom of speech clause.

Although Justice Thurgood Marshall's majority opinion began by conceding that "the use of funds to support a political candidate is 'speech'" and that the Chamber's corporate status "does not remove its speech from the ambit of the First Amendment," it proceeded to offer the belated, progressive answer to *Buckley* and *Bellotti*.[21] That answer had to be given within a certain framework, however. Because Marshall had conceded that the Chamber's political expenditures constitute political expression and that the act's requirements "burden expressive activity,"[22] he was bound to examine whether a compelling state interest existed and whether the act's provisions were narrowly tailored to uphold that interest.

Then, just as Marshall began the standard judicial script on compelling state interests carried out through narrowly tailored laws, he cited a past case that spoke of a paradigm shift: "Preventing corruption or the appearance of corruption are [sic] the only legitimate and compelling government interests *thus far identified* for restricting campaign finances."[23]

Bringing White and Rehnquist into the Fold Before naming a new compelling state interest, Marshall dwelled on its foundational concerns, drawing heavily from past opinions.

[S]tate-created advantages not only allow corporations to play a dominant role in the Nation's economy, but also permit them to use "resources amassed in the economic marketplace" to obtain "an unfair advantage in the political marketplace."[24]

Marshall assured his readers that corporate expenditure limits were not justified by the quantity of wealth that corporations may accumulate. Instead, "the unique state-conferred corporate structure that facilitates the amassing of large treasuries warrants the limit on independent expenditures."[25] White had already described that structure in terms of "limited liability, perpetual life," and "special rules relating to . . . the accumulation, distribution, and taxation of assets."[26] Corporate structure, Marshall maintained, is what "facilitates the amassing of large treasuries [and] warrants the limit on independent expenditures."[27] Indeed, Marshall considered the segregated fund requirement to be justified even in the case of corporations that do not possess much wealth, because "they [still] receive from the State the special benefits conferred by the corporate structure."[28]

White had explained the first concern behind these observations on state intervention twelve years earlier in his *Bellotti* dissent.

Massachusetts could permissibly conclude that not to impose limits upon the political activities of corporations would have placed it in a position of departing from neutrality and indirectly assisting the propagation of corporate views because of the advantages its laws give to the corporate acquisition of funds to finance such activities.[29]

This was a simple point about the fairness of state intervention. It is unfair for the state to provide corporations with a host of economic advantages over human citizens, and then allow corporations to use the fruit of those advantages to dominate the political sphere. White and Marshall's narrow reasoning along these lines is in keeping with the fact that the Court's opinions do not limit independent expenditures by spectacularly wealthy individuals. Much personal wealth is accumulated with the help of the corporate form at one stage or another, but once that wealth is transferred to a natural person it is no longer held within that organizationally superior, legally privileged framework.

Another dissenting opinion from *Bellotti* explains the second concern that lies beyond Marshall's simple point about unfairness. Supporting the Massachusetts prohibition on corporate political expenditures in state ballot initiatives, Rehnquist focused on why the state endows corporations with superior attributes and how those attributes are meant to operate in a sphere separate from politics.

A State grants to a business corporation the blessings of potentially perpetual life and limited liability to enhance its efficiency as an economic entity. It might reasonably be concluded that those properties, so beneficial in the economic sphere, pose special dangers in the political sphere . . . Indeed, the States might reasonably fear that the corporation would use its economic power to obtain further benefits beyond those already bestowed. I would think that any particular form of organization upon which the State confers special privileges or immunities different from those of natural persons would be subject to like regulation.[30]

Note the distinction Rehnquist makes between the economic sphere and the political sphere. In granting special commercial advantages to corporations, the state does not intend those advantages to be leveraged for political purposes. Regulations on the use of these economic advantages within the political sphere are justified because corporations owe their existence to the state itself and it is the state's task to confine its own creation to the proper realm.

Rehnquist's reference to corporations' use of economic power to obtain "further benefits" from the state points to a broad systemic dilemma. If corporations leverage their economic power for political gain, they bring a foreign sort of power to bear upon the political sphere. Unleashed in this territory, corporate economic prowess would surpass that of individual citizens, and could thus exercise greater control over political debate, political parties, candidates, and officeholders. The purpose would logically be to maximize profits and minimize costs, ends achieved through controlling the instruments of public policy, including the shape of legislation, administrative agencies and standards, and free-trade treaties.

Thus, the states' bestowal of perpetual life, limited liability, and unique financial terms upon the corporate form could lead, accidentally and undesirably, to a string of additional concessions achieved piecemeal. This is why Marshall embraced almost verbatim White's resolve to "prevent[] institutions . . . permitted to amass wealth as a result of special advantages extended by the State for certain economic purposes from using that wealth to acquire an unfair advantage in the political process."[31] White foresaw that the state's own creations would not be satisfied with economic power alone.[32]

Besides fairness and the importance of confining corporate power to the economic realm, the new state interest had political speech in mind. This final concern also derives from Rehnquist's and White's dissenting opinions in *Bellotti*. "[I]t might be argued," began Rehnquist, "that liberties of political expression are not at all necessary to effectuate the purposes for which States permit commercial corporations to exist."[33] "So long as the Judicial Branches of the State and Federal Governments remain open to protect the corporation's interest in its property," Rehnquist continued, "it has no need, though it may have the desire, to petition the political branches for similar protection."[34]

In contrast to today's conservative majority, Rehnquist believed that "the Fourteenth Amendment does not require a State to endow a business corporation with the power of political speech."[35] Nevertheless, he subscribed to *Bellotti*'s construction of the First Amendment as guarantor of the public's right to hear the political ideas of all speakers. "The free flow of information," he insisted, "is in no way diminished by the

Commonwealth's decision to permit the operation of business corporations with limited rights of political expression."[36] This conclusion derives from Rehnquist's premise regarding the dominion of human beings over political speech: "All natural persons, who owe their existence to a higher sovereign than the Commonwealth, remain as free as before to engage in political activity [under the challenged law]."[37]

If it is the case, as Rehnquist conceded, that the First Amendment protects a listener-oriented marketplace for speech, this political marketplace need not—indeed, must not—be fused with the economic marketplace. White provided a reason for this proposition besides the aforementioned concern over corporate control of politics.

[Corporate political] expenditures may be viewed as seriously threatening the role of the First Amendment as a guarantor of a free marketplace of ideas. Ordinarily, the expenditure of funds to promote political causes may be assumed to bear some relation to the fervency with which they are held. Corporate political expression, however, is not only divorced from the convictions of individual corporate shareholders, but also, because of the ease with which corporations are permitted to accumulate capital, bears no relation to the conviction with which the ideas expressed are held by the communicator.[38]

This passage suggests that the currency of the political marketplace is meant to convey the fervency and strength of convictions. White doubted that corporate economic power bore these marks.

Because of this concern over genuinely political speech, White could deny that the state interest in limiting corporate political expenditures was "one of equalizing the resources of opposing candidates or opposing positions."[39] Recall Marshall's point that this line of analysis turns not on the wealth of the particular corporation in question, but rather on the fact of state-conferred economic advantages. Indeed, Marshall had joined White's dissent in *Bellotti* and had taken up the task in *Austin* of making that dissent binding law. The parallels are anything but coincidental.

Readers would be right to doubt, however, that the equality concern is entirely distinct from the concerns about the political dominance of aggregated capital and the absence of a tight fit between economic resources and political convictions. In a dissenting opinion handed down five years before *Austin*, Marshall wrote that "limitations on independent expenditures . . . are justified by the congressional interest in promoting the reality and appearance of equal access to the political arena."[40] By opposing the rule against limiting the speech of some in order to further the speech of others, Marshall recanted his allegiance to *Buckley*. He also questioned *Buckley*'s assumptions about independent expenditures. "It simply belies reality," he wrote, "to say that a campaign will not reward massive financial assistance provided in the only way that is legally available."[41] Large expenditures, Marshall implied, reduce the responsiveness of candidates and representatives to ordinary Americans, who, in such a system, can never enjoy political equality.

The New Corruption and the New Compelling State Interest   Marshall's sympathy for equality as a justification for campaign finance reform should not surprise anyone familiar with his biography. He was, after all, the lawyer who prevailed in *Brown v. Board of Education* and the first African American to serve on the Supreme Court. His great-grandfather was a slave, he built his career with the National Association for the Advancement of Colored People, and he was, needless to say, far more at home on the Warren Court than the Burger Court.[42] His sympathies notwithstanding, Marshall required a viable theory of democracy for use in *Austin*, one not already foreclosed by precedent. This much was necessary if he wished to write for the Court instead of merely for himself. We should understand his reference to the only state interests *thus far* credited, and subsequent naming of a new interest in this light.

Marshall vindicated Michigan's regulation as targeting

a different type of corruption in the political arena: the corrosive and distorting effects of immense aggregations of wealth that are accumulated with the help of the corporate form and that have little or no correlation to the public's support for the corporation's political ideas.[43]

The new corruption is targeted by what Marshall called "the compelling state interest of eliminating from the political process the corrosive effect of political 'war chests' amassed with the aid of the legal advantages given to corporations."[44] He took great care in repeating his view that "corporations are 'by far the most prominent example of entities that enjoy legal advantages enhancing their ability to accumulate wealth.'"[45] "The desire to counterbalance those advantages unique to the corporate form," he continued, "is the State's compelling interest in this case."[46] This interest justified the harm to expressive activity caused by Michigan's segregated fund requirement.

Marshall's concerns tie neatly into Rehnquist's opinion for a unanimous Court in *NRWC*, suggesting that corporate political war chests accumulated through the corporate form can be used to "incur political debts from legislators," and thus create an unfair advantage over average citizens.[47] Coupled with the absence of a tight fit between money spent on politics and genuine political belief and fervency, corporate advantages corrode and distort the democratic process.

Ultimately, political equality would be well served by the new state interest validated in *Austin*. The concept of undue influence describes what the "unfair advantage" possessed by corporations over ordinary citizens produces in the political sphere.[48] What could such an advantage embody besides inequality? Still, the opinion only references the unfairness of state-conferred advantages for corporations, intended for use in the economic sphere, being leveraged for political power. There is no talk of equality itself, the importance of average citizens having a meaningful voice in the political process, or unincorporated groups being able to compete on equal terms in the marketplace for ideas. The *Austin* majority actually went so far as to reassure its readers that the "Act does not attempt to equalize the relative influence of speakers on elections."[49]

Something profound resides beneath the Court's seemingly insincere denial of the equality rationale. At base, the new state interest rests not on equality, but on its precursor, the insight that makes political equality possible. Recall that Marshall situated corporations' unfair advantage in the context of resources amassed in the economic marketplace being employed within the political marketplace. Hence, the corrosion and distortion of the political marketplace are caused by its entanglement with the economic marketplace. This separation between marketplaces is *Austin*'s central analytical postulate. All the rest—the references to state-created advantages, unfairness, genuine political speech, unstated benefits for political equality, and the avoidance of democratic corrosion and distortion—flows from this separatist architecture. If entities from the economic sphere are allowed to bring their economic superiority to bear upon the political sphere, "special dangers" arise, as Rehnquist wrote. Consider his reference to corporations obtaining additional benefits from the state, and White's admonition that the state ought not to be forced into a Frankensteinian plight. These notions, ratified just a little more than a decade after *Buckley* and *Bellotti*, made the separatist theory of democracy into law.

B. The Roots of Undue Influence:
The Auto Workers Case (1957)

What appeared to be an innovation in the Court's concept of corruption, built upon the dissenting opinions of Justices still sitting on the bench, was in reality a throwback to earlier times. This was an evolution, not a revolution. The facts confronting the Court in *Austin* resembled those in *Auto Workers*. There, Congress had limited political contributions and expenditures by corporations and unions in connection with federal elections.[50] The government alleged that the International Union Automobile, Aircraft and Agricultural Implement Workers of America had funded its political expenditure from the union's dues, not by voluntary political contributions.[51] This was akin to the Michigan Chamber of Commerce making its expenditure from general treasury funds.

Joined by Justices Reed, Burton, Clark, Harlan, and Brennan, Justice Frankfurter fleshed out the shape and effects of an unfair advantage in the political marketplace. He approvingly cited concerns that fueled, above all, the portion of the law limiting corporate contributions and expenditures: "the corroding effect of money employed in elections by aggregated power";[52] "the power of wealth threaten[ing] to undermine the political integrity of the Republic";[53] "the apparent hold on political parties which business interests and certain organizations seek and sometimes obtain by reason of liberal campaign contributions";[54] "the great railroad companies, the great insurance companies, the great telephone companies, the great aggregations of wealth . . . using their corporate funds, directly or indirectly, to send members of the legislature to these halls in order to vote for their protection and the advancement of their interests as against those of the public";[55] the "secret purchase of organizations, which nullifies platforms, nullifies political utterances and the pledges made by political leaders in and out of Congress";[56] increasing contributions and expenditures that "endanger[] the endurance of our Republic in its purity and in its essence";[57] "the absence of legislation of a liberal or sympathetic or just character, so far as it affects the interest of the wage-earners of America . . . traced with the growth of the corruption funds and the influences that are in operation during elections and campaigns";[58] and "the patience of the American workingmen [being] about exhausted."[59] Frankfurter took these quotes from other sources, a way of emphasizing that concern was widespread and long-standing.

This was a much juicier description of the dangers afoot than what Justice Marshall offered later in *Austin*. In the quotations above, cause, effect, and implications were all spelled out: aggregated power employs great sums of money in elections, gains a hold on political parties, officeholders, and candidates through political contributions and expenditures, sends its candidates to office to vote for the advancement of its interests, exercises undisclosed power in the legislative process, obtains favorable policies and nullifies unfavorable proposals, all to the considerable detriment of political integrity, the character of the Republic, and the public's trust in the same.

Frankfurter evidently shared in the concerns that he cited. Indeed, he began the majority opinion with a remarkable statement, one of a sort no longer seen in Supreme Court opinions:

The concentration of wealth consequent upon the industrial expansion in the post-Civil War era had profound implications for American life. The impact of the abuses resulting from this concentration gradually made itself felt by a rising tide of reform protest.[60]

These words introduced his review of the sources cited above, all intended to demonstrate consistent and appropriate alarm over the role of money in politics since the 1890s. Frankfurter described the popular view as holding that "aggregated capital unduly influence[s] politics"[61] and described the aim of the statute in question as "not merely to prevent the subversion of the integrity of the electoral process," but also "to sustain the active, alert responsibility of the individual citizen in a democracy for the wise conduct of government."[62]

In place of *Austin*'s references to different spheres and different marketplaces, Frankfurter supplies a view of a fractured Republic. He illustrates the operation of aggregated capital in democracy so clearly, however, as to leave the reader begging for a separation of political and economic spheres. Frankfurter's long list of concerns conveys the undoing of popular sovereignty—officeholders accountable to donors and spenders, popular platforms and legislative proposals nullified by behind-the-scenes power plays, and the role of ordinary citizens diminished, if not discarded. Such examples of undue influence form part of the motivation behind Marshall's distinction between spheres: the desire to retain the operation of popular will and popular accountability within the political sphere, a desire whose realization depends on confining the operation of concentrated economic power to the economic sphere.

If union and corporate expenditures (from dues or general treasury funds) unduly influence politics and subvert democratic integrity, and if restraint of such expenditures is justified by the "promot[ion of] individual responsibility for democratic government," the implication is clear. Individual responsibility is frustrated by the exercise of aggregated capital within the political sphere. The reasons for this derive from aggregated capital—in particular, its tremendous superiority to the resources possessed by ordinary citizens, its capacity to dominate venues for political speech, and its frequent lack of correlation with popular political support. *Auto Workers* is a case about popular sovereignty, the accountability of elected leaders to ordinary citizens and the potential for ordinary citizens to play a meaningful role within the democratic process. Frankfurter did not expect the "active, alert responsibility of the individual citizen" to manifest, or at least to have its due effect, in a political system open to aggregated capital.

These quotations amounted to dicta, however, because in the end Frankfurter's primary loyalty was to judicial restraint. Endorsing the "wisdom of refraining from avoidable constitutional pronouncements,"[63] Frankfurter concluded that consideration of the constitutional issue would be premature. Because the district court halted the prosecution prior to trial, the Supreme Court was asked to decide the constitutional questions "in the first instance" prior to "an adjudication on the merits [that] can provide the concrete factual setting that sharpens the deliberative process especially demanded for constitutional decision."[64] Rejecting this essentially legislative role for the Court, Frankfurter exercised but a fraction of the Court's power, limiting himself to reversing the district judge's construction of the Corrupt Practices Act, remanding the case for trial, and, admittedly, endorsing concerns about money in politics. Because of this restraint, it was *Austin* that first gave *Auto Workers'* principles the force of law.

C. Popular Sovereignty:
McConnell v. Federal Election Commission (2003)

The spread of *Austin* and *Auto Workers'* principles continued through various cases, reaching its pinnacle when money-in-politics crusader Senator Mitch McConnell challenged the constitutionality of the 2002 McCain-Feingold Act (also known as the Bipartisan Campaign Reform Act). The act was the first comprehensive overhaul of the federal campaign finance system left after *Buckley*. Its most important functions were, first, to eliminate the use of "soft money" by federal candidates, officeholders, national party committees, and state and local committees that wished to affect federal elections. "Soft money" refers to campaign funds donated to state and local parties by individuals, corporations, and unions. Such funds were not subject to federal limits and had exploded into the hundreds of millions of dollars in the late 1990s. Soft money made federal campaign finance limits ineffective, injecting large quantities of cash from private sources into federal elections and national parties. The act also required corporations and unions to establish segregated funds for running issue ads. This prevented corporations from relying on their general treasury funds. The sheer breadth of the case and the legislation it examined carried implications for all levels of federal politics, making *McConnell* the most important case since *Buckley*.

The majority opinion coauthored by Stevens and O'Connor took up over 150 pages in the U.S. reports. Its outcome was foreshadowed in the first few lines, where the Court endorsed *Auto Workers'* concern about "the great aggregations of wealth . . . using their corporate funds, directly or indirectly, to elect legislators who would vote for their protection and the advancement of their interests as against those of the public."[65] The Court went on to ratify the undue influence theory of corruption:

[P]laintiffs conceive of corruption too narrowly. Our cases have firmly established that Congress' legitimate interest extends beyond preventing simple cash-for-votes corruption to curbing "undue influence on an officeholder's judgment, and the appearance of such influence."[66]

This broad vision supported the government's interest in countering the role of concentrated capital in elections. On this theory, the Court upheld most of the law, including limitations on corporate expenditures and an unusual public financing scheme for presidential elections (to which we will return later in the chapter).

Addressing the evils of corporate expenditures and soft money, the majority opinion seized on three dynamics behind money in politics: legislative capture by moneyed interests, extortion by officeholders, and the prisoner's dilemma of political spending. First came a classic concern about the effort by special interests to make officeholders accountable to them over and above average citizens. Success in this regard is called legislative capture—control of the means of public policymaking by special interests. In subjugating lawmakers to the demands of donors and spenders, legislative capture stands popular sovereignty on its head. Political consumers are sovereign; ordinary citizens are disempowered. The Court cited Senator Warren Rudman's conclusion that "[s]pecial interests who give large amounts of soft money to political parties do in fact achieve their objectives." He elaborated:

They do get special access. Sitting Senators and House Members have limited amounts of time, but they make time available in their schedules to meet with representatives of business and unions and wealthy individuals who gave large sums to their parties. These are not idle chit-chats about the philosophy of democracy . . . Senators are pressed by their benefactors to introduce legislation, to amend legislation, to block legislation, and to vote on legislation in a certain way.[67]

The Court agreed, citing "manipulations of the legislative calendar, leading to Congress' failure to enact, among other things, generic drug legislation, tort reform, and tobacco legislation."[68]

In order to explain why it was that officeholders are susceptible to pressure by special interests and, ultimately, this undemocratic form of sovereignty, the Court quoted Senator Alan Simpson.

Too often, Members' first thought is not what is right or what they believe, but how it will affect fundraising. Who, after all, can seriously contend that a $100,000 donation does not alter the way one thinks about—and quite possibly votes on—an issue? . . . When you don't pay the piper that finances your campaigns, you will never get any more money from that piper. Since money is the mother's milk of politics, you never want to be in that situation.[69]

Candidates' and officeholders' preoccupation with fundraising (and subsequent vulnerability to legislative capture) is hardly avoidable in the absence of public funding for congressional elections, limits on campaign expenditures, and limits on corporate and individual expenditures. Given the tremendous competitive pressures upon candidates and officeholders to raise funds, it is only natural that members of Congress think first about political spenders and second about the vast remainder of citizens.

The majority cited political finance data suggesting that political consumers exercise systemic influence. "In 1996 the top five corporate soft-money donors gave, in total, more than $9 million in nonfederal funds to the two national party committees. In [2000] the political parties raised almost $300 million—60% of their total soft-money fundraising—from just 800 donors, each of which contributed a minimum of $120,000 . . . [And in] the 2000 election cycle, 35 of the 50 largest soft-money donors gave to both parties; 28 of the 50 gave more than $100,000 to both parties."[70] These data suggested that a relatively small number of political consumers were calling the shots, and that the majority of the most powerful players sought to influence both political parties.

The Court distinguished this practice of investing in both parties from sincere, value-based political participation: "[L]obbyists, CEOs, and wealthy individuals alike all have candidly admitted donating substantial sums of soft money to national committees not on ideological grounds, but for the express purpose of securing influence over federal officials."[71] The Court characterized this strategic behavior as "creat[ing] debt on the part of officeholders."[72]

Like its analysis of soft money, the Court's discussion of political advertisements focused on the increasing concentration of political power in a few well-funded groups capable of creating debt on the officeholders' part. The Court noted that in the 2000 election cycle, "130 groups spent over an estimated $500 million on more than 1,100 different ads" and that 75 percent of the money spent on issue ads was "attributable to the two major parties and six major interest groups."[73] On the basis of such contribution and expenditure figures, and the close relationship between politicians and their parties, the Court concluded that national parties were in "a unique position, whether they like it or not, to serve as agents for spending on behalf of those who seek to produce obligated officeholders."[74] The Court credited the perception that "the average American has no significant role in the political process."[75]

The second dynamic exposed in the opinion shows that the Court did not blame special interests alone for the decline of popular sovereignty. It pointed to a problem juxtaposed to legislative capture: "[C]andidates and donors alike have in fact exploited the soft-money loophole, the former to increase their prospects of election."[76] As opposed to special interests seeking to obligate officeholders, the Court pointed to the case of officeholders seeking to obligate corporations and the wealthy to contribute. While it stopped short of calling this behavior extortion, the Court credited testimony that "[b]usiness and labor leaders believe, based on their experience, that disappointed Members, and their party colleagues, may shun or disfavor them because they have not contributed."[77]

A fine line separated this second dynamic from a third. Even absent explicit pressure from candidates and officeholders, the Court credited evidence "that many corporate contributions were motivated by . . . a fear of being placed at a disadvantage in the legislative process relative to other contributors."[78] This followed from testimony that "competing interests who do contribute generously will have an advantage in gaining access to and influencing key Congressional leaders on matters of importance to the company or union."[79] The Court noted actual "menus" offered by six national party committees to would-be donors. For example, the Democrats made publicly available

a range of donor options, starting with the $10,000-per-year Business Forum program, and going up to the $100,000-per-year National Finance Board program. The latter entitles the donor to bimonthly conference calls with the Democratic House leadership and chair of the DCCC, complimentary invitations to all DCCC fundraising events, two private dinners with the Democratic House leadership and ranking Members, and two retreats with the Democratic House leader and DCCC chair in Telluride, Colorado, and Hyannisport, Massachusetts.[80]

Aside from any explicit pressure from officeholders, such a menu of options demonstrates how notable individuals and groups face pressure inherent in the system itself. If they do not contribute financially, others may do so and thereby gain an advantage.

These dynamics—legislative capture, extortionary behavior, and implicit pressures to spend—place all people and groups in a bind: either play the influence game or face the prospect of losses as a result of abstention.[81] On the massive scale of American democracy, this translates into a collective action problem. Those who wish neither to tie officeholders to their personal agendas nor to cave to officeholder pressure for political funds realize that the system places them in a precarious position. If they stick to their principles, others will surpass them by obtaining favorable laws and policies. Principled actors may find themselves losing out in their industry, or they may find that their industry is rendered obsolete by another industry that gained greater legislative concessions.

In contrast to aggressive, unapologetic attempts at legislature capture, money produced through officeholder extortion and the collective action problem is defensive, or at least reluctant. Absent generally applicable rules that prevent legislative capture and extortion, however, such defensive political spending is common. The Court viewed McCain-Feingold as supplying the mutual coercion necessary to enable officeholders, corporations, unions, and notable individuals to step away from these three pernicious dynamics. Legislative capture, officeholder extortion, and the collective action problem pose, in the Court's words, "the danger that officeholders will decide issues not on the merits or the desires of their constituencies, but according to the wishes of those who have made large financial contributions."[82] Noting that "the potential for such undue influence is manifest" and that "such corruption is neither easily detected nor practical to criminalize," the Court concluded that "the best means of prevention is to identify and to remove the temptation."[83] It construed the soft-money ban, limits on contributions and corporate expenditures, and the public financing mechanism for presidential campaigns in this light.

This vindication of popular sovereignty and representative democracy stood at the pinnacle of the Rehnquist Court's evolution. The Court had returned campaign finance philosophy to where Justice White would have it. In his *Buckley* dissent, White noted that "large, overhanging campaign debts . . . must be paid off with money raised while holding public office and at a time when [officeholders] are already preparing or thinking about the next campaign."[84] White hoped to "ease the candidate's understandable obsession with fundraising, and so free him and his staff to communicate in more places and ways unconnected with the fundraising function."[85] He counseled that laws devised to "insulate the political expression of federal candidates from the influence inevitably exerted by the endless job of raising increasingly large sums of money."[86] By striking down expenditure limitations and leaving candidates and officeholders "free" to raise and spend in unlimited amounts, White concluded that *Buckley* had "returned them all to the treadmill."[87]

Building on Justice White's dissent, Blasi put it succinctly: "Legislators and aspirants for legislative office who devote themselves to raising money round-the-clock are not in essence representatives."[88] Intersecting with *Buckley*'s neglected concern regarding the "protect[ion] [of] 'the integrity of our system of representative democracy,'"[89] Blasi argued that "campaign finance legislation [could] be justified . . . by resort to the constitutionally ordained value of representation."[90] His description of an unrepresentative republic was fairly implied by *McConnell*'s three dynamics, above.

The quality of representation has to suffer when legislators continually concerned about re-election are not able to spend the greater part of their workday on matters of constituent service, information gathering, political and policy analysis, debating and compromising with fellow representatives, and the public dissemination of views. Likewise, the quality of future representation has to suffer when aspirants for legislative office are not able to spend the bulk of their time learning what questions and problems most trouble voters, formulating positions on major issues, and holding themselves and their views up to public scrutiny. No doubt when candidates spend so much time fund-raising they encounter grievances, information, and ideas of potential donors that an enlightened representative would want to consider. If the candidate is not substantially free, however, to spend her time considering as well the grievances, information, and ideas of non-donors—in particular her geographic constituents—the process falls short.[91]

On this basis, Blasi proposed "protect[ing] the time of elected representatives and candidates for office" and ensuring democracy's representative quality.[92]

The Rehnquist Court's movement in this direction was clear for all to see, including Judge Roberts and Judge Alito (both serving on federal courts of appeals at the time), George W. Bush, and Bush's constituents. A broad view of corruption had been adopted, the power of aggregated capital was being limited and the power of average Americans restored, the pressures facing candidates and firms were being exposed, state and federal reforms were increasingly respected, and democracy was being construed as a mode of popular power and accountability that the government must protect. The Roberts Court eagerly accepted the mandate to reverse this move towards popular sovereignty in all of its particulars.

II. THE ROBERTS COURT'S MARKET FAITH

Roberts and Alito had been on the Court for only a year when Vermont's campaign finance law came within the Court's reach. The Vermont law defied *Buckley* by setting expenditure limits on candidates and by imposing low contribution limits on individuals. Although these limits varied depending on the race, they were approximately ten times lower than federal limits, reaching as low as $200. While it would have been fascinating to see how this regime played out in the laboratory of states, nobody was surprised when, in the 2006 case *Randall v. Sorrell*,[93] a 6–3 majority of the Roberts Court struck it down. This simple task could have been accomplished, however, without overruling the state interest in "protect[ing] candidates from spending too much time raising money rather than devoting that time to campaigning among ordinary voters."[94] The Court could have tabled that question or credited the theory, and still held that the limits were too low to satisfy any interest the state might advance. The Court's hostility to the time-protection rationale signaled that at least part of the Rehnquist Court's progressive evolution was now covered in volcanic ash—an extinction of sorts.

One year later, in *Wisconsin Right to Life*, the new conservative majority overruled *McConnell*'s restriction on corporate spending in its application to "issue ads," ads that address issues, not candidates.[95] Commentators noticed the Court's more conservative turn away from *McConnell* and *Austin*,[96] but neither of these cases was yet overruled. It was as though they had been touched by the spreading ash, but were not yet buried. Perhaps the skies would clear and the ecosystem would recover. Nobody knew for certain then, as of 2007, that the volcano was only starting to stir, and that the next three years would bring fire, lava, and smoldering landscapes.

A. The Consumer Unhands the Citizen:
Davis v. FEC (2008) and Arizona Free Enterprise v. Bennett (2011)

The Arizona legislature and the U.S. Congress had both sought to make public financing a viable choice. The Arizona law, providing public financing for candidates for state office, was the stronger of the two. *Bennett* addressed the matching funds provision of the law.[97] Participation in public financing was optional, and those who bypassed the system were subject only to preexisting contribution limits and disclosure rules. Those who chose public financing agreed to rely only on state funds in the form of an initial subsidy and, possibly, matching funds. Once a privately funded opponent spent more than the amount of the initial subsidy, the public candidate received dollar for dollar (minus fundraising expenses fixed at 6 percent) what the private candidate spent—a "matching funds" provision. Like the private candidate's expenditures, the law also counted independent expenditures in favor of a private candidate or against the public candidate in the tally of funds. Once private spending in these forms equaled the initial grant, any additional private spending triggered the distribution of matching funds. There was, however, a cap. Matching funds ceased at three times the amount of the initial grant, meaning that private spending could still prevail in the end.[98] Justices Thomas, Kennedy, Scalia, and Alito joined Chief Justice Roberts's majority opinion, striking down the matching funds provision.

Three years earlier, under the banner of Alito's majority opinion in *Davis*, these same Justices had invalidated the trigger mechanism contained in the "Millionaires' Amendment" of McCain-Feingold.[99] Although there was no public financing for congressional elections, there were limits on the amount of money parties could spend in coordination with their candidates; and individual donations to candidates were, at the time, capped at $2,300 per two-year election cycle.[100] Section 319(a) of the Millionaires' Amendment added a curious twist to this scheme. If a candidate spent more than $350,000 of her own money on her campaign, this triggered an "asymmetrical regulatory scheme" under which her non-self-financing opponents could accept unlimited coordinated party expenditures and individual contributions up to $6,900. This legal subsidy remained in place for each candidate until he or she amassed the amount of personal funds spent by the self-financing candidate. Therefore, the Millionaires' Amendment enabled non-self-financing candidates to catch up, if only to the extent that they could appeal to their party, private donors, and private spenders. Meanwhile, the self-financing candidate remained subject to the usual limits.[101]

While *Davis* concerned a legal subsidy that allowed certain forms of private wealth to be used to counteract another form of private wealth, *Bennett* dealt with a cash subsidy that pitted public funds against private funds. Aside from these differences, there are notable similarities: First, some candidates are given an advantage by the government, that advantage is pegged specifically to gains by their opponents, and the effect (and possibly the intention) is to equalize financial resources among candidates. Second, neither law limited the amount, content, form, or venue of unsubsidized candidates' speech or the amount of money they might raise to fund such speech. The same is true for independent expenditure groups, which remained free to raise and spend as much money as they wished. Any equalization of funds occurring under either mechanism resulted from an increase in the total amount of funds that could be devoted to political speech. Both cases concern subsidies, not restrictions.

We are left with a riddle. Why did the Court find in both cases that the government had abridged the freedom of speech? *Buckley* itself described the federal lump sum subsidies in force for presidential campaigns as "a congressional effort, not to abridge, restrict, or censor speech, but rather to use public money to facilitate and enlarge public discussion and participation in the electoral process, goals vital to a self-governing people."[102]

The First Amendment as the Right to an Unregulated Market The plaintiff in *Davis* reasoned that the trigger mechanism "burdens his exercise of his First Amendment right to make unlimited expenditures of his personal funds because making expenditures . . . has the effect of enabling his opponent to raise more money."[103] That novel description of the right to free speech deserves attention. The alleged burden resulted from his opponents' ability to "use [their additional government] money to finance speech that counteracts and thus diminishes the effectiveness of [his] own speech."[104] The Roberts Court agreed five to four, noting that "the vigorous exercise of the right to use personal funds to finance campaign speech produces [under the law] fundraising advantages for opponents in the competitive context of electoral politics."[105] While recognizing that the law "does not impose a cap on a candidate's expenditure of personal funds," Alito stated that "it imposes an unprecedented penalty."[106] The *Bennett* majority cited this same passage of *Davis*.[107] Both opinions construed this penalty of increased funds for public candidates as a "burden" on private candidates' speech that warrants the application of strict scrutiny.

Thus, the riddle breaks into two questions: What conception of speech and democracy caused the Court to hold that the First Amendment protects the effectiveness of privately funded speech? What type or level of effectiveness does the First Amendment require?

The answer lies within another mysterious point of disagreement between the majority and the dissent. Criticizing the Millionaires' Amendment, Alito stated that "[t]he Constitution . . . confers upon voters, not Congress, the power to choose the Members of the House of Representatives . . . and it is a dangerous business for Congress to use the election laws to influence the voters' choices."[108] He then reminded the government that it "is forbidden to assume the task of ultimate judgment, lest the people lose their ability to govern themselves."[109] Campaign finance reform was, however, popular with the general public, and it was the people's representatives who had enacted McCain-Feingold.[110] This observation applies with additional strength to the Arizona law, which was enacted by popular referendum.[111] Perhaps this is why Roberts refined Justice Alito's phrasing in *Bennett*: "[T]he whole point of the First Amendment is to protect speakers against unjustified government restrictions on speech, even when those restrictions reflect the will of the majority. When it comes to protected speech, the speaker is sovereign."[112]

Roberts did not elaborate upon the relationship between public financing and sovereignty, nor what it means for the speaker, not the majority of citizens, to be sovereign. Although *Davis* and *Bennett* reached the same conclusion, the distance between Alito's phrasing and Roberts's phrasing is significant. The former noted that the people must govern themselves, while the latter insisted that the speaker possesses the ultimate authority and must be protected from majority power.

This significant refinement did not elude Justice Kagan's dissenting opinion in *Bennett*. She praised purposes of the law that contradict Justice Roberts's brand of sovereignty: "The public financing program . . . was needed because the prior system of private fundraising had . . . favored a small number of wealthy special interests over the vast majority of Arizona citizens."[113] She built on this formulation in what was a direct response to the idea that speakers, not the general public, are sovereign: "Arizonans wanted their government to work on behalf of all the State's people . . . a law designed to sever political candidates' dependence on large contributors . . . to ensure that their representatives serve the public, and not just the wealthy donors who helped put them in office."[114] This raised the question of whether by "the speaker" Roberts really meant "the spender."

Who else could cease to be sovereign on account of government subsidies pegged to private spending? What would-be donor or spender would not be dissuaded by the knowledge that her opponents would receive free money from the government as a result of her speech? Perhaps none, except a person sincerely desiring to communicate a particular point of view and convinced of that point of view's validity and urgency. Only instrumental speakers, speakers who wish to spend in order to tip the quantity (as opposed to the substance) of speech in their favor, would be deterred for certain. To avoid any uncomfortable discoveries to this effect, Roberts waived the plaintiffs' burden of proof: "As in *Davis*, we do not need empirical evidence to determine that the law at issue is burdensome."[115] He *knew* that private speech would be rendered less effective by the matching funds.

The Court in *Buckley v. Valeo* did not know this. There, the Court required proof that the First Amendment had been violated—the traditional burden placed on plaintiffs.

Appellants voice concern that public funding will lead to governmental control of the internal affairs of political parties, and thus to a significant loss of political freedom. The concern is necessarily wholly speculative and hardly a basis for invalidation of the public financing scheme on its face. Congress has expressed its determination to avoid the possibility.[116]

The Ninth Circuit panel, reversed by the Supreme Court in *Bennett*, followed *Buckley*'s lead, holding unanimously that evidence was necessary:

In this case, as in *Buckley* and *Citizens United*, the burden that Plaintiffs allege is merely a theoretical chilling effect on donors who might dislike the statutory result of making a contribution or candidates who may seek a tactical advantage related to the release or timing of matching funds. The matching funds provision does not actually prevent anyone from speaking in the first place or cap campaign expenditures. Also, as in *Buckley* and *Citizens United*, there is no evidence that any Plaintiff has actually suffered the consequence they allege the Act imposes.[117]

The court of appeals cited undisputed evidence that "overall campaign spending in Arizona has increased since the Act's passage."[118] This did not prove, however, that campaign spending might not have increased more had the act not been passed, or that individuals instances of self-censorship did not occur because of the act.

Returning to Roberts's premise, evidence is indeed irrelevant when it is actually a principle, and not an individual instance of harm, that is being affirmed. Roberts made it known that the First Amendment required a state of affairs in which additional private funds worked only to the advantage of the candidate generating them or on whose behalf they were spent. This is the principle contravened, without any doubt—logical, factual, or otherwise—by the laws in both *Davis* and *Bennett*. Recall these cases' basic holding: the First Amendment protects the market for political speech not only from limits, but also from trigger-mechanism subsidies. We must intuit, then, that the First Amendment requires that the market for speech be both unfettered *and undistorted*. Distortion occurs (a) when the incentive to spend private funds is decreased and (b) when private funds are spent nonetheless, but a benefit to other candidates is produced as a result.

Per *Davis* and *Bennett*, the First Amendment protects not just the right to speak without government limits on one's own speech, but also a right to speak without government assistance to others. The first component contains a negative right—a right to be free from government action that directly limits one's own speech. The second appears to contain a positive right—a right so vigorous and full as to require that the government do or cease to do something that is necessary to make the exercise of one's right effective. This apparent positive right to *effective* political speech, this enhanced First Amendment, prohibits actions by the government that diminish speech.[119]

Upon reflection, however, we have good reason to doubt that the plaintiffs in *Davis* and *Bennett* were really making a positive rights claim. They did not urge the state to give them anything, to provide for them, or to otherwise boost them up. They claimed, rather, that the state's effort to provide for others had diminished what was theirs. The key to this argument lies in its underlying demand: a return to the supposedly natural, private order of things. The deceiving shape of the plaintiffs' argument was incidental to the purpose of dismantling what the state had built. The enhanced First Amendment enables candidates to assert a successful claim against the government on the grounds that it had altered the private order, which includes the preexisting distribution of resources to be devoted to political speech.

The reality is exactly the opposite of what it seemed to be: the new First Amendment *prohibits* a positive right to effective political speech. Only those who are unsuccessful in (or scornful of) the market require such a guarantee, a fact that reveals on its own why such a guarantee must be unlawful. It distorts the market mechanism for sorting out which candidates, expenditure groups, and political messages receive the most funds and obtain the loudest, most effective speech. Rather than asking the government to do anything, the *Davis* and *Bennett* plaintiffs asked the Court to issue a simple command: laissez-faire. One needs no evidence to establish that trigger mechanisms violate this principle.

"Laissez-faire" means that the current status of long-standing distributive contests between many groups must be considered final as far as the state is concerned. Let the market determine whatever gains and losses must occur from here on out. This is not a call for the natural order of things, but rather for the natural order of things absent any additional state intervention. Recall how Justices White, Rehnquist, and Marshall harped on the fact that the privileges of the corporate form are not natural, inevitable facts of nature. They are, however, well-established background conditions upon which the modern capitalist economy has been built. We are left to wonder why the First Amendment should demand the destruction of subsidies for publicly financed candidates but not for corporations.

To support the argument that one violates another's constitutional rights by helping his foe, *Bennett* rehearses the traditional gamut of First Amendment purposes, including "protect[ing] the free discussion of government affairs" and upholding "our 'profound national commitment to the principle that debate on public issues should be uninhibited, robust, and wide-open.'"[120] This raises the same riddle as before. Responding democratically, Justice Kagan retorted that the First Amendment "protects no person's, nor any candidate's, 'right to be free from vigorous debate'" and that "'falsehood and fallacies' are exposed through 'discussion,' 'education,' and 'more speech.'"[110] She praised the Arizona law for "subsidiz[ing] and so produc[ing] *more* political speech" and claimed that "[n]o one can say that [it] discriminates against particular ideas."[122] Unfortunately for Kagan, her statements are true only in a civic sense, not an economic sense.

Roberts's majority opinion easily countered Kagan's reasoning: "Any increase in speech resulting from the Arizona law is of one kind and one kind only—that of publicly financed candidates."[123] He dwelled on the selective effects of the law: "[E]ven if the matching funds provision did result in . . . more speech in general, it would do so at the expense of impermissibly burdening (and thus reducing) the speech of privately financed candidates and independent expenditure groups."[124]

Emphasizing how the Arizona law boosted the speech of just one subset of candidates, the majority portrayed the law as another impermissible effort to equalize resources. The Court returned us, once again, to *Buckley*'s omnipresent warning that "restrict[ing] the speech of some elements of our society in order to enhance the relative voice of others is wholly foreign to the First Amendment."[125] This quotation referred to FECA's expenditure limits. In *Davis* and *Bennett*, however, the government did not limit; it subsidized. The *Bennett* majority conceded this,[126] but sought to extend the anti-equality principle to cases where the *effectiveness of the speech of some elements of society* was limited (or, in the Court's words, "penalized" and "impermissibly burdened").

That new use for the anti-equality principle does not fit with the Court's articulation of the principle itself in *Buckley*. There, the Court described the First Amendment as "designed to secure the widest possible dissemination of information from diverse and antagonistic sources, and to assure unfettered interchange of ideas for the bringing about of political and social changes desired by the people."[127] Expenditure limits might conceivably frustrate this design, but the subsidies at issue in *Bennett* and *Davis* were based on it. Indeed, the effectiveness principle would allow wealthy voices to drown out the diverse sources to which *Buckley* alluded. This made it all the more mysterious: Why would the Court use cases involving an increase in diverse and antagonistic voices to lower equality to a patently illegitimate state interest?

The fact that the Court does not consider equality a problem in and of itself provides the necessary clue. A field of independently wealthy candidates and candidates with wealthy supporters could cancel out the role of wealth (albeit only after preventing poorer candidates from mounting viable campaigns). A wealthy supporter could even emerge late in the game and equalize the financial resources of candidates indirectly by funding an expenditure organization. (This in fact occurred several times over the course of the 2012 Republican presidential primary season.)[128] That organization could even carry out a "trigger mechanism policy," in which it would systematically counter each advertisement against a certain candidate with an advertisement in favor of that same candidate. The majority would apparently welcome these developments. Why is it permissible for private actors to equalize resources by bestowing one or another candidate with wealth, and yet impermissible for the state to do so? What is the difference between the private and the public in this regard? We are thus returned to the familiar command that "the existing distribution of political resources shall be respected."

The explanation for this total condemnation of state-produced equality is illuminating. *Bennett* credited *Davis* for this achievement. Alito's reasoning there was unabashedly honest. He seized on the government's view that the law intended "to reduce *the natural advantage* that wealthy individuals possess in campaigns for federal office."[129] He described the government plan as enabling Congress to "arrogate the voters' authority to evaluate the strengths of candidates competing for office."[130] Subsidies thus became a government attempt to determine which strengths should be allowed to operate, and thus an attempt to remove authority from voters.

The opposite conclusion seems more reasonable, however. The voters with authority to evaluate candidates' strengths are the same voters who overwhelmingly support campaign finance reform and believe political representatives to be unduly controlled by corporations and the wealthy. Consider Justice Stevens's dissenting view: "If only one candidate can make himself heard, the voter's ability to make an informed choice is impaired."[131] This view maintains that resource inequalities between candidates, not campaign finance subsidies, prevent voters from evaluating candidates' strengths. Tremendous variations in campaign resources enable some candidates to dominate the airwaves and characterize the issues as they see fit. In such a media market, the public can hardly hear, much less consider, competing, poorly-funded points of view.

Once again, democratic arguments miss the point. When Alito mentioned voters' authority to evaluate candidates' strengths, he was referring only to financial strength. He made this remarkably clear in a passage that appears to be taken from a political parody or dystopian novel:

Different candidates have different strengths. Some are wealthy; others have wealthy supporters who are willing to make large contributions. Some are celebrities; some have the benefit of a well-known family name. Leveling electoral opportunities means making and implementing judgments about which strengths should be permitted to contribute to the outcome of an election. The Constitution, however, confers upon voters, not Congress, the power to choose the Members of the House of Representatives and it is a dangerous business for Congress to use the election laws to influence the voters' choices.[132]

Absent from Alito's list of strengths was any attribute traditionally thought to be a sound basis for electoral choice—such as a candidate's intelligence, policy platform, political record, values, character, eloquence, and personal history. Such civic strengths and weaknesses did not concern the Court. Beyond Alito's omitting them from his list, his entire analysis served to discredit the citizens and government's intention to prevent civic strengths from being overshadowed by the role of private wealth in the political process.

By implication, Alito's viewpoint must be that discussion, education, and more speech are valid tests of truth in the market only insofar as they are produced by the market itself, including by the corporate legal structure that has done so much to define the market in recent times. If the government intervenes to facilitate that discussion, supplying the funds necessary for the discussion to occur, then this is not truly "the competition of the market." Nobody would think that the government could bleep out portions of televised speeches in order to equalize eloquence or intelligence, or limit donations and expenditures to a point where the political discourse was muted. But only a radical, laissez-faire view of the market holds that the state cannot dedicate funds to stimulate competition.

Consider what it means for every unit of private candidate success— i.e., each dollar registered by the private candidates, spent by groups supporting such candidates, or spent opposing the public candidate—to produce a unit of public candidate success. Under this regime, political donors and spenders no longer control the level at which different points of view are expressed or the level at which each candidate can broadcast or otherwise build their campaigns. As the *Bennett* majority wrote, "It is not the amount of the funding that the State provides to publicly financed candidates that is constitutionally problematic in this case. It is the manner in which that funding is provided—in direct response to the political speech of privately financed candidates and independent expenditure groups."[133] The Court noted that "an advertisement supporting the election of a candidate that goes without a response is often more effective than an advertisement that is directly controverted."[134] The proper degree of effectiveness is defined by the market-determined amount of money available to the candidate and her supporters.[135] In this view, effectiveness must vary with private preferences, not public subsidies.

The Roberts Court seeks the optimal, market-determined level of spending, not competition for competition's sake. The latter represents the outmoded neo-Keynesian conception of the First Amendment, one whose concerns include the diversity of views expressed, the robustness of competition, and the value of difference for the sake of informed electoral choice. In the economic sphere, such goals justify antitrust rules, a form of government intervention that helps maintain a competitive dynamic. They also justify regulations on environmental harms and product safety that ensure that manufacturers internalize the unintended costs of their products and present consumers with prices that reflect those costs. It is not difficult to see how, whether in political or economic markets, these same goals could justify government programs, such as public education and health care, that enable people to meaningfully participate.

Such a regulated market is one thing. The laissez-faire market conception is quite another. Here, it is acceptable for certain views and groups to become dominant, assuming that their dominance is the result of their talent and persuasiveness *as expressed and elaborated through a quantity of resources appropriate to their preexisting wealth and success in the market.* This is why the conservative majority thought it relevant to point out the obvious: that the subsidy does not increase speech in general, but rather only the speech of the publicly funded candidate. If all speech were boosted an equal amount, the market level of disparities would be respected.

What the Court means by a "chilling effect," then, is not that old-fashioned cold front of government power posing a threat to would-be speakers, but rather an icing over of the market mechanism, however slight. The market for speech presupposes that a monetary contribution or expenditure leads only to an increase in speech by the recipient of the donation or an increase in speech containing the message that has been paid for. If spending leads to an increase in desired speech as well as opposing speech, then it becomes irrational or at least less beneficial to invest one's political funds. This reduction in essentially commercial incentives cannot be compared to the far graver types of deterrence found in past understandings of a chilling effect. [136]

A hostile takeover in constitutional meanings has also occurred in other aspects of free speech law. When the *Davis* and *Bennett* majority cites precedent on *diverse and antagonistic* sources and *unfettered* interchange of ideas, a private meaning is intended there as well. "Unfettered" now means not only unlimited but also unsubsidized. "Diverse and antagonistic" does not mean diverse and antagonistic generally. It means *as diverse and antagonistic as the private order commands*—that is, as diverse and antagonistic as political investment and consumption at the moment in question. Not all citizens' views are included in this definition of diversity; the only views guaranteed representation are those of citizens who are able and willing to devote sufficient resources to participating in the market for speech.

A Mystery Resolved   This constitutional requirement of market-determined speech effectiveness explains why the *Davis* plaintiffs could successfully sue the government, but another set of plaintiffs challenging *McCain-Feingold* could not. The Adams plaintiffs in *McConnell* objected to the law's increase in contribution limits from $1,000 to $2,000. [137] They claimed that large contributions "create the appearance of unequal access and influence" and accordingly did not wish to accept them. [138] These plaintiffs alleged a "competitive injury" on this basis. This alleged injury arose through a logically similar path as the *Davis/Bennett* injury: the government increased the ability of the plaintiffs' adversaries to collect funds. In both cases, the plaintiffs themselves could accept such funds if they desired, but because they did not wish to do so, they claimed that the government had disadvantaged them.

The *McConnell* majority held that the Adams plaintiffs had no valid claim, indeed not even the standing to bring a claim, because their injury was traceable only to "their own personal 'wish' not to solicit or accept large contributions, *i.e.*, their own personal choice."[139] In order to fully exercise their First Amendment rights, the Adams plaintiffs needed only to obtain large contributions and use them to speak louder. The government had made it easier for them to raise more funds. What would the *Davis* and *Bennett* plaintiffs have argued had they found themselves in that position? They might have conceded that the law raised contribution limits across the board (just as the Arizona law offered public subsidies to all candidates), but insisted that these legislative adjustments benefited only candidates who would raise and accept large contributions. Although the law did not limit what the Adams plaintiffs could collect, it increased the amounts that other sorts of plaintiffs could collect—namely, those plaintiffs who appealed to large donors. Thus, if the plaintiffs had collected $50,000 from fifty donors, that amount could be equaled by other candidates who might collect the same amount from just twenty-five donors. In essence, their funds could be more easily countered. The same held true for the privately financed candidates facing off against the matching funds mechanism or the asymmetrical contribution limits.

And yet there are dispositive differences between the plaintiffs in *Davis* and *Bennett* on the one hand and the Adams plaintiffs on the other: first, the laws at issue in *Davis* and *Bennett* were triggered by privately financed candidates' success; second, although these subsidies were open to all candidates at the start, candidates could not opt into them at the later stages of their campaigns and thus a system of preferential treatment was created; that preferential treatment came from the government and thus constituted a subsidy (whether in the form of matching funds or asymmetrical fundraising limits); and the function of that subsidy was to neutralize, step by step, the economic advantages produced by privately funded donations and expenditures. The Adams plaintiffs could allege none of these things.

The Adams plaintiffs attacked a law that increased the role of private donations in campaigns. The *Davis* and *Bennett* plaintiffs, on the other hand, attacked a law that decreased the role of private funds (or, in *Davis*, candidates' own funds). The Adams plaintiffs argued that the government should directly limit the role of such funds. The *Davis* and *Bennett* plaintiffs argued that the government should not be allowed to do so, even indirectly. The Adams plaintiffs maintained that a relaxing of regulations disadvantaged their speech by favoring candidates willing and able to accept large donations. The source of their disadvantage, however, was private capital and the law's receptivity to the same. They urged the government to limit speech directly (inasmuch as one accepts the proposition that money is speech) because they wished to protect the effectiveness of their economically humble speech. The Adams plaintiffs argued, therefore, for a flight away from the market order of things. The *Davis* and *Bennett* plaintiffs argued for a return to the same. They did not propose limits on anyone's speech. Instead, they proposed an end to effective government assistance for speech.

The new rules of constitutional law incubated in *Davis* and announced in *Bennett* are now clear: first, the First Amendment protects the optimal, market-determined level of speech effectiveness; second, to artificially lessen or enhance that level of effectiveness is to disrupt an economic form of political accountability—accountability to donors and spenders, not citizens as a whole. *Bennett* holds that it is for the market, not the state, to determine the precise level of funding, visibility, and, ultimately, effectiveness that candidates and political viewpoints shall enjoy.

Regardless of whether it chooses subsidies or limits, and regardless of whether it aims to achieve fairness, accessibility, competitiveness, robustness, or vibrancy of political debate, government intervention disrupts the natural level of funding that stands behind each view, candidate, or party. Any government insufficiently versed in the mantra laissez-faire cannot help but to distort the market for political speech and interfere with consumer sovereignty. The Roberts Court's patience was wearing thin.

B. "We the Corporations": Citizens United v. FEC (2010)

Recall the question that stood out in 1976 after *Buckley*: Would the implications of the case extend to corporations? Justice Powell decided that question in the affirmative two years later in *Bellotti*. After *Davis* in 2008, it was unclear whether the regime of consumer sovereignty for election-period speech would extend to corporations. Justice Powell's successor, Justice Kennedy, took up the issue two years later in *Citizens United*. Echoes of Powell's memo filled the air, for the well-funded nonprofit corporation bringing the claim was dedicated to "reassert[ing] the traditional American values of limited government [and] freedom of enterprise."[140] More than history repeating itself, however, this would be a case of a historical trajectory extending itself. As we will soon see, Kennedy did not simply return to the foundation set by his predecessor. He built upwards and outwards.

The restriction on corporate and union political activity at issue in *Citizens United* had its roots in the Tillman Act, passed in 1907, and the Labor Management Relations Act of 1947.[141] Praised in *Auto Workers* and left alone by *Buckley*, it was amended by § 203 of McCain-Feingold, and affirmed by the Court in *McConnell*.[142] Section 203 did not constrain ads that addressed political issues only.[143] Rather, it prohibited the use of general treasury funds for "express advocacy" and "electioneering communications," the sorts of ads that bear specifically on a given candidate for election.[144]

Still, corporations were free to form a political action committee to transmit their views, each shareholder and employee of the corporation could communicate his or her views, and the corporation itself could make political expenditures targeting candidates most of the time (just not right before elections) and political issues (but not candidates) all the time. The only restraint concerned the use of the corporate treasury to fund the most pointed form of political advertisements. The restraint, then, pertained exclusively to where the money comes from; it did not pertain to speech itself. A parallel to the trigger mechanisms struck down on consumer sovereignty grounds was evident: the optimal, market-determined level of funds would not be spent if corporations had to form political action committees. If corporations (a) could not use as much money as they wanted (b) to run whatever sort of political ads they wanted (c) whenever they wanted, then consumer sovereignty would be violated and the market for political spending would be distorted.

The corporation challenged the law. It wished to employ general treasury funds in order to show its documentary film *Hillary: The Movie* within thirty days of the presidential primary. It was dissuaded, however, by the likelihood that this showing would run afoul of the law. The definition of prohibited electioneering communications included broadcasts made within thirty days of a primary election,[145] and Federal Election Commission (FEC) rules suggested that the movie was covered by the ban.[146]

The corporation claimed only that corporate expenditure limitations were unconstitutional as applied to its own organization and the speech it intended to produce. It did not claim that the expenditure limitations or the cases affirming them were unconstitutional per se.[147] Impatient with this humble posture, the Court ordered the parties to return to court to offer arguments about those larger questions. Through this highly unusual instance of re-argument, Roberts, Alito, Scalia, Thomas, and Kennedy gained the power to revisit the Court's own holdings on expenditure limits. They converted a case posing narrow issues into a facial challenge to campaign finance laws and the logic that sustained them.[148] Because no record on these questions had been developed at trial, the Court relied almost exclusively on amicus briefs for evidence on the overarching questions it had decided to entertain.[149]

This was the opposite of judicial restraint, the reverse of the Court's stance in *Auto Workers*. What in the hands of less-emboldened jurists might have been a narrow decision quickly blossomed into a brave declaration that swept away prior caselaw and hard-won legislation. The five conservative Justices overruled *McConnell*, supported by six Justices just ten years prior; *Austin*, also supported by six Justices; and a section of McCain-Feingold supported by a majority of the nation's legislators and the president.[150]

Justice Kennedy crafted the majority opinion as a response to censorship, stating that the "Government may regulate corporate political speech through disclaimer and disclosure requirements, but it may not suppress that speech altogether."[151] Much later in the opinion, he made his case poetically and evasively:

When Government seeks to use its full power, including the criminal law, to command where a person may get his or her information or what distrusted source he or she may not hear, it uses censorship to control thought. This is unlawful. The First Amendment confirms the freedom to think for ourselves.[152]

Under the pre-*Citizens* regime, determining whether a given corporate political advertisement constitutes express advocacy, for example, was a matter for the FEC. Even though the FEC is notoriously deadlocked by Republican appointees who believe campaign finance reform to be unconstitutional, the majority viewed the FEC's power suspiciously, noting the length of the FEC regulations, their ambiguity, and their association with open-ended and complex arguments at trial.[153] Regardless of whether these standards lead to a restriction on corporate speech in any particular case, the majority considers the process itself to represent a censor's determination of "what political speech is safe for public consumption," an "unprecedented governmental intervention into the realm of speech."[154] The precedent was, however, established over a hundred years ago, steeped in historical struggles dating from the end of the Civil War and the era of the robber barons, and had been built upon many times by Congress and state legislatures through the twentieth century.[155]

More concretely, the proposition that the government was suppressing speech and using censorship to control thought is false for reasons that Justice Stevens emphasizes in his dissenting opinion.[156] Under the law, corporations could run all kinds of ads, but some ads could not be paid for directly through general treasury funds. If a corporation must establish a political action committee to express certain views at certain times, has its speech been *censored*? Again, the parallels to *Davis* and *Bennett* shine through: has one's speech been *abridged* when it leads to matching funds for other candidates? The meanings of these terms are being enhanced so as to safeguard the optimal, market-generated balance of views.

Now we see the capitalist conception of censorship in its entirety. Because money is considered speech, regulating the source of money used to fund speech is considered censorship. "Censorship" was indeed afoot in the pre-*Citizens* regime. Although corporate views could be expressed in a number of ways and disproportionate economic power could be brought to bear in favor of those views even in the final weeks before a federal election, a corporation was not permitted to support or oppose a particular candidate through the booming voice of its general treasury in that time period. The resulting sub-optimal spending is censorship too. Plus, the political action committees formed to express corporate views had the obligation of issuing monthly financial reports and disclosing their identity within their political advertisements.[157] Without examining any evidence, the Court concluded that these requirements were simply too burdensome for corporations.[158] In order to remedy this injustice, the Court announced what *Bellotti* had whispered: "First Amendment protection extends to corporations."[159] This was Kennedy channeling his predecessor, Powell.

Because the Court conceives of the First Amendment as a lever to pry open the gates of political financing, an unregulated marketplace enforcer, it could have gone without defending the particular speech or speaker at issue. The majority opinion notes that "[c]orporations and other associations, like individuals, contribute to the 'discussion, debate, and the dissemination of information and ideas' that the First Amendment seeks to foster."[160] This is enough to satisfy the open marketplace view, but the conservative majority went further, acknowledging personal sympathy for corporate speech. They alleged that the "Government ha[d] 'muffle[d] the voices that best represent the most significant segments of the economy.'"[161] Pages later, they reminded readers that corporations "may possess valuable expertise, leaving them the best equipped to point out errors and fallacies in speech of all sorts, including the speech of candidates and elected officials."[162]

Roberts and Scalia paid additional tribute to the value of corporate speech in their concurring opinions. Scalia, joined by Thomas and Alito, stated that "to exclude or impede corporate speech is to muzzle the principal agents of the modern free economy."[163] He counseled that we "celebrate rather than condemn the addition of this speech to the public debate."[164] Roberts, joined by Alito, gave us a doomsday scenario of the effects of the government's plan: "First Amendment rights could be confined to individuals, subverting the vibrant public discourse that is at the foundation of our democracy."[165] Thus, although we are told that the government is not supposed to evaluate the worth of speech, the members of the conservative majority (themselves government employees) extol corporate speech in particular.

Even moving past this inconsistency and granting the point that corporations offer points of view on questions of public importance, a problem with the majority opinion remains. The Court would have us believe that corporate PACs, corporate leaders, shareholders, economists, and industry experts could not possibly make all the needed points, and that general treasury funds are indispensable for political speech. The position that PACs are ineffective, burdensome, and therefore unacceptable alternatives to direct corporate speech shows how extreme the Court has become.

Consider exactly what sort of influence the Roberts Court considers *insufficient*. In a 1985 dissent, well before the age of superPACs, Justice White noted "significant contacts between an organization like [the National Conservative Political Action Committee] and candidates for, and holders of, public office."[166] An example of this was the potential for "move[ment] between the staffs of candidates or officeholders and those of PACs."[167] In addition to this danger, White cited the growth in PAC spending and argued that the "infusion of massive PAC expenditures into the political process" meant that "candidate[s] may be forced to please the spenders rather than the voters."[168] He reminded the majority that "the[se] two groups are not identical." In support of this allegation of undue influence by PACs, he cited testimony by Senator Eagleton: "We see the degrading spectacle of elected representatives completing detailed questionnaires on their positions on special interest issues, knowing that the monetary reward of PAC support depends on the correct answers."[169]

Because PACs are in fact powerful vehicles for corporate political influence, and because there were countless ways to make corporate points of views abundantly clear, the conservatives' concern over "muffling, excluding, impeding, and subverting" speech is easy to decipher. In no case was such speech muffled. It may have been taken down a notch from a scream to a shout, but the numerous outlets for corporate speech available at the time do not admit the word "muffle." As to excluding, impeding, and subverting, the meaning is clear: the full use of corporate economic power was indeed thwarted by well-established legislation and caselaw.

Seemingly addressing those who would push back against corporate political power, the *Citizens United* majority alleged that regulations were pointless. The opinion informs us that *Austin* has been "undermined" and that "political speech is so ingrained in our culture that speakers find ways to circumvent campaign finance laws."[170] Normally, the circumvention of laws is cause for punishment and a reason for greater monitoring and enforcement. Here, however, the Court sides with the lawbreakers. "Our Nation's speech dynamic is changing," the Court announced, "and informative voices should not have to circumvent onerous restrictions."[171] The opinion welcomes this speech and its circumvention of campaign finance law, referring with implicit approval to the "sound bites, talking points, and scripted messages that dominate the 24-hour news cycle."[172] Without a hint of critical analysis, the Court recognizes that "30-second television ads may be the most effective way to convey a political message."[173] And then, seemingly anticipating its critics' sense that sound bites and television ads represent the demise of reasoned argument, the Court arrives at its bottom line: "The First Amendment does not permit Congress to make . . . categorical distinctions based on the corporate identity of the speaker and the content of the political speech."[174]

As though applying this same rule to itself, the majority said nothing critical about corporate political power. The Court did criticize the government, however. It described the First Amendment as "[p]remised on mistrust of governmental power" and reminds the political branches that identity-based restrictions "are all too often simply a means to control content."[175] No evidence of content control was examined. The Court determined nonetheless that "the Government deprive[d] the disadvantaged [corporate] person or [corporate] class of the right to use speech to strive to establish worth, standing, and respect for the speaker's voice."[176]

Distracted from the lack of evidence, the reader is rushed along to the next puzzle: Why should corporations be entitled to speech if that right pertains to "worth, standing, and respect"? While those rewards contribute greatly to the human quest for self-realization through membership in a community of political equals, they can offer nothing of the kind to a nexus of contracts (a corporation). Instead, they offer it instrumental economic value: trust and respect are essential to success in the economic sphere and to the ability to make one's views influential in the political sphere. The purpose of both, in the corporation's case, is profit.

Resistance to corporate political participation had long been premised on this singular interest and success in generating profit. The Court went on the defensive to explain why the superior economic resources of corporations do not justify government restrictions. These are the same resources that make it highly unlikely that qualified regulations could ever succeed in depriving a corporation of its voice, and that make it laughable to describe corporations as a "disadvantaged class." With Orwellian simplicity, the Court found corporate money to inevitably (and appropriately) pervade public discourse:

It is irrelevant for purposes of the First Amendment that corporate funds may have little or no correlation to the public's support for the corporation's political ideas. . . . All speakers, including individuals and the media, use money amassed from the economic marketplace to fund their speech. . . . Many persons can trace their funds to corporations, if not in the form of donations, then in the form of dividends, interest, or salary.[177]

The Court's points are evasive and exasperating. Of course most money is amassed in the economic marketplace. Unless inherited, gifted, stolen, found buried, taken from a foreign colony, or bestowed by the state, we can expect any given sum to have marketplace activity as its immediate source. When money is offered in exchange for something, an economic transaction has occurred, and the good or service in question has been located within a marketplace. In today's economy, it is also true that the money that accrues to natural persons is often derivative of corporate sales. But none of this should obscure the fact that people do not enjoy the same advantages as corporations in that marketplace, nor can they equal corporate economic power.

Hence it is relevant that corporate funds have little correlation to public support for corporate political ideas. If the public earns much of its money by working for or investing in corporations, as the Court alleges, should the public really then be forced to spend that money to compete with corporations in the political sphere? Or, if they cannot match corporate spending, should the public be forced to suffer legislation unfavorable to its interests? These are the logical consequences of corporate political spending that bears little correlation with public support. Because corporate funds are far greater than individual funds and are accumulated through state-bestowed privileges, the state should not allow the marketplace of ideas to be cornered by corporations.

Having forced us to belabor an obvious point, the Court then dismissed that point summarily, tersely stating that "'limited liability, perpetual life, and favorable treatment of the accumulation and distribution of assets'

. . . do[] not suffice . . . to allow laws prohibiting speech."[178] The Court considered it "rudimentary" that corporate advantages cannot trigger a diminution in speech rights and that corporate advantages are unrelated to any compelling state interest in restricting money in politics.[179] Unable to hide the differences between natural persons and legal persons, it simply decided that regulatory distinctions crafted on this basis are unlawful, at least in the area of political expenditures. What the Court called "rudimentary" was actually revolutionary.

Because the law struck down in *Citizens United* specifically exempted media corporations and because the First Amendment's text protects the press by name, it is no answer to say that Congress must be stopped from censoring media corporations. That, however, is the only specific rationale provided by the majority opinion for its conclusion that restrictions on corporate speech are unconstitutional.[180] The absence of any specific reason returns us to the Court's general theory of democracy. We ought to look intently at that theory, for it is the ultimate rationale for the Court's decision:

Austin interferes with the "open marketplace" of ideas protected by the First Amendment.[181]

Never mind ensuring fair play and competition by breaking up monopolies. The Court insisted that "ideas may compete in this marketplace without government interference."[182]

The open-market principle is now the guiding star. For instance, rather than describing the voters as having elected representatives who designed regulations to merely restrain corporate power and to ensure a competitive dynamic within the market, the Court describes the electorate as having been "deprived of information, knowledge and opinion vital to its function" by "censorship . . . vast in its reach."[131] Considering the popularity of campaign finance reform and the incredible level of popular distrust of corporate power in the political sphere, the Court's characterization of the issue strains credulity.[184] The public does not view itself as deprived of information; rather, it sees restraints on corporate power as necessary in order to make democracy accountable to citizens of average means. The Court reminded us that the First Amendment "confirms the freedom to think for ourselves";[185] but if the people, thinking for themselves, realize that concentrated wealth has corrupted the political process, this is one thought that the Court forbids them to act upon.

After displaying its prescriptions for an open market, the Court laid out a similarly dogmatic description of what corruption does not mean: "That [corporate] speakers may have influence over or access to elected officials does not mean that these officials are corrupt."[186]

Favoritism and influence are not . . . avoidable in representative politics. It is in the nature of an elected representative to favor certain policies, and, by necessary corollary, to favor the voters *and contributors* who support those policies. It is well understood that a substantial and legitimate reason, if not the only reason, to cast a vote for, or to make a contribution to, one candidate over another is that the candidate will respond by producing those political outcomes the supporter favors. Democracy is premised on responsiveness.[187]

This construction of responsiveness, indeed of representative democracy itself, is another tribute to Orwell. The Court displayed considerable mastery in torturing democratic language in order to legitimate an undemocratic state of affairs.

The inclusion of corporations into this design is *Citizen United*'s particular contribution. Kennedy cites his own dissenting opinion from *McConnell* for the proposition that favoritism towards and influence by corporations "are not avoidable in representative politics."[188] Perhaps this is true as a general rule and with regard to certain influential individuals as well, but this says nothing about the historical battles and waves of legislation that had succeeded in limiting such favoritism and influence. We see what the Court could not stomach—that corporate citizens would find their influence limited by the need to form political action committees and swear off general treasury funds in order to participate in the most pointed facets of political debate. If mild limitations on corporate financial power destroy the responsive democracy guaranteed by the First Amendment, then the Constitution protects the state of policy platforms and legislation that results from an actual, unregulated market for political speech.

Investments in this market are a function of the intensity of investors' interests (or the value to them of desired political outcomes), investors' financial means, and the projected effectiveness of the "speech" in question in producing those desired outcomes. This view of responsive democracy, solidified in *Bennett*, implies that every disorganized or poor constituency will receive less access to representatives and less influence over policy outcomes, and that this state of affairs cannot lawfully be modified by the government. Corporations, even multibillion-dollar multinational corporations, must be able to invest in political speech at the level appropriate to their commercial interests.

Less than a year after *Citizens United*, that market-determined level of speech was appropriately showcased by the defeat of Senator Russ Feingold, a towering figure in campaign finance reform and cosponsor of the legislation hollowed out in the case itself. The election that Feingold lost featured a remarkable amount of televised commercials and millions of dollars in outside spending, 92 percent of which favored Feingold's opponent, a Republican businessman.[189]

III. THE END OF CASELAW

To establish the constitutional supremacy of the free market process, the Roberts Court has used a number of analytical tools, many of which it inherited from the Burger Court. Recall from *Buckley* and *Bellotti* how money became speech, democracy a market, equality an unconstitutional rationale for limiting political spending, and corporate speech essential to political debate. To this neoclassical economic foundation, the Rehnquist Court added significant civic content. The Roberts Court responded by enhancing Burger's principles so as to make civic content unlawful. Although the political action committee requirement still permitted corporate political speech to be brought to market, it became unconstitutional the second that corporations officially acquired a First Amendment right to political speech. Although trigger mechanism subsidies placed no limit on contributions or expenditures, they became unconstitutional the second that the First Amendment began to protect the market-determined effectiveness of contributions and expenditures. Once the Court took the notion of democracy as an "open market" literally, undue influence became an invalid basis for political finance limitations. What sense could the "undue influence of aggregated capital" make, after all, if the Constitution requires an unregulated market for political spending?

Absent the market-determined effectiveness principle, standard economic notions of oligopoly and monopoly could be invoked to subsidize new political parties and candidates, and to prevent aggregated capital from cornering the market for speech. If Microsoft or AT&T had been entitled to the optimal effectiveness of their capital, they might have achieved enduring monopolies. The Court has said in numerous contexts that the remedy for undesired speech is not censorship or regulation but more speech. While tenable in contexts where speech is accessible, this argument does not fit in the context of money-in-politics cases where big spenders dominate national and regional markets.

Curiously enough, the Court's solution to monopoly is new entrants in the market. Under monopoly and oligopoly, new companies are faced with high barriers to entry, competitiveness falters, prices can be controlled by producers, and consumers are vulnerable to exploitation. The remedy to barriers and price controls cannot be the superhuman act of surmounting them. But that is precisely the Roberts Court's view of what the First Amendment demands—that parties, candidates, officeholders, citizens, interest groups, and corporations raise funds, spend, and compete on the basis of their market-determined level of political effectiveness.

There is a simple explanation behind this laissez-faire posture towards monopoly and duopoly: the effectiveness principle protects private capital only, the only source of power cognizable to an unregulated market. A monopoly or oligopoly of privately owned corporations or private citizens entails only private economic power. Therefore, the effectiveness principle does not allow the state to intervene. Justice White anticipated this state of affairs long ago: "Every reason the majority gives for treating [political finance reform] as a restraint on speech relates to the effectiveness with which the donors can make their voices heard."[190]

The movement towards market-determined speech effectiveness has been honest in this regard. Consider Scalia's dissenting opinion in *McConnell*. He began by conceding that the law did not deprive the market of corporate voices and pro-corporate points of view: "To be sure, the individuals involved in, or benefited by, those industries, or interested in those causes, could (given enough time) form political action committees or other associations to make their case."[191] "But," Scalia continued, "the organizational form in which those enterprises already *exist*, and in which they can most quickly and most effectively get their message across, is the corporate form . . . A candidate should not be insulated from the most effective speech that the major participants in the economy and major incorporated interest groups can generate."[192] So firm was Scalia's belief in the effectiveness principle that he doubted the motives of those who violated it: "It is a measure of the Government's disdain for protected speech that it would label as a sham the mode of communication sophisticated speakers choose because it is the most powerful."[193]

Justice Thomas would extend this analysis to strike down contribution limits across the board. In a dissenting opinion joined by Scalia, Thomas correctly noted that "[b]y depriving donors of their right to speak through the candidate, contribution limits relegate donors' points of view to less effective modes of communication."[194] Because the Court has long considered high donations to pose a risk of dollars for favors and it still considers the elimination of that sort of corruption (and its appearance) to be a compelling state interest, Thomas and Scalia's view is not yet law.

Consider the view that has lost out on the Roberts Court. Justice Kagan and the other three liberals on the Court believe that "[t]he best test of truth is the power of the thought to get itself accepted in the competition of the market."[195] Note, however, that the liberals limit this market to the stage at which the public hears, considers, and responds to speech. In their view, the market's robust competition and exchange is a metaphor for how differing political viewpoints ought to be sorted out, not a prescription for how political speech may or may not be financed.[196] The Liberal Four could therefore acknowledge that "responsive speech by one candidate may make another candidate's speech less effective" but maintain that this is "the whole idea of the First Amendment, and a *benefit* of having more responsive speech."[197] The liberals support government efforts to ensure that core expressive and associational activity is genuinely competitive, open, and vibrant, as one imagines a healthy market.

The conservatives, in contrast, view the financing of speech as part of an actual market. The political finance stage of market competition sorts out which candidates obtain the support of which political consumers— i.e., those individuals and groups with money to donate and spend. The market is also held to include the process through which political consumers spend money to ensure the success of their favored candidate or issue platform. Candidates and pressure groups all compete on financial terms. Therefore, we might conclude that the split within the Court centers on the question of where the market should begin. The liberals appear to maintain that the market metaphor guides our understanding of speech, association, and participation itself. The conservative view, on the other hand, extends market baselines to the *funding* of speech, association, and participation.

The deeper truth, however, is that the difference between the conservatives and the liberals centers mostly on another issue: not the scope of the market, but the type of market theory. For example, the undue influence theory of corruption aims partly at the financing of political speech. It involves the *distorting* effects of wealth, namely the lack of a close relation between the volume of capital employed and public support for the ideas promoted. The liberals still frame this as an economic concern, however. Dissenting in *Citizens United*, Justice Stevens alleged that corporate wealth "can distort the *free trade in ideas* crucial to candidate elections."[198] With the proper regulatory structure in place, Justice Brennan once opined that the "relative availability of funds is a rough barometer of public support."[199] In sum, the liberals seek a well-functioning, regulated market, one that would bring the Court back to one of the oldest articulations of the market principle: "It is the purpose of the First Amendment to preserve an uninhibited marketplace of ideas in which truth will ultimately prevail, rather than to countenance monopolization of that market."[200] This market view would demand what the Roberts Court has prohibited.

We have returned to where we started—the spillover of economic principles into caselaw. Within his account of historical change, Paul Krugman notes that "economics, circa 1975, divide[d] itself into opposing camps over the value of Keynes's views." He describes one group as "neoclassical purists [who] believe that all worthwhile economic analysis starts from the premise that people are rational and markets work." The other group, meanwhile, was "willing to deviate from the assumption of perfect markets or perfect rationality" and minimally open to regulation. Krugman marvels, however, at the great number of economists, not just committed purists, who "were seduced by the vision of a perfect, friction-less market system."[201]

Aware of cognitive errors, irrationality, imperfect information, and barriers to competition, other economists offer different prescriptions for structuring markets. As the reality sinks in that neither markets nor their participants are perfect, we might expect a resuscitation of the Keynes-ian view that markets need "a minder." Intervention might, following the market analogy, seek to break up a monopoly, inject liquidity into an arid market, or provide a counterweight to the increasing domination of oligopolies. And so we have our neoliberals (or laissez-faire conserva-tives) and our neo-Keynesians. Both agree that democracy is a market, but each maintains a distinct view of the market's prescriptions. This is not to forget the civic, non-market sentiment expressed by Justices Marshall, Rehnquist, White, Stevens, and Kagan, but such sentiment invokes even greater hostility from the Roberts Court than neo-Keynesianism.

The conservative majority relies on free market dogma to such an ex-tent that it dominates the Constitution. But why? Why should a majority of the nation's uppermost judges interpret the Constitution in this light? Does the Constitution demand it? Or is it the case that the Justices them-selves have been dominated—dominated by the major intellectual trends of their time—and are acting out the political theories that have wrought their minds?

CHAPTER 5

Why Capitalism Governs Democracy

THE SUPREME COURT'S PRINCIPLES ARE NOW FAMILIAR, BUT they remain as an unexpected topography: democracy as an unregulated market; money as its currency; corporations as vital participants; the free market value of speech as a constitutional guarantee; political donors and spenders as sovereign; and the state's role as limited to targeting quid pro quo corruption and its appearance. Equalization of funds or opportunities? Limitations on corporate spending? Effective subsidies for candidates who do not wish to indebt themselves to big donors? Democratic integrity? Unthinkable.

Having explored the cases is akin to having crested the lower summits of a mountain range. It is a good time to catch one's breath, and a look back on the trail below imparts a sense of perspective; but sooner or later, one looks up and is met by a newfound view of even higher peaks. Where does the Court's capitalist approach to democracy come from? Is there support for the decision that free market theory should govern constitutional interpretation? Indeed, is there support for the idea that capitalism should govern democracy?

I. THE FIRST AMENDMENT, THEREFORE!

Can the capitalist terrain encountered in previous chapters be fairly attributed to the First Amendment? It is tempting to think so. "Congress shall make no law . . . abridging the freedom of speech," the First Amendment commands. No law. Laissez-faire. If constitutional reality were as simple as this, then we would not need to ask why the Court uses economic ideology as a Rosetta Stone. That ideology would be built into the First Amendment and by guaranteeing an open market for political spending the Court would only be doing its duty. But, if the words of the First Amendment and the social circumstances surrounding them do not support this ideology, then a path opposite that of duty would unfold.

A. The Free Speech Clause as a Blank Check

How can the Court be sure that "the freedom of speech," a term of art, covers financial donations and unlimited expenditures? How can it be sure that this freedom extends to corporations, even for-profit ones? Is it credible to maintain that a text adopted in 1791 protects political spending by multinationals, lobbyists, superPACs, and dark money groups?

The freedom of speech referenced by the Framers encompassed no such thing. The Framers' freedom was partial, designed to prevent the censoring of speech at the outset, not the punishing of speech that later turned out to be false or unpopular.[1] The First Amendment aimed towards truth. Today's market of misleading attack ads would not have been viewed sympathetically by the Constitution's authors.[2] These were, after all, the same "men who had the street outside Independence Hall covered with earth so that their deliberations might not be disturbed by passing traffic."[3] Their modern-day counterparts, meanwhile, risk personal injury from traffic, crossing the street several times each day to access their private offices, where they spend hours making phone calls to potential donors.[4] Today's officeholders have come under fire for avoiding deliberation altogether—failing to attend meetings and sessions, forgoing debate when they do attend, and failing to read legislation before voting on it. By defining free speech as a market, the Court has pushed representatives towards fundraising and away from speech in its native context of sincere debate.

Even if we make the historically false assumption that freedom of speech was meant to achieve an open financial market in its own era, would that goal have been proposed and ratified in today's conditions? To begin with, the economic market was not what it is today. Modern multinational corporations would be unrecognizable to the eighteenth-century citizen. Even as of 1865, approximately three-quarters of a century after the First Amendment was ratified, most companies were "highly competitive, with no single company dominating any single field."[5] Forty years later, however, "one or two giant firms controlled at least half the output in seventy-eight different industries."[6] Does laissez-faire today mean the same thing it did yesterday? An open market does not make good on the same values or achieve the same ends under such different conditions.[7]

As with the economic market, so too with the political market. It makes little sense to assume that yesterday's associations and polemicists stand in direct relationship to today's large corporate speakers and more-sophisticated actors. An open market of pamphleteers and street-corner speakers serves individual rights and the need to reach the electorate in a vast expanse of terrain not yet permeated by radio waves or satellite signals. Who believes that an open market of multimillion-dollar ad campaigns, corporate speech, shadow groups, 527s, and lobbyists fulfills the same purposes or has the same social effects as the pamphleteers and street-corner speakers of the early 1800s? The potential for unhealthy dependency on those willing to defray the costs of campaign advertising was far smaller than it is today. Unlimited corporate contributions to a superPAC hardly express the same concept of rights that a speech or pamphlet does.

The social purpose of speech is not fulfilled in the same way either. In contrast to yesterday's challenge of simply getting enough information out to the electorate, the challenge today lies in making the privatized multimedia market for political advertisements accessible and perhaps less saturated by superficial and misleading ads. Yesterday's analogy is to the state of law demanded in order to facilitate the Industrial Revolution, that which places minimum burdens on productive activity by assigning the costs of accidents and other unintended consequences to the employee, the consumer, or the taxpayer. Today's analogy is to the state of law demanded a bit later, when an industrialized nation came to terms with the exploitation of workers, massive environmental pollution, and unsafe products. The resistance even today of those who stand to lose from such laws provokes a thought: Perhaps the same open, unregulated stance does further a few of the same purposes today as it did in earlier times. The industrial statesmen (or robber barons) and lesser industrialists of the late 1800s registered tremendous profits, and these groups' descendants likewise seek a lax regulatory environment.

This provokes another uncomfortable thought: At the time of the First Amendment's ratification and for almost a century thereafter, women, African Americans, and Native Americans did not benefit much from the freedom of speech, or from any of today's much-touted political freedoms for that matter. During that agonizing period of time, these groups formed an underclass toiling in support of others' speech, others' deliberations, others' self-authorship. What is the relationship of the majority of the population to political freedoms today? Although universal suffrage has been obtained, the remainder of influential political activity is out of reach for most people. Is history repeating itself? Are today's behind-the-scenes interest-group deals, corporate electioneering, and privatized multimedia environment the reincarnations of political exclusion?

These reflections need not convince anyone one way or the other. For the time being, their only contention is subjectivity itself—that it takes a great deal of subjective judgment to reach a conclusion as to the First Amendment's textual meaning, intended purposes, and application to today's conditions. That exercise is familiar to law, but it is proof nonetheless that the constitutional text and the purposes of those who wrote it do not automatically decide cases. In Cass Sunstein's words, "insistence on the text is basically unhelpful, even fraudulent."[8] He states that cases such as those we have examined "cannot plausibly be resolved simply by invoking the [Amendment's] text or history."[9]

Addressing executive authority, an area less constitutionally ambiguous than political finance, Justice Jackson memorably described the problem:

Just what our forefathers did envision, or would have envisioned had they foreseen modern conditions, must be divined from materials almost as enigmatic as the dreams Joseph was called upon to interpret for Pharaoh.[10]

The enigmatic text points us away from the law as an external, tangible reality, and towards the internal, ethereal engines of legal interpretation.

Even if the original intent behind the constitutional text could be firmly established, a court would have to exercise its will and judgment in deciding what weight to afford that intent. Many value judgments are involved in the conclusion that people in the United States should be bound for all time by the understandings of an elite cadre of eighteenth-century men— slave-holding, land-owning, tea-drinking, corporal-punishing, horse-riding, white, ostensibly heterosexual, Christian men with what in today's world would count as sexist, classist, homophobic, racist, and scientifically outdated viewpoints.[11] As advanced as they were in their own time and as superior as they were to their modern counterparts in matters of history, philosophy, debate, political vision, courage, and general sturdiness, it is unthinkable that they should rule this land in perpetuity from the crypt. Those inclined towards cryptology ought to meditate upon the convincing evidence that the Framers' intended for future generations to make the Constitution their own.[12]

Why would the Framers write out some portions of the Constitution in specific detail, and others in such open terms? If the Framers wished to achieve the Roberts Court's results, they might have written this instead: "Congress shall not abridge, inconvenience, or dissuade any utterance, writing, or representation of any kind issued on any medium by any person or entity in any context, regardless of any possible injury or detriment to any other person or entity, or indeed to the operation of democracy itself." They might also have specified: "The term 'speech' includes all financial means necessary to make speech influential. The spending of money is just as much a part of speech as verbs and nouns."

It is not that the Framers would necessarily have been against lending some constitutional protection to financial transactions aimed at speech production. It is, rather, that they did not have cause to enter such protection into the Constitution.

Electioneering during the founding era did not involve large sums of money. Candidates stood for election based on their reputation among voters and thus spent little on advertising and campaigning. For example, in Madison's first race for public office, his major electioneering cost would have been for food and drink for the electors . . . The politicians and thinkers did not reflect much on the relation of money to politics.[13]

This is the only proof we desire at this stage. The Constitution itself does not protect money in politics, because, to begin with, money in politics in the founding era was nothing like it is today.

Still, the Framers adopted a cautious approach to issues that would arise in the future. They protected copyright and patent,[14] and had inventors within their ranks. They knew that speech dynamics and technologies would change over time, but they did not know how. Their use of "the freedom of speech" instead of "all possible speech" was therefore a concession to self-authorship. The nation would decide over time, in each era, what the freedom of speech entailed. Certainly it must always include core political speech, but that is a separate matter from large donations, enormous expenditures in a privatized multimedia market, and corporate electioneering. In such cases, outside the text's embrace and the world from which the text sprang, "the freedom of speech" refers to a socially determined realm of remarkable subjectivity.

Even if the freedom of speech did cover political spending and corporate electioneering, we would still not know what to make of the word "abridge." How, for instance, does the Court know that the matching funds provision in *Bennett* abridged the freedom of speech? Is "to reduce the financial incentives for" or "to hypothetically decrease" included within the meaning of "abridge"? "Abridge" seems a stronger term than these others, a bad description of how matching funds affect speech. Sure, those wishing to control the political debate by outspending their rivals may not be willing to spend as much once they see that opposing views will continue to surface, but has the freedom of speech thereby been abridged or furthered?

The same question ought to be asked of straightforward expenditure limits, which are designed to encourage more actors to speak. At a town meeting, is the freedom of speech abridged by rules against bringing a megaphone or by rules against monopolizing the microphone? Does the First Amendment really guarantee to interest groups the right to purchase all available airtime, television and radio included, and to drown out every voice and viewpoint that is not well funded?

Let us assume for the sake of argument that the "freedom of speech" covers all expensive, loud, and incessant forms of communication and that the word "abridge" must be understood as a hypersensitive needle disturbed even by shifting incentives for particular modes of expression. Still, First Amendment protection need not be absolute. In 1883, Justice Story wrote, the free speech clause is "an expansion of the great doctrine . . . that every man shall be at liberty to publish what is true, with good motives and for justifiable ends."[15] By referencing truth, motives, and ends, Story made out the clause to be demanding and cautious. He wrote that the right was limited by the requirement that the speaker "does not injure any other person in his rights [or] disturb the public peace, or attempt to subvert the government."[16] The freedom of speech could, for example, be qualified by democratic interests in equal participation and public deliberation. The Constitution guarantees a "republican form of government,"[17] "equal protection,"[18] and it cautions that "the enumeration . . . of certain rights shall not be construed to deny or disparage others retained by the people."[19] If the people retain rights to political equality and democratic governance (either because of the Constitution's provisions on these matters or because not all rights in existence are incorporated into the Constitution), then why should a dubious construction of free speech be allowed to deny or disparage those other rights?[20]

The Constitution also prohibits officeholders from accepting "any present, Emolument, Office, or Title, of any kind whatever, from any King, Prince, or foreign State."[21] In this way, the Framers sought to prevent conflicts of interest and compromised judgment—in short, the all-too-familiar incentives that make officeholders indifferent to the interests of their constituents and the well-being of their country. While it is no longer common for a foreign king to give a U.S. officeholder "a portrait of himself set in diamonds and fixed above a gold snuff box," lobbyists for foreign corporations do take U.S. officeholders on luxurious vacations abroad.[22] And PACs accepting unlimited contributions from sources not disclosed until after the election do spend unlimited amounts promoting or tarnishing candidates as they vie for office. Could not such things have a greater pull upon officeholders' judgment than a snuffbox?

Finally, in all of these cases, the Court betrays itself. If its authority for overruling acts of Congress comes from the Constitution, and the Constitution commands that speech not be abridged, then should not the Court insist on some evidence that the plaintiffs' speech was in fact limited in every case before it? It has declined to do so in the hardest cases, relying on axioms instead of evidence.[23]

Within the realm of intellectual honesty, it is impossible to derive the Court's holdings from the text of the First Amendment. There is no way around it: In order to decide whether the First Amendment protects today's political market, significant value judgments must be brought to bear. Recent cases that hold, for example, that the First Amendment protects monetary expenditures and corporate political activity are just that: cases.

The language chosen in such cases—i.e., the First Amendment does this or that—is stylistic at best and insincere at worst. The only accurate phrasing available is *the Court hereby decides that the First Amendment shall mean this or that*. The Constitution is innocent of such autonomous meaning; prior to the case in question, it did not mean whatever a particular majority of Justices now holds.

B. *To Whom Should the Check Be Made Out (and in What Amount)?*

The absence of constitutional text concerning money in politics allows the Supreme Court to invent as much law as it wishes. This blank check does not explain, however, whom the Court chooses as a payee or the amount of money decided upon. This boils down to the question of why the Court has invented the particular body of caselaw that we have seen. Given that "[t]he Constitution is silent on virtually all the important issues regarding elections,"[24] and that the First Amendment did not anticipate multinational corporations, much less television or radio, we might expect the Court to defer to Congress or at least show a degree of caution and humility in assigning meaning to the First Amendment.

The Court has done the opposite. What should we make of receiving not deference or caution but bold neoclassical principles? Our Anglo-American legal tradition is characterized by a practice of cautious, case-by-case adjudication. As a general rule, courts should extend the law only as far as necessary to resolve the dispute in the precise case at hand—no further. Anything more is an abuse of judicial power. Consider how Justice Jackson once described the work of courts: "[D]ecisions are indecisive because of the judicial practice of dealing with the largest questions in the most narrow way."[25] Or take Justice Holmes's remark that "[g]eneral propositions do not decide concrete cases."[26] These quotations are at odds with the Court's reasoning.

They are even more at odds with the Court's procedure in *Citizens United* of ordering oral argument on issues not raised by the disputants. When the Court in *Citizens United* informs us that "we are asked to reconsider *Austin*," it means to say, "At the last minute, we ordered that the case be reargued in order to confront constitutional questions that the litigants did not ask us to confront." So much for the doctrine of constitutional avoidance that has saved countless statutes from unconstitutionality. The Court could have simply exempted nonprofit corporations from the law's reach. Instead, the Court defied the common law tradition and its own protocols in order to make way for an open-market diatribe. On the Roberts Court, general propositions and major premises do decide concrete cases, and even the narrowest questions are dealt with in the broadest way.

It would be wrong to describe the Rehnquist Court's campaign finance decisions in the same way. Although it entertained many general propositions, those were usually Congress's propositions, not the Court's. This put the legislative and executive branches of government, those accountable to the people, in charge of making broad statements about the way democracy should be. The Burger and Roberts Courts flipped this model on its head by seizing the power to make those statements in the name of the Constitution. Filling up the Constitution in this way, these Courts have shown little respect for Congress, state legislatures, and the American people.

This puts the electorate in the embarrassing position described in the tale of the emperor with no clothes. The Constitution itself does not give corporations personhood or protect their speech. This fact, together with the historically important series of congressional acts limiting corporate political power, enveloped *Austin* and *McConnell* in thick constitutional fabric. But then, seven years after *McConnell*, the citizenry is asked to believe that the Constitution demands that a century of Congress's work and decades of caselaw be erased. The Constitution has been under protective glass in the National Archives Building all this time, mind you. *Citizens United* and the robes of its authors are threadbare. Only the willing entertain the illusion.

The Court's exercise of power cannot be obscured by its use of court-created tests. Over the years, the Court has developed a formula for evaluating the constitutionality of legislation that affects individual rights. The Court asks whether any law burdening political speech is justified by a compelling state interest and is "narrowly tailored to achieve that interest."[27] The answer turns on the Court's assessment of the burden imposed and the state interest(s) that the law was designed to serve. Despite their legal packaging, these questions involve value judgments that are themselves unconstrained by law. Saying nothing at all about what state interests are compelling or what it means for legislation to be narrowly tailored—indeed, saying nothing about judicial review to begin with, nothing about the need for an interest to be *compelling* or for its pursuit to be *narrowly tailored*—the Constitution can hardly be interpreted in these ways. Justices engaging in this common exercise are adding to the Constitution, not interpreting it.

Legal realists have famously owned up to the causal role of political values, "call[ing] into question conventional efforts to anchor judicial power on a fixed legal foundation."[28] Oliver Wendell Holmes pioneered the movement with statements such as this: "Behind the [law's] logical form lies a judgment as to the relative worth of and importance of competing legislative grounds, often an inarticulate and unconscious judgment, it is true, and yet the very root and nerve of the whole proceeding."[29] This boils down to the allegation that law is, to an untoward extent, politics. And the proof is all too abundant. The Rehnquist Court affirmed a state interest in combating undue influence because Congress desired it, the Constitution did not prohibit it, and because, even assuming corporate speech qualified for First Amendment protection, there were many other avenues for corporate speech. The Roberts Court then held the undue-influence rationale unconstitutional in light of the First Amendment. The Constitution did not change during this time; the Justices did.

All of the above explains Justice White's accusation after *Buckley*: "Judges have an exaggerated view of their role in our polity." White described the Court's abuse of power with a simple formula: "The First Amendment, therefore!"[30] White objected to the Court's self-anointment as an assembly of oracles. If White found the Burger Court's reading of the First Amendment to be a stretch, what would he have said about the Roberts Court? The "therefore" has grown and threatens to burst. Where is the *there* from where the Court's principles spring? What ground is obscured when the Court attributes economic ideology to the Constitution's innocent text?

We come to what Chief Justice John Marshall called the "wishes, affections, and general theories" of Supreme Court Justices.[31] These are the factors that drive the Court's understanding of ambiguous language in the Constitution and caselaw, the Court's selection of certain principles from these sources of law, its interpretation of those principles, and its application of those interpretations to the factual predicate at hand. H. Jefferson Powell's phrase "vision[s] of constitutional principle,"[32] is a helpful pointer. When legal sources are ambiguous, such visions overwhelm traditional legal analysis. Indeterminate legal sources are given content by the Justices' "principled commitment[s] to underlying constitutional meaning."[33] Powell describes each Justice's vision and commitment, wishes, affections, and general theories, as "too deep to change."[34] He thus prepares us to hear Chief Justice Hughes's confession, "We are under a Constitution, but the Constitution is what the judges say it is."[35]

How else are we to understand the comparison of free speech in a democracy to transactions or products in a free market? Within the market principle, what accounts for the divide between Justices who think the market must be regulated to ensure that it remain competitive and diverse and other Justices who shout back "laissez-faire"? And why not derive rules for political speech in a democracy from visions of a thriving agora or an open deliberative forum instead of a marketplace? Similar questions arise as to the evaluation of the state interests that drive political finance reform. Why is political equality a constitutionally illegitimate motivation?

To say that this is so because political equality interferes with the free market is only to restate the question. In the 1919 case *Abrams v. U.S.*, Holmes posited that "the ultimate good desired is better reached by free trade in ideas—that the best test of truth is the power of the thought to get itself accepted in the competition of the market."[36] Because "time has upset many fighting faiths,"[37] Holmes hoped that people would acquire a degree of humility, realizing that many who believed deeply had later been proven wrong. This hope was addressed to those who believed so fervently and absolutely as to fashion laws to erect their views in heavy stone and "sweep away all opposition."[38]

These remarks came in a dissenting opinion that would have reversed a conviction under the Espionage Act. This was a case about an *individual's right to speak free from prosecution*, not a case about the ability of individuals, interest groups, and corporations to spend unlimited money to make their speech more influential. Indeed, such expenditures sweep away opposition, at least the poorly funded sort. Matching funds programs and restrictions on general treasury spending and unlimited expenditures would not sweep away all opposition. Quite the opposite—they would force all opposing sources to compete on a more equal footing, to contend with each other so that "truth" could prevail on the grounds of what was said instead of how many times one side's views were repeated relative to another's. As you will recall, it was in *Lochner*, a case actually about the ability of the state to regulate market dynamics, that Holmes came out on the side of regulation (or at least judicial deference), asserting that "a Constitution is not intended to embody a particular economic theory, whether of paternalism . . . or of *laissez faire*."[39] Holmes's market metaphor was just that: a metaphor. It was not intended to give moneyed actors an unlimited advantage in today's political market.

Even if we were to concede, bizarrely and unnecessarily, that the market metaphor should be authoritative, we would have to return to the fact that the market has hardly been a stable reference point. The market in 1919 was not what it is today. How are we to understand continued allegiance to the unregulated market principle in the post–Great Depression era—indeed, in the presence of more recent and more global economic crises? The debate over how to best structure the economy exposes that economic theory itself is hotly contested and that there are many different forms of capitalism.

Aside from the difficulty of choosing between different capitalist theories, the greater question is why any capitalist theory should be applied when it comes to structuring our democracy. Justices never answer these questions outright. It is unforgivably naive to imagine that their internal answers to these questions have anything to do with legal analysis, traditionally understood. We are dealing instead with visions of constitutional principle, commitments to extra-legal theories of law and society.

Although the Court does not reveal the true roots of its principles, it is possible to deduce them. As Frederick Schauer puts it, the "adoption of a[ny] free speech principle could be expected systematically over time to favor one ideology or political theory or outlook much more than it would favor others."[40] We need only ask "whether a principle of free speech is likely to have more affinity with some deeper positions than others."[41] In this way, we can identify whether a principle "is tilted rather than indifferent and if so in which direction it is tilted."[42]

II. TILTED TOWARDS DEEPER POSITIONS: VISIONS OF CONSTITUTIONAL PRINCIPLE

Writing in the same year as *Buckley v. Valeo*, C. B. Macpherson observed that "liberal democracy" can mean two things: "the democracy of a capitalist market society" or "a society striving to ensure that all its members are equally free to realize their capabilities."[43] Are the Court's principles not drastically tilted on this score? Macpherson claims that these different meanings come from the word "liberal," which can denote radically different types of freedom: "freedom of the stronger to do down the weaker by following market rules" or "equal effective freedom of all to use and develop their capacities."[44] He traced these inconsistent meanings to the fact that liberalism, although born in capitalist market societies, had justified itself through "the claim of equal individual rights to self development."[45] Note his characterization of the efforts of ethical liberals, especially John Stuart Mill, to place self-developmental freedom above market freedom: "They failed."[46]

If we agree with Macpherson that "'liberal' has consciously or unconsciously been assumed to mean 'capitalist,'" then perhaps the Court's principles are taken straight from intellectual trends, not the Constitution.[47] After all, the Court did rule in *Buckley* precisely as Macpherson saw, that the freedom of some to spend unlimited private funds on political speech could not be limited in the interest of equality. And what was the spirit of *Austin* and *McConnell*, if not a particular manifestation of Macpherson's beliefs that "the appetite for individual freedom[] has outgrown its capitalist market envelope," and that "liberal democracy depends on a downgrading of the market assumptions and an upgrading of the equal right to self-development."[48] Then came *Citizens United*. Just as Macpherson described, efforts to subordinate market freedom fail under the dominant understanding of liberal democracy. The Burger, Rehnquist, and Roberts Courts can now be seen as a microcosm of modern democratic history. Is it possible, then, that the cases are just specific manifestations of the general social understandings that Macpherson and others have described? Are the answers to our questions to be found in the annals of democratic theory?[49]

A. *There is No Such Thing as the Common Good*

The Burger and Roberts Courts' distrust of government, embrace of interest groups and corporations, faith in the open market, and celebration of consumer control have seemed out of place all along—a radically capitalist worldview from a branch of *government* interpreting a *democratic constitution*. The surprise has been all the greater given that the cases concern political speech and elections, not financial markets.

Coming upon public choice theory, everything falls into place. It is a relief to see that the Justices' intellectual loyalties belong somewhere. The Justices have transplanted select portions of a wide body of work into the lines of their opinions. Those familiar with this work could, all along, fill in the missing pieces and recognize the meaning and source of the Court's remarks. As we shall see, however, the Court's selection and portrayal of ideas from this work are unfair, transforming the disinterested inquiries of economists and political scientists into a capitalist public philosophy.[50]

While most Americans experienced the Cold War and the social turmoil of the 1960s in the vivid and dramatic terms of King, Kennedy, and Khrushchev, a particularly dry movement arose. Although it lived through the 1960s, it ignores the fact that democracy is sometimes a place of social transformation, a place where average citizens assume personal costs to achieve collective goals and where belief and principle triumph over rational calculations. This movement's names and branches are unfamiliar to most people: empirical democratic theory, rational choice theory, the pluralist elitist equilibrium model, interest-group pluralism, interest-group liberalism, and public choice theory. Economists and political scientists working within this general school of thought have employed mathematical, economic, and statistical methodologies to create the most technical assessments of U.S. democracy in existence. The goal, they claimed, was not to justify or criticize but rather to "describe the *real workings* of democracy."[51]

Those descriptions employ a particular vocabulary. All people are seen as having "preferences." Preferences are what people want. People are assumed to be self-interested; preferences tell us how people have made their interests concrete. Self-interest is defined as the maximization of "utility," which means the satisfaction of desire or pleasure: for an officeholder, reelection and greater power in her party; for interest groups, access and influence leading to favorable laws and policies; for voters, vindication of their viewpoints and better terms for their material interests. Beyond self-interested, people are also assumed to be rational. They choose the best way they know to maximize utility. Next, democracy tallies or "aggregates" individual preferences. Individuals register their preferences by voting, donating their talents or money, and spending their money. In order to most effectively achieve their interests, people associate in organizational forms that allow them to pool their funds and more effectively register their demands upon the system. Because it posits that people's preferences are formed ahead of time and are unaltered by the political process, public choice limits democracy to hosting a competition between interests and aggregating preferences. Similar to preferences, the distribution of wealth and legal rights are taken as givens.[52] Preferences, legal entitlements, and inequality become "exogenous variables," matters thought to be independent from democracy and therefore capable of being held constant. Without such assumptions, it would be more difficult to make democracy an object of quantitative inquiry.

This is paramount to dissection. The animal to be studied must be dead in order for any objective conclusion to be drawn as to its composition. In the holistic, interdependent, changing sense of its actual life, no system or creature can be understood in this way. Laying democracy out on a cold steel table, slicing it open, and viewing its innards through a microscope, public choice theory made it unrecognizable to most citizens. Still, coming across the unrecognizable dimensions of a familiar thing ought to be experienced as a discovery, and this was the case for intellectuals driving the research and reading the findings. Every economist and political scientist ought to realize that utility can arise from revenge, compassion, love, generosity, and loyalty, not just the consumer paradigm. Even the most isolated researcher must know that human behavior demonstrates both the goodness of hearts and the hunger of bellies, that the history of democracy is the story of how rules, inequalities, and preferences are formed (not just how preexisting interests are pursued), that there are certain collective interests, such as clean air and rule of law, that everyone shares, and that democracy is, accordingly, more than just a competition between self-interested actors.

Nevertheless, the discoveries of public choice theory were valuable in fleshing out the competitive and self-interested aspects of democratic politics. Perhaps in the excitement of the moment it was only natural for new discoveries to overshadow existing truths. We must ask, however, what sense it would make scientifically, intellectually, or otherwise for these aspects of democracy just uncovered to be construed as the only truth about democracy and as a commandment for how democracy must work going forward.

Public Choice as a Response to Yesterday's Problems   Shifting sovereignty from citizens to consumers was not original work on the part of the Roberts Court. In 1951, Kenneth Arrow appeared to read the public good out of democratic analysis by defining political decisions "as a sum of choices . . . of individuals pursuing private preferences."[53] Arrow's model seemed to prove that it was impossible to derive a collective set of preferences from this pursuit.[54] Translation: There is no such thing as the common good. Schumpeter elaborated: "[T]here is . . . no such thing as a uniquely determined common good that all people could agree on . . . by the force of rational argument."[55] "To different individuals and groups," Schumpeter continued, "the common good is bound to mean different things [and] ultimate values . . . are beyond the range of mere logic."[56] "[Thus] the particular concept of the will of the people," he remarked, "vanishes into thin air."[57]

Another aspect of public choice denies that collective will formation can come in through the back door, as it were, through the pursuit of benevolent private preferences. It posited that private preferences could not be altruistic, vindictive, emotive, or—in short—human. As Anthony Downs assumed in 1956, "rational behavior [is] directed primarily to selfish ends"[58]—private preferences cannot become publicly interested. Downs himself gave a wide definition of these ends, however, quipping that "self interest could be enlightenment or pizza."[59]

This was an echo of Walter Lippmann, who, thirty-four years before Downs, wrote that self-interest's crucial role was "not illuminating[] until we know which self out of many selects and directs the interest so conceived."[60] Lippmann rehearsed the various "personalities in each human being" specified by "[r]eligious teaching and popular wisdom."[61] He called them the "Higher and Lower, the Spiritual and Material, [and] the Divine and the Carnal," and noted that even if modern men would challenge these classifications, they would have to concede that "here was an authentic clue to the variety of human nature."[62] Indeed, could not human beings' self-interest include concerns over legitimacy, posterity, or reciprocity? Such concerns are harder to include in experimental models, especially quantitative ones, but do they on that account become less real?

Historical forces may best explain why an economic model of individual motivation gained prominence despite the sorts of concerns voiced by Downs and Lippmann. The rational, self-interested political actor freed from state coercion provided an attractive contrast to the view of human beings accompanying the central planning and bureaucratic dictates of the Soviet Union. John Dewey's vision of citizens in their public capacity coming together to form, identify, and implement the public interest took on a hue a bit too close to the ideology of coercive, centralized political authorities. Those authorities did, after all, conduct their business in "the public interest." Was it realistic to imagine that government could offer its services as a true servant of the public? Would the public interest really be determined freely and would its implementation prove a happy affair? The Cold War popularized a nightmare scenario of how the push for collective goals would end up. Formed during this historical period, interest-group liberalism could hardly help absorbing these suspicions about government, democracy's collective function, and a public good purportedly superior to private interests.

S.M. Amadae describes the Cold War intellectual climate as nourishing the "niggling suspicion that any attempt to censor individuals' 'raw' preferences necessarily entails the erection of an elite figure or idealist philosophy that determines what is best for individuals and society."[63] This is no doubt the heritage of Justice Scalia's view, now the majority view: "The absolutely central principle of the First Amendment . . . is that the government cannot be trusted to ensure the 'fairness' of political debate."[64] Private preferences became sacred in democracy, just like they were in the marketplace, where nobody—much less the government—is supposed to tell people what they should want or how they should spend their money.

Purchasing decisions need not bear anyone else in mind, and certainly not some abstract notion of the public and its alleged interest. Describing this model, Macpherson perceived the view central to this push against collectivism: "The purpose of democracy is to register the desires of people as they are, not to contribute to what they might be or might wish to be. Democracy is simply a market mechanism."[65] Amadae may as well have been referring to the caselaw when she recorded "broad acceptance of . . . principle[s] derived from consumer economics [being] transposed to serve as the legitimating criteri[a] for democratic sovereignty."[66]

The supremacy of private preferences and bias against government interference harmonize with a historical chord even deeper than the Cold War. As Theodore Lowi notes, they "made a happy fit with the native American fear of political power," resonating with ideas "already widely embraced before and during our Revolution."[67] Lowi asks us to remember the basic facts of our country's existence: a rebellion against colonialism (political oppression) and a rebellion against mercantilism (economic oppression). These were comprehensive governmental wrongs. The Crown oppressed the political sphere with its taxes (without representation) and denial of self-determination, and it oppressed the economic sphere as well. Recall Adam Smith's description of how governments granted monopolies to favored persons (restraints on competition), imposed tariffs ("high duties and absolute prohibitions") to protect domestic manufacturers from foreign competitors, and acquired colonies for purposes of extracting raw materials and capturing a market for goods.[68] In this context, private preferences did not receive due respect and an extreme laissez-faire view was hardly a surprising reply. What appear today to be mundane and even perverse concepts from consumer economics are, in origin, radical and emancipatory.

We can blame later generations for interpreting these revolutionary and anti-communist ideological threads too aggressively, reaching the extremes of propaganda during the Cold War. In fairness, however, corporate power in the middle of the twentieth century was not as dominant, globally, as it is today. Besides, Women and African Americans were beginning to exercise some political power, and New Deal legislation was quickly filling up the statute books. And so perhaps it is understandable that, like the supremacy of individual preferences, the role of interest groups was also construed in an emancipatory light, not as a means of domination. Writing in the 1950s, '60s, and '70s, many interest-group pluralists believed power to be "non-hierarchically and competitively arranged."[69] They found "different groups [to] have access to different kinds of resource[s]," and different kinds of resources to produce different degrees of influence across the panoply of contested political issues.[70] Thus a popular base could compete with financial power, religious authority with schooling, and so on. Financial power was not consistently singled out as dominant. The interest groups in question went far beyond chambers of commerce, corporate PACs, and unions. They included "political parties, ethnic groups, students, prison officers, women's collectives, and religious groups."[71]

Having concluded that different groups with diverse forms of power all had traction within the political system, it was hardly sinister for public choice theory to describe the state as "almost indistinguishable from the ebb and flow of bargaining, the competitive pressure of interests."[72] To portray interest groups as "the natural counterpart of free association in a . . . complex industrial system," even as "the central expression of democracy,"[73] was not to conspire against democracy. If power is distributed in diverse forms across various social groups, and if the state is untrustworthy, then it makes sense, as Lowi put it, for "[i]nterest group liberalism . . . to justify power by avoiding law and by parceling out to private parties the power to make public policy."[74] This is done by defining the role of government as that of "insuring access to the most effectively organized, and of ratifying the agreements and adjustments worked out among the competing leaders."[75] It is not for government to dictate the terms of interest-group struggle. Rather, democratic government tallies private interests, arrives at a public interest only in this sense, and thus avoids coercing anyone.

When read in this light, the Roberts Court's economic principles make a bit more sense. With free speech enlisted in the service of unlimited expression of individual preferences, free association in the service of interest groups, and government in the service of protecting this process from interference and then delivering the goods for which political consumers had bargained, democracy could avoid the errors of its enemies during the Revolution and the Cold War. At least early on, interest-group pluralists were neither describing nor justifying what the Rehnquist Court saw: the economic power of corporations, interest groups, and wealthy citizens unduly influencing elections and legislation.[76] Perhaps the Burger Court could trace its views back to the state of pluralist theory at the time. But as pluralism evolved through the 1970s and 1980s, did it learn nothing at all? Could it maintain a Cold War stance on government and financial power in the late 1980s, 1990s, and into the present day? Is it credible for the Court to insist on a rosy view of unrestrained self-interest (and interest groups) in today's era of corporate power?

Critical Trends Ignored by the Roberts Court   While the rosy view of self-interest, corporate power, and interest-group competition boasts a strong historical pedigree, so do the critical threads within public choice theory. Recall Adam Smith's warnings at the outset of capitalist theory: the concentrated wealth of certain classes enabled them to "draw to themselves the greatest share of public consideration," legislative proposals should be "carefully examined . . . with the most suspicious attention," and those with the largest capitals are "an order of men whose interest is never exactly the same with that of the public."[77] James Madison made complementary remarks one year after Smith. He warned that "the most common and durable source of factions has been the various and unequal distribution of property."[78] Although he described those who possess property and those who do not as having "ever formed distinct interests in society," Madison went on to name more specific interests within society, all possessing more power than the poor. "A landed interest, a manufacturing interest, a mercantile interest, a moneyed interest . . . grow up of necessity in civilized nations, and divide them into different classes, actuated by different sentiments and views."[79] He wrote that the "regulation of these various and interfering interests forms the principal task of modern legislation."[80] Madison did not think this an easy task, as is evident in his definition of factions as motivated by "some common impulse of passion, or of interest, *adverse to the right of other citizens, or to the permanent and aggregate interests of the community.*"[81]

Smith's and Madison's descriptions raised questions about the effects of economic power on democratic governance, questions addressed by modern pluralist thought between the 1920s and the present day. Consider, for example, the evolution of one of democracy's most famous theorists, Robert Dahl. Writing in 1956, Dahl characterized the difference between dictatorship and democracy as "government by a minority and government by minorities."[82] He said we would know democracy by the large "number, size, and diversity of the minorities whose preferences will influence the outcome of governmental decisions."[83] Paraphrasing Madison on factions, Dahl homed in on the ability of "various minorities [to] frustrate the ambitions of one another."[84] He believed the majority of citizens to be passive or indifferent, and rested democracy's hopes on "polyarchy," a system in which diverse minority groups compete for electoral power.[85]

The downside of this system, as Margaret Jane Radin put it, is that "individual maximization behavior . . . manipulat[es] wealth transfers away from the unorganized public in favor of well-organized interest groups."[86] Issacharoff and Pildes allege that public choice has failed to notice how those with political power "seek to perpetuate their political control, not by distributing benefits to their supporters, but by capturing the basic structures and ground rules of politics itself."[87] These comments bring to mind "legislative capture" as explained by Mancur Olson in 1971: Parties with the most concentrated interests in policy outcomes have increased incentives and acquire superior means to influence policy as compared with the more diffuse interests of the general population.[88] Still, if many different sorts of groups were capable of organizing themselves and drawing upon diverse forms of power to influence public policy, we might expect politics to be driven by those who care enough to take action, hardly an unattractive vision.

But would polyarchy still be attractive if the many minorities competing for power, though diverse, were all similar in their possession of economic resources? Would we still hold a rosy view of minority power if the outcome of interest-group competition, and hence governmental decisions, turned on the financial power of the groups involved? Or what if, in other cases, economic power were an entry card—not a deciding factor but a gatekeeper? Either way, Dahl would have to look elsewhere to discover the object of his study, the "processes by which ordinary citizens exert a relatively high degree of control over leaders."[89] In fact, Dahl recanted his rosy view of interest-group pluralism at almost precisely the moment as the Supreme Court did.[90] In 1985, he questioned the "liberty to accumulate unlimited economic resources and to organize economic activity into hierarchically governed enterprises."[91] He alleged that "great differences among citizens in wealth, income, status, skills, information, control over information and propaganda, [and] access to political leaders" had triggered "significant inequalities among citizens in their capacities and opportunities for participating as political equals in governing the state."[92]

These references to the influence of concentrated wealth on government might as well have been taken from the pages of *Austin* or *McConnell*. Early interest-group pluralists and early cases such as *Buckley* perceived the majority's demand for equality as a threat to democracy, while later interest-group pluralists and later money-in-politics cases have seen inequality as a threat to democracy. This is how David Held described Dahl's evolution.[93] The move from pluralism to neo-pluralism reflects the realization that interest groups are not equal and the state is not a neutral arbiter because "the business corporation wields disproportionate influence over the state"[94]—in a familiar phrase, undue influence.

Buckley and *Bellotti* grew from an earlier understanding, which Ralph Miliband describes as the "political orthodoxy" of the 1950s:

[T]he state, subjected as it is to a multitude of conflicting pressures from organized groups and interests, cannot show any marked bias towards some and against others: its special role, in fact, is to accommodate and reconcile them all. In that role, the state is only the mirror which society holds up to itself. The reflection may not always be pleasing, but this is the price that has to be paid, and which is imminently worth paying, for democratic, competitive and pluralist politics in modern industrial societies.[95]

This view of the state as an unbiased mirror of society, immune from the pressures and incentives of money in politics, characterizes the Burger Court.

The Rehnquist Court, writing later in time, followed Dahl. By recognizing that financial power could translate into political power, unduly influencing and distorting the state itself, *Austin* and *McConnell* admitted that the state might become not a mirror of society as a whole but a mirror of its dominant economic interests. Those cases challenge interest-group liberalism's claim that "[o]rganized interests emerge in every sector of our lives and adequately represent most of those sectors." They do not "effectively answer[] and check" each other,[96] *Austin* and *McConnell* maintained. Instead, the concentrated wealth possessed by *some* interests exercises undue influence.

Surveying the public choice literature, Daniel Farber and Phillip Frickey confirmed Dahl's suspicion about "significant inequalities among citizens in their capacities and opportunities for participating as political equals."[97] Their reading of the literature confirmed the "basic assumption . . . that taxes, subsidies, regulations, and other political instruments are used to raise the welfare of more influential pressure groups."[98] They noted studies suggesting that "interest group politics is skewed dramatically toward narrow economic interests"[99] and observed that producers have many more lobbyists than consumers.

The consensus view summarized by Farber and Frickey should have been familiar to the members of the Court who signed on to *Citizens United*, and even *Bellotti* and *Buckley*. Recall Posner and Landes's 1975 description:

[L]egislation is supplied to groups or coalitions that outbid rival seekers of favorable legislation. The price that the winning group bids is determined both by the value of legislative protection to the group's members and the group's ability to overcome the free-rider problems that plague coalitions. Payments take the form of campaign contributions, votes, implicit promises for future favors, and sometimes outright bribes. In short, legislation is "sold" by the legislature and "bought" by the beneficiaries of the legislation.[100]

By upholding contribution limits, *Buckley* sought to confine this market to the other forms of payment besides bribery mentioned by Posner. Ruling that money was speech and democracy was a market, the Court constitutionalized and encouraged the buying and selling that Posner perceived.

Posner's remark and many findings within public choice tend to validate the Marxist claim that "the state is not an independent and sovereign political subject but is an instrument of coercion and administration which can be used for various purposes by whatever interests manage to appropriate it."[101] The findings above regarding the political inequality among citizens by virtue of wealth and the disproportionate political influence of corporations validate the other typical component of the Marxist view: not simply that the state has been co-opted, but that it has been co-opted by "individuals of a ruling class."[102] This belief leads to the famous accusation that "the executive of the modern state is but a committee for managing the common affairs of the bourgeoisie."[103]

Instead of a Marxist, Posner became the leading proponent of economic thought within judicial reasoning. Even in this capacity, however, he questioned the use of interest-group pluralism as a model for how democracy ought to be. Writing the year *McConnell* was decided, Posner corroborated the alleged threat to popular sovereignty, noting that "interest-group pressures make elected officials frequently unresponsive to the interests of ordinary, unorganized people."[104] Then, alleging that "increasingly sophisticated techniques employed in public-opinion polling and political advertising have made political campaigning manipulative and largely content-free,"[105] he suggested that market dynamics frustrate the role of informed choice and deliberation.

This leads us to another critical trend in the literature—not the manipulation of officeholders and legislation, but the manipulation of the general public. Whereas Dahl and Posner spoke to the unequal resources that make interest-group competition a forum for legislative capture, Joseph Schumpeter and Walter Lippmann added a psychological component. What if interest groups needed public consent in order to extract rents? While officeholders and parties could be influenced rationally through costs and benefits, it would also be essential to manage public opinion, especially during election periods. Similarly, parties and politicians have a natural interest in controlling the public's viewpoints and impressions, and portraying the issues in a beneficial light. During the development of public choice theory, markets were transformed by the rising sophistication of advertising, the advent of public relations firms, and the technological gains that provided them a platform. Public choice theory could not ignore how these revolutionary changes bled over from ordinary markets into political ones.

Schumpeter saw this many years ago. In 1942, he explained that the "ways in which issues and the popular will on any issue are being manufactured [are] exactly analogous to the ways of commercial advertising."[106] Schumpeter considered consumers to be "so amenable to the influence of advertising and other methods of persuasion that producers often seem to dictate to them instead of being directed by them."[107] He observed that "mere assertion, often repeated, counts more than rational argument and so does the direct attack on the subconscious" through sexual and other cues.[108] In light of such techniques and citizens' lack of expertise on political issues, Schumpeter concluded that "groups with an axe to grind" are "able to fashion and, within very wide limits, even to create the will of the people."[109] Setting the stage for Noam Chomsky and Edward Herman's popular work, *Manufacturing Consent*, Schumpeter characterized the public's input in the political process as "not a genuine but a manufactured will" and alleged that "the will of the people is the product and not the motive power of the political process."[110]

Schumpeter's theory stated that human beings did not come to the political sphere with fixed, unalterable preferences. Instead, preferences and political consent were manufactured. This implied something that Lippmann felt was essential to understanding the operation of politics. In a book that John Dewey called "perhaps the most effective indictment of democracy . . . ever penned,"[111] a thirty-two-year-old Lippmann contemplated the workings of unions, parties, interest groups, and different types of governments. His conclusion? "Nowhere is the idyllic theory of democracy realized."[112] Still, Lippmann believed the government to be necessary in light of the complexity of group cooperation—the fact, as he put it, that "out of the private notions of any group no common idea emerges by itself."[113] His explanation for this informs Schumpeter's work: "The ordinary doctrine of self-interest usually omits altogether the cognitive function. So insistent is it on the fact that human beings finally refer all things to themselves, that it does not stop to notice that men's ideas of all things and of themselves are not instinctive. They are acquired."[114] The institutional and psychological environment in which they are acquired includes exchanges between citizens and, most important in today's conditions, countless political advertisements, smear campaigns, and organized constructions of the candidates and issues orchestrated by a handful of media conglomerates and expenditure groups. Rational candidates, officeholders, parties, and interest groups attempt to control the processes that shape citizens' ideas about policies, candidates, and parties—in sum, their ideas about what is politically desirable.

If many different types of groups with many different types of resources are no longer competing effectively, if the government is no longer a neutral ledger on which results are recorded or a neutral mediator through which results are negotiated, and if much of this is due to the disproportionate influence of financial power, then interest-group pluralism can be "plural" only to the extent that wealth is distributed among many different groups. The public choice literature has been instrumental in showing that tremendous financial inequality has stacked the deck in interest-group competition, and that even for purposes of efficiency and wealth creation a free-market free-for-all is not the way to go. Public choice does not state that competition, efficiency, and wealth creation flow naturally from an unregulated political market.

This literature contains the archaeological remains of the Court's intellectual civilization: theoretical remnants of an open market that brings about the changes desired by consumers (or "The People" in that market), and consumer sovereignty as a freedom-promoting alternative to the intervention of an untrustworthy government waving the banner of the public good. Why does today's Court ignore the subsequent, critical stages of this same civilization? Coming from public choice and the law and economics movement, the evidence seems credible enough. Even congressional evidence collected over the course of many hearings, volumes of testimony from legislators, legislation, and the nearly unanimous concern of the legal academy has not persuaded the conservative members of the Court to reconsider.

This selectivity problem goes to the heart of how public choice principles are used in the caselaw. Are public choice theory and constitutional interpretation compatible? Public choice theory describes and predicts, while the Court prescribes and dictates. The first theorizes while the second judges. In essence, the Court has held that its preferred public choice principles must remain or become an accurate description of how democracy works.[115] As a consequence, the state cannot further alter the conditions of political finance that sustain the power of capital, the influence of interest groups, and the presence of corporations as formidable political actors. The Court has read the public interest out of the equation.

And so the riddle endures: Why does the Court make some of public choice's theories and findings into requirements? It is one thing for economists and political scientists to posit or discover open political markets, political buying and selling, an apathetic public overshadowed by a committed set of vested interests, money and strategic pressure as the motors of legislation, and so on. It is quite another thing for the Court to make this vision the object of the Constitution's desire.

B. To Fashion One's Destiny Amidst a Community of Political Equals

Having seen that the Court's principles tilt towards a twisted view of public choice theory, we must now look in the opposite direction. What vision of constitutional principle has the Court tilted away from? We come to the school of thought that does not see democracy as a market, corporations as citizens, spending as speech, or citizens as consumers. Consider the "conviction that emancipated individuals are jointly called to be authors of their destiny" and the command that they shall have the "power to decide about the rules and manner of their living together."[116] These phrases belong to Jürgen Habermas, who insists that citizens should "give themselves the laws they want to obey, thereby producing their own life context."[117] "[P]olitical freedom," says Habermas, "has always been conceived as the freedom of a subject that determines and realizes itself."[118]

Anyone initiated into the caselaw might nevertheless fit a market of monied speech producers into this description. Powerful interests do give to themselves the laws they wish to obey, as Adam Smith warned, and corporations are citizens engaged in self-authorship, the Supreme Court maintains. Habermas dismisses this attempt to co-opt his approach: "This context is conceived as the product of a cooperative practice centered in conscious political will-formation."[119] The state's very reason for being is to "guarantee[] an inclusive process of opinion-and will-formation in which free and equal citizens reach an understanding on which goals and norms lie in the equal interest of all."[120] To posit cooperative practices and goals in the interest of all is also to posit that human beings might conceivably be interested in something besides their own immediate profit. The comparison is to Jeremy Bentham's view (or its legacy) of man as a self-interested utility-maximizer and John Stuart Mill's view of man: "a doer, a creator, an enjoyer of his human attributes," including a "[c]apacity for rational understanding, for moral judgment and action, for aesthetic creation or contemplation, for emotional activities of friendship and love, and, sometimes, for religious experience."[121] The exercise of these capacities could certainly produce utility, but not the sort of utility satisfied by the market.

A more well-rounded human nature, an active state, an inclusive political process, an eye-catching reference to free *and* equal citizens, and, there out in the open, a reference to goals in everyone's interest—these are some of the many contrasts between public choice theory and its principal rival. Drawing from republicanism (not associated with the Republican Party), deliberative democracy, and democratic perfectionism, a host of writers have challenged the Court's construction of speech and democracy.

The most interesting thing about these alternative approaches to constitutional values is their unconstitutionality. *Buckley* struck down the equality interest and the limitations on expenditures designed to further it; *Randall* struck down the time-protection rationale designed to allow representatives to interact with the general public and deliberate free from conflicts of interest; and *Davis* and *Bennett* struck down campaign finance mechanisms designed to produce a greater diversity of viewpoints.[122]

What the republican and deliberative critiques offer, then, is a view of the world that could have been were it not for the Supreme Court's opposition. While public choice theory clarified the way the Court believes democracy must be and must remain, republicanism reveals what the Court believes democracy must not be and must never become. Aspects of this are familiar from *Bennett*, where Owen Fiss's position on deliberative democracy was specifically foreclosed. Fiss wrote that "fostering full and open debate—making certain that the public hears all that it should—is a permissible end for the state[,] a conception of democracy which requires that the speech of the powerful not drown out or impair the speech of the less powerful."[123] He even attempted to make the state's promotion of deliberative processes palatable to the Court, framing them in terms of speech, not equality. All groups should get a "full and equal opportunity to participate in public debate" for purposes of vindicating "their right to free speech, as opposed to their right to equal protection."[124] Fiss also ties this view of speech to the listeners' rights component of *Bellotti*, portraying deliberative democracy as furthering the "interest of the audience—the citizenry at large—in hearing a full and open debate on issues of public importance."[125] Because a full and equal opportunity for all groups to participate in debate could not be accomplished without reducing the incentives for private monetary expenditures, *Bennett* forecloses the egalitarian side of the deliberative project.

Republicanism's terms hardly match up with their constitutional status as the outlaw, the rebel, the ideological fugitive and desperado. Is it really so subversive to posit a "moral right to participate on terms of equality in the governance of society?"[126] What would be subverted thereby? Is it so unorthodox to view democracy as a "deliberative process in which the public expresses social aspirations based on reasons?"[127] What orthodoxy is challenged here? What sort of constitution is threatened by a political process that shows "equal concern for the interests of all members," or by a procedure where "decisions that affect the distribution of wealth, benefits, and burdens must be consistent with equal concern for all?"[128] Instead of a ledger for recording the results of interest-group struggle or a scale for aggregating private preferences, republicanism asserts that democracy should be a forum where knowledge is gained and challenged, where proposals are aired and discussed, where citizens come face-to-face and hear each other out as equals engaged in a common task, and where, at the end of the day, preferences may be transformed. These descriptions embody the conventional account of democracy, and it is shocking to see them foreclosed in the name of the Constitution.

Still republicanism contains challenging elements. How does it propose to make citizens and interest groups comply with the norms of "respect for the facts, a commitment to reasoned argument, and an effort to reach collectively beneficial outcomes rather than to behave manipulatively, strategically, or in a narrowly self-interested manner?"[129] And as for citizens willing to abide by these norms, is it realistic to expect them to "take sufficient interest in public affairs to be able to participate . . . intelligently,

. . . discuss political issues in an open-minded fashion with other citizens [and,] base [their] political opinions and actions . . . on [their] honest opinion, formed after due deliberation, of what is best for society as a whole rather than on narrow self-interest?"[130] Do we have any realistic expectation that most citizens are willing and able to behave this way? Should the Constitution trust the State to ensure that they are and that they do?

Rawls lists the least controversial measures that republicanism would require of the State: "public occasions of orderly and serious discussion of fundamental questions and issues of public policy," "the public financing of elections," and "widespread education."[131] Improved education and public discussions could be pursued, and their connection to informed debate is obvious. But constitutional protection for donations clashes with mandatory public financing, which the logic of *Davis* and *Bennett* would prohibit. The Court does not currently credit the state interests behind such a plan.

As protracted as this constitutional conflict is, it is mild compared to the others that republicanism would instigate with a seemingly innocent question: What does it mean for deliberation to be properly democratic? Michelman asks whether this label applies "only in the absence . . . or only in the presence . . . of certain controls on economic inequality or of certain positive social and economic guarantees—subsistence, health care, housing, education?"[132] Can any ongoing process of democratic debate be considered fair and open to all citizens when a significant portion of the population is uneducated, distracted (or worse) by curable health problems, and struggling to make ends meet? Is debate under conditions of high inequality properly democratic?

Michelman lists other contested issues with implications for this issue, including collective bargaining, affirmative action, electoral design, federalism, access to the media, political spending, controls on religious expression, legislative structure, and checks and balances. To these, we might add greater regulation of markets, for example mortgage products and derivatives, so as to avoid events of mass impoverishment that disproportionately affect the lower and middle classes. Members of the political community disagree vehemently on the proper outcomes on these fronts, which, in turn, determine whether a system of democratic governance can meet the highest standards for deliberation. And, if republicanism is to be consistent, all such questions would themselves have to be decided by fair and open decision making. This is the basic paradox. The conditions necessary for republicanism would have to be determined through properly republican conditions, but that cannot happen at present. The monumental struggles ongoing on all those fronts are far from decided, and none is occurring in a rigorously deliberative and inclusive fashion.

While public choice takes existing social conditions—such as the distribution of wealth, property rights, and entitlements—as a given, republicanism considers them to be essential questions to be decided by the political community pursuant to the establishment of a democratic political process. And those who push republicanism today tend to support the ethical concept of man's powers, which includes "not only [man's] natural capacities (his energy and skill) but also his ability to exert them."[133] This conception of democracy requires that each citizen have "access to whatever things outside himself are requisite to that exertion."[134]

Not surprisingly, republicanism supports egalitarianism. Its goal is not deliberation of all imaginable sorts, but rather deliberation in a community of political equals under conditions of reciprocity, including equal concern and respect for all.[154] This makes it a common tool for justifying public financing and expenditure limitations. As if republicanism were not already controversial enough, its stance on political finance tends to blend into a stance on the redistribution of wealth within society. Owen Fiss's description of expenditure limitations illustrates the implications: "a way of enhancing the power of the poor, putting them on a more nearly equal political footing with the rich, *thus giving them a fair chance to advance their interests and enact measures that will improve their economic position.*"[136]

What exactly would the great majority of citizens do with political equality if they had it? This is the elephant in the room, a question that can hardly be bracketed for the sake of advancing equality for purposes besides redistributing wealth. Despite the fact that diverging interests in redistribution may determine where many people stand in the money-in-politics debate,[137] that debate does bracket the issue. This is especially true for the constitutional dimensions of the debate, where republicanism's support for campaign finance reform alone (never mind the potential for redistribution) earns it a fascinating group of enemies.

C. Critics of Deliberation on Equal Terms

One can question the premises of deliberative democracy without ruling out campaign finance reform, but often enough the fates of each are linked. This can be demonstrated by exploring Posner's assessment of republican debates: "indeterminate and interminable—and in any event far above the head of the average, or for that matter the above-average, voter."[138] "Few citizens have the formidable intellectual and moral capacities (let alone the time) required," he writes. John Samples reaches the same conclusion without insulting the citizenry: deliberative democracy's norms are "unrealistic for a nation where most people do not like politics or care much about participating in public affairs."[139] In his assessment, "the costs of voting (and getting information about candidates for office) almost always outweigh the direct benefits of participation."[140] Samples implies that citizens may be smart enough, but not irrational enough to participate.

For those who have seen with their own eyes that many citizens are smart enough and willing (whether rationally or not) to engage in debate, Posner has another reply. He alleges that deliberation is counterproductive: "A Pentecostal and an atheist, a pro-lifer and a pro-choicer, a pacifist and a foreign-policy 'realist,' a hunter and a vegan, do not reach a modus vivendi through discussion; discussion exacerbates their differences by bringing them into open contention."[141] By implication, Posner's view on the value of peace talks between Israelis and Palestinians is clear; but why treat all disagreements within society as quite so deep-seated and impossible to resolve? "There is no consensus," states Posner, "on what the goal of American society should be or even on whether the attainment of a goal or goals is the right way to think about the social good."[142] Posner seems to imply that there *can never be* any such consensus, not merely that there is none at present.

If this is true, then debate on a great many public policy issues is pointless at best. This restates a familiar position: preferences cannot be transformed by a deliberative political process, human beings are self-interested automatons who do not revise their positions in light of creative, intellectual, or moral considerations born of sincere exchange and contemplation, and the market is the best vehicle for providing the information useful for each citizen in deciding what course of action will maximize her utility.

Once benefits from a more equal and more deliberative process are ruled out, limitations on financial power impose only costs. Integral to this viewpoint, as developed by the Court, is the belief that through limitations on corporate speech "the electorate has been deprived of information, knowledge and opinion vital to its function."[143] The Court assigned corporations a role in "advising voters on which persons or entities are hostile to their interests."[144] This generous evaluation of the value of corporate electioneering and denial that political advertisements can confuse and mislead stands behind the listeners' rights rationale developed in *Bellotti*. There, the Court held that corporate speech was protected due to its function in informing the electorate, calling it "the type of speech indispensable to decisionmaking in a democracy."[145] As to the argument that the wealthy could drown out other viewpoints, Justice Powell admitted, "[C]orporate advertising may influence the outcome of the vote," but insisted that "the fact that advocacy may persuade the electorate is hardly a reason to suppress it."[146] Building on the Court, Bradley Smith describes big spending and lobbyists as integral to the processes through which voters and representatives make up their minds, criticizing the republican posture as one that holds that "democracy itself is corrupt."[147]

These statements imply that Posner and Samples are both mistaken about the public. The judgment that corporate advertising campaigns are good for democracy rests on the assumption that citizens are sophisticated political consumers who are not easily manipulated or misled by big spenders. As Scalia put it in his *McConnell* dissent, the "premise of the First Amendment is that the American people are neither sheep nor fools, and hence fully capable of considering both the substance of the speech presented to them and its proximate and ultimate source."[148] *Citizens United* rests on this premise. We need not fear unlimited corporate expenditures because they produce speech that "is public, and all can judge its content and purpose."[149] The First Amendment "confirms the freedom to think for ourselves,"[150] the Court informed the people, who, it turns out, think corporations have hijacked the political process. As evidence of the strength of its coercive faith in citizens, the Court assigned to them the duty to control factions: "Factions will necessarily form in our Republic but [they] should be checked by permitting them all to speak . . . and by entrusting the people to judge what is true and what is false."[151]

These notions not only go against restricting political finance, they also defy republicanism's model of an orderly, deliberative process. Justifying unlimited corporate speech, Scalia wrote: "Given the premises of democracy, there is no such thing as *too much* speech."[152] Building on this, the *Citizens United* majority approved of "sound bites, talking points, and scripted messages that *dominate* the 24-hour news cycle."[153] It told us that the "Nation's speech dynamic is changing," that "30-second television ads may be the most effective way to convey a political message,"[154] and that "informative voices should not have to circumvent onerous restrictions."[155] Republicanism's emphasis on the political process could not be further removed from the Court's emphasis on the maximization of informational content—"an uninhibited marketplace of ideas."[156]

Note the contradictory and comprehensive shape of the arguments against republicanism. A properly deliberative political process is seen as undesirable regardless of the condition of the citizenry. If citizens are mediocre and incapable, republicanism is an unobtainable ideal. But if citizens are intelligent and capable, deliberation is unnecessary and republicanism's constraints on political finance are cast in a coercive light. And regardless of their level of intelligence, the very nature of all citizens has been judged.

The massive assumptions necessary to dismiss republicanism are not unpacked or justified within any of the Court's opinions. This is partly because they are obviously wrong. Clearly, some citizens are foolish and others intelligent, and surely all citizens are well informed about some questions and ill informed about others. It is also undeniable that some citizens are more collaborative and others more adversarial, some more empathetic and generous, and others more greedy. But, as with intelligence, questions of collaboration and empathy vary not just in terms of each particular citizen, but also in terms of each particular issue in its effect on each particular citizen, and on the expectations about politics and patterns of political engagement that each citizen has already formed. It is curious for one-sided axioms about intelligence and human nature to be decisive within caselaw. The political branches and the general public have been hogtied by amateurish and cynical positions.

Advocates of Money in Politics   We have yet to hear a defense of money itself. Bradley Smith, Martin Redish, and John Samples are colossal figures in taking up such an unpopular cause. Smith fights egalitarianism with a powerful weapon: egalitarianism. "[A]re all individuals treated with equal concern and respect when they are not allowed to equally employ the fruits of their labors and talents to political action?"[157] This is curious phrasing. The political finance limits that Smith opposes do allow all individuals to equally employ their wealth. The limits are applicable to all and all can spend up to the specified amount. Smith means to say that all individuals are not equal unless they are free to spend *all the fruits of their labors on political action*, but this is the same absurd idea that political equality is satisfied by the universal right to fund ad campaigns. Smith's view derives not from equal concern, equal respect, reciprocity, or community concerns, but from a libertarian defense of freedom. To borrow from Edward Foley's summary of libertarianism, "citizens lack true political freedom unless they have the right to use their private property to communicate their political opinions to each other."[158]

Still, Smith presses forward with a civic defense of money in politics. He casts political spending not in the light of transactions in a market, but as substantive political activity. "Many individuals, such as small-business owners, have time constraints that prevent them from working on a campaign," Smith laments. The sorrow continues, for, even if they had time to give, "[m]ost individuals lack skills directly transferable to political campaigning." "For such individuals," Smith informs us, "money contributions are the primary source of political participation."[198] At one point he puts it bluntly: "Money is how people who lack talent participate."[160] And at another point he puts it urgently: "[F]or a great many Americans, [money] is the only realistic form of direct political participation."[161]

This appears to be a way of adapting republicanism to the conditions alleged by its critics. Recall that we have been asked to believe that people lack the time or the talent to participate in substantive political activity. If this is so, then money can be used as a proxy and it ought to be viewed as participation. But of course these descriptions wear one's patience thin. Skills useful for political campaigning include fitting papers into envelopes, making phone calls, updating websites, sending e-mails, researching political issues, managing funds, greeting the public, organizing events, knocking on doors to hand out flyers, and holding up a sign in a town square. Someone who lacked all such abilities would be unemployable, unable to care for himself even.

It is also hard to believe that anyone lacking all such skills would have made enough money to spend generously on political causes. Smith later describes political talents in terms of speech writing, debating, authoring law review articles, and testifying before Congress, but it is not just the wealthy who lack such skills. (In fact, those who make above $100,000 per year probably possess such skills in the highest quantities.) In terms of basic skills transferable to genuine political activity, all citizens have something to offer. And in terms of making time for genuine political activity, it is hardly just small-business owners who have trouble finding sufficient hours in the day. In this, they have something in common with parents and low wage earners working multiple jobs.

Perhaps what Smith means to say is that citizens who make lots of money are less likely to participate, genuinely participate, in politics because they conceive of their time as money. Whatever money they later spend on political causes, it follows that the wealthy see such contributions as either less costly or more effective than devoting their time to political activity. Perhaps Smith is really saying that wealthy citizens comply with public choice theory's definition of the self-interested, rational actor, and as long as they are able to use their excess wealth instead of their actual time and energy to influence politics, they will continue to do so. The irony is that their ability to do so is precisely the factor that convinces most average citizens that genuine political activity is pointless. Why, most citizens ask, should I stand for hours in the town square holding a sign or sit for hours at my desk sending e-mail alerts when candidates' and officeholders' first priority is to satisfy the interests of those who fund their campaigns and their affiliated political action committees? If genuine political activity is overshadowed by donations and expenditures, it is not just the rational actor who desists. It is also the average citizen who feels disappointment, betrayal, and disgust.

Smith, however, does not desist. He refines his point, noting that "very few citizens have the talent, physical and personal attributes, luck of time and place, or wealth to influence political affairs *substantially.*"[162] Conceding that wealth is influential in politics and that few people have the ability to deploy it, Smith finds cause for celebration in strange places. Of the roughly 100 million voters in the 1996 federal elections, only 235,000 people contributed large donations—less than half a percent. "235,000," Smith tells us, "is a considerably larger number than those given op-ed space in daily newspapers, or the number of people who served as managers for political campaigns, or who filed amicus briefs in the United States Supreme Court, or who sat on the boards of foundations that awarded six-figure grants to groups that lobby for campaign finance reform."[163] This is surely true, and we might share his concern about six-figure grants, but still something seems amiss. Is it appropriate, democratically speaking, for those few citizens and many corporations with lots of money to spend to exercise substantial political influence, just like the even fewer citizens who manage campaigns, write editorials, and file amicus briefs? Should economic and political talents be on equal footing within the political sphere?

Martin Redish takes the baton from Smith. He advocates including the "profit-making corporation as a *participant* in the policy *deliberations* of the government and as a performer of a leadership role in the political-economic order."[164] If we bracket momentarily his fusing of the political order and the economic order, it could be said that Redish is speaking the democratic language of participation and deliberation. Emphasizing *Bellotti*'s familiar listeners' rights justification, Redish calls corporate speech and participation a "valuable input into the exercise of [citizens'] *self-governing power.*"[165] Redish alleges that Meiklejohn's view on the function of free speech applies to corporate speech, casting it as one of the conditions through which voters "acquire . . . intelligence, integrity, sensitivity, and generous devotion to the general welfare."[166]

Even compared with deliberative and informative functions, these final words point to something more profound. Redish describes corporations as instruments for one of democracy's most transformative purposes: "The profit-making corporation should be seen as an important catalyst in the process of individual self-realization."[167] Through associating in the corporate form, Redish says, people "use and develop their human faculties and control their destinies by pursuing their chosen purposes in society."[168] This adds an interesting twist to the Court's framing of the issue in *Citizens United*: "[T]he Government deprives the disadvantaged [corporate] person or [corporate] class of the right to use speech to strive to establish worth, standing, and respect for the speaker's voice."[169] Through aggregating their talent and resources in the corporate form, Redish says, people "self-realize by engaging and investing in businesses and by participating in and personally benefitting from the political-economic system."[170] The advantages of the corporate form serve a "catalytic" function, speeding up the process of self-realization by allowing individuals to accomplish their goals more efficiently and effectively.[171] This concern over the effectiveness of speech, itself rooted in spending more than others do, recalls *Davis* and *Bennett*. The goal is not self-realization per se, but the catalytic function—i.e., the function of monetary power in speeding up the process of self-realization.

To the extent that Redish does speak of self-realization itself, he seems to mean profit maximization. This is clear from his description of self-realization above, focused on "investing in business" and "personally benefitting from the political-economic system." As Redish's concept of self-realization moves closer to profit maximization, he moves further away from republican, perfectionist, and transformative conceptions of democratic participation. His theory verges on insincerity all along. The listeners' rights justification always hinged on the belief that corporate "expertise, resources, and incentives" favor supplying the sort of information the electorate needs to achieve its goals. This is incompatible with what interest-group pluralism has told us all along: powerful interests are generally engaged in rent-seeking, not the disinterested provision of high-quality information conducive to each person's interest in informed decision making. Adam Smith and Judge Posner are clear on this, not just a hoard of progressive activists.

The same naive belief in corporate neutrality or public-spiritedness attends Redish's conclusion that citizens' judgments are "reasonably influence[d]" by the "fact that a major profit-making corporation is of the opinion that a particular candidate or a particular policy is important to the community's prosperity."[172] Corporations, especially "major profit-making" ones, are concerned with their own prosperity. Their legal duty to maximize shareholder revenue cannot be equated with an interest in the well-being of any particular community. Although corporations necessarily provide jobs in the communities where they operate, the imperative of reducing costs associated with labor, employee benefits, raw materials, environmental protection, and taxes has led countless corporations to relocate their operations in developing and underdeveloped nations, and to take advantage of tax shelters. When jobs are moved overseas and tax revenues cease to flow to communities, it is unclear that corporate opinions on candidates and policies provide a reliable bearing on what is best for community prosperity.

Those who associate in the corporate form to more effectively achieve their goals and investors who stand to gain the most from corporate prosperity are not representative of any geographic community or the general public. Redish has anticipated the reply that his flirtations with republicanism are mere show, given their questionable relationship to equality. Attempting to justify corporate political power as egalitarian, he quotes James Hurst and Ronald Seavoy: "[T]he corporate form should be available by a simple procedure on equal terms to all who [see] use for [it]" and thus the corporate form can "equalize the opportunities to get rich."[173] Now Redish's views come into sharper focus. If all can employ the corporate form, then all can use the corporate form within political circles to "speak in support of attaining economic goals in a stronger, more effective voice."[174] And this analysis, Redish clarifies, is equally as valid in the "economic arena" as in the "political arena."[175] As a consequence, those who are successful economically can, by virtue of that fact, be successful politically. Smith had already conceded that money is the means of exchange through which people without time or political talent can nonetheless obtain political success.[176]

Republicanism's critics inadvertently illustrate the justifications for campaign finance reform. Because they understand its justifications to be its critiques, they succeed in illustrating one of their premises: that incompatible worldviews do exist and that, under such circumstances, debate is unlikely to breed consensus. If not a consensus, then one hopes for transparency, for attention to be brought to bear upon the rationales for the Court's stance.

D. *Justice Is More Important Than Democracy*

While public choice and republicanism maintain an interest in the ends to be achieved (whether predicting them or prescribing them), the "deontological" view cares more for the means. As John Samples puts it, "[V]otes [should] be allocated equally, but other forms of political participation [should] not have to meet the standard of equality in part because meeting that standard would impinge deeply on fundamental rights."[177] Fundamental rights can trump social goals. Those committed to the right against torture would tolerate more terrorism if that were a necessary consequence of treating detainees humanely. Similarly, those committed to rights of political spending would tolerate more corruption, more commercialization, and less popular accountability in order to guarantee open avenues for contributions and expenditures.

When the Court voted six to three to uphold Michigan's prohibition on political advertisements financed by general treasury funds (*Austin*), the dissenting Justices did not focus their efforts on justifying corporate political power. Granted, they depicted corporations in a favorable light and defended their role in politics; but the essence of their dissent was not that corporate power was a good thing. Instead, the accusation was that the law "prevents distinguished organizations in public affairs from announcing that a candidate is qualified or not qualified."[178] The result, said the conservative Justices, "is an unhappy paradox[:] this Court, which has the role of protecting speech and of barring censorship from all aspects of political life, now becomes itself the censor."[179]

It is all too easy for the conservative Justices to make this claim in the cases discussed so far, cases concerning speech they applaud. But Scalia has suggested their position to be a principled one nonetheless. In his *McConnell* dissent, he recounted the "inconsequential forms of expression" that the Court had recently defended from censorship, including virtual child pornography, tobacco advertising, dissemination of illegally intercepted communications, and sexually explicit cable programming.[180] In light of its defense of these objectionable forms of speech, Scalia marveled at the Court's tolerance of limitations on political speech. His argument is a strong one: the First Amendment protects many forms of speech, whether we approve of them or not. If the state cannot illegalize cigarette ads in the interest of health, pornography in the interest of morality, or virtual child pornography in the interest of both morality and child safety, why should it be able to illegalize corporate political advertisements in the interest of equality or democratic integrity? Censorship is wrong, the argument goes, regardless of the benefits it pursues.

The centrality of censorship rhetoric in the caselaw lines up with deontological liberalism. Consider Michael Sandel's revealing description: "If the happiness of the world could be advanced by unjust means alone, not happiness but justice would properly prevail."[181] Stanley Fish has fit this description to the conservative majority in *Citizens United*, noting that "even if they were persuaded by the dire predictions Stevens and those he cites make [about corruption], they would come down where they do."[182] Fish does not allege that the Justices welcome corruption; rather, he believes they prioritize the "categorical imperative of the First Amendment [which] forbids the suppression of voices."[183] That imperative leads to familiar forms of fatalism: "The question of where [corporate speech] might take the country is of less interest than the overriding interest in assuring that [speech] is full and free . . . open to all."[184]

Deontological liberalism also does a good job of explaining the Court's reliance on principles over evidence. Sandel notes that the deontological "claim for the priority of the subject [i.e., each person and their rights] is not an empirical claim."[185] As Chief Justice Roberts put it in *Bennett*: "[W]e do not need empirical evidence to determine that the law at issue is burdensome."[165] Of the Justices' "belie[f] that free trade in ideas . . . will inevitably produce benign results for a democratic society," Fish writes that "their confidence . . . is a matter of theoretical faith and not of empirical or historical observation."[187] Deontological liberalism would defend individual freedom in an open market against claims, empirical and otherwise, about collective goals.

The deontological view does not match up, however, with some of the Court's justifications of free speech and market principles. The Court has told us that the marketplace of ideas produces a great deal of information from diverse sources, informs the electorate, and brings about the changes desired by the people. By stipulating such goals, the Court abandons deontology for consequentialism. Once desirable consequences have been specified, it follows that types of speech that go against those objectives must be regulated. If certain types of speech are found to monopolize the debate or mislead the electorate, for example, then they would not deserve to be protected. "If such forms of speech appear," Fish argues, the Court would be "obligated—not in violation of the First Amendment, but in fidelity to it—to move against them."[188]

Deontological liberalism is not concerned with social welfare or the public good, but rather with what is right in and of itself; it is concerned with means over ends. Hence, the subject, man, triumphs over the possible objects men may seek to obtain, whether health, morality, safety, equality, or democratic integrity.[189] It will never be the case that everyone agrees as to the priority of these goals or the means chosen to obtain them—hence government and the collective against man and his rights. In order to avoid advocating anarchy, some deontological liberals entertain a fiction by holding that society should be "governed by principles that do not themselves presuppose any particular conception of the good."[190]

This view is circular enough to cause motion sickness. What authority bestows rights independent of any conception of the good? To posit that some rights are above human judgment and authority is to posit a conception of the good—namely, that a particular superior order, whether divine or natural, is better than the alternatives. The rights granted by that order also represent a particular conception of how society is best ordered. If it were not for a particular conception of the good, how could deontological liberalism know which order to prescribe? If not for a particular conception of the good, how would it have anyone to defend it? Is it really so persuasive to posit a series of rights and then defend them on the ground that they require no justification?

That sums up the choice made in bestowing corporations with First Amendment rights. A case of censorship is not upon us in *Citizens United* any more than when police restrain activists from using megaphones inside the Capitol building. Corporations were free to form political action committees—powerful ones at that. They did not need to rely on their general treasury funds in order to express their views; indeed, unlimited general treasury funds are necessary only if one's goal is to take the Capitol by force. And what of the rights of others, the great majority of the population with no disposable income to spend on politics? To what extent are their political rights usable or effective? Could a fascination with rights really be so one-sided?

This returns us to where we began this chapter, the subjectivity of the First Amendment and the unavoidability of value judgments in its application to political finance. The deontological view attempts to make an end run around this issue. Returning to Scalia's opening quote, how does he know that the restriction on the use of corporate general treasury funds is censorship? That can be true only if corporations are speakers and large expenditures are speech. Scalia's majority view posits a superior principle, one above collective meddling, that must always be adhered to: the open market. Censorship is wrong because it violates the free market principle. Corporate electioneering and large expenditures are speech because that is consistent with the free market principle. Trigger mechanism subsidies are unconstitutional because they interfere with the free market principle. And so on. Neither the Court nor the theorists explain, however, why justice is defined by the exercise of market freedoms within the political sphere. Their deontological vision requires a justification. How do we know the freedoms to spend and to spend without pesky public subsidies getting in the way are good in and of themselves, and logically prior and morally superior to all other principles of decision?

The free market principle is a particularly bad candidate for deontological liberalism. By resisting all government intervention starting in the present moment, the status quo would become sacred, including the present distribution of wealth, property, and educational capital. Far from positing no notion of the good, the unregulated market principle holds that it is good for us to be ruled by "all of the economic, social, cultural, and psychological forces that operate even when the state does not."[191] And the state is not so easily read out of the equation. Declaring the defeat of government and retiring its forces at present means that all the conceptions of the good pursued by the government up until now—the laws and government policies of the past that have led us to our present station—should rule over us. The forces within government that have won out and pressure groups behind them shall not be subject to correction.

Where does one begin in explaining the present distribution of wealth, property, and marketable skills among citizens in this nation, or even among the community of nations? Wars, inquisitions, conquests; monarchy, feudalism, theocracy; countless campaigns against particular minorities and majorities; countless forms of social control that discriminated on the basis of sex, religion, race, ethnicity, social class, sexual orientation, political views, and so on; and recently in the United States, the usual litany of wrongs beginning with the treatment of Native Americans and slavery. There is no escaping the fact, for example, that women and African Americans were long restrained in political and economic circles, and that therefore all the wealth made in America—and its distribution—has never been a pure reflection of talent and energy.

Surely today's distribution of wealth is also shaped by talent and effort, but the talented and industrious have relied on policies pursuing a particular conception of the good countless times in order to arrive at their present station. Need we rehearse the thousands of government subsidies and tariffs that have protected our talented and industrious from the progress of the talented and industrious residing in other nations? Nobody should be fooled by deontological liberalism's siren song. No conception of the good today is a concession to the good that ruled yesterday.

III. REDRAWING THE BORDERS

The Court's principles tilt towards a variety of deeper positions contained within the theories of democracy discussed above. But it turns out that the tilt is really more of an orbit, one that leads the Court to pass by all of the theories, aligning with each of them temporarily. How else could the Court overlap with so many, but remain within the reach of none for long? The Court's star is not competition, efficiency, deliberation, or even rights, but rather a different concern that can never be openly confessed within political circles. To what is the Court gravitationally bound? What motivates its unusual trajectory?

If the Court orbited public choice theory or law and economics, it would rely on evidence in order to fashion legal rules conducive to efficiency, robust competition, or wealth creation. It would also be affected by critical trends in the public choice literature warning of legislative capture and the manufacture of consent. If the cases revolved around competition, they would require the restraint of monopoly power, and the promotion of diverse and unrepresented views. The Court is not interested in actual, verifiable competition between actual, verifiably diverse sources. The design of unregulated competition indicates a separate course.

Deliberative democracy, republicanism, and perfectionist theory are poor suitors as well. If the Court gravitated towards an informed electorate capable of carrying on substantive deliberations, it would be at least somewhat critical of misleading, false, and superficial speech.[192] It might seek out evidence on the effect of attack ads on public understandings, and it might support efforts to subsidize underrepresented views. Alongside this clue, keep present Redish's teachings on how corporations themselves participate in political deliberation and speed up individual self-realization. The Court supports the self-realization of actors that are economically powerful enough to obtain access and influence.

The Court is hostile to republican and transformative approaches only to the extent that they require limitations on financial power. Its holdings bring us deliberation between candidates, representatives, and political parties, on the one hand, and members of ALEC, the Business Roundtable, the Chamber of Commerce, and lobbyists on the other hand. The Court does not describe unlimited expenditures or corporate electioneering as a way of aggregating self-interested preferences. Its emphasis on informing the electorate and injecting maximum content into democracy speaks more to a deliberative system of financial elites with valuable trickle-down effects. Even so, informed deliberation is not the Court's guiding purpose. Were deliberation the goal, we would see attention to evidence of substantive deliberation and support for the inclusion of diverse voices, not just those with money to spend. Deliberative theory and even transformation are perfectly acceptable theories in the Court's view, so long as the natural advantage of monied actors is preserved. This protection of capital explains why the Court sides with the critics of republicanism, instead of the critical trends within public choice theory.

Although the Court flirts with deontological theory, that theory proves a poor match as well. To begin with, a truly deontological approach need not justify the consequences of upholding its principles. The Roberts

Court's praise for corporations and the role of *all speech* in informing the electorate proves that the majority does not justify rights on the basis of justice alone. The most influential voices in the economy have valuable information to share, information vital to informed decision making. Such remarks prove that the Court's view is at least partially consequentialist or instrumental.

Commentators suspect that deontology is at work, nonetheless, because the Court appears willing to tolerate a host of undesirable consequences. For example, in order to prevent the *censorship* of corporate voices, corporate political power becomes disproportionate, and in order to prevent the *abridgments* caused by limits on large expenditures and trigger mechanism subsidies, citizens and candidates have to contend with big spenders. In reality, undue influence and a dependence on private donors and spenders are not undesirable consequences in the majority's view. The Court has noted that favoritism and unequal access are unavoidable in democracy, and that most people can trace their funds, in one way or another, back to corporations anyhow. In fact, Roberts, Alito, Thomas, and Scalia's view of corruption is so limited that they voted in *Caperton v. Massey Coal* to allow a state judge to hear a case involving a party who had contributed more than $3 million to further that judge's election, more than all of the judge's other supporters put together.[193] They do not believe that a judge can be biased in a case involving the man who single-handedly made possible the judge's election to office. The money-in-politics cases rarely involve loyalties of this magnitude. The conservatives believe either that human beings are incorruptible or that a bias in favor of one's financial constituents is not a form of corruption. The deontological view would offer a more accurate description if only the Court believed that corporate political power and dependence on big donors and spenders are undesirable.

Then there is the case of widespread voter abstention and apathy among the citizenry, two other predicted (and observed) consequences of allowing unlimited expenditures and corporate electioneering. *Citizens United* simply denies that these consequences will occur: "The appearance of influence or access, furthermore, will not cause the electorate to lose faith in our democracy."[194] A truly deontological approach would not bother denying its consequences. The Court justifies the open marketplace as a place of robust competition between diverse social forces, and as a system that informs the electorate and legitimizes the ideas that gain acceptance. "Open" is a misleading term, however. The Ferrari dealership is also open to all, but in practice few people can do any business there. The T-shirt with a horse on it is no substitute for the car. In essence, the same is true of the marketplace for speech.

What the Court intends, then, is an unregulated marketplace—commerce as settled on by private actors whose property rights and contractual freedoms are secure. Here, then, is a principle that the Court vindicates as an end in itself, or as a means to some undisclosed end. True conviction emerges only on the question of financial resources: those must be free. The Court celebrates all democratic theories insofar as they justify the role of capital within the political sphere.

There can be no fatalism at this stage. If sophisticated, strategic, intellectual decision makers go to tremendous lengths to vindicate a particular vision of rights with serious consequences, they must be comfortable with those consequences. Like other citizens, the Justices observe the political world. Many of them are ensconced in it. They are affiliated with ideologically driven organizations, they give speeches, some write books, and several have high-profile conflicts of interest.[195] It is difficult to believe that the conservative justices are not at least secretly instrumental. They must be comfortable with the reality of the unregulated regime they have forced upon the nation; but, as sophisticated political actors, they know better than to say so. The right of capital to enjoy political power commensurate to its economic power is a purpose too unpopular to be professed.

The Court's application of its unregulated market vision, case after case, redraws the lines between capitalism and democracy. When market actors are allowed to spend unlimited amounts on political advertisements, when public financing is ineffective and all candidates and parties must indebt themselves to large donors and spenders, and when lobbyists permeate the legislative process, the borders of the market have been extended and the borders of the political sphere reduced. Walzer describes boundaries as "vulnerable to shifts in social meaning" and informs us that "we have no choice but to live with the continual probes and incursions through which these shifts are worked out."[196] As regards the market's occupation of the political sphere, this new stage in "market imperialism," the issue has been the same in each case: "the dominance of money outside its sphere, the ability of wealthy men and women to trade in indulgences, purchase state offices, corrupt the courts, exercise political power."[197] When Walzer notes that "[d]ifferent principles guide the process at different points in time and space,"[198] we see the caselaw for what it is.

The Court's principles are precisely those that are necessary to enable markets to march forward, offering them a new terrain to exploit. Viewed in this light, the Court's principles can be categorized. They are not deliberative, republican, perfectionist, transformative, or pluralist. They are all these things at once: deliberative insofar as moneyed interests deliberate, republican insofar as moneyed interests are virtuous, perfectionist and transformative insofar as economic power can be a catalyst for self-realization, and pluralist insofar as a variety of interests use money to pursue their political goals.

In order to round out our understanding of the Court's approach, it is necessary to move towards results and away from theories. Where have *Buckley*, *Bellotti*, and their Roberts Court progeny taken us? What system of governance makes political donors and spenders sovereign? In the state of affairs that the Court protects, just below its surface, the free market Constitution displays the truth of our political society.

CHAPTER 6

Plutocracy

TO NATIONS, PLOTS OF LAND, AND PERSONAL SPACE, THE SAME four truths apply. First, there is a line. One need only try to run into North Korea without stopping, open a farmer's gate, or plant a kiss on the lips of a passerby to comprehend that not all territory is alike. The jail of a foreign sovereign, the barrel of a farmer's shotgun, and the well-placed kick of a furious stranger are all effective teachers. Next, there is a motivating principle. Whether encapsulated in the Peace of Westphalia, a deed, or a person's emotions and right to bodily integrity, there are always principles in play. And there is no such thing as a principle without a justification. Nations supplanted empires, private property the commons, and individual rights the laws of the jungle and the collective for reasons practical and philosophical alike. (Law school tuition is a small price to pay to find out.) Finally, physical borders have effects. Their location may shape the identity of peoples, determine the distribution of natural resources, decide whether there is room to install a swimming pool, or mark the difference between friendship and romance.

In the context of market actors crossing political lines, the Supreme Court has played the role of foreign sovereign, farmer, and passerby. Its offers have varied considerably, however: to those running across the border, luxurious dinners with high-ranking officials instead of prison gruel; to those opening the gate, a bouquet of flowers instead of lethal force; and to that lascivious stranger, outstretched arms instead of an outstretched foot. Welcoming financial power into the political sphere, the Court has redrawn the borders between the economy and the state, the vehicles of market and government, and the systems of capitalism and democracy.

Like physical borders, borders between social systems have a quadruple existence of *lines* drawn in accordance with *principles* justified by *reasons* that, all together, produce *effects*. Whether the lines are more or less tangible, the principles agreeable, the justifications persuasive, and the effects desirable are separate questions. Regardless, those with anything riding on capitalism or democracy have an interest in locating these borders. Let us take well-known principles in the way of a familiar place, and measure the distance between these principles and those used by the Roberts Court. This supplies a sense of how far to walk and in which direction.

In his seminal work, John Rawls wrote:

[T]he constitution must take steps to enhance the value of equal rights of participation for all members of society . . . [T]hose similarly endowed and motivated should have roughly the same chance of attaining positions of political authority irrespective of their economic and social class . . . The liberties protected by the principle of participation lose much of their value whenever those who have greater private means are permitted to use their advantages to control the course of public debate.[1]

Austin and *McConnell* served Rawls's principles, which are also familiar from our discussion of egalitarianism; however, in *Citizens United, Davis,* and *Bennett*, the Court effectively made these revisions:

[T]he Constitution must take steps to *safeguard* the *market-calibrated* value of rights of participation for all members of society *including corporations* . . . [T]hose similarly endowed *with the strengths of wealth and wealthy supporters,* and *similarly* motivated *to exploit those strengths* should have roughly the same chance of attaining positions of political authority *and influencing the public debate* . . . The liberties protected by the principle of participation lose much of their value whenever those who have greater *public* means are permitted to use their advantages to control the course of public debate.

Rawls's description of the "fair value of political liberties" also provides a bearing that could be followed:

[T]he worth of the political liberties to all citizens, whatever their social or economic position, must be approximately equal, or at least sufficiently equal, in the sense that everyone has a fair opportunity to hold public office and to influence the outcome of political decisions.[2]

The Roberts Court appeared to set this course instead:

> [T]he worth of the political liberties to all citizens *of approximately equal* economic position must be approximately equal, or at least sufficiently equal, in the sense that everyone has an *effective, market-based* opportunity to hold public office and to influence the outcome of political decisions.

These principles dictate that economic power be given traction in matters of political offices, political influence, and lawmaking. On these fronts, the state retreats and the market pushes forward in accordance with the Court's instructions: start at the sites of familiar political processes, parcel out more and more of their components as private property, enforce contractual rights, and stand by while the forces of supply and demand establish prices and allocate entitlements. The lay of the land comes into focus.

I. A MARKET, *AN ACTUAL MARKET,* FOR POLITICAL POWER

Gone are the days of comparisons and metaphors. Politics is a place where things are bargained for, invested in, bought, and sold. It is not *like* a market; it *is* one, or several.[3] The admission is not an easy one, but the cases themselves compel it: Some candidates wish to contribute millions of dollars of their own money to their campaigns, as do some of their supporters; some individuals, interest groups, and corporations want to spend millions of dollars on political advertisements and lobbyists; some corporations wish to give millions of dollars to one or both political parties, and some officeholders would like to make that wish come true; if the government gives aggressive subsidies to public candidates, then the money of privately financed candidates and their financiers does not go as far. Most of these plaintiffs, and countless other would-be financiers, investors, buyers, and sellers, have prevailed in court and proceeded to flood politics with money. What does this reveal about democracy?

Is it not strange that private funds are spent on elections in the first place? Our privatized system of campaigns and parties leaves political finance in the hands of consumers, producers, and investors, drastically affecting what politics is all about. Take, for example, the billions of dollars spent in an election cycle by millionaire candidates, large donors, interest groups, wealthy outside spenders, and corporations. Do these funds primarily promote ideas, debate, and publicly minded policies? The cigarette companies giving heavily to the Republican Party, the law firms giving heavily to the Democratic Party, the insurance companies giving heavily to both, the financial services firms finding every possible way to route funds to the politicians on the congressional committees best positioned to decide their fate after the latest economic crisis, the industry associations that draft model legislation—are such groups promoting deeply held ideas or profits? Are they defending political commitments for the sake of a civic sense about what is right or wrong, or are they defending their bottom lines for the sake of their salaries and shareholders? One can never finish articulating such a question before the answer impatiently arises. Those who run Philip Morris and Fannie Mae may believe in the *ideas* (or products) their corporations promote, but the volume of their spending and their material interests in particular government policies reveal a business sense, not a civic sense.

What is the difference between the profiteer and the average citizen? Politics provides opportunities to invest money and to sell goods and services in the expectation of making a profit.[4] Many people and organizations stand ready to offer goods and services for this purpose. In contrast, the woman next door who gives $100 to her favorite candidate is not on account of this fact a capitalist. She has no more expectation of reaping a profit than does a man who gives flowers to his wife. The candidate may expect to profit, however; certainly the florist does.

The logic of capitalism cuts across all possible contexts in which money can be exchanged for commodities that yield a greater amount of money.[5] A pimp rents an apartment, invests in a knife and a gun, reaches an agreement with his laborers, eventually recovers his costs, and finally receives in return more money than he initially invested. So long as his income outpaces his costs, he is a successful capitalist. It does not matter that sex is his commodity. In this sense, what is true for the pimp is also true for the car manufacturer; and what is true for the methamphetamine dealer and record label is also true for the accounting firm. Who would have thought that sex, drugs, and rock and roll had this much in common with station wagons and taxes? Marx simplified the process as a continuous loop of accumulation: Money-Commodities-Money. As far as capitalism is concerned, "[i]t is not the nature of the activity itself that matters but the possibility of making a profit out of it."[6]

Still, many players in a capitalist system are not capitalists. The people donating $100 and buying flowers are not motivated by profit, at least not economic profit. They are consumers in a market, however. The woman demands political representation that suits her tastes (and perhaps the satisfaction of strengthening the economic position of her candidate) and the man demands an item with pleasing symbolic, visual, and olfactory qualities that he can give to his wife. Instead of donating money, the woman could have volunteered her time. Instead of purchasing a flower, the man could have picked one along the roadside. Such alternatives do not represent participation in an economic market or consumer behavior.

So long as people lack the means or the will to fulfill their political desires through non-market means, they need private producers, who in turn need investors. And producers and investors need consumers, for without demand there can be no profit, and without profit there would be no commercial incentive for investment. The fact of the political market, and a multibillion-dollar market at that, reveals that there is a profit to be made from political spending (or, at least, that there are losses to be avoided). Some then proceed to draw a line between political consumers and political capitalists, maintaining that the latter are less legitimate than the former. Should it matter, for example, why Newt Gingrich's largest supporter, Sheldon Adelson, has given him $17 million? Although Adelson is a casino magnate and no doubt desires a president who would support his business interests, he "has long been enamored of Mr. Gingrich's full-throated defense of Israel."[7] Are Adelson's ideological interests more democratic and less market-based than his business interest in maintaining political conditions favorable to casinos? As long as he pursues both sets of interests through political spending, the answer is no.

The first and most important question is not whether a given political actor is on this or that side of the consumer-capitalist divide. That divide is a symbiotic relationship, after all, and it would be artificial (and fatal for the participants) to break it up. The fundamental question, rather, is whether political desires are pursued and fulfilled through market channels.

Imagine a series of pairings: a publicly financed candidate and a privately financed one; a political speech given in a public square, local high school, or public access television slot, and a political speech excerpted, laid over patriotic images, and broadcast on prime-time television slots; a person writing her congresswoman a letter and a person hiring a lobbying firm to convey the same points. We must concede that the public candidate, the town square speaker, and the letter writer are not necessarily more sincere or better intentioned. And the content of their messages need not vary from that of the expensive messages offered by others. Nonetheless, there are profound differences between the actors in the pairings above.

Examples from other fields help us to locate them. What is the difference between the flower growing along the roadside and the flower growing in the florist's pot? Could it be the type of flower or the care it receives? What is the difference between sex on one's wedding night and sex in a brothel? Is it love and commitment? What is the difference between the liver you are born with and one that you purchase on the black market fifty years later? Is it the familiar genetic imprint of your parents, and the likelihood that your body will react favorably to one versus the other? The answers are perplexing. The liver on the market could have been extracted from your brother, sister, child, or parent, so genes do not necessarily mark the difference. Next, some people marry without love and some people fall in love with prostitutes, so sex on the market is not necessarily distinct on the grounds of love or its absence. And the 50 percent divorce rate has revealed commitment to be driven by other factors besides a formal promise sanctioned by civil or religious authorities. Finally, the flowers on the roadside and in the shop could be identical to the naked eye. Some roadside plots are better fertilized and endowed with a healthier mix of sun and shade than those in the florist's refrigerator or windowsill; other roadside plots are blanketed with pollution and trampled by feet.

The first difference in every case is a function of whether the thing or activity is for sale or not, whether it has become a *good*, not a thing; a *service*, not an activity. The transformation process is essentially geographic: flowers occur in nature, livers in our bodies, and sex—most naturally—between two people who are genuinely attracted to each other. When these things and activities are taken from their home context and brought to market, they travel the respective distances from the natural realm, the biological realm, and the most intimate social realm to the impersonal economic realm, where anyone can have them for a price. The flower, liver, and sexual service purchased at market do not cease to be natural, biological, or even intimate (albeit in a narrower sense of the word), but they cease to be located in the domains defined by those adjectives. They have been extracted in order to be allocated by market actors in accordance with market rules. The ways of their customary or natural settings are lost.

The second difference concerns those market rules. Once a good or service is brought to market, each person can generally consume as much of it as his cash and credit permit. Absent a market, a person's possession of flowers depends on that person's energy, knowledge of where flowers grow, and charm, for flowers can be given when one least expects them just as much as they can be sought out. Sex follows a similar rule. And, like flowers, organs can be given by family or friends. Here, if nowhere else, one finds an incentive to keep one's self in high esteem. The market does away with these personal ties and incentives. It also does away with the limits of one's natural abilities. The wealthy man can have as many flowers and as much sex as he wants, and probably more organs than he could use over a lifetime of bad luck or reckless living.

The application to our public candidate, town square speaker, and letter writer is simple. Each of them could be mean-spirited, ignorant, and low. The private candidate, televised ad, and lobbyist's client could be better-intentioned and more sincere, and could end up working a pleasing upward motion upon the state of political debate. Or the opposite could occur. The *necessary* difference is only that the market-based political actors operate through goods and services, and, accordingly, they can have as much of those as they can afford. Hence, the public candidate, town square speaker, and letter writer can be outgunned by their market-based counterparts, regardless of character, intentions, intelligence, skill, message quality, or anything else besides their wealth and the wealth of their supporters. Like flowers, sex, and organs on the black market, political power is also available on the basis of money—those with deep pockets and voracious appetites are free to have much more of it than others do.

As before, the market diminishes the importance of one's natural abilities within customary settings. It used to be that a speaker would attract a large audience if she were eloquent, entertaining, or enlightening. A speaker who worked up a reputation that way, bit by bit, speech by speech, could eventually expand her circle of influence. Today, with consultants and ad producers, a bumbling oaf can be made to appear eloquent, entertaining, and enlightening in a videotaped message and then teleported directly into the living rooms of more people than our more deserving speaker could ever hope to reach.

Bradley Smith agrees, conceding that "[m]oney allows individuals, quickly and easily, to convert the things that they produce efficiently, and which other people value, into those things that they value but are not able to produce, at least not with any degree of efficiency or quality."[8] Hence, if you are good at producing computers, derivatives, or machine guns you will earn money, and you can then use that money to acquire political goods and services. Smith calls money "the single most important means by which people who lack talents with direct value in the political arena, such as production of advertising, writing, campaign organization, speaking, and the like, can participate in politics beyond voting."[9] It is also true, however, that money marks the difference between two talented speakers, catapulting one to prominence while the other goes about enlightening the shadows, hoping, eventually, to make it to neighboring cities.

What has happened, then, with political parties, campaigns, political insiders (e.g., lobbyists), the airwaves, and even legislation? The word "commodification" describes how a thing or activity is made cognizable to the market—how it is transformed from exactly what it is, inherently, into a good or a service that can be valued in economic terms and exchanged for currency. Commodification increases where there is money to be made from trades and where profits can be kept by those who bring the new goods and services to market—hence, capitalism's tendency to "extend market relations to a wider and wider range of social phenomena."[10] As commodification spreads, money becomes a "generalizable source of power," tradable for more and more things.[11]

The necessary conditions for commodification can be as simple as possession, desire, and the ability of the buyer and seller to reach an agreeable price. Possession need not be equated with ownership, for black markets do not require any such thing. Possession need not be lawful either. Cocaine, mountain lions, and weapons of mass destruction can be legally possessed in precious few contexts, and legally owned or lawfully exchanged in fewer yet; but still there are markets for such things. And the price need not be agreeable to all participants, only the buyer and seller—today's thriving global market for sexual slaves, for example, is hardly consensual all-around.[12] These black market dimensions do in fact apply to the political market. Consider the many political scandals over the years regarding bribery. A politician drafting legislation in a given way in accordance with a bribe fulfills many conditions of black markets: the service itself cannot be legally traded for money, the politician does not own the lawmaking process or the eventual legislation, and the consent of other parties directly involved in production (such as the other legislators working on and eventually voting for the bill) has not been obtained.

Limiting ourselves to the legal portion of political markets, there is a simple answer as to how democracy is parceled out as a series of goods and services. The Supreme Court prevents state and federal lawmakers from limiting private ownership and making major portions of democracy public. The legal portion of political markets is precisely the portion that is protected by the Supreme Court or permitted by the political branches. When the political branches move to constrain the market, the Court provides a legal remedy for private parties whose financial transactions have been prohibited, limited, or even indirectly diminished (as in *Bennett*). The Court maintains the sanctity of private property and freedom of contract under the guises of protecting political freedoms. So long as the Court does this work, there will be a market whenever political goods and services are demanded and supplied for a price.

What are the goods and services demanded and supplied in the political market? We must look to two interrelated markets: the market for government offices and the market for public policy.

A. The Market for Government Offices

Recall that *Buckley* struck down limits on independent expenditures and expenditures by candidates, establishing the unconstitutionality of "restriction[s] upon the freedom of a candidate to speak without legislative limit on behalf of his own candidacy."[13] The Court considered this stance necessary in "the free society ordained by our Constitution."[14] It reminded the Congress and the president that "it is not the government but the people—individually as citizens and candidates and collectively as associations and political committees—who must retain control over the quantity and range of debate on public issues."[15] Without flinching, the Court directed that remark to an elected government that had implemented a highly popular measure. Its remark amounts not to empowering the people in the collective sense, but to empowering each person who wishes to continue bargaining. Rather than allowing the people to retain control over debate on public issues, it decided the system in which debate would unfold: not government, but market.

When "those seeking to finance economic activities and those with money to invest" are free to bargain for mutual gain, then a market exists.[16] Because campaigns and parties are privately financed, the demand for capital is easily explained. Besides a decent salary and employment benefits, public office brings the satisfaction of a prestigious job with opportunities to affect social and economic change, and the knowledge that many private and public sector jobs will be available once one's tenure in office comes to an end. Candidates, especially candidates for reelection, have staked their good names, years of their lives, and often their own personal fortunes on winning. Political parties have train-sized momentum of their own, living out a centuries-long war for control of government. Let us assume that these conventional factors of career and party provide most of the motivation behind the tremendous demand for offices.

Still, in the cases of party officials and candidates, motivations may veer away from service to one's country and fellows and towards profiteering. It was not until 2012 that the Senate and House voted to ban "insider trading"—the use of privileged information, obtained by lawmakers in the course of their public duties, to guide lawmakers' own investments.[17] That information includes details about which companies or industries are on course to receive subsidies, government contracts, taxpayer bailouts, and all manner of other favorable or unfavorable arrangements that are part of legislation and earmarks. Such information, including that which industries share with congressional committees but not with the general public, is of tremendous value to members of Congress, 244 of whom were millionaires as of 2009.[18] With an average net worth of $725,000 in the House and $2.4 million in the Senate, members of Congress are much wealthier and more heavily invested than average Americans. The ban was motivated by a news exposé that left Congress little choice, and yet, its terms, diluted through the bicameral process, verge on ineffectual.

Access to the so-called "revolving door" also strengthens the demand for government office. The fundraising necessities of campaign and party life make officeholders particularly well versed in private-sector interests. Officeholders' substantial contact with lobbyists over the course of their careers, including trips and conferences paid by lobbyists, provides a thorough education. Many officeholders trade their roughly $160,000 annual salary for one ten times greater in private industry and lobbying.[19] Between 1998 and 2005, for example "[t]wo thirds of the Republican senators who went into private life . . . have become lobbyists, compared with one-third of Democratic senators . . . In the House, nearly half of the Republicans eligible to become lobbyists have registered to do so over that period—46 of 94."[20] By 2010, 172 former congressmen had registered as lobbyists,[21] and still more render political services by other names. This is why congressional service has become known as "a farm league for K Street," where most prestigious lobbying firms have offices.[22]

In light of the desirability of holding public office, especially at the federal level, and the need to raise tremendous sums of campaign cash, candidates' and parties' demand for campaign funds is straightforward. As of 2011, the average winner in the House raised over $1 million, and in the Senate the figure was over $10 million.[23] Even among well-funded candidates, the better-funded candidate has a meaningful advantage. The combined House and Senate figures show that the best-funded candidate wins 85 percent of the time.[24] Richard Hasen notes that "the modern party organization is the fundraiser and media handler of the candidate. It depends upon infusions of cash. In this system, interest groups have much that parties need in order to deliver votes to the parties' candidates."[25]

Given the importance of money, candidates spend most of their time raising it, while officeholders spend roughly half of their time doing so.

Investigations of congressional activity have concluded that officeholders have two jobs: lawmaker and telemarketer.[26] As Senator Dick Durbin put it, "I think most Americans would be shocked—not surprised, but shocked—if they knew how much time a United States senator spends raising money."[27] Besides spending several hours a day, on average, at private call centers across the street from their public offices, officeholders also work a third job: speaker for hire. Perhaps the most industrious in this category is Nancy Pelosi, the Democratic Party's top fundraiser, who attended 400 fundraising events in 2011 alone.[28]

Courting political donors means spending time with the wealthy and the well-off. Results from the 2000 election are typical: "95 percent of those donors making substantial campaign contributions came from households earning over $100,000."[29] As Representative Robert Borski put it, "[Y]ou can't raise $1,000 from people who make $45,000 or $50,000 a year."[30] Certainly average Americans can afford to make smaller donations; but even Bradley Smith, who praises the U.S. system of private financing for obtaining "so broad a base of voluntary support," concedes that "this support still amounts to less than 10 percent of the voting age population."[31] A very narrow group of suppliers meets the candidates' tremendous demand.

Besides increasing officeholders' contact with wealthy constituents, the realities of fundraising make it more likely that wealthy citizens will themselves become officeholders. In the words of Representative Tim Roemer, "the amount of time it takes to raise the money . . . [and] some people's inherent access to the political system [because] they come from money . . . certainly precludes poor and low income people from ever running."[32]

The demand for cash is only becoming more extreme. For example, the Democratic Party's national finance committee and advisory board asked President Obama's top 450 donors to raise $350,000 each in preparation for the 2012 campaign.[33] This is $100,000 more than they were asked to raise in 2008. Party leaders rightly anticipated that $750 million, the amount raised for that election, would be insufficient in 2012.[34]

Increases in campaign fundraising, presidential and congressional alike, relate to another facet of money in politics. Although campaign contributions are limited, individuals, interest groups, unions, and corporations can spend as much money as they wish on independent political speech. Candidates with stronger support from political action committees and other nominally independent groups have a clear advantage. But if the balance of independent spending swings in the other direction, the only thing that can save a campaign is its own cash reserves—hence the need to raise even more money than before. It is nearly impossible to raise enough money to ward off superPAC threats, however. A recent news story illustrates the source of officeholder insecurity: "Imagine the oil industry wants a small, technical change in a law setting environmental standards. It's an issue few voters are following, or will even hear about. But it's worth billions of dollars to the industry. So oil companies establish a super-PAC and send lobbyists to every congressional office with a simple message: Legislators who support the change will receive a donation, and each legislator who votes against it will be subject to $1 million in super-PAC attack ads in their district in the last week of the campaign."[35]

Such scenarios are much harder to track than candidate-superPAC alliances, relationships forged to indirectly increase campaign resources. Speeches by candidates' staff members at PAC events make it clear that donations to the candidate are to be routed through this channel.[36] Federal law prevents them and other independent expenditure groups from coordinating their messages with candidates and their campaigns, but this rule is hardly worth the paper it is printed on. A campaign and a PAC may share the same political consultants, former campaign officials often run PACs, and groups working for campaigns and PACs sometimes work in the same office suite.[37] And aside from such arrangements, it is easy to discern a campaign's message and devise communications to strengthen that message or harm the campaign's opponents.[38] A recent newspaper article stated what everyone already knew: "In practice, super PACs have become a way for candidates to bypass [donation] limits by steering rich donors to . . . ostensibly independent groups, which function almost as adjuncts of the campaign."[39]

Campaigns outsource a portion of their advertising needs to super-PACs, which front a tremendous amount of the costs without receiving a penny in return from their preferred candidates. And while candidates might suffer fallout when they endorse an offensive ad campaign, superPAC advertisements do not bear a candidate's stamp of approval. SuperPACs can be discredited or become unpopular without bringing down the candidate herself, offering the relief known as plausible denial.

Citizens United has come to stand not only for record-breaking expenditures by corporations, but also for the nudging out of direct party control. SuperPACs, such as American Crossroads and Americans for Prosperity, coordinate strategies for spending their funds. The meetings where efforts in battleground states, ideological messages, and particular tasks are all debated and defined look a great deal like a meeting of party officials; indeed, former party officials and former campaign staffers are usually present. Whereas only the money was private before, today the money, planning, and execution increasingly lie beyond political parties. SuperPACs are appropriating party functions regarding ideological messages and their best possible distribution.[40] As such essential functions are sourced to outside organizations, a privatization process occurs.[41]

B. The Market for Public Policy

Moving from the market for offices to the market for law and policy, the roles of candidates and the donor class are reversed. Candidates consume campaign funds in the market for offices and then supply favorable terms in the market for policy. Donors and spenders supply funds in the former in order to consume policies in the latter.

What explains the supply of political funds? Imagine candidates as entrepreneurs or start-up companies seeking capital in order to mount a business venture.[42] Early success might be judged by drumming up a great deal of financial support and initial orders—i.e., mounting a competitive bid for office or winning a presidential primary. The final goal is obtaining office itself, which is akin to the moment when a young company has its initial public offering—the moment when it "goes public." This phrase applies quite literally to the moment when political candidates, awash in a sea of private capital, offer themselves up for public election. Their major suppliers of campaign funds are essentially venture capitalists who got in on the ground level, fronting the start-up funds necessary to mount a campaign. The amount of those funds in relation to the amount of those provided by others can be converted into a number of shares, which will be worth a great deal if the public offering is successful. As a company thrives, its shares pay increasing dividends and additional investors buy in.

Here is the trouble with the analogy, however: no matter how much legislation a "company" of this kind sponsors or defeats, no matter how many congressional committees it chairs, no matter how many wise solutions to social problems it engineers, it will never make its own money directly. Its products and services cannot be placed on the market, except indirectly as dividends paid to investors. And every two to four years, each of these "companies" spends nearly all of the money investors had put in. Under the repetitive pressure of electoral challenge, even the most successful officeholder is in constant need of capital investment. This situation makes them especially sensitive, vulnerable even, to the interests of donors and spenders. Because political finance has been privatized and it is extremely expensive to win an election, officeholder term limits may backfire, ensuring private accountability instead of public accountability.[43]

A varied group of investors and consumers supplies the funds. This entails the usual list of individuals, corporations, and interest groups and a wide array of organizational vehicles, many of which are tax-exempt—such as 527 and 501c organizations.[44] Lobbyists fulfill an important function in finding willing donors and "bundling" contributions so as to become indispensable to candidates in tight races. In sum, the major investors and their respective shares are well known to candidates, officeholders, and party officials. Donors and spenders do not lend their support arbitrarily. If their investments yield low returns, they may take their money elsewhere.

The logic of investments, shares, and dividends should seem foreign to politics, but it is crucial for understanding why the supply of political funds is so plentiful and why those who benefit sue to establish their right to spend. Saul Anuzis, a member of the Republican National Committee, offers an interesting prediction: "A third of all the money spent on federal elections will come from candidates, a third will come from the parties, and a third will come from these independent groups and superPACs."[45] What does each of these three basic sources have in common? Private parties supply their funds, fulfilling the crucial functions of campaign finance, party finance, and the financing of independent political advertisements. Often the same people fulfill multiple functions. For example, just 172 of Mitt Romney's donors during the 2012 Republican primary "gave the campaign a total of $444,000—and they gave the [Restore Our Future] superPAC more than $16 million."[46]

Political donors and spenders can be shy, however. They may receive bad press as an unintended consequence of registering their demand for policy. Money in politics is unpopular, especially corporate money. Although broad public support exists for greater disclosure of the source of donations and expenditures, Republicans in Congress have blocked disclosure efforts.[47] The public would distrust ideas being paid for by large corporations, or possibly would retaliate by boycotting certain corporations. The market has responded to this qualified demand for political influence by providing political influence without bad press. The U.S. Chamber of Commerce, for example, "has increasingly relied on a relatively small collection of big corporate donors . . . mak[ing] no apologies for its policy of not identifying its donors [and] vigorously oppos[ing] legislation in Congress that would require groups like it to identify their biggest contributors when they spend money on campaign ads."[48] SuperPACs have done something similar, often distributing their funds to nonprofit affiliates that do not have to disclose donors. American Crossroads, for example, founded by Karl Rove and two former Republican national chairmen, operates alongside Crossroads GPS, its nonprofit sister organization. The former must disclose its donors but can run all sorts of political advertisements; the latter is limited to "issue ads" but need not disclose its donors. To put the power of these two groups into perspective, note that they raised $51 million in 2011. The Republican National Committee itself raised $88 million that year.[49]

Besides pure political spending, political investors find creative ways to ingratiate themselves to officeholders, including infamous congressional "junkets," lavish trips paid for by lobbyists and corporations. The *New York Times* examined 1,150 such trips to an entertaining effect. Imagine Representative F. James Sensenbrenner Jr. "tour[ing] a prince's vineyard and castle in Liechtenstein and spen[ding] an afternoon at a ski resort in the Alps—all at the expense of a group of European companies." Or envision Representative Ileana Ros-Lehtinen's "privately sponsored trip [to] the historic King David Hotel in Jerusalem and . . . a gala party near the

Western Wall as part of a weeklong conference that lobbyists and executives paid as much as $18,500 to attend."[50] In order to avoid violating revised congressional guidelines passed in the wake of the Jack Abramoff affair, "companies finance much of this travel indirectly, getting around the spirit of the rules by giving money to nonprofits, some of which seem to exist largely to sponsor trips[,] obscuring who is actually paying for a lawmaker's junket."[51] Abramoff himself, who was famous for flying members of Congress to the best golf course in Scotland and doling out the most coveted seats at sporting events, has come forward to warn us of the ineffectiveness of the reforms passed after the scandal he caused.[52]

Other spending seems to take the form of congratulatory wishes or a thank-you card. For example, in 2009 President Obama refused "corporate [and] federal lobbyist money to pay for his inauguration" itself, but private companies wrote checks for inauguration parties—including $40,000 from American Airlines and $80,000 from Exelon donated to an Illinois State Society ball. At such private "lobbyist-sponsored soirees," attendees "schmooze with members of Congress and congressional staff."[53] In 2013, Obama reversed his policy, welcoming such gifts more openly.[54]

What do the donors and spenders want in return? Sometimes the answers are specific, too specific in fact. Koch Industries and Exxon Mobil are among the largest funders of the American Legislative Exchange Council (ALEC) which hosts conferences for legislators and supplies model legislation. In Virginia, at least 50 of ALEC's bills have been "introduced . . . practically word for word" on matters including voter identification, private education companies, the legalization of deadly force in defense of property, the reduction of asbestos liability, and weakening the Environmental Protection Agency.[55]

Other examples of specific demands include: lowering capital gains taxes, weakening antitrust enforcement, and deregulating the financial industry;[56] abolishing the EPA;[57] reducing emissions standards for automobiles;[58] "fighting proposed rules that would impose tighter security requirements on chemical facilities[, and] weaken[ing] the historic rewrite of the nation's financial regulations";[59] defeating regulations and eliminating fines on tobacco companies; "reforming" tort law; directing military spending to certain private contractors; keeping tax breaks for ethanol fuel producers, oil companies, and corporate jet owners;[60] defeating proposed taxes that would affect private equity firms and hedge funds in particular;[61] preserving "mortgage interest deductions for higher-priced residences and second homes";[62] and shaping the precise terms of health care legislation.[63] A government that tries to reduce pollution, regulate the financial industry, sustain courts of law and rights of action, and tax luxury goods necessarily threatens powerful interests. As the president of the American League of Lobbyists put it, "everybody's at risk."[64]

Lobbying conveys interests and demands, reinforced by the delivery of bundled contributions or with the threat of placing similar bundles at others' doorsteps. Lobbyists are often former officeholders, cabinet officials or campaign staffers, and industry insiders. Even before offering officeholders bundled contributions, gifts, trips, and useful information, many lobbyists are respected in their own right. Studies confirm that money spent on lobbyists tends to be money well invested: "[O]n average, for every $1 that an average firm spends to lobby for targeted tax benefits, the return is between $6 and $20.83."[65] In a more favorable case, dollars spent lobbying for a tax benefit in the American Jobs Creation Act of 2004 yielded a 22,000 percent rate of return.[66]

Lobbying does not cause policy outcomes that can be pinpointed in every case, but it is effective enough to be demanded by those who have much to gain or lose from political outcomes. Consider the $3.3 billion spent on lobbying in 2008.[67] With negotiations over government bailouts for banks and automakers ongoing, the extra $400 million spent over the previous year is hardly surprising. With the $825 billion stimulus package in the works for the following year, not to mention the larger overall bulk of all other government policies, "what companies spend (on lobbying) is only a tiny fraction of what they can reap from the government."[68] Indeed, the U.S. Chamber of Commerce's $62 million investment in lobbying proved to be money well spent in light of the $700 billion bailout for the financial industry. The same can be said of GM's $3.3 million investment in lobbying in the three months immediately preceding the government's decision to award GM $13.4 billion in federal loans.[69]

As with government spending, so too with cuts in government spending. The twelve lawmakers on a congressional committee charged with $1.2

trillion in debt reductions "are suddenly among the most popular people in town, with lobbyists and executives from powerful interest groups angling to schedule meetings, distribute checks at fundraisers, and deliver petitions."[70] Because those who hire lobbyists tend to be strategic actors who pay for lobbying year after year, it stands to reason that such payments produce overall gains (even if only through avoiding losses).

The specific desires of political investors are almost infinite, spanning whatever investors might desire from legislation, agency rulemaking, the decisions of courts of law, executive decisions, the composition of administrative agencies, and the judicial appointments process. Categories of desire are few in comparison: (1) "secure special tax breaks and tax loopholes that reduce the tax burden of an individual firm or industry"; (2) "thwart actions of regulatory agencies that are viewed as too costly or as a threat to private control over investment decisions"; (3) "funnel self-serving advice and information selectively to state officials to influence which facts are available to government decision-makers"; (4) "secure favorable legislation [including earmarks] for a particular company or industry (e.g., antitrust exemptions, tariffs[, and subsidies]) through legislative bodies";[71] (5) undermine unfavorable legislation—a far easier task than securing favorable legislation, as "[t]here is only one way to pass a bill in Congress, and a million ways to kill it";[72] (6) learn of policies before the general public does, and gain an advantage by exploiting that information—hence the "political intelligence industry"; and (7) promote particular candidates, parties, and ideas because they are viewed as good in and of themselves.[73]

Sometimes desires are subtler than these categories would allow, seeking at first to build trust and trigger a budding sense of gratitude.[74] But for donors who are not friends of candidates, the ultimate goal of political spending lies with what trust and gratitude can get you. Officeholders readily admit that "money buys access to members [of Congress]."[75] They might lose their jobs if they admitted that money bought more than access, but members of the Supreme Court are free to make that admission.

Take, for example, Justice Kennedy's defense of the role of money in politics: "It is well understood that a substantial and legitimate reason, if not the only reason, . . . to make a contribution to one candidate over another is that the candidate will respond by producing those political outcomes the supporter favors. Democracy is premised on responsiveness."[76] Another example is the case of Senate Banking Committee chairman Christopher Dodd, who was one of the most influential figures in deciding the terms of bailout negotiations. It can hardly be a coincidence that "[s]ince 1989, he has taken more than $13 million (out of $43 million total) in campaign contributions from the financial services sector."[77] Is the responsiveness of Congress to the powerful interests that it is tasked with regulating a democratic sort of responsiveness? Once we begin to talk about responsiveness to donations and expenditures, not just votes, then we are talking about a market.[78]

But what of the vote? As opposed to simply purchasing the policies they desire, political investors have to contend with elected officeholders. The presence of the popular vote in the market for political office is just as notable as the absence of its equivalent—that is, political referenda or direct democracy—in the market for public policy. The market for policy can be thought of as the financial equivalent of referenda; individuals can register their demands in between voting cycles in this way. Still, there are many regulations that limit and burden the supply of funds. Political investors have to contend with those, as well as the vote. Can political capitalism survive these government interventions into political markets?

C. Universal Suffrage, but Capitalism Nevertheless

Given the persistence of the popular vote, is it possible to maintain that government offices and public policy are allocated through the market? Capitalism requires only that production and distribution be "entrusted *primarily* to the market mechanism, based on private ownership of property."[79] Universal suffrage does not violate this rule, although it seems to at first.

Each citizen gets only one vote, and, with it, two options: cast it or sit on it. Votes cannot be bought, sold, traded, or even gifted. Therefore, the vote is not part of the market mechanism. Even when casting a vote, citizens are not consumers. It is wrong to characterize voting as a "transaction in the political market . . . between politicians supplying policy promises and the electorate which has a demand for particular policies."[80] Citizens do not spend money in order to acquire their votes and they receive nothing of tangible value for casting them.[81]

Politicians routinely betray their campaign promises anyhow. In contrast to parallel situations in real markets, voters cannot sue for breach of contract when the recipients of their votes fail to deliver the goods as promised.[82] Moreover, the goods that officeholders do deliver generally remain invisible to the electorate. How many voters are aware of the details of international trade treaties, government contracts in the reconstruction of Iraq, the particulars of financial bailouts, all the subsidies in effect to particular industries and companies, the earmarks that flank bills on virtually every topic, the appointments to the various administrative agencies that administer complex statutes (on matters such as environmental protection, election law, and food safety, for example), the effects of the loopholes in the tax code, or the likely effects of the latest health care legislation on insurance companies?

Everyone knows that his or her vote will not be decisive for the election and that election promises are rarely decisive for public policy; and still, people take the time to get to the polls. Few hope for any payoff besides being part of the collective motion that leads to the election of one's preferred candidate. And regardless of electoral outcomes, one may still find satisfaction in exercising a political right and duty. A civic sense is at work, even if only in the form of anger towards a particular candidate and the corresponding, essentially symbolic need to vote for his opponent.

Perhaps the most powerful recognition of the power of collective action and public sentiment comes in the form of efforts to restrict and dilute the vote. Here, restrictions are the sincerest form of flattery. How better to recognize the power of collective action than to restrict suffrage to property-owning white males? The time it took for landless men, African Americans, and women to claim what democracy promised them reflects on this. Other founding-era restrictions on the vote have endured, however. The framers settled on a representative democracy, not direct democracy, and even the general presidential election remains protected to this day from rash popular sentiment by the Electoral College. And non–founding era restrictions have been added: many areas have been zoned so as to dilute the power of racial minorities and poor majorities; controversial voter ID laws promise to reduce the participation of many qualified minority voters even as they prevent a few cases of fraud; regulations affecting newly registered voters reduce the time frame for submitting forms and, in the process, complicate the plight of civic organizations seeking to recruit new voters; other laws simply shorten voting periods.[83]

While it is not part of the market, the vote is not the *primary* means of decision about matters of political office or public policy either. It may be the most celebrated and most visible of the various handles of power, but it does not choose which citizen is to be lifted from obscurity to a seat of power. As Walter Lippmann put it, "The Many can elect [only] after the Few have nominated."[84] Lippmann's quote is true in a technical way with regard to how votes are allocated in many primary elections, but it is true in a much more comprehensive way with regard to the role of money itself.

A tremendous amount of money from private donors and spenders is necessary for a candidate to get her message out in the first place, the purpose of which, ironically, is to enable her to raise additional money. "Donor-investors use fundraising prowess as a heuristic to assess the 'electability' of primary candidates."[85] The same is true of political parties, which use the same measure to decide which candidates to support.[86] As a former chairman of the Democratic Congressional Campaign Committee put it: "The first third of your campaign is money, money, money. The second third is money, money, and press. And the last third is votes, press, and money."[87] Indeed, much of the electoral process can be summed up by the phrase "the wealth primary." The election, then, subjects the political market to the *filter of democracy*.[88] This is the filter of the general public beyond the donor class, where the preferences of those who are not political consumers, investors, or entrepreneurs are finally activated. Because the vote is limited to deciding which of the market-dominant candidates will be selected in the end, the allocation of political offices is still entrusted *primarily* to the market mechanism.

Besides determining which candidates are viable, private wealth provides the great majority of information that bears upon how citizens vote. The post–*Citizens United* regime of unlimited corporate expenditures has begun a new chapter in this story. What the Court has framed innocently in terms of "providing useful information to the electorate" has been framed quite differently by psychologists, media experts, and political insiders. Attention and information retention are both limited. The market for political speech serves as a forum for the "struggle for salience," "a marketing effort in which the goal is to achieve a strategic advantage by making problems that reflected owned issues the criteria by which voters make their choice."[89] And so political spenders exercise the powers of selection and portrayal over candidates and issues. It is not the market's fault when political advertisements present an unfair and even factually inaccurate take on candidates and issues. The market's only permanent rule concerns the volume of speech, not its content. Airtime and print space are allocated according to the simple formula of ability and willingness to pay. Accordingly, well-funded candidates and interest groups can "effectively and completely drown out the other's message to the voters."[90]

Voters take what the market gives them. They are in this sense consumers, destined for the most part to passively absorb mass media messages, the views, rhetoric, and pet issues of the market-dominant candidates and their financial backers. They make a choice, much in the way of voting for the contestants on reality television shows, which, incidentally, have from time to time rivaled political contests in terms of public participation.[91]

In the end, the vote is not autonomous from political markets. It is a government-owned sector, true enough, but that sector is a tiny parcel in a great expanse of private land. The government sector receives shipments from the private sector, does what it can with those materials, and then ships its products back out to the private sector. Even affirming that voting is significant non-market activity and that the perseverance of the vote signifies the perseverance of a government sector, we have not shown that capitalism is second to democracy. "[A] market-dominated economy has often existed alongside a government-owned sector."[92]

D. A Regulated Market, but Still Capitalism

The vote is only the first of many government interventions. It came alongside a more significant intervention into the realm of private affairs: the establishment of a government with a limited number of officeholders. Whether voted for or not, a government takes certain functions away from private citizens, even if only those of keeping the peace and building roads. But in the case of a powerful government operated by a limited number of officeholders who legislate on many topics, the supply of offices is fixed, but the demand for favorable laws is virtually endless.[93] Every person and organization could benefit from public policies of one sort or another, and yet there are only a few people with the authority to make those policies and the policy-making procedure has been set in advance.

Consider the criminal law prohibition on bribery, a rule that helps maintain the proper policy-making procedure. Is public policy really allocated through a market, given the fact that bribery is illegal? Indeed, the word "bribery" is telling enough. Why not call it "purchasing"? And why not call the acceptance of a bribe "selling"? In sum, can democracy be a capitalist market if neither offices nor public policy can be purchased directly? Numerous other limitations on the political market survive—including the prohibition on corporate and union contributions to candidates, various limits on individual contributions, congressional ethics rules, lobbyist registration rules, fiscal requirements for ideological associations, and disclosure requirements for PACs.

For our purposes, it does not matter that even law school courses on election law are hard-pressed to provide a map of this regulatory jungle. The fact of regulations on political finance follows the general trend of capitalism in other markets: "Almost nowhere . . . have production and distribution been determined purely by free exchange in the market."[94] Plus, a great deal of the regulations in force are not really *in force*. The Federal Election Commission, charged with the interpretation and enforcement of campaign finance laws, has long been deadlocked. For some time, at least half of its members have been ideological opponents of campaign finance laws—perhaps an ironic testament to the power of money in politics.[95]

The broader set of regulations that are enforced, especially the vote, the public employment of officeholders, and the prohibition on bribery, makes political markets dense and layered—mediated as opposed to direct. Because legislative provisions cannot be purchased directly, they are pursued indirectly by acquiring the power to influence officeholders, parties, and voters. On the other hand, ad space, airtime, lobbyist services, political speechwriters and consultants, well-staffed interest groups, and political intelligence services can be purchased directly. Media companies, lobbying firms, and consulting firms are straightforward capitalist enterprises offering goods and services directly to consumers. Successful lobbyists and speechwriters are in high demand and receive larger fees than others in their industry. They offer a proven product.

Still, that product, like campaign and party donations, serves only as an investment in political influence. Lobbyists influence officeholders who then produce the desired public policy, a consultant frames a message that induces citizens to vote in the desired way, and so on. Investments in candidates and parties, airtime, political advertisements, and the services of lobbyists are all intermediate products desired for their ability to produce ultimate goods. Even the tangible perks given to big donors—such as a night in the Lincoln Bedroom or a retreat at Camp David—are generally not the ultimate goods desired. The markets for government office and public policy are mediated by other markets.

This makes the legal portion of political markets inherently speculative. Even investors who succeed in obtaining political influence do not necessarily obtain favorable public policy. Having spent sizable sums, hired lobbyists, and met with officeholders and party officials, a particular person may become politically influential. But that person still has to contend with other politically influential people. Indeed, her lobbyists may be doing battle with other people's lobbyists, and her ads with others' ads. Such buffer effects and competitive spending situations make political markets a risky place for investment and help to explain why there is not even more money in politics.

Still, the vote and many other limitations on money in politics fail to remove politics from the market. Lobbying firms, political consulting firms, the media, many politicians, and many donors and spenders invest their own capital in political goods or activities that, in the end, generate a greater sum of capital than was initially invested. Lobbying firms, for instance, are capitalist enterprises that make a profit by offering political services (the representation of clients' interests) through political goods (political access and influence). Most political messages are brought to the public through capitalist enterprises that reap profits, such as privately owned television stations and newspapers. Reporting CBS's additional $180 million profit in the 2012 election year, CEO Les Moonves said, "Super PACs may be bad for America, but they're very good for CBS."[96] Remember: capitalism requires only that production and distribution of political goods be "entrusted *primarily* to the market mechanism, based on private ownership of property."[97]

Ruling out the abolition of government,[98] there are many less-regulated forms of political capitalism. Here are a few basic examples: (1) Abolish the vote, abolish the system of government-paid officeholders, and scale back the public policy machinery to administrators who respond only to financial bids. People and associations would literally vote with their dollars and the resulting "public" policies would respond only to the overall balance of spending. This would not be a democracy, mind you, but it would be a form of politics. (2) Keep the vote but make votes tradable on the market, to be bought and sold at will. Each person would be entitled to theirs, but would then be free to do whatever they wanted with it. (3) Keep a system of officeholders, but allow offices to be sold to the highest bidder. Instead of an auction for public policies, there would be an auction for a limited number of seats at the bargaining table where public policy is made. (4) Keep the vote, the current system of officeholders, and the prohibition on bribery, but abolish all other limits on financial power. Contributions could be made in million-dollar sums or more even by corporations, disclosure rules could be eliminated, and unlimited expenditures by private parties would no longer need to be independent of campaigns. For those desiring an even stronger political market, this last option is the only realistic one for the time being.

Even though U.S. political markets could be further liberalized, comparative studies of political finance describe the United States as one of the most laissez-faire models among all advanced democracies.[99] Citing its relatively high openness to private influence, the Marxist literature refers to the United States as a "weak state."[100] As seen in other advanced democracies, more regulated forms of political capitalism are possible. Expenditures by parties, candidates, and even citizens could be limited, corporate expenditures could be abolished, public financing for parties and campaigns could be much stronger or even mandatory, the media could offer rights of public access or the government could fund serious alternatives to dominant private players, and the election season could be restricted so as to prevent the need for constant fundraising. In all of these cases, there would still be capitalist markets, such as those for political speech in the private media or at least a market for political consultants helping to prepare speech destined for public channels, and for access to representatives through lobbyists. Overall, however, such regulations would constrain political markets.

E. Private Control of the Means of Decision

Politics is unlike any other market in existence. As C. B. Macpherson points out, politics has to "produce and sustain a government[—]it has recurrently to confer on identifiable persons the power to make . . . the laws and orders by which political goods are distributed."[101] In other economic markets, activity is focused not on ensuring suitable leadership or governing authority over the market, but on the goods and services themselves—bringing them to market, producing them efficiently, developing new products, and so on.[102] In fact, nobody is supposed to have authority over a market. Markets are widely considered the only voluntary, non-coercive way to organize society. Consumer choices and producer decisions are not to be made by any outside group. Prices and distribution flow from competition and the conditions of supply and demand, all of which are coordinated, for the most part, through private property and freedom of contract, not government intervention (or so the theory goes).[103]

The reality is one part irony, one part paradox. Defying the conventional wisdom that "markets are . . . the mechanism by which the private realm can organize its tasks without the direct intervention of the public realm,"[104] the political market is the mechanism by which the direct intervention of the public realm is controlled. The political market is the *meta market*, the market for control of all other markets. This is why Walzer calls politics "probably the most important, and certainly the most dangerous, good in human history."[105] Market champions complain of government intervention in private affairs. But what if government control is actually a veiled form of private control? Then, the private realm would itself control the intervention of the public realm into . . . well . . . the private realm.

And still, we cannot say that the private realm thereby dissolves the public realm—we cannot reduce this chain of control to the private realm controlling itself. The vote, government employees, and government decisionmaking and enforcement bodies remain intact. Private investors and capitalist enterprises provide the funds and materials that produce the government and pull the strings of public policy. Although these transactions are voluntary, their produce is coercive, "applying to, and often imposing costs on, those who did not vote for it or did not want it."[106] Taxpayers are forced to bail out the financial sector, in many cases the same firms whose negligence and malfeasance caused the crisis in the first place; a minimum-miles-per-gallon requirement for automobile production narrows the range of contracts that consumers and producers can make; health care legislation forces insurers to cover some conditions they would otherwise exclude, and requires all citizens to purchase a policy when some would prefer to gamble. These and other laws are not necessarily a bad thing. It is just that law, as a market product, is unique in binding parties who did not take part in the transaction, and especially in binding parties who did take part but desired opposite results. It stands to reason that those parties are often disadvantaged by the law, a result that Ayn Rand described as "the good of some men tak[ing] precedence over the good of others, with those others consigned to the status of sacrificial animals," "the concept of man as a slave to the absolute state embodied by 'the people.'"[107]

The irony of the meta market that we call democracy, however, is that it is not controlled by "the people." The "good of some men" that dominates over others is often the good of a particularly influential group of wealthy concerns. Only some private actors spend appreciable sums to influence the government's work. Hence, the sequence of the meta market is: *a select portion of the private realm* seeks to control the interventions of the public realm into *the entire private realm*.

There is something devastatingly familiar about the way the meta market works. Private investors and enterprises provide the funds and materials, citizens vote and officeholders make legislative gestures (amidst continuous signals from investors and associated enterprises), and public policy is produced. This recalls how private ownership of the means of production and wage labor define capitalism. By owning "the workplace, the machinery, and the raw materials" and paying wages instead of sharing profits, capitalists are able to keep the surplus value generated by productive activity. Laborers keep their wages, not the money that corresponds to the value they produce by working their employers' machinery.[108] The added value accrues to the owners of the means of production and registers as profits when it exceeds expenses. For this reason, laborers who own the machinery are not laborers at all but craftsmen. Craftspeople, like other small-business owners, keep their profits (and absorb their losses), but they are not responsible for much of the total volume of production.

As the Supreme Court deregulates political markets, the workplace, machinery, and raw materials of democracy can be privately owned to a greater and greater extent. Investors, entrepreneurs, and mature enterprises are gaining *ownership of the means of decision* within society. They fund political parties and campaigns. They own the media that distribute political advertisements; the lobbying firms that sell political access and influence; the political intelligence firms that obtain inside political information and sell it to hedge funds; and they can own an unlimited quantity of political speech commodities—including advertisements, political events, and websites. All who invest within the political market seek to capture the surplus value, which could, for example, accrue from a lobbying firm charging handsome rates, the savings generated by a government subsidy, a competitive advantage achieved through legislation affecting other firms or industries, or the higher prices charged thanks to the weakening of antitrust enforcement.

Great comfort flows from the mistaken perception that candidates, officeholders, parties, and voters own the processes of political speech, elections, and lawmaking. Unfortunately, it is more accurate to conceive of all these actors, including ourselves in our capacity as citizens, as laborers working tools owned by others, shaping raw materials owned by others, and mulling about in a workplace owned by others. Might it then be the case that the motions of electoral contest, lawmaking, and political speech—like all other uses of capital and labor in the market—serve to generate profits for the owners of the means of production?

The answer depends on the precise political good or service in question. For political advertisements broadcast on private television or printed in newspapers, and the services of lobbyists and political consultants, the answer is yes. In other facets of political markets, however, private ownership of the means of decision is not as complete. Although capitalists cannot produce without laborers, tools, parts, and suppliers of parts and tools, they employ those laborers directly and they can order parts and tools at will. Political capitalists do not employ officeholders or party officials. They help to fund campaigns and parties, but officeholders and parties are not employed directly by their financiers. After making their initial investments, financiers cannot lay claim to the surplus value generated by politicians as they can with the laborers they employ. If the politicians and parties produce public policy of value, political capitalists are pleased. If they do not, they are disappointed and may decide to fund other politicians and parties. Admittedly, failing to fund a politician's election campaign is not the same as firing a disobedient laborer. If joined in by enough big donors and spenders, however, the effect is identical.

Because the market is layered, multifaceted, and regulated, the proper description is *private control of the means of decision*. Although that control is not so complete as to entail ownership, it is substantial and it is increasing.

II. CAN POLITICAL MARKETS BE JUSTIFIED?

The question may seem odd. Why would the consensual activity of buyers and sellers require a justification? Because the vote remains intact, contributions have been limited (at least for the time being), and bribery has been prohibited, political markets can be rationalized away from view. If voters disapprove of a given candidate's fundraising tactics, donor base, or political advertisements they can elect someone else. And if voters are tired of corporations' and interest groups' negative advertisements and sound bites, let them punish those interests by voting against the candidates benefiting from them or even boycotting the goods and services of the corporations in question. If officeholders do not condone the policy goals of particular donors and spenders, they are free to disregard them. Potential donors to campaigns and PACs are also free to abstain. In a market, no one is obligated to spend their money and no one is obligated to sell their products.

Even a brief look at some of the effects caused by political markets refutes this disingenuous narrative. A justification is required, but first let us be clear on what, exactly, requires justification.

A. *The Effects of Political Markets*
That Everybody Must Concede

Not everyone agrees about the definition of corruption or the importance of political equality. Some debate surrounds the questions of whether congressional voting can be linked directly to large donations and expenditures, whether lobbyists twist officeholders' arms or merely offer them valuable information, and whether negative advertisements are effective. Leaving aside scandals and the most heated allegations, there are several dynamics caused by political markets that most observers and participants own up to, and these—the least-controversial evils in play—are serious enough.

Stacking the Deck—The Dependency of Officeholders and the Distortion of Democracy   Because officeholders owe their station to donors and spenders, and continue to depend on them for their reelection bids, they can make no comprehensive claim to independent judgment. Lawrence Lessig calls the "improper, or conflicting, dependency" on donors "dependence corruption."[109] The problem with dependency is not that donors necessarily cause disagreeable outcomes. For instance, Sheldon Adelson's and Foster Friess's multimillion-dollar donations to Gingrich's and Santorum's superPACs prolonged the contest for the Republican nomination, enabling millions of additional voters to weigh in.[110] Absent these tremendous investments by two billionaires, Romney would have likely wrapped up the primary contest months earlier, confining its scope to the first few states, and thus reducing democratic choice. Roger Cohen observed that large donors did something similar by underwriting Eugene McCarthy's challenge to Lyndon Johnson in 1968, making possible McCarthy's notable run for the White House.[111] Dependence corruption does not impute the particular effects of the money to the course of a campaign or to the policies later supported by the officeholder. It imputes the effects to officeholder judgment and the disproportionate power of the wealthy to skew that judgment their way.

Discussing the studies on financial influence, Susan Rose-Ackerman concludes that "it is difficult to distinguish between politicians who bend their positions to favor contributors and those who were elected because they share contributors' point of view."[112] Some officeholders and party officials lean towards a particular policy because it will earn them continued financial support from major donors or will avoid an onslaught of negative spending by a powerful group. Other officeholders and party officials lean towards that same outcome because they believe it to be superior on the merits. Is it such an important difference that some modify their judgment to please powerful donors while others are in a position to exercise their judgment to begin with because their views are naturally favorable to powerful donors? Either way, the deck is stacked against those with little money to spend; either way, the interests of donors and spenders are overrepresented, taken into account more often for the simple reason that they determine where political money is allocated.

Across the candidates, officeholders, parties, and decades, the central role of private wealth in all aspects of political finance does have a distorting effect, as the *Austin* majority alleged. Dependency on donors, including the lobbyists who bundle contributions, leads to a distortion in policy outcomes—again, not that the resulting policies are necessarily better or worse, only that they respond to the needs of The Funders, not those of The People.[113] Surveying the political science literature, Lessig reports that "there is a wide gap in the policy preferences" of these two groups, i.e., between the 90 percent of the American public that does not donate a dime and the 10 percent that donates the billions of dollars it takes to finance all parties and campaigns.[114] The priorities of lobbyists vary substantially from those of the overall population, as shown in public opinion surveys.[115]

That gap between the preferences of The Funders and those of The People translates into policy distortion through many channels besides the receipt of checks in the mail. Take the lobbyist component, for example: if "a member went to Washington after campaigning on two issues, the need to stop Internet 'piracy' and the need to help working mothers on welfare, on day one she'd find a line of lobbyists around the block eager to help with the first issue, but none there to help her with the second."[116] But at least she would have strong financial support for part of her platform. Imagine the sorry plight of a member seeking to help working mothers *and* pass strict financial regulations to prevent another financial crisis. The numbers are staggering: 1,537 lobbyists represented the interests of finan-

cial firms in the latest financial reform bill, twenty-five times more than the number of lobbyists representing the likes of consumer groups and unions.[117] Among those lobbyists working for the financial sector stood 70 former members of Congress.[118]

Officeholders are affected not just by the lopsided balance of lobbyists, but by their own everyday routine as well. The demands of fundraising on their schedules hasten the decline of substantive political activity, including congressional meetings, meeting attendance rates, and attention to the text of proposed legislation in the first place.[119] Today, nobody can expect members to have read the legislation they vote on or to participate in any substantive debate on it. Remember: officeholders have several jobs and it is hard to do them all well. Deliberation is also increasingly unnecessary when decisions on how to vote are formed in accordance with donors' preferences, not independent judgments formed in conjunction with one's fellow officeholders or one's geographic constituents. Their fundraising needs naturally put officeholders in frequent contact with the 10 percent, not the 90 percent. Big donors and spenders have far greater access to candidates, officeholders, and party officials than average Americans. There is simply no comparison.

Justice Scalia conceded the point in 2003: "It cannot be denied . . . that corporate (like noncorporate) allies will have greater access to the officeholder, and that he will tend to favor the same causes as those who support him . . . That is the nature of politics-if not indeed human nature."[120] Justice Kennedy agreed. "Access in itself . . . shows only that in a general sense an officeholder favors someone or that someone has influence on the officeholder . . . Favoritism and influence are not, as the Government's theory suggests, avoidable in representative politics."[121] How can this statement be read as anything besides a telling-off? The favoritism and influence at issue are the type that flow from officeholder dependency on donors and spenders. Favoritism and influence have reached overwhelming levels because the Court has struck down so many limits on money in politics. The Court has made access, influence, and favoritism unavoidable. Kennedy himself went on to author *Citizens United* seven years after making this remark, granting corporations and big spenders even more leverage. And he claims that access, influence, and favoritism are unavoidable?

Conscience Becomes Self-Eliminating   Justice Kennedy's remark can be easily refitted to reality: "[S]o long as the Court prolongs the unconstitutionality of spending limits for campaigns, restrictions on corporate expenditures, and effective public financing, then favoritism and influence are unavoidable." Under such conditions, what becomes of candidates who take a principled stand against large donations or against PAC expenditures? They severely decrease their odds of winning.

Recall that this was the Adams plaintiffs' argument in *McConnell* against the increase in contribution limits—they wished to avoid the appearance of unequal access and influence caused by the acceptance of large donations. This was not an easy wish to act on, however. Candidates who refuse large donations are at a disadvantage to those who accept them. Imagine the time and energy it takes to collect $500,000 from 1,000 or even just 500 donors, and compare that to the energy it takes to collect the same amount from 250 donors. Given that there are plenty of big donors out there, candidates who appeal to them can hit their fundraising targets much more easily than their more scrupulous adversaries can. The Court came out unanimously against the Adams plaintiffs, holding that it was their choice to spurn larger donations and that the law's provision for larger donations did not amount to an injury that could be remedied in court. Therefore, the Court disavows responsibility for the life-and-death incentives produced by market liberalization. Opening up the political market to greater sums of money leaves candidates with the "choice" of playing the money game or losing the election.

Citizens United has had the same effect in facilitating the creation of superPACs. A candidate who finds unlimited spending, billionaire sponsors, and corporate political influence objectionable has the same choice: swallow your morals and buddy up with a superPAC or assume a tremendous risk of losing the election. Although President Obama initially rejected superPACs in the 2012 election, he quickly changed course: "[W]e've got some of these super PACs that have pledged to spend up to half a billion dollars to try to buy this election and what I've said consistently is, we're not going to just unilaterally disarm."[122]

Interest groups, corporations, unions, and wealthy individuals often face a similarly illusive choice. Either spend a lot of money on politics or be placed at a disadvantage relative to one's competitors. Just like candidates and parties, economic and ideological interests cannot afford to unilaterally disarm. The incentives for investors and corporations are clear. Rational actors will engage in political activities if the benefits outweigh the costs. Investors need not avoid companies that use general treasury funds for political expenditures, only the companies that are not savvy enough to do so at a profit. Capitalism itself fuels these dynamics. Lobbying and media consulting firms will design products that are increasingly effective. "Creative destruction" occurs in political industries too—note how super-PACs have surpassed PACs and how shadow groups threaten to surpass superPACs. The campaign finance lawyers who wish to earn their keep will find loopholes for their clients. Interest groups will search for more effective vehicles for applying political pressure. Like many industries, the political influence industry does not merely satisfy demand. It also creates it.[123]

Beyond such general incentives facing players on all sides of the political market, there are more specific incentives. For candidates and parties having made the choice to indebt themselves to big spenders: further the interests of one's investors or risk "capital flight" come election season. It would be feasible to act independently if only other officeholders and parties were not eager to offer one's investors better terms, and if one's particular investors were not essential for countering those of other candidates. This can take the form of extortion: a lobbyist comes into a member's office and describes the bundled contributions he has to offer to members who will vote to tweak a particular provision of a bill. Either agree and receive the money, or disagree, watch the money go to another officeholder, and prepare for potential reprisals from the superPAC aligned with the opposite platform.

Similar forms of extortion are applied to hesitant donors and spenders.[124] From a survey of three hundred corporate managers in 2000, the Committee for Economic Development concluded that "51 percent of business executives fear adverse legislative consequences to themselves or their industry if they turn down requests for campaign contributions from high-ranking political leaders and/or political operatives."[125] John Samples reports that business extortion has motivated some economic interests to support campaign finance reform.[126]

All of the above are collective-action problems, problems in which no rational actor will make the right choice unless she has a guarantee that all others will follow suit. Without such a guarantee, the temptation to defect from the deal and gain an advantage over one's fellows poses too great a risk. The situation was best described by Garrett Hardin, who used the example of public grazing land, where access is open and greater usage brings greater individual profit—a commons.

> The rational herdsman concludes that the only sensible course for him to pursue is to add another animal to his herd . . . But this is the conclusion reached by each and every rational herdsman sharing a commons. Therein is the tragedy. Each man is locked into a system that compels him to increase his herd without limit . . . Freedom in a commons brings ruin to all.[127]

The commons becomes barren; the grass does not have time to grow back; the soil dries out; the tragedy is overuse and exhaustion of precious terrain.

Candidate and officeholders are likewise locked into a system that compels them to increase their . . . well . . . *hoard* without limit. The results are disastrous for democracy's terrain. Hardin advocates "mutual coercion mutually agreed upon" as a solution to the tragedy, reasoning that individuals locked into the logic of constant consumption are "free only to bring on universal ruin; once they see the necessity of mutual coercion, they become free to pursue other goals."[128]

Adding one tragedy to another, the Court has undermined the "mutual coercion" imposed by officeholders and business leaders to end the financial arms race. So long as the Court strikes down political finance reforms, a peculiar result obtains: those who act out of conscience and do the right thing are easy prey for the rest. As this general rule plays out over time and across contexts, the less scrupulous obtain higher stations. Conscience becomes self-eliminating.

Losing Confidence in Democracy   Understanding that officeholders are locked into this logic of mutual self-destruction, the general public has become increasingly cynical. Scandals make matters worse, but the essence of the problem is that even earnest souls are corrupted by the money game. This lends the impression of hopelessness. Justices Souter, Stevens, Ginsburg, and Breyer have recognized that "the demand for campaign money in huge amounts from large contributors . . . has produced a cynical electorate."[129] The Roberts Court has denied that this is the case, however. *Citizens United* states flatly: "The appearance of influence or access, furthermore, will not cause the electorate to lose faith in our democracy."[130] Evidence collected since the ruling suggests that this victory for corporations has in fact caused the electorate to lose faith in democracy or, at least, to lose faith in the Court.[131]

Even before *Citizens United*, 77 percent of Americans believed that "elected officials in Washington are mostly influenced by the pressure they receive on issues from major campaign contributors"; 60 percent believed that "public officials don't care much what people like me think"; and only 24 percent believed that Congress is not owned by special-interest groups.[132] Despite these numbers, the Court has continued to open the floodgates, exacerbating the financial arms race responsible for the loss in public confidence. A 2011 CBS News–*New York Times* poll found that public approval of Congress stood at just 9 percent.[133] Indeed, how could the general public approve of a Congress that spends so much of its time telemarketing, courting powerful donors, communicating with lobbyists, and bailing out and subsidizing the very interests that the general public conceives of as having caused the major problems of the day? The extent of public dissatisfaction was aptly conveyed by Representative Michael Bennet, who noted that "more people support the United States becoming communist . . . than approve of the job that we're doing."[134]

B. Justifications

The incentives governing political markets explain why candidates, parties, and interest groups behave as they do. There is no mystery there. In the absence of limits on money in politics, actors in political markets have little choice how to behave. But why should the Court put them in that position to begin with? Why should it prevent officeholders, parties, reluctant individual spenders, and corporations from setting themselves free from the money race?

We must assume that the Court is aware of the effects that money works upon democracy. While I hesitate to allege that members of the

Court consciously agree with both of the following justifications for political markets, it is a matter of public record that these justifications divided political conservatives and political liberals for over a century. Why should they not do so within a judicial body polarized along the same party lines?

The Virtues of the Wealthy and the Pursuit of Wealth   Why preserve an aristocracy of the wealthy and the well-connected? Is there anything special about donors and spenders, something that would justify a system that gives them greater traction? Or perhaps it is not so much a matter of including the wealthy as it is a matter of excluding the poor and the middle class. Is there any particular wisdom to increasing the influence of the rich or to decreasing the influence of the middle class and the poor?

Those who today hold a tremendous amount of money, a form of property, were preceded in political privilege by those who held real property—land—and those who could pay a poll tax. Granted, the arguments in favor of restricting suffrage to the propertied class were used to justify wholesale political exclusion. Universal suffrage would seem to make such arguments irrelevant today. But because our present system still rewards the propertied class with political power and privileges unknown to the rest of society, arguments for partial suffrage remain relevant.

Chilton Williamson has cataloged many of these arguments, beginning with "the concept that the freeholders [i.e., landowners] were and should remain the backbone of state and society because they were the repository of virtues not found in other classes."[135] Williamson notes that "[i]t was the freeholders who would have, in a phrase as old as Aristotle, a common interest in and a permanent attachment to society and the state." He adds that figures as ancient as Cato, Cicero, and Pliny "had extolled the virtues of rural life" and that "[f]arming virtues became political virtues—independence, stability, good character, and respect for the personal and property rights of others."[136] Those who were excluded, "that element of the population which was relatively poor and lacked education and standing in the community," were deemed "not likely to develop an active interest in the affairs of state."[137]

The "attachment to society and state" argument comes at a curious time. Today's most powerful freeholders are those whose fortunes are tied up in multinational corporations with questionable attachment to society or state. Operations are moved abroad, tax shelters are employed, and assets are hidden. Those most rooted in place in today's times are the middle class—not the lower class that might go anywhere in search of work or the corporation that might go anywhere in search of cheaper materials and labor. Moreover today's market virtues are not yesterday's farming virtues—the differences between agribusiness and small family farms ought to suffice to make the point. And if we look more broadly to today's economy, we find that short-term notions of efficiency and profit maximization, and even short-term wealth-making schemes, are highly associated with wealth. Analysts question how much money is left to be made from traditional investments in companies that produce "real value," rather than speculative financial products.[138]

Another facet of the view that "freeholders are the strength of this [republic] not the freemen" was tied specifically to freeholders' financial responsibility.[139] The United States inherited the theory from England, where, at least from the emergence of the House of Commons, fiscal responsibility was tied to electoral privilege. Landowners paid most of the taxes, and naturally those were the funds that bankrolled governmental functions. Hence the Maryland Upper House, alongside many other authorities in the 1700s, justified partial suffrage on the basis that the "persons, purses and stocks [of freeholders] must bear the burden of government, and not the freemen who can easily abandon us."[140] While the wealthy do bear a tremendous share of the tax burden, this justification comes at the moment when Warren Buffett publicized the fact that he was taxed at a lower rate than his secretary.[141]

Besides their lack of education, lack of attachment to the state, and lack of financial responsibility for the acts of lawmaking bodies, democracy's pariahs were considered uncivilized and dependent on their masters. Williamson uses an English law from 1430 as an example: "[A] restriction of the electorate to the freeholders was desirable in light of the disorder and confusion which the poorer and meaner sort of person had caused at the polls."[142] This goes back to Montesquieu who described the poor as "in so mean a situation as to be deemed to have no will of their own."[143] Hence, Blackstone's concern that "working people were as vulnerable, if not more so, to the blandishments and threats of their employers as were tenants to those of their landlords."[144]

Although these notions bring us far back into time, they are hardly ancient history. The poll tax and property tax qualifications were major political issues in U.S. states into the early 1900s.[145] Brought into the present as grounds for exclusion not from the vote but from the major channels of political influence, the possession of property (especially money) serves a slightly more moderate function than it did before. The concentration of wealth remains highly unequal, mind you—moderation is not to be found here. The "top 1.0 percent of American families own 61 percent of all outstanding corporate stock in the United States, and 41 percent of total personal income goes to the top one-fifth of families."[146] The bottom 80 percent, on the other hand, receive "less than half of [all] total income."[147] The top 1 percent receives almost 25 percent of all income and controls 40 percent of total wealth.[148] Joseph Stiglitz reports that "[a]ll the growth in recent decades—and more—has gone to those at the top" and that "most citizens are doing worse year after year."[149] This means, quite literally, those at the very top: "[E]ssentially all of the upward redistribution of income away from the bottom 80 percent has gone to the highest-income 1 percent of Americans." [150] As far as inequality of income, the United States is the most unequal country in the world, most comparable to Russia and Iran.[151] How then can wealth work a moderating function on the means of political exclusion?

Whereas in earlier times women and African Americans could not own property to begin with and the landed aristocracy was essentially constituted by family lineage or royal prerogative, wealth is more fluid, more democratic today. Stiglitz writes that "the chances of a poor citizen, or even a middle-class citizen, making it to the top in America are smaller than in many countries in Europe."[152] Still, the business aristocracy is not as impenetrable as other aristocracies. Consider, for example, that "70 percent of U.S. corporate executives are not upper class by family origin."[153] Although opportunities are far from equally distributed and being born into a well-off family counts for a great deal, many of today's entrepreneurs, bankers, lawyers, doctors, CEOs, traders, investors, and inventors did not come from wealth.[154] Are we not better off with people competing to make money and join the wealthy class than with people competing for a privileged position within a given aristocracy?

Capitalism may well be the most just system of social stratification yet invented. Indeed, it is not intended to stratify society in the least. Its intention is for differences in intelligence, effort, creativity, and aptitude to reap their due reward, and thus to incentivize the development and exertion of these virtues, over and over again. Absent the disadvantages caused by birth into unfortunate circumstances, birth into poor regions of the world, and bad luck, the inequalities created by capitalism are at least correlated with differences in effort and skill. Of course many other factors are in play, but capitalism's magnanimity as regards sex, race, religion, social class, ethnicity, sexual orientation, political orientation, and national origin says a great deal. No other dominant social system in history has been tolerant along all such lines. Discrimination exists in spite of capitalism, not because of it.

And so, despite the passage of roughly a century since political restrictions on the basis of property, the age-old bias against the poor is still capable of arising, at least in the back of our minds. Given the official absence of discrimination and emphasis on talent, how did the poor arrive at their station? C. Wright Mills notes that the "test of ability . . . in a society in which money is a sovereign value is widely taken to be money-making." He asks, "'If you are so smart, why aren't you rich?'"[155] That test goes back at least to Hobbes, who wrote that "the value or worth of a man is, as all other things, his price, that is to say, so much as would be given for the use of his power."[156]

This is a tough argument to sell to schoolteachers, stay-at-home parents, nurses, college professors, artisans, low and mid-level government employees, gardeners, professional athletes in non-mainstream sports, and all others who make less than $100,000 per year but have failed to lose all self-esteem by virtue of that fact. Many people love what they do and create tremendous social value, but do not find themselves paid nearly as well as the CEO of a failing company.[157] As Stiglitz puts it, "Those who have contributed great positive innovations to our society, from the pioneers of genetic understanding to the pioneers of the Information Age, have received a pittance compared to those responsible for the financial innovations that brought our global economy to the brink of ruin."[158] But then, of course, the government bailed out a number of the offending companies, thus sending a message quite opposite to that of personal responsibility and reward in accordance with value added. Again, who exactly should have the privilege of heightened political access and influence? Even conceding that many wealthy citizens and interest groups have positive insights and worthy demands, are those of the schoolteacher and the small-business owner thereby upended? Is it really the Constitution's judgment that the day trader possesses more wisdom and virtue than the kindergarten teacher?

Aside from the elitist question of who deserves to be included in substantive political activity, a more politically correct question arises. What could society gain by premising full political inclusion on wealth? Part of capitalism's justification rests on the creation of wealth: "With a liberal state guaranteeing a free market, everyone's natural desire to maximize his own utility, or at least not to starve, would bring everyone into productive relations which would maximize the aggregate utility of the society."[159] One man, one vote, is an entitlement and a limit to how much power a person can obtain. The political market, on the other hand, provides unlimited opportunities for advancement. Anyone could become a Koch brother. Jeremy Bentham, one of capitalism's godfathers, understood the appeal of equality but maintained that it "had to yield to the case for productivity." After all, "[w]ithout security for unequal property there would be no incentive to capital accumulation, and without [that] there would be practically no productivity."[160]

Bentham's logic underlies *Bennett*'s intolerance for effective public campaign financing and offers a promising theory for why *Buckley* condemned political equality so categorically. Even more clearly still, it describes the logic of political markets in all facets, not just the ones at issue in *Bennett* and *Buckley*. Markets reward those who create and exploit competitive advantages. Incentives for profit fuel the "constant revolutionizing of the techniques of production," which leads to innovation and growth.[161] This brings us to the adage that what is good for General Motors is good for America—that what is good for the leaders of the economy leads to profits, which lead to reinvestment and expansion, which lead to better goods and services, and increased employment. The downward trickle of benefits looks more like a cascade and, at least for a moment, it appears sensible to constitutionally enshrine superior access and influence for the wealthy.

But this justification in reality requires another. While the products of major corporations tend to be of use to a large portion of the public, and a portion of the public is employed thereby, the same cannot be said about the capitalists operating within political markets. SuperPACs and 527s, advertising consultants, lobbying firms, and political intelligence firms, for example, offer the public little of value—neither much employment nor many useful products. Indeed, the public generally supports banning or reducing these products. Furthermore, for reasons we will soon see, it is doubtful that the wealthy use their superior political access and influence for the purpose of overall economic growth and social welfare, as Bentham hypothesized with regard to the real economy.

Money in Politics as a Check on Government Authority The second possible justification for political markets would prove easier to confess than the first, but it is controversial nonetheless. It increases in step with the move towards popular empowerment. Ballots were not always secret. Public voting provided an obvious form of accountability—accountability of the masses to their private employers. A particular fear surrounded the move away from public voting: "The poor of both town and country might combine to attack property rights and pull down the pillars of the established order."[162] Now, in the era of universal suffrage by secret ballot, what provides the counterweight to democracy? There are a number of mechanisms—such as representative democracy and the absence of popular referenda; a bicameral legislature, one part of which is a more elite body; the presidential veto; a federal court system of unelected judges with secure pay and life appointments; and strong individual rights, including vehement protection of private property and contractual freedoms.

These are among the primary counterweights in play. But what if they prove insufficient to protect property rights and the established order? Private control of the means of decision keeps officeholders in line. Better yet: it sets conditions of campaign and party finance and media advertising that make it difficult for the "wrong sort" of leaders to get elected in the first place.

Echoing Powell's memo, John Samples alleges that "'[b]ig business' has become highly unpopular with the public and thus an inviting target for ambitious demagogues."[163] "Given those incentives for exploitation and the government's monopoly on violence," Samples concludes, "we should be concerned that businesses and unions have the means to counterbalance the power of the state."[164] More than a counterbalance, Martin Redish calls corporations an appropriate "rival for societal authority."[165] This strong political function of corporations fits with Redish's view that there is a single "political-economic system" in which "three powerful entities— the government, the press, and private organizations—provide competing views and messages . . . and a check on one another."[166] Following the logic of this model, Redish opines that "[o]ne can never be sure whether restrictions on corporate expression are in reality nothing more than governmental attempts to curb or intimidate a potential rival."[167] In this view, money in politics preserves the rivalry, the ability of powerful economic actors to serve as a check on government. Consistent with this, Samples describes lobbyist spending as a way for business and unions to "defend their interests" and concludes that contribution limits should be repealed along with disclosure laws.

Samples does not believe that deregulating the political market even further will be sufficient, however. He counsels that "[t]o prevent extortion, we . . . should reduce the power of the state over the rest of society"— i.e., that the scope of government must be reduced.[168] Let us return to his claim that big business has become highly unpopular. Decades before Samples, Ayn Rand made the same point more forcefully: "In Soviet Russia, the scapegoat was the bourgeoisie; in Nazi Germany, it was the Jewish people; in America, it is the businessmen."[169] Like Samples, she alleged that money in politics was a response to government overreaching. Bearing in mind her definition of the common good as "the good of the majority as against the minority or the individual," consider this view: "So long as a concept such as 'the public interest' (or the 'social' or 'national' or 'international' interest) is regarded as a valid principle to guide legislation—lobbies and pressure groups will necessarily continue to exist."[170] Rand's conception of the common good as an excuse for majority tyranny required a defense of minority rights, but she observed that such rights applied only to racial and religious minorities. "The defense of minority rights is . . . not applied to that small, exploited, denounced, defenseless minority which consists of businessmen,"[171] she wrote. Although this may smell of satire, Rand's prose is earnest. She felt that officeholders behaved as looters, despite all the structural checks on government power described above. And the consequence, again, was what Rand called the "grotesque profession" of lobbying.[172]

How has the state gone too far? What has it done to force private interests to defend themselves through lobbies and pressure groups? Rand singled out the concept of economic rights pushed by Franklin Roosevelt, essentially state welfare programs, including entitlements and social services. She cited supposed rights to work, adequate food, clothing, recreation, education, and medical care, among others. She counseled that we simply add this question at the end of every supposed entitlement: "At whose expense?" Observing that medical care and education "do not grow in nature," Rand concluded that "[i]f some men are entitled by right to the products of the work of others, it means that those others are deprived of rights and condemned to slave labor."[173]

Although the money-in-politics cases never comment on the scope of the welfare state and the costly regulations that monied interests naturally oppose, it is plain to see from other bodies of caselaw that the Roberts Court opposes the government's more progressive functions and favors its more conservative ones. The majority's interest in economic freedom and strong law enforcement accompanies a disdain for entitlements and regulations of the sort that allegedly decrease profits. This, coupled with frequent praise for corporations in political finance cases, makes it likely that the majority protects money in politics partly because of its function: to allow those with the most money to effectively defend their interests in the face of an ambitious government.

Distrust of the U.S. government by business interests is a tremendously ironic position. The U.S. economy is highly privatized. Our government companies are a rarity. Our private companies are too, but for another reason entirely: many of them have ventured into areas of society that were previously not industries. Two somber examples come to mind: the massive military firms that not only make the missiles but apportion the mercenaries; and the private companies that build and operate prisons. We are dealing not just with private hospitals, insurance companies, schools, universities, broadcasting, and elder-care companies, but also plans for additional privatization: "Water and power utilities, police, fire and emergency services[,] Social Security[,] airports[,] genes[,] the electromagnetic spectrum, public parks, and highways . . . are being considered for full or partial privatization."[174]

Privatization, itself a political decision, provides a baseline for claims that government regulations interfere with the private sphere. As the private sphere expands, even a diminishing quantity of state regulations could lend the impression of growth. In sum, there is greater private incentive to influence government regulations when those regulations concern areas of society that have been parceled off to business concerns. That, today, includes most areas of society.

Despite providing increased incentives for market control of government, massive privatization has the unexpected effect of casting doubt on Samples's, Redish's, and Rand's explanations for money in politics. As Lindblom observed early on, "Because public functions in the market system rest in the hands of businessmen, it follows that jobs, prices, production, growth, the standard of living, and the economic security of everyone all rest in their hands."[175] Accordingly, "government officials cannot be indifferent to how well business performs its functions."[176] Government and industry are built on a two-way street. Most "decisions about investment, job creation, and wages . . . are made by private capitalists," but "capitalists do not invest unless there is a reasonable guarantee that their capital is physically (and legally) secure and that it will return a profit to them."[177] The state looks to maintain business confidence by ensuring a favorable business climate.

Markets have powerful mechanisms besides money in politics to keep governments in check: "reduced investment, unemployment, declining public revenues, . . . lower standards of living . . . unwillingness or reluctance to finance public debt [and] capital flight."[178] The importance of a favorable business climate and the ability of companies to pick where they operate have led to "competition among countries for business, which drives down taxes on corporations, weakens health and environmental protections, and undermines what used to be viewed as the 'core' labor rights."[179] Jessup was not exaggerating when he noted the "veto power of business confidence."[180] Can the state really afford to show indifference towards the conditions required by capitalism?

Lindblom points out that hard economic times "can bring down a government,"[181] but this is true not just because voters value employment and the growth of their retirement funds. The state itself—including all of its employees and agencies—also has a vested interest in economic growth: tax revenues shrink or grow with the economy itself. Here the dependence principle from before is written in capital letters. It is not just that officeholders depend on their contributors and often the very industries that their contributors tend to inhabit. It is also the case that the "policy capabilities of the state are always dependent upon the success and continuity of the accumulation process."[182] Massive privatization controls regulations in another way as well: "[T]he information required by the [government] agency may be obtainable only from the regulated industries; lack of expertise in the subject-matter may mean that the agency has to recruit officials from those industries; and the industries may threaten the agency with costly, or even trivial, time-wasting appeals should it fail to be 'co-operative.'"[183]

Why is so much money in politics necessary, given these "constraints [on government] imposed by the requirements of private accumulation"?[184] Is the political market really necessary in order for capitalism to keep democracy in check? A naive answer to that question is that lobbyists, special interests, and political spending serve only as "transmission belts between capital and the state," communicating to the state "what business 'needs' to restore its confidence."[185] Given the government's interest in business confidence, it does not follow that useful information would be received only if accompanied by a large check. Moreover, it is the Court itself—the defender of the rights of capital—that maintains political finance as a market, which in turn is what makes access to officeholders so expensive to begin with. So elaborate a scheme is hardly necessary to ensure that business interests can communicate capitalism's general requirements.

Let us assume for the sake of argument that the veto power of business confidence is not enough to keep the U.S. government in line, and that the welfare state and government regulations really are suffocating capitalism.

If money in politics functioned to secure general conditions favorable to capitalism, what would we expect to see? Those who feel themselves "condemned to slave labor" by virtue of helping the worse off in society would logically respond by pressuring government to reduce taxes to the minimum level—presumably that required to fund the military, police, basic infrastructure, and the courts. This does occur, and money in politics is one of the ways this goal is pursued, but money in politics pursues far more than tax issues, far more even than a reduction in costly regulations.

The "defensive spending" explanation is unsatisfactory because money in politics is also used to obtain government subsidies and regulations that harm commercial rivals. A great deal of money in politics pursues the "short-term interests of capitalists in maintaining or increasing the immediate profitability of their particular company or business sector."[186] This is an expensive endeavor because government would not naturally favor particular capitalists or particular industries over others. Capitalists would have to distinguish themselves in order to give officeholders and parties reasons for favoring them over their competitors. Indeed, we would expect a great deal of money in politics if business interests were competing for government favors, not providing valuable information for how to achieve overall economic growth and maximize business confidence.

Rent seeking is not a principled response to the regulatory state or a principled defense of overall economic health. The interests of capitalism itself are like the public interest. Who has the incentive to pursue them? When particular companies and interests use money in politics to "manipulat[e] wealth transfers away from the unorganized public" and towards themselves, they do not don the dignified garb of capitalism's emissaries.[187] They don the trench coat of the crony capitalist.

CHAPTER 7

Capitalism and Democracy Reconciled

DESPITE JUST SUFFERING THROUGH THE WORST FINANCIAL crisis since the Great Depression, almost 70 percent of Americans believe that "people are better off in a free-market economy."[1] The 2009 survey revealing this belief even cautioned respondents that free markets undergo "severe ups and downs from time to time." A related 2010 poll found that "86 percent of Americans have a positive image of free enterprise." Arthur Brooks summarized the results: "[N]o matter how the issue is posed, not more than 30 percent of Americans say they believe we would fare better without free markets at the core of our system[—]we are essentially a 70–30 nation."[2]

The destruction of campaign finance reform and the flourishing of political markets would seem to respond to the public's view that markets should reside at the core of our system. And yet, Americans reject money in politics by at least that same 70–30 margin. More than 70 percent of Americans, Democrats and Republicans included, oppose the holding in *Citizens United*.[3] More than 70 percent of Americans support campaign finance reform.[4] Can widespread support for free market capitalism be reconciled with widespread opposition to free market democracy? Can Americans have it both ways?

Let it be. The Court's command to state and federal lawmakers appears neutral, as though by stepping back and removing limits on money in politics, democracy would be freer, more democratic, more inherently its own self. But the object of laissez-faire in money-in-politics cases is not democracy at all, much less neutrality. The Court's command is that lawmakers let political markets be, that the tethers on capitalism within the political sphere be untied, and that political capitalists be free to make democracy their own. At its root, this is a case of market expansion. Theories, legal analysis, and political ideology aside, the fact of the money-in-politics cases is that the Court has kept profitable fields open for exploitation. So long as there are profits to be made, investors and firms will come, and the logic of competition and innovation will sweep aside ethics that are less immediately productive.

To let it be is to open up a particular terrain to whatever motivations and plans flourish there. The profit motive is among the most universal and the most indelible. Who among us would not like to have a greater facility to acquire whatever it is we value? Who among us would not like to gain, indeed to gain in ever-increasing amounts? Few can imagine a scenario in which human beings would cease to count this as a powerful behavioral drive. That said, the profit motive is not a good judge of what is just or even what is conducive to material prosperity in the long run.

Observe how these formulations make no sense: "He made a profit on it, so that must be good." "She has found ways to do it more efficiently and produce more of it than her competitors, and therefore we admire her." "He has improved on it, and so we're delighted." "They've eased the rules on it, making it cheaper to do. This is good news." The profit of each individual capitalist may be justification enough for most individual capitalists, just as getting something of high quality for a low price is usually justification enough for whoever wants that thing. But for many capitalists, many consumers, and certainly for the remainder of the general population, there are other factors in play. And so whether we agree with the formulations above depends on whether we are talking about a market for slaves, cocaine, gigolos, body parts, sexual tourism, elephant tusks, standardized test scores, iPads, running shoes, or hybrid cars. Americans support markets, but on this score we come out 7–3 against them (and even when we favor markets, we oppose sweatshops and desire safety regulations). The terrain itself matters—its flora, fauna, and customary ways. The social goals and values located there are not always amenable to profit.

Such encounters between the profit motive and other goals and values embody a conflict between capitalism and another social system, such as a religious creed, a particular version of family values, educational precepts, or medical ethics. These are cases in which the expansion of the economic sphere is opposed by the conceptions that dominate some other part of society. Overall gross domestic product would almost certainly rise if abortion were deregulated and marijuana and prostitution were legalized. What would be good for the economy, however, need not be good for all other parts of society and their associated value systems. The resulting turf wars are viciously subjective, for one social sphere and its associated value system must yield to the other in the end. Of course there may be rifts within the same sphere—multiple value systems—such that many consider abortion, drug use, and prostitution acceptable within the realms of body and soul. Be that as it may, capitalism will lose out only if the prerogatives of another value system defeat it.

Occasionally, though, one comes across a different sort of case: one where the profit motive is operational, where the terrain, when liberalized, is saturated by capitalists, but where the expansion of markets defies capitalist precepts and threatens the economy itself. This sort of case arose most recently with certain mortgage products and speculative investment instruments that made a great deal of money for some capitalists at the expense of the general public and the integrity of capitalism. Although regulatory failures in these areas led to the efficient production and wide distribution of these products, they also led to a massive decline in overall wealth and a widespread loss of confidence—in sum, a systemic failure. No defender of capitalism would endorse the behavior of those particular capitalists, who will be remembered, one hopes, as traitors, not traders. Capitalism transcends individual profit and, indeed, must guard against some applications of the profit motive.

This brings us back to the political influence industry and the incentives facing candidates, officeholders, and parties in a privately financed system. Are the markets for political office and public policy that are home to those viciously subjective turf wars resolvable only when one system triumphs over another? Is this capitalism versus democracy? Or is this a case of capitalists versus capitalism and democracy? If the incentives within political markets go against the integrity of capitalism itself, then capitalism and democracy would be allies in the struggle for political finance reform. The terrible irony would be that the Court, in using capitalist ideology to liberalize political markets, has undermined capitalism itself. The cause for hope, on the other hand, would be the American public's clarity of mind, its vehement support for both capitalism and campaign finance reform.

I. MONEY IN POLITICS:
AN ASSAULT ON CAPITALISM

In the era of corporate conglomeration, rising inequality, sweatshops, faulty financial products, and a full frontal assault on unions and environmental laws, it is easy to forget capitalism's emancipatory pedigree. Capitalism responded to the injustice of mercantilism, the system that happened to be subjugating the American colonies at the time of the Revolutionary War. The same empire that oppressed the people's capacity for self-authorship in politics was doing something similar in the economy. Mercantilist doctrine provided for the sort of capitalism that strengthens the state first and foremost—state capitalism. A primary goal, observed Adam Smith, was to "increase the quantity of gold and silver in any country by turning the balance of trade in its favour."[5] It led governments to grant monopolies to favored people, impose tariffs to protect domestic manufacturers from foreign competitors, and acquire colonies for purposes of extracting raw materials, capturing a market for goods, and increasing tax revenue. Mercantilism routed self-interest through crooked and inefficient channels, seeking to ensure that its produce accrued to the state.

Smith saw his way through the mists of centuries. He noted in human beings "the propensity to truck, barter, and exchange one thing for another."[6] Individuals could not freely exercise those propensities in a market controlled by the state. Without free exchange, effort and ability would not reliably translate into results, and incentives to make the most of one's abilities were absent. Smith proposed cooperation through voluntary exchange as an alternative. This is what Milton Friedman would come to call "the central principle of a market economy."[7] Its driving force was simple: "Individuals co-operate with others because they can in this way satisfy their own wants more effectively."[8] Smith ascribed a collective purpose to self-interest, writing that "[t]he natural effort of every individual to better his own condition, when suffered to exert itself with freedom and security, is so powerful a principle, that it is alone, and without any assistance . . . capable of carrying on the society to wealth and prosperity[.]"[9]

In Smith's view, the pursuit of self-interest and the resulting benefit to the individual and the collective alike is a function of freedom, not the reason freedom is due. Smith located something more than materialism and social welfare in voluntary exchange, making the free market more than a euphemism for greed or gains. He believed in "sacred and inviolable" rights, which included each person's property in their own labor. The workman had the right to dispose of his labor as he pleased and others had the right to offer him employment if they wished.[10] If nobody, not even the government, could obligate anyone to go into a particular line of work, serve a particular master, hire a particular laborer, buy a particular product, or sell at a particular price, then society would move closer to an ideal later articulated by Ayn Rand, one that would have pleased Smith: "[M]en [must] deal with one another as free, independent individuals, on the premise that every man is an end in himself."[11] Smith called government interference on these scores "a manifest encroachment upon . . . just liberty."[12] Absent such interference, he predicted, "the obvious and simple system of natural liberty [would] establish[] itself of its own accord."[13] He counseled that while respecting the "laws of justice," "[e]very man [be] left perfectly free to pursue his own interest his own way, and to bring both his industry and capital into competition with those of any other man."[14]

The right of individuals to compete on the basis of their resources and abilities brings us back to the collective purpose of self-interest—Smith's assertion that, under the right conditions, the natural effort of each individual would carry society to prosperity. Instead of the "authoritative allocation of work or rewards," capitalism aimed at "contractual relations between free individuals . . . who calculate their most profitable courses of action and employ their resources as that calculation dictates."[15] The rights to do as one pleased and keep what one earned provided powerful incentives. The other side of the coin offered powerful motivation as well, the sort that arises from the possibility of failure and the certainty that if one does fail there will be no recourse other than getting up and trying again. Thus motivated to generate the greatest possible value with his labor and capital, Smith famously posited that each man would increase society's wealth, "led by an invisible hand to promote an end which was no part of his intention."[16]

Capitalism's design does not tolerate all ways of using one's capital to generate value. Smith's stipulation about respecting the laws of justice tells us only so much: one cannot use one's capital to purchase guns and rob banks. This might generate more gains than any other use of one's capital, but it would be unlawful and it would not benefit society as a whole. In reality, the invisible hand theory is a brilliant deductive device. If we expect beneficial collective results from a bunch of individuals freely employing their labor and capital, what does this tell us about *how* that labor and capital are to be employed?

A. The Pull Peddler, the Crony Capitalist, and the End of Economic Competition

Consider the basic design laid out by Smith and his descendants, the one that we continue to rely on to this day. Once individuals have a right to what is theirs (property), feel confident in their ability to make binding agreements for mutual gain (contract), and are assured that the state will protect them from coercion (police powers), then they can focus their energies and assets on what they do best (freely chosen, productive activity), sell it to others, and acquire from others what they are less suited to produce themselves. The division of labor that forms from these incentives for specialization leads to increases in skill through repetition, efficiency through focusing on the implements of one calling instead of many occupations, productivity from all of these, innovation from the material incentive and practical knowledge to increase quality and production, and an efficient (and morally defensible) allocation of resources from all of the above.[17]

Again, bank robbery is ruled out. Although the bank robber could certainly increase his skill, efficiency, and productivity, and even pioneer new techniques, he is using force and taking other people's property. And he is not offering anyone else anything of value in exchange. Although the bank robber might get rich and become a leader in his "industry," an economy cannot be built or sustained in this way. What, then, about the lobbyist? The lobbyist is not technically robbing anyone. He does increase his skills and productivity, and his profession has led to innovations in political access and political influence, two perfectly legal and highly valuable commodities offered for exchange. Or what about the businesswoman who devotes some of her capital to the lobbyist's services, obtains political influence and special legislative terms, and thereby surpasses her competitors?

Rather than rely on a progressive activist to make the point, let us ask Ayn Rand, one of capitalism's most notable celebrators and a dedicated conservative icon. Are there limits to the freedom of choice guaranteed by capitalism? Should we rejoice in the freedom to spend one's money on lobbyists and campaign contributions, in the freedom to choose one's own career as a political influence peddler and offer one's services in the market? Rand initially gives a wide-open view of preferences: "Since values are to be discovered by man's mind, men must be free to discover them—to think, to study, to translate their knowledge into physical form, to offer their products for trade, to judge them, and to choose, be it material goods or ideas."[18] "Every man must judge for himself," she writes, "in the context of his own . . . goals and interests."[19] Economic power, she continues, "is the power to produce and to trade what one has produced."[20] Thus far, it would seem as though capitalism would rejoice at one's decision to work as a lobbyist, bundle campaign funds, leverage political contacts, produce as much political influence as one is able, and allow others to reach their own decisions as to whether they value that product enough to purchase it.

Then Rand enlightens us with a distinction. On the one hand, she gives us Andrew Carnegie and Commodore Vanderbilt, among other "giants of American industry[,] self-made men who earned their fortunes by personal ability, by free trade on a market."[21] On the other hand, she gives us "another kind of businessmen . . . the men with political pull, who made fortunes by means of special privileges granted to them by the government."[22] Citing the leaders of the Central Pacific Railroad, Rand contends that "the political power behind their activities—the power of forced, unearned, economically unjustified privileges— . . . caused dislocations in the country's economy, hardships, depressions, and mounting public protests."[23] In his contribution to Rand's book, a young Alan Greenspan criticized the "kind of promoters who always exist on the fringe of the business community and who are constantly seeking an 'easy deal.'"[24] These fringe capitalists acquired land grants from the government—massive subsidies that were offered to individual companies without competitive bidding.

Rand and her coauthors saw lobbying as an inevitable response to a government legislating "in the public interest."[25] With vast legislative powers to be directed in the pursuit of whatever was deemed the public interest,

Rand notes how a fight ensues to define that interest in one's favor, such that "so grotesque a profession as lobbying (selling 'influence') becomes a full-time job."[26] In what she called "a civil war of pressure-groups looting and devouring each other," Rand understood that government policy "has to swing like an erratic pendulum from group to group, hitting some and favoring others, at the whim of any given moment."[27] She described exactly what we see in today's political market, noting that legislators "who would not sell out their country for a million dollars are selling it out for somebody's smile and a vacation trip to Florida."[28] Rand considered "actual corruption . . . not a major motivating factor in today's situation," citing instead "the manipulations of little lawyers and public relations men pulling the mental strings of lifeless automatons."[29]

Rand understood that political markets are not a legitimate part of the free market economy itself. This is the crux of the issue. The pendulum swing of government favor awards "legislative actions which grant[] special privileges (*not obtainable on a free market*)" such as "special franchises, licenses, [and] subsidies."[30] It is easy to tell that businesspeople who obtain such privileges do not fit into the capitalist design, as articulated by Nathaniel Branden, another one of Rand's coauthors: "[A]ny man or company that can surpass competitors is free to do so"; this is how "the free market rewards ability and works for the benefit of everyone—except those who seek the undeserved"; "[n]o one can morally claim the right to compete in a given field if he cannot match the productive efficiency of those with whom he hopes to compete."[31]

The political market bypasses the economic market, achieving economic advantages in a way that is corrupt from a capitalist standpoint. Subsidies can mask productive inefficiencies and enable producers to offer artificially low prices. Then it is not necessarily the "purveyor of the best product at the cheapest price who wins the greatest financial rewards in the field,"[32] as capitalism stipulates, but rather the beneficiary of government favors. Competition is then re-routed from the economic market into the political market. We all know, however, that firms are supposed to triumph or be vanquished on the basis of their ability to offer good products at competitive prices, on their ability to innovate and capitalize on talents, resources, and technology. If it must be the case, as John Kenneth Galbraith quipped, that "the purpose of economic competition is to eliminate competition," capitalism at least requires that such a cutthroat affair be properly conducted.

Competition is, in Galbraith's words, "[t]he first requirement of the classical system,"[33] thought to lead to better products, lower prices, and overall social gains. But with channels of political influence open, capitalists have three ways to compete, instead of only one: improve their products and their efficiency of production; pursue political conditions (subsidies, special tax breaks, and the like) favorable to their business or unfavorable to their rivals; or, to be safe, pursue both channels simultaneously. As Lessig puts it, "It's one thing to invent the light bulb and thereby become a billionaire . . . and another thing to use your financial power to capture political power, and then use political power to change the laws to make you even richer."[34] Thomas Edsall sums up the forms of these laws: "[T]he companies and trade associations that dominate top-dollar lobbyists' clientele are seeking to protect their own legislated competitive advantages, including special tax breaks, favorable procurement rules and government regulations that prevent new challengers from entering the marketplace."[35]

Examples are commonplace. Citing the price protection measures won by the steel industry during Carter's presidency, and the auto industry's political victory under Reagan, limiting Japanese competitors in the U.S. market, Robert Lekachman concluded: "For large corporations, it frequently makes better sense to lobby in Washington and state capitols than to improve the efficiency of their operations or the quality of their products."[36] Lessig provides several modern-day examples, including high-fructose corn syrup, sugar, steel, lumber, and dairy products. These are only several of the areas in which the government gives handouts to domestic producers, sets prices, or charges tariffs on foreign products being brought to the U.S. market. Reviewing the studies on point, Lessig reports that government price controls and subsidies have "increase[d] the price of milk by about 26 percent" and have made it so that cheese and butter cost 37% and 100% more, respectively, than in other countries.[37] Meanwhile, tariffs on foreign sugar producers have given the domestic sugar industry "about $1 billion in extra profits a year [while costing] the overall economy (through increased prices and inefficiency) about $3 billion."[38]

The pattern is simple: lobbying by special interests, especially the most powerful and most organized special interests, increases profits at consumers' expense. Archer Daniels Midland, for example, made over $69 billion in 2009, but almost half of those profits came from products "heavily subsidized or protected by the American government."[39] "[E]very $1 of profits earned by ADM's corn sweetener operation costs consumers $10, and every $1 of profits earned by its ethanol operation costs taxpayers $30."[40] Lessig notes that the "world's richest and most powerful corporate farmers" receive the largest agricultural subsidies."[41] His conclusion supports Lekachman's: the "beneficiaries of these policies spend an enormous amount to keep them."[42] Regulations, subsidies, taxes, and tax breaks are justified as being in the "public interest" but are most often the products of fierce lobbying by business or industries seeking a competitive advantage over one another.[43]

Perhaps the simplest form is a no-bid contract from the government awarded in earmarks attached to legislation.[44] Patrick Bernhagen spots "price-fixing and other anti-competitive behaviour rais[ing] entry barriers to new competitors," which "thwart the efficiencies of the market economy."[45] Take, for example, the 2008–2009 bailouts of failed banks and automakers. When the government comes to the rescue of businesses, bailing them out with taxpayer money, it socializes losses. When the remedy for failure is bankruptcy and the disappearance of companies, only to be replaced by incipient ones, intent on doing things differently, employing a different business plan, and, one hopes, a different corporate culture, then we have a powerful incentive for responsible planning and a powerful disincentive for unnecessary risk taking. What do bailouts say to those firms' competitors who avoided making the sorts of decisions that led to failure? In sum, firms thus come to triumph over others on the basis of their ability to secure favorable legislation and, this being common knowledge, political spending becomes a cost of doing business.[46]

In economic terms, political spending is a deadweight loss. It does not contribute directly to productive activity, to efficiency, to innovation, or to any other purpose of capitalism. This would be bad enough if all groups spent the same amount of money and received the same amount of attention from legislators. In that case, there would be tremendous waste, but public policy on the whole need not be compromised. Gary Becker, a Nobel Prize–winning economist at the University of Chicago, has studied the relationship between interest groups and government policies that promote efficiency and growth. He notes that inequalities in the relative power of interest groups can lead to government policies that are wasteful and inefficient for society as a whole, policies that promote the well-being of numerically small groups at the expense of the rest of us. Becker writes that "if all groups have the same number of members and the same skill of producing influence, costly redistributions would not survive the political process because losers would be willing to spend more opposing them than gainers would spend supporting them."[47] Imagine just how wasteful this would be. Still, Becker describes an even worse scenario—the status quo. "[I]f groups have highly unequal access to political influence, costly redistributions would be common, and many programs that raise social output would not be undertaken because of strong opposition from powerful groups that would be harmed."[48]

This is a common result within the economic literature, where it is generally found that "interest group politics is skewed dramatically toward narrow economic interests."[49] As the wealthy obtain government favors, they obtain more advantages in the market, greater profit, and consequently an ever-greater ability to extract additional rents from the government. As economist Lawrence Katz put it, "[H]igh inequality can generate further high inequality and eventually poor economic growth."[50] Citing the financial sector's "lobbying clout" and the elite's "superior access to the political system to protect their interests," Francis Fukuyama concludes that the "current concentration of wealth in the United States has already become self-reinforcing."[51] When the tilt of interest-group competition towards the wealthy reaps its harvest, we get familiar produce: corporate bailouts, rising inequality, "socialism for tycoons and capitalism for the rest of us," or the privatization of profits and the socialization of risk.[52]

The union of government with the economic elite portends a change in our economic and political systems, an unholy union between the two. The result is a strange parallel to the economic system that Adam Smith condemned and the American revolutionaries overthrew. Mercantilism consisted in the state commandeering economic actors and processes for its own benefit. Today, private parties lobby the state to interfere in the economy for their own benefit, a sort of reverse mercantilism. To put it more strongly, economic actors commandeer the state just as state actors before had commandeered the economy. The beneficiaries have changed, but the economic interference is similar. And the general public still loses out as before, because competition is unfair, the price mechanism distorted, and the invisible hand tethered. It is no wonder that the economic tides of late have not raised all boats.

Robert Heilbroner predicted that "[t]he twenty-first century will be dominated by a spectrum of capitalisms, some successful, some not."[53] "The crucial question for Americans," he noted, "is where our own nation will be located along that spectrum."[54] In light of what we have seen, owning up to our current location will be an uncomfortable exercise. Economist Richard Freeman writes that the "economic interests of small groups of 'crony capitalists' have come to dominate government responses to the financial crisis and ensuing recession."[55] "The danger," he concludes, "is not an ever-expanding state, per Hayek's road to serfdom, but of a move to economic feudalism, in which a small set of wealthy masters dominate markets and the state and subvert or outsmart efforts to regulate their behavior or rein them in."[56]

Similar to economic feudalism and crony capitalism is the Marxist designation, state monopoly capitalism, "a distinct stage of capitalism characterised by the fusion of monopoly forces with the bourgeois state to form a single mechanism of economic exploitation and political domination."[57] Monopoly forces are the large firms that dominate industries. The calling cards of this sort of capitalism are the "close, organic connection between monopoly capital and the state" and the purpose of "advanc[ing] the struggle to consolidate the economic and political domination of monopoly capital in the face of opposition from the oppressed classes."[58] Bob Jessup characterizes the transition to monopoly capital in all-too-familiar terms: the "public finance of private investment and production"[59] and the expansion of the state's economic role "in order to maintain the profitability of monopoly capital."[60]

As if this were not enough to send shivers down one's spine (in light of notable bailouts, subsidies, and tariffs), Jessup adds that during the transition to monopoly capital the state "must also step up its political and ideological role to protect the political power of the [monopoly capital]."[61] Now he has taken us from bailouts and subsidies to the ideological function of the Supreme Court, which insists, case after case, upon legitimizing the political role of monied interests. The transformation of money into speech and corporations into citizens exemplifies this ideological function.

Although interest-group competition and government favors are tilted in favor of the most powerful economic interests, it is an exaggeration to speak of a single mechanism of economic and political domination, as though monopoly capital were entirely coordinated and as though it had cornered the market for political influence. Even present-day Marxists tend to recognize that "corporate elites are inherently incapable of organizing themselves as a class" and so their use of capital for domination is not the all-encompassing conspiracy that the familiar caricature suggests.[62] On the whole, it is more accurate to speak of "market rivalries between individual companies and conflicts of interest between different industries [that] direct corporate elites towards pursuing the specific interests of their particular company or industry."[63] "Crony capitalism" is an accurate description of our present economic system because it allows for all sorts of rent seeking by all sorts of actors. There need be no conspiracy. But even somewhat uncoordinated rent seeking by a variety of interests for a variety of purposes still connotes severe damage to the capitalist design for the essential reason given before: it routes economic competition through political channels, bypassing the mechanism of economic competition and nullifying capitalism's moral and collective justifications.

Crony capitalism, with its responsiveness to the largest political spenders, is a particularly bad model for global economic competition. The national goal should be to generate the sort of capitalism that makes the United States competitive enough that protectionism would be against our interests—the sort of capitalism that would make the elimination of subsidies and tariffs a smart move. This would mean fomenting a dynamic economy, not an oligarchic one in which large firms maintain their positions through political spending. Innovations often come from smaller and newer companies, precisely those that are disadvantaged in interest-group competition. These entrepreneurial forces can be artificially restrained by their larger competitors who pull political strings more forcefully. Plus, entrepreneurial capitalists have only limited overlap with large, entrenched firms.

While start-ups may require subsidies in order to get off the ground, that sort of government intervention is forward-thinking and more likely to be short-lived. Progressive measures—such as research grants available on an equal basis to all firms pioneering valuable technologies, and tax breaks for sustainable energy companies and for consumers buying hybrid cars—could indeed benefit entrepreneurial capitalism and lead to overall wealth creation in the midterm. But these sorts of interventions tend to be the kind that independent officeholders would make of their own accord, not the kind that indebted officeholders are induced to make by the wealthier interests and well-established industries that supply the better part of political funds. Given its bias towards large firms, crony capitalism is the enemy of entrepreneurial capitalism and, indeed, competitive capitalism itself.

The 70 percent of the public that supports free market capitalism surely has competitive capitalism in mind. Besides the strong intuition that most people would not support crony capitalists and large firms that gain economic advantages through political influence, we already know that 70 percent of the public favors campaign finance reform and opposes corporate political expenditures. This proves that the public is against crony capitalism. The political finance limitations supported by the overwhelming majority of Americans can now be seen as protecting capitalism, not just democracy. This is the less obvious purpose of those important reforms, the same reforms ruled out, ironically enough, by the Court's capitalist ideology.

B. The Invisible Hand or the Invisible Fist?

The crony capitalist corrodes the mechanism of economic competition by using political favors to get ahead. Those offering the best products and the lowest prices can find themselves outpaced by less-efficient or less-talented (or possibly equally efficient and talented) competitors who obtain any number of government advantages—advantages not available in a free market.[64] Because many government favors take the form of economic intervention (whether at the behest of pressure groups or officeholders attempting to extract concessions from private interests), it would seem that the remedy would be the scaling back of government itself, not merely the reform of political finance. Given the biased, unprincipled government actions we have seen thus far, perhaps Ayn Rand was right on all counts—not just that the pull peddlers and crony capitalists corrupt capitalism, but that capitalism's fate is sealed so long as the government possesses broad authority to legislate in the public interest.

The function of money in politics is not merely to produce inefficient government interventions into the economy, however. Pull peddlers and crony capitalists also seek to *prevent efficient government intervention*. The truth is strange indeed: capitalism's competitive mechanism can be jammed just as effectively by government inaction as by government action itself. Consider what it means, for example, when money in politics targets environmental standards and enforcement, tort law, and automobile emissions standards. Here interest groups ask the government to refrain from doing things that are essential for the integrity of capitalism.

What oil company has the incentive to clean up its spills in the absence of oversight? Responding to spills is costly, as are pollution controls on smokestacks, automobile emissions rules, and product safety requirements. Without well-enforced government rules in such areas, companies could offer lower prices by foisting the cost of cleanups, pollution, and injuries onto others: in the case of air pollution, society in general (including future generations); in the case of unsafe products, the unlucky consumers who get injured and are denied a legal remedy; in the case of oil spills, taxpayers (the government would have to pay to clean up the mess).

These harms are often hard to trace. Birth defects from chemicals in water or food show up years later. The same is true of asthma in children who grow up breathing dirty air and the decline of ecosystems altered by deforestation (say, for example, to clear land for the grazing of cows soon to become hamburgers). When harms are hard to trace, social pressure on offending companies is rarely forthcoming, and consumers are likely to choose, all other things equal, the cheaper product. Indeed, in today's economy, ignorance is bliss. The sound of one's enjoyment going down the drain becomes audible as soon as one realizes how technological gadgets are manufactured (e.g., the iPad sweatshop controversy), how meat is produced (fertilizer run-off into water supplies, the use of antibiotics and growth hormones later absorbed by humans, or the unconscionable treatment of animals), or what is involved in driving that practical SUV or exciting sports car (carbon emissions, global warming, and increased dependency on foreign oil often produced in countries that sponsor terrorism or abuse human rights).[65]

Capitalism can live with unclean consciences. Distortions in the price mechanism, on the other hand, it detests and ultimately cannot survive. Take, for example, the situation of consumers in the market for a new car. They weigh many factors, price being just one of them. But between two equally appealing models manufactured by two reputable companies offering similar warranties and similar financing, it is reasonable to assume that price will be the decisive factor. Now, imagine that Company A has distinguished itself in a number of respects from Company B, minimizing its environmental footprint, perhaps even running a carbon-neutral production facility, constructing a safe workplace for its employees, and investing in top-of-the-line product-safety checks so as to ensure that defective parts are screened out of the assembly process.[66] If Company B does not have to pay for its environmental harms, its workplace injuries, or accidents caused by defective parts, it will have a sizable advantage over Company A in the form of lower operational costs. All other things equal, Company B can then price its cars lower than Company A, gaining an advantage in the market that can be compounded through investing profits in advertising, equipment upgrades, or research and development.

So long as pollution control, workplace safety, and product safety are voluntary, and the associated harms are hard to trace, no rational company will internalize those costs.[67] A well-intentioned company that pushes ahead in the name of social responsibility risks being surpassed by its competitors or pushed into niche markets that cater to conscientious consumers, a small subset of all consumers—those who are concerned about the effects of their purchasing behavior and can afford to pay higher prices.

In order to avoid the cost and inconvenience of making companies pay for all injuries case by case, the government establishes generally applicable standards as law—such as standards for pollution control and automobile safety. Also, the government does sustain a case-by-case mechanism, tort law, that allows injured parties legal recourse against a variety of parties, including employers and product manufacturers. In the contexts of general regulations and tort law, government intervention forces producers to incorporate the unintended costs of their products into their operational costs, thus allowing economic competition to do its work (here, through the integrity of the price mechanism). The price of products is supposed to reflect the operational costs undertaken in order to produce them and maintain them on the market. As operational costs come to reflect the overall cost of the product, it can be said that something closer and closer to the true price is set.

If negative externalities—these unintended costs of products—are not incorporated into prices, careless and destructive companies gain an advantage over their more conscientious rivals, those who have invested in safety measures, pollution controls, and the like. This is the obvious effect of government inaction. The less obvious effect is buried within capitalism's suicide course. Facing artificially low prices, consumer behavior is distorted. Consumers will buy the wrong products, the right products from the wrong producers, or the right products in the wrong amounts. It is in this sense that Heilbroner remarks, "[E]xternalities undermine a vaunted function of the market, which is to guide resources to their most rational use."[68] The price mechanism is what "coordinate[s] the activity of millions of people, each seeking his own interest, in such a way as to make everyone better off" and it does so "without central direction."[69] This returns us to the collective functions of capitalism, and the essential role of government in setting the conditions under which the price system can obtain accurate measurements.

Once government requires that externalities be incorporated into firms' operational costs, the invisible hand can begin, once again, to do its work. The self-interest of each company will then lead it to adopt some pollution controls and product safety measures, at least at the level required by law. The self-interest of the person shopping for a car will lead that person to choose the more responsible manufacturer only when responsible manufacturers cannot be undercut by unscrupulous rivals who save money by forgoing such measures. When regulations targeting externalities are passed as generally applicable measures that do not contain favors for the particular companies that fund campaigns and parties, those regulations favor capitalism.

The interest-group pressures of crony capitalism do not always prevent the government from acting. When externalities visibly affect many individuals in shocking ways, then social mobilization stands a chance of overpowering the pull peddlers and their clients. Such was the case with unsafe working conditions and inhumane wages and hours in the wake of the Industrial Revolution, exploding gas tanks and the consumer rights movement in the 1970s, lung cancer and lawsuits against cigarette manufacturers in the 1990s and 2000s, and even local pollution regulations for companies operating alongside rivers and ocean bays when the river becomes so polluted as to catch fire or the bay so polluted as to prevent local residents from swimming. Such battles still require significant funds and organizational clout on the side of affected parties. They often go on far too long, thanks to the disproportionate political power of moneyed interests; and when victory is obtained, the balance of political spending softens the penalties for offending companies. Indeed, the deck is stacked so mercilessly that many battles are not begun in the first place. Still, tangible and shocking externalities stand a chance of being corrected. The victims, being singled out and affected in extreme ways, have an incentive to press their case.[70]

Other times, externalities have only general, long-term effects such that few concrete victims are shocked into action. In such cases, social concern does not generate enough economic or organizational capital to rival the concentrated interests responsible for the externalities. Consider the fact that the United States is one of the most lenient countries in terms of vehicle emissions and mileage standards, "lagging as much as 10 m.p.g. behind the rest of the world."[71] This is partially the result of intense lobbying by the automotive industry, which insists that high-emissions cars are cheaper to make and, naturally, easier to sell. Because climate change inflicts long-term costs on society—indeed, on the world as a whole—few particular actors have the incentive to oppose the concentrated interests in the oil and automotive industries, and convince government that it must act more forcefully. And even though some do take action, there are hardly any associations in any sector of society that could match the concentrated economic power emanating from these industries.

The status quo promises to linger even though the latest polls show that we are a 70–30 nation in this regard as well: 70 percent of Americans believe climate change is responsible for the severe weather of recent years.[72] When candidates funded by these industries and their various allies are elected to office, it is of little surprise that environmental protection is one of the first government activities to be placed on the chopping block.[73] As with climate, so with clean air, clean water, and the protection of endangered species.

Free markets have led to dirty air, dirty oceans, and climate change, and, if we let them, they would also lead to insufficient police protection, the disrepair of highways, and insufficient national defense. This is something that all economists know, but the Supreme Court refuses to acknowledge. Cass Sunstein explains that "it is not feasible to provide defense or clean air to one person without simultaneously providing it to many people or to everyone."[74] That is why these goods are "nonexcludable." Why would one person pay for clean air or national defense knowing that all others, even non-payers, would get the same benefit? That person would rightly expect others to pay too and would be hesitant to absorb all the costs. Absent government coordination and spending, public goods will suffer from the "free rider" problem: those who do not pay for clean air get the same benefits as those who do, and therefore everyone has an incentive to sit back and wait for someone else to foot the bill. When it comes to the political market, then, it is disastrous for the system to "produce just that set of decisions (or, that allocation of political goods) which the citizens are willing to pay for."[75]

We come at last to a market view of the Constitution that possesses greater wisdom than the Roberts Court's ode to crony capitalism. Richard Epstein maintains that "the business of constitutions is . . . to ensure that legislation will work on those things for which markets fail—such as defense, social order, and other common pool problems."[76] Jon Elster concurs, citing cases in which the common good "cannot be realized as the aggregate outcome of individuals pursuing their private interests."[77] Noting that "uncoordinated private choices may lead to outcomes that are worse for all than some other outcome that could have been attained by coordination," Elster describes political institutions as necessary "to remedy . . . market failures[—]an inability to provide public goods or . . . a breakdown of the self-regulating properties usually ascribed to the market mechanism."[78]

The dynamics above are not the only reasons why public goods are under-produced. It is not just that the free market economy will fail to produce them, absent government intervention; it is also the case that political markets will oppose that sort of government intervention. Government responses to pollution, climate change, dangerous products, and sharp dealing in financial markets involve trade-offs. Companies that impose costs on others stand to lose money, at least in the short term. No company wants to pay for its negative externalities, and no company wants to have to make costly changes to its operations in order for the government to protect a public good. Companies that avoid such costs through political spending gain an advantage over their rivals, and industries that do so gain an advantage over rival industries. Therefore, to the extent that the policy process is a function of the resources of the varying groups, the wealthiest interests will be better able to avoid the internalization of their externalities and to kill off regulations that protect the public good.[79] The Roberts Court's capitalist Constitution protects the political markets through which firms can avoid paying for externalities and frustrate the move to secure public goods. Accordingly, capitalism, as an approach to constitutional interpretation, calls into question the sustainability of capitalism as an approach to the economy.

Properly understood, however, the interests of capitalism are aligned with the public interest itself. Society as a whole depends on economic competition being based on economic criteria—the quality of products, the efficiency of production, and so on. The invisible hand will not work if the crony capitalists are defeating the true capitalists, or if the true capitalists are forced to moonlight as crony capitalists in order to survive. Society further depends on the integrity of the price mechanism so that consumer choices reflect the informed consent of consumers, as evidenced by their willingness to pay the true price of the product. And, by definition, society depends on the protection of public goods. As with climate instability, so too with market instability, unclean air, unclean water, and dangerous products: society suffers when capitalism is corrupted.

But who has the incentive to pursue the interests of capitalism itself? The capitalist seeks to make a profit, while capitalism seeks to maintain an overall framework in which the drive to make a profit accords with moral values of economic freedom and social goals of economic health.

Capitalists and capitalism do not have the same goals. That is the trouble. No particular company or industry has a specific incentive to sustain the capitalist system. This is another free-rider problem and another instance in which those who make conscientious choices may incur a competitive disadvantage relative to firms that cut costs, sacrificing the stability of the system in order to get ahead.

By providing for public goods, solving collective-action problems, and internalizing externalities, the government sets up a structure within which the self-interest of consumers and producers can exert itself justly and lead to social gains.[80] Take the case of firms that succeed in the market even though their products are priced at their true cost and their operations do not threaten public goods beyond levels set by law. Those firms have proved their worth and honored the system's constraints. By forcing the internalization of externalities and the protection of public goods, government harmonizes self-interest with the public interest.[81] The invisible hand then becomes benevolent.

Compare this state of affairs to one in which firms that do not wish to incorporate externalities or maintain public goods are able to use their economic power to frustrate government action. The oceans are polluted and overfished; dirty fuels continue to edge out renewable energy; the climate changes; the public bears the costs of subsidies and tariffs; and economic competition is corrupted. In the absence of limits on money in politics, the invisible hand clenches to form an invisible fist propelled by an invisible arm, delivering a beating. The victim is capitalism itself, which, in its crippled state, is proving unsustainable. Congress's repeated attempts to limit political markets ought to be understood as repeated attempts to sustain the integrity of democracy *and capitalism*.

II. TO PROTECT CAPITALISM AND DEMOCRACY, A LIBERAL ARCHITECTURE

Democracy is not designed to socialize economic production any more than capitalism is designed to privatize political representation. True, under mercantilism the state controlled the economy. But the people did not control the state; the king did, and this control was unjust from most perspectives, not just the economic one. Aristocracy and mercantilism ended simultaneously; the state and the economy were emancipated from the same master. Then, the political and the economic were parsed into distinct spheres, one encompassing "the exercise of the traditional political tasks of rulership—mainly the formation and enforcement of law" and the other "limited to the production and distribution of goods and services—that is, to the direction of the material affairs of society."[82] It was not until state and economy were liberated and separated that democracy and capitalism were born.

Heilbroner describes the resulting power-sharing arrangement as "the divided secular authority within a capitalist society."[83] Noting that "[t]his duality of realms . . . has no counterpart in noncapitalist societies," he ventures a well-informed guess: the "idea that the material provisioning of society, gladly left to the self-motivated activities of farmers, artisans, and merchants, was not in some ultimate sense under the authority of the state would never have occurred to Aristotle or Cicero or Machiavelli."[84] If we are not careful, however, a new time will come. Naming the great theorists of political future, a historian will write, "The idea that the political tasks of lawmaking and rulership were not in some ultimate sense under the authority of the economy would never have occurred to them." It is this duality of realms that blurs together today.

Having entered the economic era some time ago, seeing corporate consolidation, the globalization of big-firm capitalism, the growth of inequality, and the commercialization of countless facets of society, how should the architects of liberal democracy respond? Will the boundaries between capitalism and democracy be maintained, or will the economy become so dominant as to incorporate politics as one of its sectors? The question is whether it is problematic for economic actors to treat the state the same way that kings treated the economy during mercantilism.

A. Democracy's Invisible Hand

The economy dominating the state: it would almost be fair in the way of settling a score or as a reckoning for the plight of sister economies still enslaved in places such as China. But in the United States at least, as history's pendulum swing works its way back, the economy subjugates the people alongside the state. The old aristocratic state no longer exists, and so the economy has nothing upon which to act out its revenge. Curiously enough, having grown as strong as they have and directing their force back at the state, economic actors themselves form a new aristocracy. This is why Jefferson's warning about "a single and splendid government of an *aristocracy* founded on banking institutions and moneyed incorporations" is so interesting.[85] His solution to this "aristocracy of our monied corporations which dare already to challenge our government to a trial of strength" was to "crush [it] in its birth."[86] This terminology—aristocracy and a foreign source of power challenging our government—matches up with the domination that Jefferson knew firsthand, the one that inspired him to write the Declaration of Independence in just a few weeks' time.[87] The king was the head of an aristocracy that dominated society. Did corporations aspire to the same station?

Jefferson comes to mind for another reason as well. The breakup of economy and state into separate realms was not liberal democracy's only division. Jefferson's concern over corporate political power had a parallel in his views on another part of the First Amendment: the separation of church and state. Jefferson believed that "the church should be walled off from the state in order to safeguard secular interests (public and private) 'against ecclesiastical depredations and incursions.'"[88] Lawrence Tribe notes Jefferson's interest in barring clergy from public office and his "conviction that only the complete separation of religion from politics would eliminate the formal influence of religious institutions and provide for a free choice among political views."[89] We see in Jefferson the separatist instinct of keeping democracy autonomous from the forces that would co-opt it. Expressing this sensibility, Walzer compares "the kind of economic power that shapes and determines public policy" with "the high ecclesiastical authority that routinely calls upon the 'secular arm.'"[90]

If the Supreme Court does not blink at this sort of economic power and defends the market metaphor to such an extreme as to transform politics into an actual market, why could it not permit other constructions of the First Amendment that align the Constitution with another social system? If capitalism, then why not Christianity? Imagine that instead of linking the First Amendment with an open market, Justice Holmes's 1919 dissenting opinion linked it to an open confessional or an open mass. Given that the market metaphor has led to money as speech, corporations as citizens, and political donors and spenders as sovereign, the confessional metaphor could also be taken quite far. It could provide enhanced protection to the activities of religious organizations, so much so that these could come to dominate the political sphere.

It might seem strange to construe the First Amendment as desiring all viewpoints to be aired out in the open so that all faithful brothers and sisters could bare their souls, so that religious organizations could spread the good word, and so that the citizenry could be guided by a higher authority in its civic duties. But why is that construction any more foreign than the construction the Court has given us? Take Radin's description: "[p]olitics as a competitive market; rationality as maximizing profits[,] political theory as a species of economics, [and] man [a]s an egoistic, rational, utility maximizer."[91] Why could the human being not be understood as religious instead of economic, political theory as a species of revelation instead of a species of economics, and politics as a divine quest instead of a competitive market?

Redish writes that the First Amendment does not "prohibit the enactment of . . . a free market philosophy through the democratic process."[92] If he is referring to a philosophy to guide economic policy, then nobody should disagree. But if he is referring to a philosophy to guide constitutional interpretation and democracy's design, then all should disagree. How could Redish lose that age-old awareness that the democratic process could cease to be democratic? It is precisely that contextual grounding—a *democratic* right within a *political* document—that gives the First Amendment its inherent meaning. Why should the Constitution permit plutocracy if it does not permit theocracy, aristocracy, or dictatorship? If the Court interprets it to allow any of these alternatives to democracy to gain traction, then the Court has failed in its most elementary task.

The Supreme Court's validation of economic power within democracy interests us at its core, in its *constitutionally* misguided nature. Liberal democracy's essential structure consists of a series of separations, more than just a separation of economy and state. Here its makeup and deepest sensibilities are laid bare. The first three articles of the Constitution divide government into legislative, executive, and judicial branches. Madison called this design a "foundation for that separate and distinct exercise of the different powers of government."[93] The purpose of the separation of powers is often quoted: "Ambition must be made to counteract ambition. The interest of the man must be connected with the constitutional rights of the place."[94] This referred to the ambition of the members of the various branches who might seek to augment their powers by usurping those of another branch. The Framers wished to prevent any strong executive from bringing about the reincarnation of monarchy. The ambition of religious leaders was also accounted for—but other ambitions were not dealt with so explicitly.

Religion, the state, and the various branches within the federal government are not the only spheres in play. Our society also gives autonomy to the family, education, the professions, and of course the economy. Different values and procedures govern these spheres, such that those who gain power in one have not for that reason acquired the goods to gain power in any other.[95] Social systems that violate this design are easily named. Monarchy premises political power on family lineage—royal birth. Theocracy does so on status within a religious hierarchy. Dictatorship rests on control of the military. Plutocracy premises political power on wealth. Communism, meanwhile, premises economic power on political power. It is one thing for the patriarch or matriarch to exercise control of their clan; the priest, bishop, or cleric, his followers; the general, his soldiers; the CEO, investor, and capitalist, their companies and commercial acquisitions; the party leadership, its members, or its latest proposal for public infrastructure; and so on. But converting success in one sphere into success in another turns a pluralistic society of diverse freedoms and equalities into a regime of domination. This is why Walzer defines tyranny as "the systematic coordination of social goods and spheres of life that ought to be separate."[96] Walzer tells us that we will know the tyrant because he seeks to make his power "dominant everywhere."[97]

That recipe is evident in homages to money in politics. According to Bradley Smith, "the virtue of money contributions" is that money "allows people to use talents in one field to fulfill desires in another."[98] Hence, those who are economically successful on the basis of talents for plumbing and investment banking can use their economic power in lieu of political talents. Lumping it all together, Smith insists that "citizens are free to use their differing abilities, financial wherewithal, and personal disposition to become more or less active in political life."[99] This recalls Alito's majority opinion in *Davis*, listing candidates' "different strengths" as wealth, wealthy supporters, celebrity status, and a recognizable family name, and concluding that the government lacked the authority to decide "which strengths should be permitted to contribute to the outcome of an election."[100]

John Samples elaborates on the importance of maintaining the political role of financial power. Political finance reform "attracts people with the abilities to write well, to speak persuasively, and to manipulate the legislative agenda."[101] In light of this, he concludes that freedom of speech under conditions of economic equality will "create an inequality of influence in American politics" and "permit inequalities in talents in writing and speaking to translate into inequalities in political power."[102] "If egalitarianism is a consistent doctrine," he writes, "the expression of these talents, too, should be restricted by the state."[103] This colossal misunderstanding requires a full explanation.

Discussing political talents, Bradley Smith concludes that reducing financial inequality in politics "will make everyone more equal, even though other forms of inequality remain."[104] Walzer dispels the confusion, explaining that egalitarianism "aims at eliminating not all differences but a particular set of differences, and a different set in different times and places."[105] "The aim of political egalitarianism is a society free from domination . . . It is not a hope for the elimination of differences."[106] But Smith has a word for the state of affairs in which the role of unequal wealth has been limited within politics but inequalities in political abilities remain: "Orwellian."

In Samples's and Smith's futuristic dystopia, campaign managers, editorializing intellectuals, activists, and lawyers exercise more political influence than the rich. Or, more precisely, they fear a world in which people with talent directly applicable in politics exercise more influence than people with talent well rewarded in the economy. Would it then be dystopian for those with talents in the economic field to wield more influence over economic affairs than those with political talents? Should we hope that the influence of those with religious talents—preaching, charity work, prayer and devotion—be counterbalanced within religious affairs by those talented in sports, product advertisements, or investment banking?

Bradley Smith views money as having a natural application to politics. He alleges that money is accessible to all sorts of campaigns whose "non-economic resources may equally be traded for money";[107] then he proceeds to describe the role of volunteer canvassers, campaign managers and publicists, brain trusts, personality, good looks, good voice, and volunteer labor in drumming up donations, free press, and access to the media. He sums up "[s]uccess in electoral politics" as a function of "*capitalizing* on the assets with which a candidate begins to create the necessary assets the candidate initially lacks."[108] Walzer objects, describing money as "a dominant good . . . monopolized by people who possess a special talent for bargaining and trading."[109] But Smith believes money to be more evenly distributed than political talents,[110] and holds that democracy should come down to capitalizing (literally) on one's talents and using economic resources to generate the political talents one lacks. Again, politics as an actual market.

This returns us to the problem of economic power becoming dominant in politics. Most Americans do not believe that electoral success should depend on each candidate's and party's ability to curry favor with those who have money to fund campaigns and superPACs. Most Americans do not believe that legislative success should depend on the amount of money at one's disposal and the ingenuity of one's lobbyists. Few Americans, on the other hand, fret that a particularly powerful orator will come along and, by mere force of her eloquence, inspire the legislative agenda. Few would object if such a soul gained electoral success on the basis of her vision for the nation and her ease of connection with the body politic. The same holds for a powerful essayist, a courageous activist, or a dedicated civil servant. Political power gained through these political talents and channels would be well deserved. It need only be compared to political power premised on the political access that money buys, politicians' need to satisfy donors and spenders in order to be elected or reelected, or the financial rewards that come from aligning one's platform with that recommended by wealthy interest groups. The question today is what has happened to good faith consideration of public policy issues and genuine debate. Where have the political talents gone?

Just as money in politics disrupts the invisible hand of economic competition, it disrupts the invisible hand of democratic competition and collaboration. Rights of speech and association should naturally lead to greater political power in the hands of those with greater eloquence, energy, writing ability, charisma, aptitude for comprehending social problems, conflict resolution skills, and organizational talent. The resulting inequality is a necessary premise of liberal democracy. How else would individuals have an incentive to study the issues, develop viewpoints, explain them thoroughly and persuasively, associate with each other, engage their peers, and, on the basis of this, constantly refine and improve their positions on the issues and their political talents? If such skills, activities, and social orientations were essentially powerless—indeed, if political power turned on a separate medium altogether—then why would anybody bother to behave in a civic fashion?

Plutocracy's advocates imply that equality requires us to bleep out the most eloquent portions of a speech in order to equalize the effects of education or rhetorical skill on political outcomes, or to diminish the creative energy of a grassroots organizer in order to equalize organizational talent. They suggest that if financial resources were restricted (and thus equalized), then intellectual consistency requires equalizing all other sources of inequality. No, strange calls to equalize political talent must yield to the case for political productivity.

Capitalism and democracy both require that differences in energy, talent, creativity, shrewd deal-making, entrepreneurial spirit, and leadership reap their due rewards. The energy, talent, and creativity that we have in mind, however, are not the same in both cases, nor are the rewards that they reap. But, still, if an officeholder believes his talents have economic applications, let him abandon his post, enter the private sector and apply himself. That is a different recipe than leveraging his political power to nationalize the company he has his eye on, or leveraging his political contacts to gain favors for particular companies eager to employ him as a consultant. Similarly, if the talents of a particular capitalist are applicable to political challenges, this is not bad news. Quite the contrary: let her enter the political sphere and apply her talent for deal-making, her ability to coordinate diverse activities, her vision for possible futures, and her entrepreneurial spirit there. She may bring much-needed understanding to social problems and gain widespread support. Democracy's only requirement is that she not take the money that these skills have earned her in the economy and employ it within the political sphere, thus forgoing the political mechanism. If her talents have political applications, let her prove it.

The political energies of politicians, the electorate, and civil society groups come in many forms and are conveyed in many different spirits. Some are inclined to collaborate, others to compete, and most to do a bit of both. This is the right place to reinterpret Alito's rule that government lacks the authority to decide which strengths can be employed. The government must remain neutral on the question of whether people participate in politics with competitive fury or collaborative magnanimity, just as it must do so on the substance of their speech. Neither interest-group pluralists nor deliberative democrats have any claim to preferential treatment. The libertarian, egalitarian, and democratic perfectionists are all welcome. Democracy's only rule is that participants not compete, collaborate, or transform themselves on the basis of financial power, or any other foreign form of power, for that matter.

What if political power flows to a candidate, party, or interest group because of its particular experience with financial issues, matters of faith and devotion, military valor, or long-standing family history of noble acts? All of these experiences and many of their associated talents have political value. The task of governing an extensive and diverse nation certainly touches on markets, faith, and national defense, and government could certainly be enhanced by piety, discipline, and nobility making their way into the dispositions of officeholders and citizens. A great many energies and players can invigorate democracy so long as they abide by democracy's rules. And so if any of those alternative forms of power were to coopt the political process as economic power has, democratic integrity would demand that they be disentangled, set aside, and invited to return to their proper place.

When state and federal legislatures, time and time again, have limited the most poignant forms of financial power and provided for campaign subsidies, they have defended democracy's invisible hand. The judgment is that intelligence, energy, and talent should all be allowed to reap their natural rewards. Absent political finance reforms, politicians catering to wealthy interests acquire other people's talent through money. And absent such reforms, wealthy candidates can buy themselves the public attention and campaign apparatus that democracy would have them earn through civic sweat and public toil.[111] Are the parallels not obvious? Crony capitalists acquire economic power in the same way, not through employing their economic talents, but through employing their money in a different sphere, gaining an improper advantage. And so the legislatures that have reformed political finance were not just defending democracy's invisible hand. They were defending capitalism's as well. Striking down these reforms, the Court has harmed capitalism and democracy.

Limits on money in politics complicate the efforts of crony capitalists to gain economic advantages through political channels. And they complicate the efforts of plutocratic politicians to gain political power through economic channels. Such reforms seek to maintain the integrity and efficacy of each sphere's vital mechanisms. Democracy's mechanism, as glorified as it is, is initially nothing but a logical sequence of incentives. If political power is conditioned on raising a great deal of money, that is how candidates and officeholders, at least successful ones, will spend their time. When politicians spend their time courting constituents with money to spend, meeting with lobbyists, strategizing for and against PACs, and otherwise negotiating the pathways of our privatized regime of political finance, they are exposed to certain issues (those that interest donors and spenders) and certain positions on those issues (those of donors and spenders). Furthermore, they gain certain skills (those necessary for fundraising), they travel the country and world widely (on junkets and to fundraising events), and they learn to maintain the requisite popular support despite having little time to devote to their average geographic constituent (making promises, dragging out polarizing issues, finding emotionally charged but substantively trivial ways to characterize their adversaries, and disguising the way politics really works). They do all of these things in reasonably good conscience, knowing that this is the way the game is played, and that if they do not participate, others will.

To expect officeholders to gain a more comprehensive sense of the issues affecting society, to develop well-informed positions on the merits, to get to know their geographic constituents, to debate with their peers in good faith, and to enact the policies that they think, in all sincerity, are best for their region and country is incredibly naive in today's conditions. If campaigns and parties were publicly financed, on the other hand, and if significant grassroots activities were necessary to gain enough support to qualify for that financing, then the political game would have gained a new set of rules, the activities that unfolded would vary, and, perhaps, additional types of leaders would participate at the outset. There would still be lobbyists, interest groups, and other political associations of many kinds, but they would not possess the power of the political purse, the power to create a relationship of dependency. Officeholders could afford, quite literally *afford*, to listen to them with a critical ear and to compare the information and perspectives thus gleaned with others from different sectors of society, including sectors with little organizational or economic capital.

In all settings governed by generally applicable rules, customs, or incentives, participants unintentionally bring about collective results.[112] Whether we like it or not, the aggregation of individual incentives, subsequent behaviors, and final effects occurs constantly. There are two questions as to the tireless invisible hands following us everywhere: first, whether their produce will be agreeable or not to the social goals and values attending the setting in question; and second, whether their produce intrudes upon another sphere's domain, leading to domination and tyranny.[113] We know that officeholders, constituents, and associations, pursuing their own self-interest, are "led by an invisible hand to promote an end which was no part of [their] intention."[114] This could be public cynicism and costly private-interest legislation, or human flourishing arising from well-studied approaches to externalities and public goods. It depends on the design of the system and the resulting incentives. Will officeholders be given the incentive to exercise political talents or the incentive to exercise fundraising talents? Will average citizens be given the incentive to participate or to abstain? Will capitalists be given the incentive to devote money to electioneering or product improvement? The answers vary in accordance with the rules governing political finance, and so we return to the law.

B. Separatism Emergent

What legal principles would be necessary to protect the political sphere from economic encroachment? How could capitalism be confined to its own rightful place? Separatist principles have been welling up all along in the caselaw—often in dissenting opinions and sometimes in majority opinions, such as *Austin* and *McConnell*, that have been reversed. These principles are an important piece of the jurisprudential record, evidence that plutocracy has not gone unopposed and guideposts for an alternative future. The following excerpts show that separatism would not be an affront to the Supreme Court as an institution; it would only defy those who currently control the Court—Roberts, Scalia, Kennedy, Thomas, and Alito. Numerous other Justices have advocated a radically different course, one that ought to be taken as supplying basic demands for the reform movement.

Money Is Not Speech   Chief Justice Burger's market formulation holds that the First Amendment "protect[s] a marketplace for the clash of different views and conflicting ideas."[115] Chief Justice Rehnquist believed that the First Amendment aimed "to assure the unfettered interchange of ideas," a description similar to Burger's, except that Rehnquist assigned a particular purpose to that interchange: "the bringing about of political and social changes desired by the people."[116] While Burger stopped at "the clash," as though a conflict of views and ideas were the amendment's final goal, Rehnquist substituted "interchange" for "clash" and went on to assign to that interchange a democratic purpose—popular sovereignty.

In order for the Constitution to value the opinions of The People, not just donors and spenders, money must not be mistaken for speech. Justices White and Stevens have developed what we now recognize to be a separatist approach to this question. Adding to his *Buckley* and *Bellotti* dissenting opinions, White elaborated on his views in 1985:

The First Amendment protects the right to speak, not the right to spend, and limitations on the amount of money that can be spent are not the same as restrictions on speaking . . . [E]xpenditures [may] "produce" core First Amendment speech . . . But that is precisely the point: they produce such speech; they are not speech itself . . . I cannot accept the identification of speech with its antecedents. Such a house-that-Jack-built approach could equally be used to find a First Amendment right to a job or to a minimum wage to "produce" the money to "produce" the speech.[117]

"I cannot accept the cynic's 'money talks' as a proposition of constitutional law," he added.[118] Foreshadowing *Davis* and *Bennett*, White noted that "[e]very reason the majority gives for treating [the law at issue] as a restraint on speech relates to the effectiveness with which the donors can make their voices heard."[119] What the majority framed in terms of the protection of speech, White framed in terms of the protection of "the right of the contributors to make contributions."[120] The key is to differentiate between speaking and spending.

Justice Stevens has fleshed out that distinction. Ten years before *Citizens United*, Stevens proposed "a new beginning[:] Money is property; it is not speech." He described money as a medium of exchange and speech as a democratic force:

Speech has the power to inspire volunteers to perform a multitude of tasks on a campaign trail, on a battleground, or even a football field. Money, meanwhile, has the power to pay hired laborers to perform the same tasks. It does not follow, however, that the First Amendment provides the same measure of protection to the use of money to accomplish such goals as it provides to the use of ideas to achieve the same results.[121]

Note the invisible hand question implicit above: Would democracy be moved by the use of ideas or the use of money in enlisting volunteers and conducting campaigns? The answer depends on how the Court interprets the First Amendment and how that interpretation guides self-interested behavior to collective consequences beyond any particular actor's intentions.

Stevens honored the importance of individual freedom in deciding how to use one's property; he even conceded that the "right . . . to fund 'speech by proxy' certainly merits significant constitutional protection."[122] But he insisted that even speech by proxy involved the exercise of a property right, which is "not entitled to the same protection as the right to say what one pleases."[123] Justices Breyer and Ginsburg also would have held that money is not speech.[124] If money were conceived of property and spending as conduct, then legislatures would have greater leeway for enacting political finance reforms. The Court's scrutiny of the state interests that motivate reforms would become less strict, requiring a valid and sufficiently important objective instead of a compelling one.

Still, that increased leeway would be worthless once the Roberts Court got hold of the case. Since the Court has stated that it will only honor state interests in reducing quid pro quo corruption and its appearance, no legislature can contemplate limiting expenditures (by campaigns, individuals, or corporations), enacting effective public financing, or further limiting contributions. With contribution limits in place, such measures do not respond to fears of bribery. They respond to an interest in curbing undue influence, freeing officeholders from the fundraising treadmill, protecting political equality, and, consequently, restoring democratic integrity.

Democratic Integrity is the Essential State Interest   How would constitutional interpretation have to change in order for the state to maintain the primacy of political talents and the operation of democracy's invisible hand? How would it have to change in order for citizens to enjoy popular sovereignty instead of being subjugated by a regime of consumer sovereignty? The Court would have to recognize a compelling state interest far broader than the elimination of concrete favors for dollars.

In his 2006 *Randall* dissent joined by Ginsburg and Souter, Stevens described campaign costs as "so high that only the rich have the reach to throw their hats into the ring."[125] He noted how the absence of expenditure limitations forces candidates into a "fundraising straightjacket[:] fundraising devours the time and attention of political leaders, leaving them too busy to handle their public responsibilities effectively."[126] In light of these problems, Stevens considered two state interests constitutional: "protect[ing] equal access to the political arena, [and] free[ing] candidates and their staffs from the interminable burden of fundraising."[127] Two years later, in his *Davis* dissent, Stevens argued for an "independent governmental interest in reducing both the influence of wealth on the outcomes of elections, and the appearance that wealth alone dictates those results."[128] This work had been done thus far by the state interest in maintaining democratic integrity.

A 2007 dissenting opinion by Souter, joined by Stevens, Ginsburg, and Breyer, describes political integrity as "value second to none in a free society."[129] These four Justices sought to protect the "capacity of this democracy to represent its constituents and the confidence of its citizens in their capacity to govern themselves."[130] This harks back to White's defense of democratic integrity in his *Buckley* dissent.[131] It also recalls Rehnquist's unanimous opinion in *NRWC*, vindicating "the integrity of our electoral process [and] the responsibility of individual citizens for the successful functioning of that process."[132]

NRWC connects these two priorities to officeholder dependency and the violence it does to political accountability. The opinion cautions that "political 'war chests' [can] be used to incur political debts from legislators . . . aided by the contributions."[133] As Stevens put it in his *Citizens United* dissent, democratic integrity is compromised when officeholders decide issues not on the "merits or the desires of their constituencies," but "according to the wishes of those who have made large financial contributions."[134] Justices Ginsburg, Breyer, and Sotomayor joined in this sentiment. Perhaps the clearest statement along these lines was given by Justice Rehnquist in 1985. Leading a majority of the Court in *NCPAC*, he defined corruption as the "subversion of the political process" that occurs when "elected officials are influenced to act contrary to their obligations of office by the prospect of financial gain to themselves or infusions of money into their campaigns."[135]

Recall from Chapter 4 how Justice White's dissenting opinion in that case challenged the majority's assumption that PACs democratically influence public opinion and officeholders. He referenced "significant contacts between an organization like NCPAC and candidates for, and holders of, public office" and "move[ment] between the staffs of candidates or officeholders and those of PACs."[136] In addition to this danger, White felt that "candidate[s] may be forced to please the spenders rather than the voters."[137] As an example, he cited the "degrading spectacle of elected representatives completing detailed questionnaires on their positions on special interest issues, knowing that the monetary reward of PAC support depends on the correct answers."[138] On the basis of these concerns, White credited Congress's belief that "elections . . . should not turn on the amount of money spent" and that the "dangers of spiraling campaign expenditures" required action.[139]

White had already found similar problems in the referenda context. In a 1981 dissent, he juxtaposed the declining role of individual participation with "skyrocketing" contributions from corporate sources. He noted "[s]taggering disparities . . . between spending for and against various ballot measures"[140] and "increasing evidence that large contributors are at least able to block the adoption of measures through the initiative process."[141] This brought him to the conclusion that "enormous contributions from a few institutional sources can overshadow the efforts of individuals[, and] may . . . discourage[] participation in ballot measure campaigns."[142] All of this suggested that *Bellotti* was wrongly decided.

Justice Souter later grounded the same line of analysis in the context of political parties.[143] Disturbing his fellow Republican appointees with a pointed majority opinion in 2001, he alleged that parties "act as agents for spending on behalf of those who seek to produce obligated officeholders."[144] Pages later, he re-emphasized the point: "Despite decades of limitation on [their] spending . . . parties continue to . . . function for the benefit of donors whose object it is to place candidates under obligation."[145] Justices Stevens, Ginsburg, and Breyer joined the opinion, contradicting the Respondent's theory (and conventional wisdom) that "[p]arties exist precisely to elect candidates that share the goals of their party."[146] Souter deemed the Respondent's view a "refusal to see how the power of money actually works in the political structure."[147] He wrote that "it would ignore reality to think that the party role is adequately described by speaking generally of electing particular candidates."[148] Describing those who provide parties with their funds as "contributors with their own personal interests,"[149] he concluded that "[p]arties are . . . necessarily the instruments of some contributors whose object is not to support the party's message or to elect party candidates across the board, but rather to support a specific candidate for the sake of a position on one narrow issue, or even to support any candidate who will be obliged to the contributors."[150]

These defenses of democratic integrity suggest that the role of money compromises both the system of popular representation and the rights found within it, rights that must be interpreted differently in democratic and economic spheres. Equality is a special case. If political access is highly unequal, it follows that officeholders will be locked into a struggle to secure support from the financial elite. Put another way, if the financial elite are allowed to employ their economic resources in quantities that dwarf those available to average citizens, then campaigns, officeholders, parties, and interest groups will all seek to obtain those resources, and the great majority of the population will become second-class citizens. The rights of ordinary citizens will be trivialized if the game is conducted on an economic playing field.

Justice Marshall sought to prevent this outcome in *NCPAC*. Weakening his allegiance to *Buckley*, his dissenting opinion states that "limitations on independent expenditures . . . are justified by the congressional interest in promoting the reality and appearance of equal access to the political arena."[151] "It simply belies reality," Marshall wrote, "to say that a campaign will not reward massive financial assistance provided in the only way that is legally available."[152] Eleven years later, Stevens and Ginsburg resuscitated this "important interest in leveling the electoral playing field by constraining the cost of federal campaigns."[153] Consider their view of how fairness and integrity relate to political debate: "It is quite wrong to assume that the net effect of limits on contributions and expenditures— which tend to protect equal access to the political arena, to free candidates and their staffs from the interminable burden of fund-raising, and to diminish the importance of repetitive 30-second commercials—will be adverse to the interest in informed debate protected by the First Amendment."[154] Tying the rights of ordinary citizens to the integrity of the system as a whole, these remarks challenge the Roberts Court's assumptions about political finance reform.

To posit that democratic notions of accountability and equality will run contrary to the First Amendment is to posit an inconsistency within the Constitution and democracy itself. The Roberts Court takes this tack, holding that the First Amendment and democracy require economic rights to be honored as political. That course naturally maximizes profit for particular capitalists. Compare this to what happens when those rights are honored in their proper sphere. Economic rights validated within capitalism produce profits for individuals and gains for society as a whole. It is plain to see what happens when the lines are crossed in the opposite direction: political rights leveraged within capitalism produce profits for individual officeholders and bureaucrats (perhaps through nationalizing a company or exacting a bribe). Returning to equilibrium, political rights leveraged within democracy produce civic empowerment for individuals and vitality for society as a whole. What is good for each person and each place is good for them only there, in that context. When the contexts are confused, both systems and most of those who depend on them lose out. A precious few win: the crony capitalist who gains economic power through political channels, the plutocrat who wins office through economic channels, and the politicians who acquire economic power through political channels.

In order to prevent the harm caused by crony capitalists and plutocrats, many Justices have validated a state interest in preventing undue influence. The construct that flourished in *Auto Traders, Austin, and McConnell*, and perished in *Citizens United*, aims precisely at the conversion of economic power into political power. "Undue influence" refers to the specific result achieved by money in politics; when it is an apt description of democratic affairs, political equality and popular accountability are not.[155] As democracy's rights are violated, its collective purpose is interrupted. And nowhere is capitalism's dependence on democratic rights better illustrated. When economic actors and interests gain political traction and then economic advantages, upending capitalism's design, they do so by infringing upon political equality and popular sovereignty.

Is it not remarkable that capitalism and consumers can be harmed in this way only when the rights of citizens and the design of democracy are harmed as well? Consumers and citizens, and capitalism and democracy are interdependent pairings that depend, curiously enough, on separation. That is the paradox: a mutually supportive relationship premised on distance. This is the distance between different rights, values, and procedures, not a distance of miles and open spaces, for every citizen is also a consumer, and each laborer and capitalist is also a citizen. Economic and political flourishing demand distinctions between the spheres that people rely upon each day, sometimes from one second to the next.

The Importance of Restoring Citizen Confidence   Healthy, wholehearted reliance on capitalism and democracy depends on perceptions. Just as investors are scared off by an unstable market or an overreaching government, citizens will be hesitant to engage in the political process if they sense that its integrity has been compromised. This explains *Buckley*'s validation of a state interest in combating even the appearance of quid pro quo corruption. As we have seen, however, a great deal of the apathy and cynicism within the general population is not due to the perception of flagrant wrongdoing. It is due to the perception of officeholder dependency, lobbyists' prominence, politicians' frequent trips and meetings with donors and spenders, and corporate domination of public affairs—phenomena that, on the whole, are perfectly legal.

Justice Souter validated these perceptions in 2001 by interpreting *Austin*'s view of corruption broadly: "corruption being understood not only as quid pro quo agreements, but also as undue influence on an officeholder's judgment, and the appearance of such influence."[156] In this formulation, endorsed by the Court in *McConnell*, the government could successfully assert a compelling interest in reducing the appearance of undue influence.[157] Naturally, citizen confidence would be best restored by attending to the reality of undue influence, not just its perception. By paying more attention to evidence from officeholders, lobbyists, CEOs, wealthy individuals, and political spending data, the Court could build a bridge between perceptions and reality, as it did in *McConnell*.[158] Perhaps Souter's point is best understood as emphasizing the importance and fragility of citizen confidence. By placing a premium on its restoration, Souter would give states more leeway in addressing the reality of money in politics.

Corporations Are Not Citizens   Corporate political power makes up a significant piece of that disappointing reality, especially after *Citizens United*. Recognizing the dangers posed for democracy, many Justices have elaborated an alternative approach. Dissenting in *Bellotti*, the original validation of corporate speech, Justice White characterized the electoral process as "the essence of our democracy[,] an arena in which the public interest in preventing *corporate domination* . . . is at its strongest."[159] As with the distinction between money and speech, Justice Stevens carried on White's legacy. Dissenting in *Citizens United*, Stevens lamented "corporate domination of politics."[160] To Stevens, the constitutional validation of that domination is the death knell of democratic integrity.[161] On this score,

White opposed Powell in *Bellotti*, and Stevens opposed Powell's successor, Justice Kennedy, in *Citizens United*.

Concerns over corporate power are heightened with regard to wealthy, for-profit companies and diminished in cases involving less wealthy and non-profit corporations. In a 1986 dissent joined by Justices Blackmun, Stevens, and White, Justice Rehnquist acknowledged that "large and successful corporations with resources to fund a political war chest constitute a more potent threat to the political process than less successful business corporations or nonprofit corporations."[162] Although the case at hand involved a non-profit corporation publishing a newsletter, Rehnquist concluded that "these distinctions . . . are 'distinctions in degree' that do not amount to 'differences in kind.'"[163] He wrote that only the legislature could draw distinctions between for-profit and non-profit corporate political activity, not the judiciary, and that prophylactic measures are appropriate in the case of "groups that organize in the corporate form."[164]

Rehnquist went on to support Congress's judgment that "the corporate shield which the State has granted to corporations as a form of *quid pro quo*" poses distinct advantages in the economic sphere, which, in turn, pose dangers for the political sphere. Rehnquist reminded the majority that the restriction at issue, a prohibition on the use of general treasury funds for expenditures in connection with a federal election, targeted only "the *form* of otherwise unregulated spending" and that the corporation could have established a segregated fund.[165] This is the same thing that was asked of *Citizens United*—that if it wished to participate in the political sphere, it set up a special fund under distinct rules, thus converting its economic power into a more politically appropriate form.[166]

Seeing how this design was undone in *Citizens United*, Justice Stevens pressed fundamental points in dissent. "Campaign finance distinctions based on corporate identity tend to be less worrisome," he wrote, "because the 'speakers' are not natural persons, much less members of our political community."[167] "Corporations have no consciences, no beliefs, no feelings, no thoughts, [and] no desires," he continued.[168] "[T]hey are not themselves members of 'We the People' by whom and for whom our Constitution was established."[169] To prove his point, he listed concerns of the First Amendment that do not support corporate electioneering: "protecting the individual's interest in self-expression," helping to "make men free to develop their faculties," respecting "their dignity and choice," and "facilitat[ing] the value of individual self-realization."[170] In sum, corporations are not citizens.

Stevens thus offers two separatist notions: First, corporations, at least when "speaking" through their general treasuries, are entities from the economic sphere and have no place as such within the political sphere. Second, the political sphere is different from the marketplace—it is, Justice Stevens suggested, a place where citizens develop their humanity through membership in a community of political equals.

These notions do not represent the view that politics ought to be a well-regulated, competitive market. They are, rather, anti-market. If money is not speech and corporations are not political citizens, then politics is free to become a public sphere. Goals of self-expression, development of human faculties, respect for dignity, and facilitation of self-realization continue the march away from market relations. Not even a neo-Keynesian view can bear them. A well-regulated market is still a market, and markets—as much as they may satisfy preferences, generate wealth, provide choices, and develop human capacities—are commercial in nature. They provide fora for financial exchanges, and aid human dignity and self-realization only insofar as those deeper values are tied to gainful activity or purchasing behavior.[171] This, ultimately, is what democratic integrity cannot abide.

Different Spheres with Different Values   To speak of dignity and self-realization in the political sphere, as Justice Stevens does, and to contrast that sphere with the economic sphere, is to recognize different territories with different interpretations of the same values. Equal access to the political sphere is different from equal access to the economic sphere. In the latter, all people are guaranteed access to the market without discrimination. From that point on, they may go only as far as their own financial resources permit or only as far as others are willing to permit by transferring their own. Surely capital is thought to flow to those with talent, vision, and drive, but the evaluation of those merits lies in the hands of those with money to spend or lend. Endorsing Cass Sunstein's view, Stevens concluded his Davis dissent by positing that "a well-functioning democracy distinguishes between market processes of purchase and sale on the one hand and political processes of voting and reason-giving on the other."[172]

Justice Kagan, Stevens's successor, built on this distinction by defending popular sovereignty in her *Bennett* dissent. Notice how she characterizes the public financing scheme that the majority struck down: "Arizonans wanted their government to work on behalf of all the State's people . . . [, to] serve the public, and not just the wealthy donors who helped put them in office . . . [and to run] campaigns leading to the election of representatives not beholden to the few, but accountable to the many."[173] "[T]hat government may be responsive to the will of the people"—this is how Kagan described the "values underlying both the First Amendment and our entire Constitution."[174] Absent effective public financing, she worried that officeholders would act on behalf of "wealthy contributors" instead of "all the people."[175] She described the majority as having "invalidate[d] Arizonans' efforts to ensure that in their State, '[t]he people . . . possess the absolute sovereignty.'"[176] This paints popular sovereignty as the alternative to consumer sovereignty, which served as the underlying principle of the majority opinion.

Kagan called the majority's view of the First Amendment tenable only in "a world gone topsy-turvy,"[177] an apt description of democracy under the free market Constitution. *Bennett*'s insistence on private spending having its market-determined effect is the key to consumer sovereignty and free market democracy. The influence that the Rehnquist Court had called "undue"—the powerful effect of large aggregations of wealth on officeholders' judgment and the balance of viewpoints within the market for political speech—was "due influence" in the Roberts Court's view. Under the free market Constitution, undue influence describes influence obtained through a government subsidy or through political finance limitations that increase the relative power of small donations and expenditures.

The same transformation has occurred in the meaning of the word "distortion." While *Austin* held "immense aggregations of wealth" to be a source of distortion and corruption, *Bennett* held government subsidies to be a form of distortion within the political market and hence an unconstitutional interference with speech.[178] *Bennett*'s position makes sense if one assumes that the distribution of economic resources is the appropriate baseline for the exercise of political rights.

These contradictions show that what is undue and distorting, democratically speaking, can be due and rectifying, economically speaking. The economic sphere would also be turned upside down if democratic notions of freedom and equality were applied there. Indeed, the Rehnquist and Roberts Courts' understandings of "undue influence" and "distortion" are mirror images of each other. The reason, quite simply, is that the Rehnquist Court located political speech within a democratic state, while the Roberts Court locates it within a capitalist economy. Perhaps it was best put in 1978. Justice Rehnquist's warning about corporate power was specific: it poses "special dangers in the political *sphere*."[179] And White's description of the "the essence of our democracy" also bears repeating: "an *arena* in which the public interest in preventing corporate domination . . . is at its strongest."[180]

The Value of Judicial Opinions   The foregoing principles, now constituting the minority view on the Court, provide valuable building blocks for reform. Virtually every time the majority has struck down limits on money in politics, a strong dissenting voice has sounded, laying the groundwork for those who would someday repair the damage. Even a majority of Justices cannot propose new laws to do this work, however; they can only strike down existing ones. Proposals for the mandatory public financing of elections, for example, could never originate in the judicial branch.[181]

While changes to the Court's roster could lead to *Austin* and *McConnell* being resurrected and the offending portions of *Buckley*, *Bellotti*, *Davis*, *Bennett*, and *Citizens United* being struck down, the roster could become more conservative instead. And even if a conservative were replaced by a liberal, the balance were to shift, and the new majority were inclined to be as aggressive as the present one in overruling the Court's own precedent, such changes could be decades in the making. Whatever achievements a new liberal heyday on the Court could eventually bring, the balance could tip back in the other direction just a few years later. And so, while it is essential to look to the Court for an understanding of the principles that maintain plutocracy and for contrary principles issued in dissent, the matter of money in politics calls for a broader focus.

C. The Next Constitutional Amendment

Once the Court has spoken on the meaning of the Constitution, a majority of both houses of Congress and the president together are powerless to change it. They can tinker around the edges, but history has shown the Court's willingness to tie up loose ends and reverse the work of legislatures, state and federal alike. The states and the Congress retain the ultimate authority, however. Two-thirds of Congress can propose an amendment to the Constitution and two-thirds of states can instruct Congress to call a constitutional convention for the same purpose.[182] Although our Constitution may well be "the most difficult to amend of any constitution currently existing in the world today,"[183] it has been amended twenty-seven times. The first question, therefore, is not whether it *can be* amended, but rather whether it *should be* amended.

That depends on the issue at stake or, more specifically, on how the issue is understood. The foregoing chapters have suggested a particular understanding of money in politics and the Court's judgments on the topic. That understanding is sympathetic to a variety of reforms, not just constitutional ones, but in the end it suggests that the issue of money in politics runs so deeply and profoundly through our political system as to be constitutional in essence. This is true in two ways. The issue goes to the heart of both democracy and capitalism, and is therefore constitutional in the sense of affecting the nation's makeup and nature. And it is constitutional in the strict legal sense as well, centering on the meaning of constitutional text. Both aspects of the issue bode in favor of foundational reform.

Despite its doubly constitutional nature, political finance is unaccounted for by the Constitution itself. The Constitution is silent on the issue and the First Amendment was not drafted with it in mind. The radical variations in the Court's rulings stand as a reminder of this and as a suggestion that this area of law has not been properly committed to the judicial branch. The United States has fallen into this dangerous malaise of legal subjectivity only because of the incredible age of its Constitution—the oldest constitution in continuous use today.[184] If the Constitution were to be amended to account for political finance, legal disputes would still arise, but at least then there would be a concrete baseline from which to derive specific principles. The disagreements across the Burger, Rehnquist, and

Roberts Courts on political finance have not been caused, in the first instance, by the juxtaposed ideologies of their members. Many courts host a diversity of political worldviews without issuing such radically contradictory decisions. The primary cause of the Supreme Court's contradictions is that the Constitution gives personal ideology free rein in disputes over money in politics.

This points to what is missing: an authoritative benchmark for adjudication. And because the issue is constitutional in a general sense as well, that benchmark must be grounded in a principled understanding that protects the integrity of capitalism and democracy. The underlying questions—democracy or plutocracy, capitalism or crony capitalism—are for the people and their representatives to decide, not the Supreme Court. The answers should become part of the Constitution, leaving the details for adjudication. The current constitutional silence, in contrast, leaves the political judgment, ideology, and the details for adjudication. Some matters are too important to be left to the changing ideological composition of an unelected body.

Thinking Like a Framer The language of spheres and arenas would hardly be available to Rehnquist and White if it were not for the American political tradition of separatism. Because of the Framers' experience with monarchy and familiarity with theocracy, they understood that popular sovereignty and political equality were vulnerable to alternative means of allocating power, especially those premised on birth and belief. Extending this separatist tradition from nobility and religion to the power of wealth and corporations would require more authority than the Court possesses. It is a question for the people and their representatives in state and federal government.

The separatist instinct of ensuring reasonable autonomy for society's various spheres motivated major features of the Constitution. For example, the separation of powers provides an architectural framework within which power struggles and adjudication play out. It ensures that no branch of government becomes unduly powerful. Rather than oppress each other, the Framers made clear on the face of the Constitution their intention that the various branches of government should check each other.

The connection to monarchy is clear: the separation of powers stands in the way of self-aggrandizing officials who wish to become supreme. This separation has by no means prevented conflict from arising between the branches of government. The wisdom lay in recognizing at the outset that conflict was inevitable and that it required resolution at the hands of a principled framework. Citizens and officeholders (including the Justices) know that framework. Each branch has its own domain, its own powers, and its own separate functions. These different branches are not be conflated—no branch is allowed to take over another's territory. This system has made it difficult for leaders to become tyrants. Each, by law, has a sense of place. As a consequence, the three branches have not preyed upon each other as much as they otherwise would. Having escaped an unprincipled power struggle, they have become strong and reasonably diverse.

The same separatist instinct has also favored the development of religion in America, producing a similar strength and diversity. Religious freedoms have thrived here precisely because religious leaders and state actors have been confined to their rightful places. The separation of church and state has not permitted religious organizations to acquire as much political power as they otherwise would, nor has it allowed the state to acquire religious power or to prefer one religion over another. (Naturally, offenses are still committed from time to time, but surely they would be more numerous were it not for the Constitution's disapproval.) This truce, enforced by law, maintains a reasonably secular state and religious freedom.[185]

Rawls notes that "[s]ome citizens of faith have felt that this separation is hostile to religion and have sought to change it." He concludes that these citizens "fail to grasp a main cause of the strength of religion in this country and . . . seem ready to jeopardize it for temporary gains in political power."[186] Without constitutional separation, religious leaders could pursue theocracy. Religious political power harms religion not just when the dominant sect oppresses the rest. It is the road to dominance that inflicts the initial damage. The various faiths set upon each other, competing for state power, knowing full well the stakes. The better course is the one we have taken: theocracy was ruled out in advance, as a matter of constitutional structure.

The Argument for a Third Separation   What Rawls says about some citizens with faith in God must also be said about some citizens with faith in the market. They fail to grasp the cause of capitalism's strength, and they are ready to jeopardize it for temporary gains in political power. Do they really believe that an open political market bodes well for capitalism? Are companies to compete on the basis of their ability to secure favorable government treatment? Can that sort of competition be expected, like proper economic competition, to increase overall social wealth?

Of course not. Naturally, innovation, better goods and services, increased efficiency, and lower prices might still result, but not in the economic sphere of goods and services. The improvement, the creative destruction, and their motor, self-interest, have been redirected into the markets for political goods and services. And hence it is easy to explain the remarkable "progress" in the various vehicles of influence—527s, PACs, superPACs, bundlers, political advertising, and the like. This productive pressure also explains the miserable routines into which officeholders have sunk in order to raise the cash necessary for reelection.

There are two reasons the Court can remark, "[M]oney, like water, will always find its way in": a political market with tremendous potential for profit, and caselaw that keeps that market open for business. In this way, conservative Justices, plaintiffs, and other citizens of market faith distort capitalism. They have made it so that economic competitors can be undermined not through being surpassed initially in terms of price or quality, but rather through encountering unfavorable background conditions produced by government at the behest of another firm or industry. There are many forms: no-bid contracts, subsidies, regulatory exceptions, earmarks, selective enforcement of rules, the defeat of environmental regulations, and so on.

Just as capitalism holds that politics is not an economically legitimate form of competition, democracy holds that the market is not a politically legitimate form of governance. The design of consumer sovereignty interrupts the natural operation of political talents and popular preferences, injecting a foreign system into the political sphere. Citizens now participate on the basis of their ability and willingness to pay. From this, a new collective measurement is obtained: the overall balance of donations, expenditures, and hired political insiders vying for or against a particular outcome. Whether the outcome is a legislative provision or an election itself, the result is the same: citizens and corporations with the greatest capital have a tremendous political advantage over their fellows. They can tip the balance of media time and public attention in favor of their preferred outcome.

Every system has a point of equilibrium, a gentle oscillation to and fro, varying healthfully and appropriately from a central point of balance. Those who would substitute markets for politics are faced with a question that they can never answer to the satisfaction of their fellow citizens: What justice is there in taking the overall balance of donations and expenditures as a state of equilibrium? The market system carries out the judgment that campaigns should be launched and continued when candidates and their supporters have enough cash on hand and believe it worth their while to spend it. In this system, political viewpoints are aired and repeated in relation to the ability and willingness to spend of those who are promoting them. The rule appears to be that the platforms of political parties ought to be adjusted in relation to their effects on party funding. In sum, this system holds quite simply that the 0.37 percent of the population that supplies the majority of funds for campaigns and political speech knows what is best.[187]

The essential design of democracy stands in the way of such proxies for wisdom and such criteria for authority. If political influence can be obtained by virtue of wealth, then democracy has accepted a foreign form of power. The same structural dilemma presents itself again. Our subject is a nation that has achieved popular suffrage, robust civil and political rights, a separation of church and state, separation of powers, and an end to formal class structures. Does it make sense for such a nation to link political power with economic power? If political power does not lie with religious leaders, nobility, a military junta, any one branch of government, or any foreign government, and if elections are decided by citizens of all races, ethnicities, religions, sexual orientations, sexes, and political viewpoints whose rights of political participation are well established, then economic power represents the last available source of domination. An informal class structure arises, every bit as powerful as the formal hierarchies of past eras.

Domination is not the same thing as economic inequality. No citizen is dominated by the bigger houses, better cars, nicer clothes, and extra leisure time belonging to their wealthier countrymen. But when money buys political access and influence, then the wealthy have a greater say in governance itself. It is of no use disguising the issue with economic language, construing democracy coldly as "a means by which men as they are now can register their wants as political consumers in the political market."[188] The "goods" provided by the political market impose forceful consequences on others, society as a whole, and even future generations. There is no comparison to yachts, mansions, and fancy cars. More or less regulation of greenhouse gases, more or less public education, one immigration policy or another, one foreign policy or another—these are not anything like decisions over what kind of dress to buy or what main course to order from the menu. When public policies are predictably and necessarily affected by the wealth of those who favor or oppose them, when wealth is institutionalized as a mechanism for political power, then a system of domination has been implemented. Economic inequality is one thing; its translation into political inequality is another.

Our democracy's historical trajectory contains the key: birth by revolt against a royal aristocracy with an actual king, followed by an adolescence of struggles to overcome aristocracies of race and sex. Has the nation come this far only to succumb, in middle age, to an aristocracy of corporations and wealth? The Supreme Court once noted how our "conception of political equality" has a trajectory from "the Declaration of Independence, to Lincoln's Gettysburg Address, to the Fifteenth, Seventeenth, and Nineteenth Amendments."[189] To this, we can now add the Twenty-Third, Twenty-Fourth, and Twenty-Sixth Amendments as well. The abolition of slavery, national citizenship based on birth, a guarantee of equal protection, the banning of racial and gender discrimination at the polls, senators elected by a popular vote, and the abolition of poll taxes all reflect an ongoing evolution towards political maturity.[190]

It would not be fitting for this long-standing project to go from "the cry of the oppressed, their claim for recognition as equal human beings" and the pursuit of a society in which all people "could enjoy and develop their human capacities" to a market in which all can exercise political power to the extent that they can pay for it.[191] The view of history implicit in the free market Constitution holds that self-governance is a bridge from the power of emperors, kings, and nobles to the power of their modern-day equivalents in the era of capitalism. That is not a satisfactory end point for centuries of social struggle. The nation has achieved universal suffrage only to see the vote become secondary to the power of political finance and, after the election, to the access and influence that money buys within the legislative process.

Is the dilemma not familiar by now? The conservatism of the free market ideologue and the plutocrat has the same flavor as yesterday's conservatism, imbued with the "fear that the liberal project of democracy would destroy all the traditional privileges of men over women, employers over workers, rich over poor, educated over uneducated, whites over other races, and the like."[192] Given just how entrenched those privileges were, the liberal project required several constitutional amendments to do its work. In the case of money in politics, state and federal lawmakers have taken many steps to reduce the political privileges of the rich over the poor. By reversing those steps, the Court has frustrated the course of political evolution and forced the issue of a constitutional amendment.

Ideology and Authority   The Court heads up the only branch of the federal government that is immune from the pressures of money in politics—its members appointed for life, their salaries and their tenures secure from politics itself. And yet it is the one branch that maintains the free market conditions that keep monetary power on top of democracy. The prospect for personal gain does not motivate the Court's choice. In explaining the dominance of capitalist thought in the 1800s, Lowi writes that "it was not a question of influence *on* the policy-maker; capitalism was so pervasive because it operated as an influence *in* the policy-maker."[193] Heilbroner describes the power of ideologies in a complementary fashion. They are the "systems of thought and belief," he stresses, "by which dominant classes explain to themselves how their social system operates and what principles it exemplifies."[194]

This suggests that the Court does not intend its explanations to be means of manipulation or propaganda. As Heilbroner puts it, ideologies "exist not as fictions but as 'truths'—and not only evidential truths but moral truths."[195] The power of ideology explains the Court's stance and emphasizes the fact that social systems, even oppressive ones, are commonly believed to be just by those who administer them. Theocracy, monarchy, dictatorship, and communism all have their true believers. Why should plutocracy be any different?

Those interested in the integrity of capitalism and democracy have no choice but to confront the cases that constructed the free market Constitution. Chapters 2 to 4 have facilitated that work, exposing the substance behind what, to the unindoctrinated, appears as sleights of hand: corporations as citizens; money as speech; donations and expenditures as so important as to be entitled to their optimal effectiveness in the political market; political spenders as sovereign; bribery as the only true form of corruption; political equality, democratic integrity, and the protection of officeholders' time as coercive agendas; and political finance reform as censorship. We have seen how the Court has bestowed the force of supreme law upon this series of delusions, striking down limits on money in politics and retrofitting the First Amendment with a capitalist worldview.

Meaningful political finance reform cannot survive under these conditions. These are, in fact, the conditions that reforms have sought to eliminate. We have seen how this polarity between the campaign finance reform movement and the free market Constitution did not emerge accidentally. The diametrical opposition between the components and directions of each, this chain of contrasts and contradictions, has arisen as the Court constitutionalized the state of affairs that campaign finance laws have sought to correct. The present chapter and Chapters 5 and 6 before it laid bare the theory and consequences of this state of affairs now known to us as free market democracy—the extensive system of political and economic corruption preserved by constitutional interpretation.

The path forward ought to be decided through a proper exercise of political power. There could hardly be a problem more deserving of massive engagement by citizens of all stations. The Court has given the nation an economic vision of self-governance, ceding our political values and procedures to the market, but it is ultimately for the nation to decide its own identity. The commercialization of politics should be only as permanent as popular consent. Are the real-world consequences for democracy and capitalism desirable? Are they suitable for our life contexts and opportunities?

If a critical mass of citizens reject the Court's ideology and its consequences, then a more practical set of questions arises. What reforms are required to restore the integrity of capitalism and democracy? What rules should be implemented to govern political finance and moderate corporate political power? The Court cannot do this work. It can only undo it, and it has proven itself resolute on this score. And so, as it should be, these questions fall to the people and their representatives. Nobody else has the rightful authority to amend the Constitution.

Notes

PREFACE

1. I do not mean to suggest that the quest for equal rights has come to an end or that social stratification along the lines of wealth represents the last stage. Additional struggles have been unfolding along the lines of sexual orientation and immigration status, for example.

2. The Constitution is first among all sources of the "supreme Law of the Land," and the remaining two sources—federal law and treaties—depend upon it, respectively, for their existence and proper procedures. U.S. Const., art. VI, cl. 2.

3. The formulation of "saying what the law is" comes from Marbury v. Madison, 5 U.S. (1 Cr.) 137, 177 (1807), the case that is generally credited with establishing judicial review. Hamilton's famous assessment of the judicial branch can be found in "The Federalist No. 78," in *The Federalist Papers* (Clinton Rossiter ed.), 465. Whether or not the judiciary is the least dangerous branch is a question whose answer depends on the values of the inquiring person, his or her ranking of dangers, and so on; but regardless, it ought to be a context-sensitive inquiry. The judiciary's power varies from area to area. Nobody believes the judiciary to have acquired the power of the purse or the sword, but it has acquired a substantial power to define democracy. The context of political finance plagues Hamilton's assertion with doubt.

CHAPTER I

1. The Associated Press, "Louisiana Congressman Pleads Not Guilty in Bribery Case," *New York Times*, June 9, 2007, http://www.nytimes.com/2007/06/09/washington/09jefferson.html.

2. You can see the Abramoff photo at the Ronald Reagan Library in Simi Valley, California, or in Thomas Frank, "The Wrecking Crew," *Harper's Magazine,* August 2008, 38.

3. Ken Silverstein, "Beltway Bacchanal," *Harper's Magazine*, March 2008, 49.

4. This information comes from NPR's list of donors who have given $1 million or more to superPACs. "The SuperPAC Superdonors," February 13, 2012, http://www.npr.org/2012/02/13/146836082/the-superpac-super-donors.

5. Seth Cline, "Sheldon Adelson Spent $150 Million on Election," *CBS News*, December 3, 2012, http://www.usnews.com/news/articles/2012/12/03/sheldon-adelson-ended-up-spending-150-million.

6. David Firestone, "Bad News for Campaign Finance," *New York Times*, December 7, 2012, http://takingnote.blogs.nytimes.com/2012/12/07/bad-news-for-campaign-finance/?ref=campaignfinance.

7. Mike McIntire, "Conservative Nonprofit Acts as a Stealth Business Lobbyist," *New York Times*, April 21, 2012, http://www.nytimes.com/2012/04/22/us/alec-a-tax-exempt-group-mixes-legislators-and-lobbyists.html?pagewanted=all&_r=0.

8. Ibid.

9. Ibid.

10. Robert Pear, "In House, Many Spoke with One Voice: Lobbyists'," *New York Times*, November 15, 2009, http://www.nytimes.com/2009/11/15/us/politics/15health.html.

11. This trend was noted as early as 1977. Lindblom, *Politics and Markets*, 190.

12. Eric Lipton and Eric Lichtblau, "Ethics Inquiry Focuses on Fund-raisers and House Vote," *New York Times*, July 15, 2010, http://www.nytimes.com/2010/07/15/us/politics/15lobby.html. A similar story can be told about the special Congressional committee charged with debt reduction, how it is lobbied by interested parties that will be affected by tax legislation and debt legislation, and how its members use their role on the committee as a lever for increased fundraising. Eric Lichtblau, "Lobbyists Line Up to Sway Special Committee," *New York Times*, September 22, 2011, http://www.nytimes.com/2011/09/22/us/politics/lobbyists-line-up-to-sway-debt-reducing-special-committee.html.

13. Ibid.

14. These numbers reflect the candidates' own fundraising, coupled with money raised by their national committees and parties' joint fundraising efforts. Nicholas Confessore and Derek Willis, "2012 Election Ended with Deluge of Donations and Spending," *New York Times*, December 7, 2012, http://thecaucus.blogs.nytimes.com/2012/12/07/2012-election-ended-with-deluge-of-donations-and-spending/?ref=nicholasconfessore.

15. The sums listed for Senate and House fundraising are the average amounts raised by candidates who win elections. Andrea Seabrook, "Who's Weighing Tax on Rich? Congress' Millionaires," *National Public Radio*, September 20, 2011, http://www.npr.org/2011/09/20/140627334/millionaires-in-congress-weigh-new-tax-on-wealthy?sc=17&f=1001.

16. Schweizer catalogs tremendous evidence to this and other effects in *Extortion*.

17. Ibid., 4.

18. OpenSecretsblog, "2012 Election Spending Will Reach $6 Billion, Center for Responsive Politics Predicts," *October 31, 2012*, http://www.opensecrets.org/news/2012/10/2012-election-spending-will-reach-6.html; Jeanne Cummings, "2008 Campaign Costliest in U.S. History," *Politico*, November 5, 2008, http://www.politico.com/news/stories/1108/15283.html (noting that Obama and McCain raised over $1 billion and that "[t]he 2008 campaign was the costliest in history, with a record-shattering $5.3 billion in spending by candidates, political parties and interest groups on the congressional and presidential races").

19. See Jonathan D. Salant, "Spending Doubled as Obama Led Billion-Dollar Campaign (Update 1)," *Bloomberg.com*, http://www.bloomberg.com/apps/news?pid=newsarchive&sid=anLDS9WWPQW8 (providing numbers for total spending and individual candidate spending in the 2008 election); Lewis, *The Buying of the President* 2004, 4 (recording the expenditures of the 2000 elections); Jeff Zeleny, "$350,000 Goal Is Set for Re-election Donors," *New York Times*, March 18, 2011, A20, http://www.nytimes.com/2011/03/18/us/politics/18democrats.html. For useful information on public financing, see Federal Election Commission, "Public Funding of Presidential Elections," February 2011, http://www.fec.gov/pages/brochures/pubfund.shtml#anchor686308.

20. OpenSecrets.org, "2012 Overview", http://www.opensecrets.org/pres12/.

21. Nicholas Confessore, "Result Won't Limit Campaign Money Any More Than Ruling Did," *New York Times*, November 11, 2012, http://www.nytimes.com/2012/11/12/us/politics/a-vote-for-unlimited-campaign-financing.html?_r=0.

22. Michael Barbaro and Ashley Parker, "With Rich Donors, a More Candid Romney Emerges," *New York Times*, September 22, 2012, http://www.nytimes.com/2012/09/23/us/politics/with-donors-a-more-candid-romney-emerges.html?pagewanted=all.

23. Stephen Braun and Jack Gillum, "Final Campaign Reports: 2012 Spending Nears Record," *Yahoo News*, December 6, 2012, http://news.yahoo.com/final-campaign-reports-2012-election-nears-record-231024887-election.html; Albert R. Hunt, "In Politics, More Can Mean Less," *New York Times*, December 9, 2012, http://www.nytimes.com/2012/12/10/us/10iht-letter10.html; Times Topics (Campaign Spending), "2012 Elections: The Aftermath,"

New York Times, November 12, 2012, http://topics.nytimes.com/top/reference/timestopics/subjects/c/campaign_finance/index.html. Another article put independent expenditure group spending at $834 million. Firestone, "Bad News for Campaign Finance."

24. On political party fundraising, see OpenSecrets.org, "Political Parties Overview," http://www.opensecrets.org/parties/index.php?cmte=&cycle=2012. On the role of million-dollar donations, see Firestone, "Bad News for Campaign Finance" (describing such donations as constituting 60% of total third-party spending).

25. Paul Abowd, "Obscure Nonprofit Threatens Campaign Finance Limits beyond Montana," Center for Public Integrity, October 22, 2012, http://www.publicintegrity.org/2012/10/22/11577/obscure-nonprofit-threatens-campaign-finance-limits-beyond-montana.

26. Such groups fall under 501(c) under the tax code, most notably 501(c)(4) organizations, dubbed "social welfare organizations." These nonprofit groups must claim that political activity, especially express political advocacy, is not their primary purpose. S. V. Date, "Crossroads GPS Redefines 'Social Welfare' Political Action," *NPR News*, November 5, 2012, http://www.npr.org/blogs/itsallpolitics/2012/11/05/164364802/crossroads-gps-redefines-social-welfare-political -action?sc=17&f=1014. See also Meredith McGehee and David Vance, "Outside Group Spending Controlled the 2012 Election Conversation," *The Hill*, November 15, 2012, http://thehill.com/opinion/op-ed/268071–outside-group-spending-controlled-the-2012–election-conversation.

27. Eric Lipton, Mike McIntire, and Don Van Natta, Jr., "Top Corporations Aid U.S. Chamber of Commerce Campaign," *New York Times*, October 21, 2010, http://www.nytimes.com/2010/10/22/us/politics/22chamber.html?pagewanted=all; Carol D. Leonnig, "Corporate Donors Fuel Chamber of Commerce's Political Power," *Washington Post*, October 18, 2012, http://articles.washingtonpost.com/2012–10–18/politics/35501119_1_center-for-political-accountability-political-donations-chamber. For more on the Chamber's disclosure policies, see Dan Eggen, "Chamber Says It Will Evade Disclosure by Tweaking Ads," *Washington Post*, May 30, 2012, http://articles.washingtonpost.com/2012–05–30/politics/35454730_1_issue-ads-groups-disclosure.

28. Lipton, McIntire, and Van Natta, "Top Corporations Aid U.S. Chamber."

29. Sheryl Gay Stolberg, "For Corporate Donors, Inauguration Details," *New York Times*, December 12, 2012, A30, http://www.nytimes.com/2012/12/09/us/politics/obama -team-outlines-four-corporate-donor-packages-for-inauguration.html?ref=politics.

30. Presidential Inaugural Committee 2013, "Online Solicitation for Inaugural Funds," https://www.documentcloud.org/documents/536326–picdonationformv8.html (if this should become unavailable online, many of its terms will still be viewable in Stolberg's article, above).

31. Nicholas Confessore and Sheryl Gay Stolberg, "Well-Trod Path: Political Donor to Ambassador," *New York Times*, January 18, 2012, http://www.nytimes.com/2013/01/19/us/politics/well-trod-path-political-donor-to-ambassador.html?_r=0; T. W. Farnam, "The Influence Industry: Obama Gives Administration Jobs to Some Big Fundraisers," *Washington Post*, March 7, 2012, http://articles.washingtonpost.com/2012–03–07/politics/35447935_1_bundlers-obama-administration-steve-spinner; Michael Beckel, "Big Donors & Bundlers Among Obama's Ambassador Picks," *Center for Public Integrity and OpenSecrets*, May 28, 2009, http://www.opensecrets.org/news/2009/05/big-donors-bundlers-among-obam.html.

32. Jake Tapper and Kirit Radia, "Report: Nearly 80% of Obama's Top Bundlers Given 'Key Administration Posts,'" *ABC News*, June 15, 2011, http://abcnews.go.com/blogs/politics/2011/06/report-nearly-80–of-obamas-top-bundlers-given-key-administration-posts/.

33. Consider, for example, Editorial, "A Landslide Loss for Big Money," *New York Times*, November 10, 2012, http://www.nytimes.com/2012/11/11/opinion/sunday/a-landslide-loss-for-big-money

.html; Eduardo Porter, "Get What You Pay For? Not Always," *New York Times*, November 6, 2012, http://www.nytimes.com/2012/11/07/business/pitfalls-of-spending-on-politics.html?pagewanted=all; Peter Overby, "Post-'Citizens United' Senate Snapshot: Money Doesn't Guarantee Victory," *NPR News*, November 7, 2012, http://www.npr.org/blogs/itsallpolitics/2012/11/07/164547856/post-citizens-united-senate-snapshot-money-doesnt-guarantee-victory.

34. Alex Blumberg, "Senator by Day, Telemarketer by Night," *NPR News*, March 30, 2012, http://www.npr.org/blogs/money/2012/03/30/149648666/senator-by-day-telemarketer-by-night. Studies show that it is common for members to spend between "30 and 70 percent of their time raising money." Lessig, *Republic Lost*, 138.

35. For example, Romney was harmed by superPACs and millionaire donors aligned with Gingrich and Santorum. Consider this report: Liz Halloran, "Did SuperPAC Money Hurt Romney More Than It Helped?" *NPR News*, November 7, 2012, http://www.npr.org/blogs/itsallpolitics/2012/11/07/164632802/did-superpac-money-hurt-romney-more-than-it-helped?sc=17&f=1014.

36. Bill Moyers, "Trevor Potter on Big Money's Election Effect," *BillMoyers.com*, November 16, 2012, http://billmoyers.com/segment/trevor-potter-on-big-moneys-election-effect/.

37. Ibid.

38. Meredith, McGehee, "Only a Tiny Fraction of Americans Give Significantly to Campaigns," The Campaign Legal Center, October 18, 2012, http://www.clcblog.org/index.php?option=com_content&view=article&id=482:only-a-tiny-fraction-of-americans-give-significantly-to-campaigns.

39. Center for Responsive Politics, "2012 Overview: Donor Demographics," *OpenSecrets.org*, http://www.opensecrets.org/overview/donordemographics.php.

40. Robert E. Mutch, "Three Centuries of Campaign Finance Law," in Lubenow, *A User's Guide*, 1.

41. George Washington, candidate self-funding, and the origin of corporate political power are discussed in Lubenow, *A User's Guide*, 3–20.

42. Jefferson, "Letter to William Johnson," (1823), in *Writings*, 1476.

43. Quoted by Noam Chomsky, "Consent Without Consent: Reflections on the Theory and Practice of Democracy," *Cleveland State Law Review* 44 (1996): 415.

44. Jefferson, "Letter from Thomas Jefferson to Tom Logan" (Nov. 12, 1816), in Ford, *The Writings of Thomas Jefferson*, 10:69.

45. Lincoln, "Letter from Abraham Lincoln to William F. Elkins" (Nov. 21, 1864), in Hertz, 2 *Abraham Lincoln: A New Portrait*, 2:954.

46. Ibid.

47. Smith, *The Wealth of Nations*, bk. 1, 87–88, 231–232.

48. Ibid.

49. Ibid.

50. Ibid. For another sound introduction to campaign finance law, including its historical trajectory, consider: Corrado, Mann et al., *The New Campaign Finance Sourcebook*.

51. For a discussion of state laws, see Malbin and Gais, *The Day after Reform*, and Schultz, *Money, Politics, and Campaign Finance Reform Law in the States*.

52. Many of these cases are discussed in Chapters 2–4.

53. McConnell v. FEC, 540 U.S. 93, 224 (2003).

54. Citizens United v. FEC, 130 S. Ct. 876 (2010). It is important to note that this case allows corporations to spend unlimited sums only insofar as that spending is not coordinated with candidates and campaigns. It does not allow corporations to donate money to parties or campaigns, or to coordinate their unlimited spending with parties or campaigns. This case is discussed in Chapter 4.

55. Arizona Free Enterprise v. Bennett, 131 S. Ct. 2806 (2011), consolidated with McComish v. Bennett, 611 F.3d 510 (9th Cir. 2010).

56. Eliza Newlin Carney, "Bevy of Fixes Might Complicate Efforts to Reshape Campaign Finance System," *Roll Call*, November 21, 2012, http://www.rollcall.com/news/bevy_of_fixes_might_complicate_efforts_to_reshape_campaign_finance_system-219338-1.html. Nicholas Confessore, "Result Won't Limit Campaign Money Any More Than Ruling Did," *New York Times*, November 11, 2012, http://www.nytimes.com/2012/11/12/us/politics/a-vote-for-unlimited-campaign-financing.html?_r=0.

57. Federal Election Commission, McCutcheon, et al. v. FEC Case Summary, http://www.fec.gov/law/litigation/McCutcheon.shtml.

58. For information on contribution limits, see Federal Election Commission, Contribution Limits 2013–2014, http://www.fec.gov/pages/brochures/contriblimits.shtml.

59. This would be the aggregate sum in play for maximum contributions to joint fundraising committees and candidates for both houses of Congress. Trevor Potter, Trevor Potter's Opening Remarks on McCutcheon v. FEC at The National Press Club's Newsmaker Event, The Campaign Legal Center Blog, October 1, 2013, http://www.clcblog.org/index.php?option=com_content&view=article&id=533:trevor-potters-opening-remarks-on-mccutcheon-v-fec-at-the-national-press-clubs-newsmaker-event-october-1-2013.

60. The center's positions on these and other campaign finance provisions can be viewed at http://www.campaignfreedom.org/research/.

61. "About Center for Competitive Politics," http://www.campaignfreedom.org/about/.

62. James Bennet, "The New Price of American Politics," *The Atlantic*, October 2012, http://www.theatlantic.com/magazine/archive/2012/10/the/309086/.

63. Ray Long, "Quinn Signs Super PAC Campaign Finance Law," *Chicago Tribune*, July 6, 2012, http://articles.chicagotribune.com/2012-07-06/news/chi-quinn-signs-super-pac-campaign-finance-law-20120706_1_contribution-limits-political-party-donations-campaign-finance-law.

64. Bennet, "The New Price of American Politics."

65. Buckley v. Valeo, 424 U.S. 1, 92–93 (1976), discussed in Chapter 2, upheld contribution limits and a limited public financing system for presidential elections. Two U.S. courts of appeals recently upheld bans on corporate contributions directly to candidates and campaigns: United States v. Danielczyk, No. 11–4667 (4th Cir. 2012); Minnesota Citizens Concerned for Life v. Swanson, No. 10–3126 (8th Cir. 2012).

66. Even the Rehnquist Court was unsympathetic to claims by political candidates, challenging the weakening of contribution limits. *McConnell*, 540 U.S. at 227–229 (deciding the fate of the "Adams Plaintiffs").

67. Ben Pershing, "As White House Candidates Abandon Public Funding, Republicans Look to End System," *Washington Post*, November 28, 2011, http://articles.washingtonpost.com/2011-11-28/politics/35282626_1_presidential-election-campaign-fund-general-election-general-election.

68. , "The First Amendment," 1021.

69. Tucker, "Rational Coercion," 1132. Tucker goes on to note, "The future focus of corporate campaign finance regulation, thus, must come from the corporations and the shareholders themselves. For corporations this means creating or strengthening corporate political spending policies and voluntary disclosures. For shareholders this means increased monitoring, reporting, and analyzing corporate political expenditures in order to educate shareholders and to draft successful shareholder resolutions that limit corporate spending policies and encourage internal corporate governance mechanisms."

70. Consider Kent Greenfield's and Siebecker's assessments of corporate power: Green-

field reminds us that "only 57 of the 100 largest economic entities in the world are nations[,] the other 43 are corporations," and Siebecker warns that "*Citizens United* . . . will affect democracy at its core by allowing corporations to dominate the political agenda and public opinion." Kent Greenfield, "The Stakeholder Strategy," *Democracy Journal*, Fall 2012, Issue 26, http://www.democracyjournal.org/26/the-stakeholder-strategy.php?page=all; Siebecker, "A New Discourse Theory of the Firm," 162.

71. Greenfield, "The Stakeholder Strategy," 48.

72. "Instead of amending the constitution to weaken corporate 'personhood,' we should focus on changing corporations [into 'associations of citizens'] so that overturning Citizens United would be unnecessary." Kent Greenfield, "A New Strategy to Fight Citizens United," *Huffington Post*, October 4, 2012, http://www.huffingtonpost.com/kent-greenfield/a-new-strategy-to-fight-c_b_1882744.html.

73. Winkler, "Beyond Bellotti," 165.

74. Fairfax, "Making the Corporation Safe for Shareholder Democracy," 53 (quotation taken from the abstract).

75. "Purpose and Summary," Shareholder Protection Act of 2010, H.R. 4790, 111th Cong. (2010), H.R. Rep. No. 111–620, at 4 (2010).

76. Bebchuk and Jackson, "Corporate Political Speech," 98–99.

77. Tom Hamburger and Brady Dennis, "More Shareholders Call on Companies to Disclose Their Political Spending," *Washington Post*, May 21, 2012, available at http://articles.washingtonpost.com/2012–05–21/business/35457217_1_corporate-governance-center-for-political-accountability-political-campaigns. On the push for SEC regulations on corporate political disclosure, see Kevin Bogardus, "Activists Press Obama's FEC to Expose Political Giving of U.S. Companies," *The Hill*, November 29, 2012, http://thehill.com/blogs/on-the-money/economy/270005–activists-press-sec-to-expose-political-giving-of-us-companies. The U.S. Chamber of Commerce provides the greatest opposition to this proposal, alleging that it would "silence the business community by creating an atmosphere of intimidation under the cover of investor protection." Ibid.

78. Winkler, "'Other People's Money,'" 873.

79. *Citizens United*, 130 S. Ct. at 977 (Stevens, J., concurring in part and dissenting in part).

80. Greenfield, "The Stakeholder Strategy," 52. On how corporate law may be drifting toward such broader concerns and away from a pure focus on profit maximization, see Stout, "Bad and Not-So-Bad Arguments for Shareholder Primacy."

81. Greenfield, "The Stakeholder Strategy," 59.

82. Siebecker, "A New Discourse Theory of the Firm," 165–166.

83. For a broad discussion of corporate economic power and its spread into areas of public concern, see Marx et al., *Private Standards and Global Governance*; on the disintegration of categories such as public and private authority, see Cafaggi, Scott, and Senden, *The Challenge of Transnational Private Regulation*; on corporate political spending, see Derber, *Corporation Nation*, 33.

84. Siebecker, "A New Discourse Theory of the Firm," 167.

85. Greenfield, "A New Strategy to Fight *Citizens United*."

86. Ted Barrett, "Senate Republicans Block DISCLOSE Act for a Second Straight Day," *CNN.com*, July 17, 2012, http://www.cnn.com/2012/07/17/politics/senate-disclose-act/index.html.

87. Alexander Bolton, "McConnell Pushes Back Against Campaign Finance Reform Efforts," *The Hill*, December 6, 2012, http://thehill.com/homenews/senate/271343–mcconnell-pushes-against-campaign-finance-reform-.

88. For a convenient overview of these and other terms, see Congressman Chris Van Hollen, "The 'DISCLOSE 2012 Act' Summary," http://vanhollen.house.gov/uploadedfiles/disclose_summary_020912.pdf.

89. HR 5175 (2010), 111th Congress, 2d Session, Sections 101–102, available at http://www.gpo.gov/fdsys/pkg/BILLS-111hr5175pcs/pdf/BILLS-111hr5175pcs.pdf. For a basic summary of the act's terms as of 2010, see "The Van Hollen 'DISCLOSE ACT,'" http://vanhollen.house.gov/uploadedfiles/disclose_summary_042910.pdf.

90. Rosalind S. Helderman, "DISCLOSE Act, New Donor Transparency Law, Blocked in Senate," *Washington Post*, July 16, 2012, http://www.washingtonpost.com/blogs/2chambers/post/disclose-act-new-donor-transparency-law-blocked-in-senate/2012/07/16/gJQAbm7WpW_blog.html.

91. See, for example, *Buckley*, 424 U.S. at 66–84, *Citizens United*, 130 S. Ct. at 914–916, and Doe v. Reed, 561 U.S., 130 S. Ct. 2811 (2010). The Court recently refused to grant certiorari in The Real Truth About Abortion v. FEC, No. 11–1760 (4th Cir. 2012), confirming its unwillingness to weaken disclosure rules.

92. Joan Aikens, Lee Ann Elliott, Thomas Josefiak, David Mason, Bradley Smith, Hans A. von Spakovsky, Michael Toner, and Darryl R. Wold, "Chuck Schumer vs. Free Speech," *Wall Street Journal*, May 19, 2010, http://online.wsj.com/article/SB10001424052748703460404577524477207071037 4.html.

93. Presidential Funding Act, S. 3312 (112th Congress), *govtrack.us*, http://www.govtrack.us/congress/bills/112/s3312.

94. HR 6448, 112th Congress, Second Session, Sept. 20th, 2012, http://www.gpo.gov/fdsys/pkg/BILLS-112hr6448ih/pdf/BILLS-112hr6448ih.pdf.

95. Adam Skaggs, Brennan Center Senior Counsel, quoted in "Brennan Center Applauds Introduction of Empowering Citizens Act," *Brennan Center*, Sept. 21, 2012, at http://www.brennancenter.org/content/resource/brennan_center_applauds_introduction_of_empowering_citizens_act/.

96. On disclosure and coordination, respectively, see HR 6448, Title V, Section 501 and Title III, Section 324. For general information on the legislative effort, see Albert R. Hunt, "In Politics, More Can Mean Less," *New York Times*, December 9, 2012, http://www.nytimes.com/2012/12/10/us/10iht-letter10.html.

97. For a summary of terms, see "The American Anti-Corruption Act: Summary of Provisions," http://anticorruptionact.org (scroll down toward the end of the page). For a popular press analysis, see Eliza Newlin Carney, "Lobbyists Could See More Curbs Arising from Campaign Finance Movement," *Roll Call*, December 5, 2012, http://www.rollcall.com/news/lobbyists_could_see_more_curbs_arising_from_campaign_finance_movement-219658-1.html.

98. "The American Anti-Corruption Act." For an analysis of the constitutionality of the act's terms, seehttps://s3.amazonaws.com/s3.unitedrepublic.org/docs/AACA_Constitutionality.pdf.

99. Associated Press, "Executives Urge Public Financing for Campaigns," *New York Times*, January 23, 2010, available at http://www.nytimes.com/2010/01/23/us/politics/23letter.html?_r=0.

100. U.S. Const., art. V. ("The Congress, whenever two thirds of both Houses shall deem it necessary, shall propose Amendments to this Constitution, or, on the Application of the Legislatures of two thirds of the several States, shall call a Convention for proposing Amendments, which, in either Case, shall be valid to all Intents and Purposes, as part of this Constitution, when ratified by the Legislatures of three fourths of the several States, or by Conventions in three fourths thereof, as the one or the other Mode of Ratification may be proposed by the Congress.")

101. George Washington, "Letter to Bushrod Washington," quoted in Levinson, *Responding to Imperfection*, 3.

102. Still, some argue that Article V does not represent the only path for amending the Constitution. See Amar, "The Consent of the Governed."

103. James Madison, "The Federalist No. 43," in *The Federalist Papers* (Isaac Kramnick ed.), 284. On Article V's two procedures for amending the Constitution and recent amendment proposals, see Freedman, *The Naked Constitution*, 307–319.

104. Robert Weissman, "One Year Later, Movement Is Growing to Overturn Citizens United," *Public Citizen*, January 21, 2011, http://www.citizen.org/pressroom/pressroomredirect.cfm?ID=3264. The terms of *Public Citizen*'s proposed amendment are available at http://www.citizen.org/Page.aspx?pid=5008.

105. Carney, "Bevy of Fixes"; Paul Blumenthal, "Obama Endorses Anti-Citizens United Amendment in Reddit Chat," *Huffington Post*, August 29, 2012, available at http://www.huffingtonpost.com/2012/08/29/barack-obama-citizens-united-reddit_n_1841258.html.

106. On state ballot initiatives, see Common Cause, "Fed Up with Runaway Campaign Spending, Voters Back Constitutional Amendment to Overturn Citizens United," *Amend 2012*, http://amend2012.org/2012/11/07/fed-up-with-runaway-campaign-spending-voters-back-constitutional-amendment-to-overturn-citizens-united/.

107. See Hart Research Associates, "Free Speech for People Nationwide Survey," http://freespeechforpeople.org/sites/default/files/FSFP%20Nationwide%20Voter%20Survey-1.pdf, discussed in Bob Edgar, "The Only Way to Revive Real Democracy," *New York Times*, October 24, 2012, http://www.nytimes.com/roomfordebate/2012/10/24/amend-the-constitution-to-limit-political-spending/the-only-way-to-revive-real-democracy.

108. Move to Amend's Proposed 28th Amendment to the Constitution states that "Artificial entities, such as corporations, limited liability companies, and other entities, established by the laws of any State, the United States, or any foreign state shall have no rights under this Constitution." See https://movetoamend.org/democracy-amendments. Senator Bernie Sanders's Save American Democracy Amendment contains similar terms: "The rights protected by the Constitution of the United States are the rights of natural persons and do not extend to for-profit corporations, limited liability companies, or other private entities established for business purposes or to promote business interests under the laws of any state, the United States, or any foreign state." See http://www.sanders.senate.gov/imo/media/doc/S.J.Res.pdf.

109. Alliance for Democracy, Mission Statement, at http://www.thealliancefordemocracy.org/about.html.

110. "Move to Amend's Proposed 28th Amendment to the Constitution," https://movetoamend.org/democracy-amendments.

111. Public financing has been proposed by several reformers, including Representatives Yarmuth and Jones. See http://yarmuth.house.gov/uploads/Money%20Out%20of%20Politics%20CA-Yarmuth%2012.5.11.pdf.

112. Representative Deutch's proposed amendment, endorsed by *Public Citizen* and referred to as the OCCUPIED Amendment, can be accessed at http://teddeutch.house.gov/uploadedfiles/deutch_036_xml.pdf.

113. See, for example, Lawrence Lessig's proposed amendment, http://lessig.tumblr.com/post/14010963493/proposed-28th-amendment-beta-v-9 ("Congress shall by law establish an agency for federal elections which shall enforce the provisions of this article, and whose principal officers shall be non-partisan commissioners who have served at least 10 years as a federal judge. The agency shall have standing to enforce the provisions of this article ju-

dicially in the federal courts, and the judicial power shall be construed to extend to actions by the agency against Congress").

114. It bears repeating that this conception of freedom was not initially extended to women or African Americans. Although one does observe a favorable progression in this regard, its time span is notable: voting rights were not completely implemented in the American South, for example, until the beginning of the 1970s. On democracy's late arrival, see Denning, "Neither Capitalist nor American," in Purdy, *Democratic Vistas*, 145.

115. The Court has adopted such language in several cases, as will be discussed in Chapter 3. "Political 'free trade' does not necessarily require that all who participate in the political marketplace do so with exactly equal resources . . . Relative availability of funds is after all a rough barometer of public support." FEC v. Massachusetts Citizens for Life, Inc. [hereafter *MCFL*], 479 U.S. 238, 257–258 (1986). "It is the purpose of the First Amendment to preserve an uninhibited marketplace of ideas in which truth will ultimately prevail, rather than to countenance monopolization of that market." Red Lion Broadcasting Co. v. FCC, 395 U.S. 367, 390 (1969).

116. I do not mean to deny that religion, economic planning, power-hungry presidents, and sometimes even royalty can exert significant pressure within the liberal-democratic state in today's world. Rather, I suggest that such influence is no longer institutionalized. In the case of economic planning, all democratic governments regulate the market, but that is a different proposition from a planned economy. It is one thing for the state to provide for certain public goods, force economic actors to internalize the unintended consequences of their activities (pollution and injuries from defective products, for example), and break up monopolies. It is another thing entirely for the state to dictate levels or areas of production, nationalize industries, and so on. These matters are explored in Chapter 7.

117. Michael Walzer's *Spheres of Justice* and *Thinking Politically* have been the most successful efforts to frame the problem in these terms.

118. Most advanced democracies have gone further than the United States in limiting the role of economic power in politics. Ewing and Issacharoff, *Party Funding and Campaign Financing in International Perspective*; Gunlicks, *Campaign Finance and Party Finance in North America and Western Europe*.

119. Issacharoff and Pildes, "Politics as Markets," 713.

120. Powell, *Constitutional Conscience*, 45.

121. Ibid., 47.

122. Lindblom, *Politics and Markets*, ix.

123. Ibid.

124. PBS News Hour, "Greenspan Admits 'Flaw' to Congress, Predicts More Economic Problems," *PBS.org*, October 23, 2008, http://www.pbs.org/newshour/bb/business/july-dec08/crisishearing_10-23.html.

125. Thomas Frank, "Obama and the K Street Set," *Wall Street Journal*, September 30, 2009, A21, http://online.wsj.com/article/SB10001424052748704471504574443355332223162.html.

126. Dworkin, *Is Democracy Possible Here?* Makinson, *Speaking Freely*; Blasi, "Widening Gyre of Fund-Raising."

127. Sunstein, "Political Equality," 1392.

128. Hasen, "The Political Market Metaphor," 730.

129. Fiss, "Free Speech and Social Structure," 1406.

130. Ibid.

131. Ibid., 1407. Others too deserve mention. Epstein, "Modern Republicanism,"

1637 (describing interest group pluralism, at its best, as "see[ing] politics as an extension of market behavior into the political realm"); Overton, "The Donor Class," 104. "The antireformers' lack of concern about disparities in wealth stems, in part, from an unwavering acceptance of economic market norms, even though such norms often conflict with democratic values and objectives." Cass Sunstein writes, "The extraordinary transformation of the First Amendment from a Madisonian principle into a species of neoclassical economics—into a celebration of laissez-faire and the 'invisible hand' for speech—is an important and largely untold story." Sunstein, *Democracy and the Problem of Free Speech*, Kindle Location 200–204.

CHAPTER 2

1. Paul Krugman, "How Did Economists Get It So Wrong?" *New York Times Magazine*, September 6, 2009, http://www.nytimes.com/2009/09/06/magazine/06Economic-t.html.

2. Ibid.

3. Akerlof and Shiller describe this history as one of "sharp reversals" in *Animal Spirits*, 172–173.

4. Krugman, "How Did Economists Get It So Wrong?"

5. Justin Fox, *The Myth of the Rational Market: A History of Risk, Reward, and Delusion on Wall Street* (New York: HarperCollins, 2009), xiii.

6. Ibid.

7. Justin Fox explains that Friedman cannot be taken as subscribing entirely to the efficient market hypothesis: "Friedman didn't believe markets were perfect. He just thought that they were better, and more accommodating of human liberty, than government. He may have oversold that argument on occasion. But don't go calling the man an efficient marketeer." Justin Fox, "Milton Friedman on the Efficient Market Hypothesis," November 21, 2006, http://www.byjustinfox.com/2006/11/milton_friedman.html.

8. Friedman, *Capitalism and Freedom*, vi, 5.

9. Friedman, quoted in Rosanvallon, *Democracy Past and Future*, 151.

10. *Buckley*'s timing makes it part of a broader social change, more a feature of a widespread trend than an isolated development within the caselaw. Deane, *The State and the Economic System*, 192. Dean notes the "distinctly monetarist bias [of] policy decisions taken (even by left-wing governments) in the late 1970s and the 1980s."

11. Buckley v. Valeo, 424 U.S. 1 (1976).

12. Hohenstein, *Coining Corruption* 3–201; Anthony Corrado, "Money and Politics: A History of Federal Campaign Finance Law," in Corrado, Mann et al., *The New Campaign Finance Sourcebook*, 7–47; Robert E. Mutch, "Three Centuries of Campaign Finance Law," in Lubinow, *A User's Guide*, 1–24.

13. Washington Post.com, "Campaign Finance Special Report," http://www.washington post.com/wp-srv/politics/special/campfin/intro3.htm.

14. Pasquale, "Reclaiming Egalitarianism," 612.

15. Ibid.

16. Fleishman, "The 1974 Federal Election Campaign Act Amendments," 885.

17. The most important provisions for our purposes are these: individual contributions to candidates were set at $1,000 and later increased by the Bipartisan Campaign Reform Act of 2002; presidential candidates could not use more than $50,000 of their own money; the same limit in the case of congressional candidates varied between $25,000 and $35,000; candidates for nomination for election to the presidency could not spend more than $10 million; and candidates for election to the office of the president could not spend more than

$20 million. These and other limits are detailed in the appendix to the per curiam opinion. *Buckley*, 424 U.S. at 187–199.

18. Randall v. Sorrell, 548 U.S. 230 (2006).

19. *Buckley*, 424 U.S. at 14.

20. Ibid.,14–15.

21. Ibid., 15.

22. Ibid., 14.

23. Ibid., 18n17.

24. Ibid., 19.

25. Ibid.

26. Anne Marie Helmenstine, "Turning Lead into Gold: Is Alchemy Real?" *About. com*, http://chemistry.about.com/cs/generalchemistry/a/aa050601a.htm. "Today particle accelerators routinely transmute elements. A charged particle is accelerated using electrical and/or magnetic fields. In a linear accelerator, the charged particles drift through a series of charged tubes separated by gaps. Every time the particle emerges between gaps, it is accelerated by the potential difference between adjacent segments. In a circular accelerator, magnetic fields accelerate particles moving in circular paths. In either case, the accelerated particle impacts a target material, potentially knocking free protons or neutrons and making a new element or isotope."

27. *Buckley* simultaneously concedes and obscures this in noting that "[a] restriction on the amount of money a person or group can spend . . . restrict[s] the number of issues discussed, the depth of their exploration, and the size of the audience reached." 424 U.S. at 19. A paper posted on a blog could (and would almost inevitably) cover more issues in greater depth than any television advertisement purchased for millions of dollars. Money secures a large audience and attractive packaging for political advertisements. It has much more to do with these things than with the number of issues discussed or the depth of their exploration. These latter variables may well be inversely correlated with expensive political communications.

28. *Buckley*, 424 U.S. at 16.

29. Brief for Appellees Center for Public Financing of Elections, Common Cause, League of Women Voters of the United States et al. at 90 and 76, *Buckley*, 424 U.S. 1 (Nos. 75–436, 75–437).

30. Ibid., 12 (quoting Paul Freund, "Commentary," in Albert J. Rosenthal, *Federal Regulation of Campaign Finance: Some Constitutional Questions*, 71–72 [Milton Katz ed. 1970]).

31. The Court added that this would "reduc[e] the overall scope of federal election campaigns." *Buckley*, 424 U.S. at 17.

32. The Court described these limitations as additional to those on "any reasonable time, place, and manner regulations otherwise imposed." Ibid. at 18.

33. Karlan, "Politics by Other Means," 1699.

34. Schumpeter, *Capitalism, Socialism, and Democracy*, 266.

35. Mutch, *Campaigns, Congress, and the Courts*, 55.

36. Mill, *Principles of Political Economy*, bk. 3, ch. 1, 208.

37. *Buckley*, 424 U.S. at 21.

38. Ibid., 20–21.

39. Ibid., 21–22.

40. Ibid., 24–26.

41. Ibid., 26.

42. Ibid., 26–27.

43. Ibid., 27.

44. Ibid., 47.

45. Ibid., 53.

46. Marshall alluded to this in his separate opinion. "In the Nation's seven largest States in 1970, 11 of the 15 major senatorial candidates were millionaires. The four who were not millionaires lost their bid for election." Ibid., 288n1 (Marshall, J., concurring in part and dissenting in part).

47. Fiss, "Free Speech and Social Structure," 1409.

48. Walzer, *Spheres of Justice*, 101.

49. Ortiz, "Democratic Paradox," 901.

50. Peter Buttenwieser, "Why I Participate in a Corrupt System," in Corrado, Mann, and Potter, *Inside the Campaign Finance Battle*, 311.

51. Paul Simon, "How the Senate Was Corrupted by Soft Money," in Corrado, Mann, and Potter, *Inside the Campaign Finance Battle*, 317.

52. *Buckley*, 424 U.S. at 288 (Marshall, J., concurring in part and dissenting in part). Most to the point is Justice Marshall's recognition of millionaires' disproportionate success as senatorial candidates. Ibid., n1.

53. Tocqueville, *Democracy in America*, vol. 1, 3.

54. Contribution limits came in the 1974 amendments to FECA. Corrado, Mann et al., *The New Campaign Finance Sourcebook*, 21–25.

55. As an example of this, consider the illegalization of employment discrimination in Title VII of the 1964 Civil Rights Act, Pub. L. No. 88–352, 78 Stat. 241 (codified as amended at 42 U.S.C. § 2000 (2006)).

56. Rawls, *A Theory of Justice*, 224–225.

57. Rawls, *Political Liberalism,* 327. Consider, along these lines, Ronald Dworkin's remark: "It is another premise of democracy that citizens must be able, as individuals, to participate on equal terms in both formal politics and in the informal cultural life that creates the moral environment of the community." "The Curse of American Politics," *New York Review of Books*, October 17, 1996, at 19, 21.

58. As Sunstein put it, "A system of unlimited campaign expenditures should be seen as a regulatory decision to allow disparities in resources to be turned into disparities in political influence." Sunstein, "Political Equality," 1399.

59. *Buckley*, 424 U.S. at 48.

60. Ibid., 48–49 (internal quotations removed).

61. Harper v. Canada (Attorney General), SCC 33 at ¶ 91 (2004).

62. The Canadian Court was not solely interested in equality's effects on liberty. It also emphasized an "egalitarian model of elections." Still, I find it difficult to separate their concern for equality from their concern for liberty. For example, the Court wrote that "[a]dvertising expense limits may restrict free expression to ensure that participants are able to meaningfully participate in the electoral process." Ibid., ¶ 87.

63. Jackson, "Fiss's Way," 312.

64. Good sources on donors include: Overton, "The Donor Class," and Bartels, *Unequal Democracy*.

65. *Buckley*, 424 U.S. at 49n55. There the Court notes the appellees' lack of support for the proposition that "the First Amendment permits Congress to abridge the rights of some persons to engage in political expression in order to enhance the relative voice of other segments of our society."

66. As H. Jefferson Powell puts it, "The constitutional text itself presupposes that its interpreters will go outside the four corners of its language." Powell, *Constitutional Conscience*, 45.

67. *Buckley*, 424 U.S. at 55.

68. Smith, *Unfree Speech*, 165–166.

69. Ibid. In keeping with our ideological theme, Smith has named his nonprofit advocacy group the "Center for Competitive Politics" and has chosen as its URL "www.campaign freedom.org."

70. *Buckley*, 424 U.S. at 48–49.

71. Cato Institute, http://www.cato.org/about.php (last visited June 26, 2009).

72. Samples, *The Fallacy*, 133. On the role of Samples at CATO, see http://www.cato.org /people/john-samples. Above his photo, these words appear in large type: "Individual Liberty, Free Markets, and Peace."

73. Kara, *Sex Trafficking*.

74. Robert Lekachman, "Capitalism or Democracy," in Goldwin and Schambra, *How Capitalistic Is the Constitution?*, 129.

75. Issacharoff and Karlan, "The Hydraulics of Campaign Finance Reform," 1705. This article demonstrates that piecemeal reforms and eviscerated statutes tend to simply reroute money into other, increasingly elusive and often increasingly harmful channels.

76. *Buckley*, 424 U.S. at 56.

77. Ibid.

78. Ibid.

79. Ibid., 57.

80. Ibid. (my italics).

81. Lekachman, "Capitalism or Democracy," 128.

82. A present-day example of such competition arises from the debate over health care reform. Katherine Q. Seelye, "Competing Ads on Health Care Plan Swamp the Airwaves," *New York Times*, August 16, 2009, A1. Seelye notes that one ad opposing Obama's plan ran 115 times in 36 hours in the media market where Obama was speaking, and that most of the $57 million spent on television ads was spent within a 45-day period.

83. Wagner, *Social Reformers*, 25.

84. Ibid., 20.

85. Dahl, *Dilemmas of Pluralist Democracy*, 108–109.

86. Galbraith, *American Capitalism*, 27–28 (discussing how competition solves the "problem of power").

87. Posner, *Law, Pragmatism, and Democracy*, 152–153. Posner criticizes the "duopolistic competition" of the two parties, noting that certain groups are not represented, and concluding that this system "induces parties to compete in the general election for the median voter."

88. *Buckley*, 424 U.S. at 237 (White, J., dissenting).

89. Ibid., 238.

90. Ibid., 237.

91. Ibid., 45n55.

92. Ibid. at 67n79.

93. Ibid. at 67.

94. Abrams v. United States, 250 U.S. 616, 630 (1919) (Holmes, J., joined by Brandeis, J., dissenting). On the market theory of speech, consider Meiklejohn, *Free Speech*.

95. Blocher, "Institutions in the Marketplace of Ideas," 824.

96. Holmes, *The Common Law*, 77. "[T]he prevailing view is that [the state's] cumbrous and expensive machinery ought not to be set in motion unless some clear benefit is to be derived from disturbing the status quo."

97. 198 U.S. 45 (1905).

98. Ibid., 53. Concerns over paternalism are clear within the opinion: "There is no contention that bakers as a class are not equal in intelligence and capacity to men in other trades or manual occupations, or that they are not able to assert their rights and care for themselves without the protecting arm of the state, interfering with their independence of judgment and of action. They are in no sense wards of the state . . . [W]e think that a law like the one before us involves neither the safety, the morals, nor the welfare, of the public, and that the interest of the public is not in the slightest degree affected by such an act. The law must be upheld, if at all, as a law pertaining to the health of the individual engaged in the occupation of a baker." Ibid., 57.

99. Ibid., 75–76 (Holmes, J., dissenting).

100. Rawls, *Political Liberalism*, 362. Cass Sunstein has made the same point. "Just as the due process clause once forbade government 'interference' with the outcomes of the economic marketplace, so too the First Amendment now bans government 'interference' with the political marketplace, with the term 'marketplace' understood quite literally." Sunstein, *Political Equality*, 1398. Sullivan makes a complementary point in *Discrimination, Distribution and Free Speech*, 440.

101. Walzer, *Spheres of Justice*, 102.

102. Ibid.

103. Radin, *Contested Commodities*, 108.

104. Sunstein, *Political Equality*, 1397.

105. Ibid., 1397–1398.

106. Dahl, *Dilemmas*, 108.

107. *Buckley*, 424 U.S. at 26–27. There, the Court stated: "To the extent that large contributions are given to secure a political *quid pro quo* from current and potential office holders, the integrity of our system of representative democracy is undermined." On the significance of *Buckley*'s definition of corruption, consider Teachout, "The Anti-Corruption Principle," 386: "As the first Supreme Court decision to mention '*quid pro quo*' as the core harm against which anti-corruption measures are fighting, *Buckley* suggested a new, more mechanical way of thinking about the power of money."

108. *Buckley*, 424 U.S. at 27. The Court stated: "Of almost equal concern as the danger of actual *quid pro quo* arrangements is the impact of the appearance of corruption stemming from public awareness of the opportunities for abuse inherent in a regime of large individual financial contributions."

109. *Buckley*, 424 U.S. at 26. The role of the media and the particular structure of the U.S. media market should not be ignored in generating conditions that raise candidates' and parties' demands for money—conditions such as deregulation, ownership concentration, and advertising costs. Croteau and Hoynes, *The Business of Media*; Bennett, *The Governing Crisis*.

110. Landes and Posner, "The Independent Judiciary," 877.

111. Ibid.

112. Schumpeter, *Capitalism, Socialism, and Democracy*, 287.

113. Ibid., 263. "The ways in which issues and the popular will on any issue are being manufactured is exactly analogous to the ways of commercial advertising. We find the same attempts to contact the subconscious. We find the same technique of creating favorable and unfavorable associations which are the more effective the less rational they are. We find the same evasions and reticences and the same trick of producing opinion by reiterated assertion that is successful precisely to the extent to which it avoids rational argument and the danger of awakening the critical faculties of the people." And ibid., 283: "The psycho-technics of party management and party advertising, slogans and marching tunes, are not accessories.

They are the essence of politics." Galbraith had noted the same thing about the commercial realm, just as Schumpeter alleged: "The large corporation can have significant power over the prices it charges, over the prices it pays, even over the mind of the consumer whose wants and tastes it partly synthesizes." Galbraith, *American Capitalism*, 7.

114. Schumpeter, *Capitalism, Socialism, and Democracy*, 298n8. In the same passage, Schumpeter explains how this phenomenon would be viewed by an economic theory of democracy: "From the . . . standpoint [of economic theory], the result reads that those private means are often used in order to interfere with the working of the mechanism of competitive leadership."

115. The market makes no apologies for this. Besides viewing the advantages of wealth as an incentive to succeed in the market (and thereby obtain wealth) and aside from the view that wealth is a sign of hard work and desert, defenders of the market system focus on freedom, not equality. It would not be a free market if individual advantages were coercively removed or artificially lessened by the state.

116. In the 1998 congressional elections, for example, contributions of $200 or more accounted for 66% of all contributions made. Three-quarters of these contributions came from people who made at least $100,000 per year, and a majority of those characterized as the "most active donors" made at least $500,000 per year. Clyde Wilcox, "Contributing as Political Participation," in Lubenow, *A User's Guide*, 117–118 (labeling income "the best single predictor of giving in politics"). Wilcox cites studies showing that it is actually the wealthiest of the wealthy—those in the top 5% of the total population—who give drastically more and drastically more often. This group gives seven times more frequently than the bottom two-thirds of the population combined.

117. A major study of contributors to congressional campaigns reveals a number of distinguishing traits. They are much more highly educated than the average American. Even among the occasional donors, 80% went to college, and 64% of the most active donors completed at least some graduate education. They are 99% white across the board—even among those who donate merely occasionally. A great majority are male—between 72% and 82%. They are most likely to be mainline Protestants or Catholics. And the great majority is over 46 years of age. And yet donors are not representative of any of these groups on the whole, not typical college-educated, wealthy, white males of some years. They are in fact a special cross-section of each group to which they belong. Their defining characteristic across all the groups to which they belong, even the group that is the wealthy elite, is their especially conservative views on economic issues. From eight years of American National Election Studies data, Wilcox concludes that "donors are significantly more conservative than other wealthy and well-educated citizens on economic issues—guaranteed jobs, spending on social programs, affirmative action—but not on social issues such as women's role or abortion, or on foreign policy." Ibid., 116–119.

118. Even in 1952, roughly two-thirds of all money spent on federal elections came from donations of $500 or more ($2,300 or more in today's dollars). Urofsky, *Money and Free Speech*, 24. Senate fundraising as early as the 1960s is discussed in Miliband, *The State in Capitalist Society*, 151n3.

119. Overton also notes *Buckley*'s validation of a market for political power: "According to the class-blind assumptions about political participation underlying *Buckley* and its progeny, the private economic market determines the allocation of entitlements to financial resources for use in the political sphere. The donor class is a natural product of the market and requires no legal acknowledgment or remedy." Overton, "The Donor Class," 80–81.In Overton's reading of the data, the donor class is constituted as follows: "70.2% are male, 70.6% are age 50 or older, 84.3% have a college degree, 85.7% have family incomes of $100,000 or more, and 95.8% are white." Ibid., 102.

120. Bartels, *Unequal Democracy*, 254.

121. "[R]egardless of how the data are sliced, there is no discernible evidence that the views of low-income constituents had any effect on their senators' voting behavior." Ibid., 280.

122. Overton, "The Donor Class," 80.

123. Ibid.

124. Blasi, "Widening Gyre of Fund-Raising," 1281. Numerous members of Congress discuss the difficulty and undesirability of the private fundraising system in Makinson, *Speaking Freely*.

125. Blasi, "Widening Gyre of Fund-Raising," 1281. Blasi references "bazaars staged by political parties to display their candidates for the inspection of potential contributors." He also notes that "[m]any political action committees require candidate-supplicants to fill out questionnaires pertaining to how they would vote on hypothetical legislative proposals." Ibid., 1281n2.

126. Galbraith, *American Capitalism*, 15.

127. Ibid., 14.

128. Galbraith also discusses the "strong humanitarian basis for this preoccupation" with efficiency among early economists. Ibid., 24.

129. Ibid., 14.

130. Galbraith notes extensive corporate consolidation, its negative effects on standard capitalist notions of consumer sovereignty and competition among firms too small to control prices, and describes new theories of imperfect competition and oligopoly, which show that price competition subsides and advertising competition thrives. Ibid., 32–49.

131. *Buckley*, 424 U.S. at 235 (Burger, C.J., dissenting). Burger's concerns are expressed in that familiar form of the slippery slope: "[D]elegate selection and the management of political conventions have been considered a strictly private political matter, not the business of Government inspectors. But once the Government finances these national conventions by the expenditure of millions of dollars from the public treasury, we may be providing a springboard for later attempts to impose a whole range of requirements on delegate selection and convention activities." Ibid., 250.

132. Ibid., 256–257.

133. Ibid., 259. Justice White further notes that many federal laws have had incidental effects on speech, including labor laws, antitrust, and taxation. Ibid., 262–263 (White, J., dissenting). He deepens this approach somewhat in his dissent in Fed. Election Com'n v. Nat'l Conservative Political Action Comm., 470 U.S. 480 (1985), as discussed in Chapter 7.

134. *Buckley*, 424 U.S. at 265 (White, J., dissenting).

135. Ibid. Vincent Blasi later expanded on this point.

136. Ibid., 263 (White, J., dissenting).

137. Ibid., 266.

138. Ibid., 265.

139. Ibid., 266.

CHAPTER 3

1. I refer to Chief Justice Burger's and Justice Blackmun's separate opinions in *Buckley*, 424 U.S. 1.

2. 435 U.S. 765 (1978).

3. Powell added, "It is time for American business—which has demonstrated the greatest capacity in all history to produce and to influence consumer decisions—to apply their great talents vigorously to the preservation of the [American] system [of free enterprise] it-

self." Memorandum from Lewis F. Powell Jr. to Eugene B. Sydnor Jr., Chairman, Education Committee, U.S. Chamber of Commerce, August 23, 1971, http://old.mediatransparency. org/story.php?storyID=22. The Chamber of Commerce published the memo after a reporter exposed it: U.S. Chamber of Commerce, "The Powell Memorandum," *Washington Report*, Supp. No. 2900, 1971. Professor Houck was one of the first to write about the effect of the memo on interest-group politics. Houck, "With Charity for All," 1457–1460.

4. This memo was addressed to Lawrence Higby, assistant to Nixon's chief of staff, as discussed in Chester, *Watergate*, 81, 269.

5. Dean Memo, August 16, 1971, quoted in Kutler, *The Wars of Watergate*, 104–105, 248.

6. Examples are documented in many places, including the Articles of Impeachment themselves. H.R. REP. NO. 1305, 93rd Cong., 2d Sess. (1974).

7. Powell memo (accessed online, without page numbers).

8. Ibid.

9. Ibid.

10. Ibid.

11. Although the ideologies of Supreme Court Justices eventually become common knowledge and the outcome of many cases can be predicted, it is rare for Justices to have already opined, in detail, about a matter submitted for decision.

12. *Bellotti*, 435 U.S. at 768.

13. Ibid., 769.

14. Ibid., 770n4.

15. Powell Memo.

16. Ibid.

17. *Bellotti*, 435 U.S. at 776.

18. New York Times Co. v. Sullivan, 376 U.S. 254, 266 (1964).

19. *Bellotti*, 435 U.S. at 777.

20. Ibid., n11.

21. Smith, "The Wealth of Nations," in Wagner, *Social Reformers*, 18.

22. *Bellotti*, 435 U.S. at 777.

23. Ibid. He does, however, mention only corporations, unions, associations, and individuals as possible speakers.

24. Potter, "The Current State of Campaign Finance Law," in Corrado, Mann et al., *The New Campaign Finance Sourcebook*, 59–60.

25. Ibid.

26. Powell memo.

27. *Bellotti*, 435 U.S. at 778–784.

28. Ibid., 777.

29. A utilitarian view of the Due Process or Cruel and Unusual Punishment Clauses, for example, would take a similar form: trials without rights and torturous punishments are prohibited because they tend to trigger both decreased respect for law and social rebellion. Such prohibitions might be ignored, however, if it were found that the benefits exceeded the costs.

30. *Buckley*, 424 U.S. at 15. "In a republic where the people are sovereign, the ability of the citizenry to make informed choices among candidates for office is essential, for the identities of those who are elected will inevitably shape the course that we follow as a nation."

31. *Bellotti*, 435 U.S. at 777n12.

32. Ibid.

33. Ibid.

34. Examples from other areas of constitutional law may help illustrate this point. Ap-

plying this particular deontological view to the Eighth and Fourteenth Amendments, Kafka-esque trials and medieval punishments should be forbidden because they are wrong per se. This judgment flows respectively from "a principle of justice so rooted in the traditions and conscience of our people as to be ranked as fundamental" and "the dignity of man." See Palko v. Connecticut, 302 U.S. 319, 325 (1937) and Trop v. Dulles, 356 U.S. 86, 100 (1958).

35. *Sullivan*, 376 U.S. at 266.

36. *Buckley*, 424 U.S. at 16.

37. It even became irrelevant whether corporate speech was directed at an issue materially affecting the corporation's business interests. *Bellotti*, 435 U.S. at 781–784.

38. Ibid., 787.

39. Ibid., 789–790.

40. Ibid., 789.

41. Ibid., 790.

42. Ibid., 791.

43. Schumpeter, *Capitalism, Socialism, and Democracy*, 263.

44. *Sullivan*, 376 U.S. at 266.

45. I see this as a parallel within economics to the rights-based rationale for free speech.

46. Consider Galbraith's discussion of the factors that influence new entrants in *American Capitalism*, 34.

47. Smith, "The Wealth of Nations," in Wagner, *Social Reformers*, 14.

48. Ibid.

49. Ibid., 25.

50. Ibid.

51. Galbraith, *American Capitalism*, 37.

52. Ibid., 41.

53. Ibid., 43–44.

54. Ibid., 44.

55. Ibid., 43. Amazon.com has been host to interesting controversies along related lines. Lynn Neary, "Publishers and Booksellers See a 'Predatory' Amazon," *NPR.org*, January 23, 2012, http://www.npr.org/2012/01/23/145468105/publishers-and-booksellers-see-a-predatory-amazon; "Daily Report: The E-Books Pricing Controversy Continues," *New York Times*, June 8, 2012, http://bits.blogs.nytimes.com/2012/06/08/daily-report-the-e-books-pricing-controversy-continues/; Anita Ramasastry, "Web sites change prices based on consumer habits," *CNN.com*, June 24, 2005, http://edition.cnn.com/2005/LAW/06/24/ramasastry.website.prices/.

56. Galbraith, *American Capitalism*, 44.

57. Ibid., 43.

58. Ibid., 46. Galbraith refers to the phenomenon of price-cutting. Ibid., 44–45.

59. Ibid., 46–47.

60. *Bellotti*, 435 U.S. at 792n32. Here, Powell wrote: "Corporate advertising, unlike some methods of participation in political campaigns, is likely to be highly visible. Identification of the source of advertising may be required as a means of disclosure, so that the people will be able to evaluate the arguments to which they are being subjected."

61. Ibid.

62. Ibid., 791.

63. Powell memo.

64. Ibid.

65. Ibid.

66. Ibid.
67. Ibid.
68. Ibid.
69. Ibid.
70. Ibid.
71. Ibid., quoting a *Fortune* magazine article.
72. Lindblom, *Politics and Markets*, 195.
73. Ibid.
74. Ibid., 196–197.
75. Ibid., 197.
76. *Bellotti*, 435 U.S. at 810 (White, J., dissenting).
77. Ibid.
78. Perhaps the most recent, blatant example of this is detailed in Caperton v. Massey Coal, 129 S. Ct. 2252 (2009). There, a corporation's chairman and principal officer spent $3 million to ensure the election of Brent Benjamin to the West Virginia State Supreme Court of Appeals, the court that was poised to hear the corporation's appeal of a $50 million verdict. Now-Justice Benjamin was elected and supplied the vote that tipped the Court 3–2 in the corporation's favor. The Supreme Court held that due process required Benjamin's recusal. Still, Chief Justice Roberts and Justices Scalia, Thomas, and Alito dissented.
79. *Bellotti*, 435 U.S. at 807 (White, J., dissenting).
80. Ibid., 804–805. Justice White goes on to distinguish corporations formed for the express purpose of advancing certain ideological causes shared by all their members, or, as in the case of the press, of disseminating information and ideas. Under such circumstances, association in a corporate form may be viewed as merely a means of achieving effective self-expression. But this is hardly the case generally with corporations operated for the purpose of making profits. On this expressive or dignitary theory of speech, consider Thomas Emerson's linkage of expression to human dignity. Emerson, *The System of Freedom of Expression*.
81. The common practice of lending financial support to both major political parties illustrates how instrumental speech varies from expressive speech—the goal of strategic speakers is to gain access and influence, nothing more.
82. John Dewey described democracy as "more than a form of government[:] a mode of associated living, of conjoint communicated experience" that can produce "a liberation of powers." Dewey, *The Middle Works*, 93. Ralph Waldo Emerson discussed the need to focus on personal transformation, beyond social transformation: "All men plume themselves on the improvement of society, and no man improves." Emerson, *The American Scholar*, 77. Walt Whitman called democracy a "formulator, general caller-forth, [and] trainer" and went on to say this about its ends: "[T]o become an enfranchised man, and now, impediments removed, to stand and start without humiliation, and equal with the rest; to commence, or have the road clear'd to commence, the grand experiment of development, whose end . . . may be the forming of a full-grown man or woman—that *is* something." Whitman, *Complete Poetry and Prose*, 947–948. All of this melds together nicely with Brandeis's remarks in Whitney v. California, 274 U.S. 357, 375 (1927) (Brandeis, J., concurring): "Those who won our independence believed that the final end of the State was to make men free to develop their faculties; and that in its government the deliberative forces should prevail over the arbitrary. They valued liberty both as an end and as a means."
83. *Bellotti*, 435 U.S. at 809.
84. Ibid.
85. Ibid., 825 (Rehnquist, J., dissenting).

86. Lindblom observed in 1971 that "the federal government has often deferred, for example, to requests from industrial corporations to postpone or soften proposed antipollution legislation." *Politics and Markets,* 190.

87. *Bellotti,* 435 U.S. at 809 (White, J., dissenting).

88. Ibid.

89. Ibid., 826 (Rehnquist, J., dissenting). Among the benefits already bestowed, we might note the following superior attributes granted to corporations by state law and Supreme Court caselaw: perpetual life, simultaneous existence in multiple places, limited liability, and possession of due process and equal protection, among other certain civil rights. Santa Clara County v. S. Pac. R.R. Co., 118 U.S. 394 (1886). Corporate personhood, the constitutional rights of corporations, and the advantages they enjoy in the commercial sphere are described in Cox and Hazen, *Corporations,* 2–6.

90. *Bellotti,* 435 U.S. at 809 (White, J., dissenting).

91. Mancur Olsen is credited with demonstrating that incentives for collective action apply most when private goods are generated for group members, as compared to public goods for the general public, and thus explained why concentrated interests defeat diffuse social interests. Olsen, *The Logic of Collective Action.* Kenneth J. Arrow cast doubt on whether it is possible to produce a rational social ordering through the aggregation of individual preferences and whether any voting system based on individuals' ranked preferences can satisfy basic requirements of fairness and stability. *Social Choice and Individual Values,* 1–21, 46–60.

92. Rousseau, *Discourse on the Origin of Inequality,* 105, 116.

93. Dodge v. Ford Motor Co., 170 N.W. 668, 684 (Mich. 1919): "A business corporation is organized and carried on primarily for the profit of the stockholders. The powers of the directors are to be employed for that end. The discretion of directors is to be exercised in the choice of means to attain that end and does not extend to a change in the end itself, to the reduction of profits or to the nondistribution of profits among stockholders in order to devote them to other purposes." Schwartz discusses these economic priorities within the corporate legal form in "Defining the Corporate Objective," 512–513. The voluntary reforms of the corporate social responsibility movement are dependent on the profitability of good behavior. Several general studies offer guidance on this question: Frederick, *Corporation Be Good!*; Vogel, *The Market for Virtue.*

94. Joel Bakan, *The Corporation,* 60. Bakan's concern about corporate nature deserves to be quoted in full. "[T]he corporation can neither recognize nor act upon moral reasons to refrain from harming others. Nothing in its legal makeup limits what it can do to others in pursuit of its selfish ends, and it is compelled to cause harm when the benefits of doing so outweigh the costs. Only pragmatic concern for its own interests and the laws of the land constrain the corporation's predatory instincts, and often that is not enough to stop it from destroying lives, damaging communities, and endangering the planet as a whole." Ibid.

95. *Bellotti,* 435 U.S. at 826.

96. Ibid., 809.

97. We should recall Justice White's admonition that the sort of economic power controlled by corporations "may, if not regulated, dominate not only the economy but also the very heart of our democracy, the electoral process." Ibid.

98. Ibid., 810.

99. Ibid., 826.

100. *Bellotti,* 435 U.S. at 807 (White, J., dissenting). Corporate wealth can even distort the market for individual speech, however. An example is how oil company employees

were bussed in from work by their employers to protest against proposed federal emissions limits. Clifford Krauss and Jad Mouawad, "Oil Industry Backs Protests of Emissions Bill," *New York Times*, August 19, 2009, at B1.

101. *Bellotti*, 435 U.S. at 807.

102. Ibid., 826.

103. Ibid., 821.

104. Galbraith, *American Capitalism*, 109.

105. Ibid.

106. Walzer, *Spheres of Justice*, 316.

107. Galbraith, *American Capitalism*, 111.

108. Ibid.

109. Consider Galbraith's discussion of the role of "strong buyers" in a market of only a few sellers. Ibid., 112.

110. Ibid. As Karlan puts it, campaign finance reform is a "species of antitrust law. . . . Regulation seeks to prevent illegitimate tying arrangements where actors with economic power in one 'market'—the economy—seek to leverage that power into an unfair advantage in another 'market'—the political process." "Politics by Other Means," 1702.

111. Clyde Wilcox, "Contributing as Political Participation," in Lubenow, *A User's Guide*, 169, 48–51.

112. Galbraith, *American Capitalism*, 136.

113. Galbraith writes that "[m]uch of the domestic legislation of the last twenty years, that of the New Deal episode in particular, only becomes fully comprehensible when it is viewed in this light." Ibid., 127–128.

114. Ibid., 136.

115. Ibid.

116. Ibid., 151.

117. Ibid.

118. Akerlof and Shiller, *Animal Spirits*, 172.

CHAPTER 4

1. "Text, State of the Union Address," *New York Times*, January 28, 2010, http://www.nytimes.com/2010/01/28/us/politics/28obama.text.html?ref=state_of_the_union_message_us&pagewanted=all.

2. Alito's body language can be seen in the video of the address. "Obama's State of the Union Address," http://video.nytimes.com/video/2010/01/28/us/politics/1247466761306/obama-s-state-of-the-union-address.html?ref=state_of_the_union_message_us

3. Bill Mears, "Chief Justice Chides State of the Union as 'Political Pep Rally,'" *CNN .com*, March 11, 2010, http://edition.cnn.com/2010/POLITICS/03/10/obama.supremecourt/index.html.

4. Lisa Mascaro and Peter Nicholas, "Obama Chides Republicans on Campaign Finance," *Los Angeles Times*, July 26, 2010, http://articles.latimes.com/2010/jul/26/nation/la-na-obama-campaign-finance-20100727/2.

5. Citizens United v. FEC, 130 S. Ct. 876 (2010).

6. Memorandum from Lewis F. Powell Jr. to Eugene B. Sydnor Jr., Chairman, Education Committee, U.S. Chamber of Commerce, August 23, 1971, http://old.mediatransparency.org/story.php?storyID=22.

7. David D. Kirkpatrick, "Lobbyists Get Potent Weapon in Campaign Ruling," *New York Times*, January 21, 2010, http://www.nytimes.com/2010/01/22/us/politics/22donate.html.

8. SpeechNow.org v. FEC, 599 F.3d 686, 689 (D.C. Cir. 2010). An FEC advisory opin-

ion after the rulings states: "Following Citizens United and SpeechNow, corporations, labor organizations, and political committees may make unlimited independent expenditures from their own funds, and individuals may pool unlimited funds in an independent expenditure-only political committee." Commonsense Ten, FEC Advisory Opinion 2010–11, 3 (July 22, 2010), http://saos.nictusa.com/aodocs/AO%202010–11.pdf. The Supreme Court denied certiorari in *SpeechNOW*, meaning that the appeals court judgment stands as final.

9. Quoted in Adam Liptak, "Courts Take on Campaign Finance Decision," *New York Times*, March 27, 2010, A13.

10. NPR reports that "more than two dozen people or groups" have donated this much or more. NPR maintains a list of donors who have given $1 million or more to superPACs. "The SuperPAC Superdonors," http://www.npr.org/2012/02/13/146836082/the-superpac-super-donors.

11. David M. Herszenhorn, "Campaign Finance Bill Is Set Aside," *New York Times*, July 27, 2010, http://www.nytimes.com/2010/07/28/us/politics/28donate.html?_r=1&hpw.

12. Dan Eggen, "Poll: Large Majority Opposes Supreme Court's Decision on Campaign Financing," *Washington Post*, February 17, 2010, http://www.washingtonpost.com/wp-dyn/content/article/2010/02/17/AR2010021701151_pf.html.

13. *Bellotti*, 435 U.S. at 826 (Rehnquist, J., dissenting).

14. FEC v. National Right to Work Committee, 459 U.S. 197, 207–208 (1982).

15. Ibid.. *Buckley*, 424 U.S. 58. It is remarkable that Justices Burger, Blackmun, Stevens, and Powell joined the majority opinion in *NRWC* given their stance in *Bellotti*. What is more, Stevens would later become the Court's leading critic of money in politics prior to retiring in 2010. In 2000, for example, he claimed that "[m]oney is property; it is not speech." Nixon v. Shrink Miss. Government PAC, 528 U.S. 377, 398 (2000) (Stevens, J., concurring). His stance in this and other cases is detailed in the final portions of Chapter 7.

16. *NRWC*, 459 U.S. at 209.

17. Austin v. Michigan Chamber of Commerce, 494 U.S. 652 (1990). Such expenditures are defined at 655.

18. Ibid. These facts are detailed at 654–656.

19. Ibid., 656.

20. Ibid., 664.

21. Ibid., 657. One could say that *Austin* is the liberals' belated answer to *Buckley* and *Bellotti*'s most conservative principles. The terms "liberal" and "conservative" are useful here only in the biographical sense of liberal and conservative Justices.

22. Ibid., 657–658.

23. Ibid., 658 (quoting *NCPAC*, 470 U.S. 480, at 496–497) (my italics).

24. Ibid., 658–659 (quoting Federal Election Committee v. Massachusetts Citizens for Life, 479 U.S. 238, 257 (1986)).

25. Ibid., 660.

26. *Bellotti*, 435 U.S. at 809 (White, J., dissenting)

27. *Austin*, 494 U.S. at 660.

28. Ibid., 661.

29. *Bellotti*, 435 U.S. at 809–810 (White, J., dissenting).

30. Ibid., 826–827 (Rehnquist, J., dissenting).

31. Ibid., 809.

32. Ibid.

33. Ibid., 826.

34. Ibid.

35. Ibid., 827n6.

36. Ibid., 828.

37. Ibid.

38. Ibid., 809–810 (White, J., dissenting).

39. Ibid., 809.

40. *NCPAC*, 470 U.S. at 521 (Marshall, J., dissenting).

41. Ibid., 519.

42. Neil A. Lewis, "A Slave's Great Grandson Who Used Law to Lead the Rights Revolution," *New York Times*, June 28, 1991, http://www.nytimes.com/1991/06/28/us/a-slave-s-great-grandson-who-used-law-to-lead-the-rights-revolution.html.

43. *Austin*, 494 U.S. at 660.

44. Ibid., 666.

45. Ibid., 665.

46. Ibid.

47. *NRWC*, 459 U.S. 207–208.

48. Undue influence was identified most clearly in Federal Election Commission v. Colorado Republican Federal Campaign Commission, 533 U.S. 431 at 441 (2001) (noting that "undue influence on an officeholder's judgment" is a form of corruption).

49. *Austin*, 494 U.S. at 660.

50. "It is unlawful for any national bank, or any corporation organized by authority of any law of Congress, to make a contribution or expenditure in connection with any election to any political office, or in connection with any primary election or political convention or caucus held to select candidates for any political office, or for any corporation whatever, or any labor organization to make a contribution or expenditure in connection with any election at which Presidential and Vice Presidential electors or a Senator or Representative in, or a Delegate or Resident Commissioner to Congress are to be voted for . . . " U.S. v. UAW-CIO, 352 U.S. 567, 568–569 (1957), quoting 18 U.S.C. Section 610 (June 23, 1947, 61 Stat. 136, 159).

51. The Court explained that "the indictment charged appellee with having used union dues to sponsor commercial television broadcasts designed to influence the electorate to select certain candidates for Congress in connection with the 1954 elections." Ibid., 585.

52. Ibid., 582 (discussing congressional concern).

53. Ibid., 570 (quoting historians).

54. Ibid., 576 (quoting Senator Robinson).

55. Ibid., 571 (quoting Elihu Root).

56. Ibid., 573 (quoting Perry Belmont).

57. Ibid., 574 (quoting Samuel Gompers).

58. Ibid. (quoting Samuel Gompers).

59. Ibid. (quoting Samuel Gompers).

60. Ibid., 570.

61. Ibid., 571.

62. Ibid., 575 and 590.

63. Ibid., 590.

64. Ibid., 591.

65. McConnell v. FEC, 540 U.S. 93, 115 (2003).

66. Ibid., 150.

67. Ibid., 150–151.

68. Ibid., 150.

69. Ibid., 149.

70. Ibid., 124–125, and 125n12.

71. Ibid., 270.

72. Ibid., 146.

73. Ibid., 128n20.

74. Ibid., 145 (quoting *Colorado II*).

75. Ibid., 120n5.

76. Ibid., 146.

77. Ibid., 125n13.

78. Ibid., 124–125.

79. Ibid., 125n13.

80. Ibid., 151.

81. Again, evidence to this effect was substantial. The Court cited testimony from the 1970s as well: "The disclosures of illegal corporate contributions in 1972 included the testimony of executives that they were motivated by the perception that this was necessary as a 'calling card, something that would get us in the door and make our point of view heard,' . . . or 'in response to pressure for fear of a competitive disadvantage that might result.'" Ibid., 120n5.

82. Ibid., 153.

83. Ibid.

84. *Buckley*, 424 U.S. at 264.

85. Ibid., 265.

86. Ibid.

87. Ibid., 264–265.

88. Blasi, "Widening Gyre of Fund-Raising," 1283.

89. *Buckley*, 424 U.S. at 26–27. *Buckley* added, "Of almost equal concern as the danger of actual quid pro quo arrangements is the impact of the appearance of corruption stemming from public awareness of the opportunities for abuse inherent in a regime of large individual financial contributions." Ibid., 27. *McConnell* called *Buckley*'s concern over integrity of our system "[j]ust as troubling to a functioning democracy as classic *quid pro quo* corruption." *McConnell*, 540 U.S. at 153.

90. Blasi, "Widening Gyre of Fund-Raising," 1283.

91. Ibid., 1282–1283.

92. Ibid., 1282.

93. Randall v. Sorrell, 548 U.S. 230 (2006).

94. Ibid., 243–245.

95. FEC v. Wisconsin Right to Life, Inc., 551 U.S. 449 (2007).

96. According to Pasquale, "The great virtue of deliberative democratic theory was its compatibility with the moderate campaign reform agenda tentatively endorsed by the Supreme Court in its 'New Deference' cases. But this advantage was lost with WRTL, a case that demands a fundamental rethinking of the aims and rationale of campaign finance regulation." Pasquale, "Reclaiming Egalitarianism," 601. Hasen, "Beyond Incoherence."

97. Arizona Free Enterprise v. Bennett, 131 S. Ct. 2806 (2011).

98. For the facts of the case, readers may also wish to consult McComish v. Bennett, 611 F.3d 510, 514–515 (9th Cir. 2010).

99. Davis v. FEC, 128 S. Ct. 2759 (2008).

100. Ibid., 728.

101. Ibid., 728–731.

102. *Buckley*, 424 U.S. at 92–93.

103. *Davis*, 554 U.S. at 736.

104. Ibid.

105. Ibid., 739.

106. Ibid., 738–739.

107. *Bennett*, 131 S. Ct. at 2809.

108. *Davis*, 554 U.S. at 742.

109. Ibid.

110. Clyde Wilcox, "Contributing as Political Participation," in Lubenow, *User's Guide*, 48–51, 115. Wilcox notes that 77% of Americans say that "elected officials in Washington are mostly influenced by the pressure they receive on issues from major campaign contributors"; 76% believe that "Congress is largely owned by special-interest groups"; 71% agree that "[m]oney makes elected officials not care what average citizens think"; only 19% said that officials were most influenced by the "best interests of the country"). Corporate political spending, for example, is tremendously unpopular. Dan Eggen, "Poll: Large Majority Opposes Supreme Court's Decision on Campaign Financing," *Washington Post*, February 17, 2010, http://www.washingtonpost.com/wp-dyn/content/article/2010/02/17/AR2010021701151_pf.html. Eggen notes that 85% of Democrats, 76% of Republicans, and 81% of independents polled are opposed to the *Citizens United* ruling (with a margin of error of plus or minus 3 percentage points).

111. *Bennett*, 131 S. Ct. at 2829 (Kagan, J., dissenting).

112. Ibid., 2828.

113. Ibid., 2842 (internal quotations removed).

114. Ibid., 2845 (Kagan, J., dissenting).

115. Ibid., 2823. Roberts described *Davis* as "requiring no evidence of a burden whatsoever." Ibid.

116. *Buckley*, 424 U.S. at 93n126.

117. *McComish*, 611 F.3d at 525.

118. Ibid., 517.

119. The roots of this view can be found in Scalia's *McConnell* dissent. "In the modern world, giving the government power to exclude corporations from the political debate enables it effectively to muffle the voices that best represent the most significant segments of the economy and the most passionately held social and political views. People who associate—who pool their financial resources—for purposes of economic enterprise overwhelmingly do so in the corporate form . . . To be sure, the individuals involved in, or benefited by, those industries, or interested in those causes, could (given enough time) form political action committees or other associations to make their case. But the organizational form in which those enterprises already *exist*, and in which they can most quickly and most effectively get their message across, is the corporate form . . . A candidate should not be insulated from the most effective speech that the major participants in the economy and major incorporated interest groups can generate." *McConnell*, 540 U.S. at 257–258.

120. *Bennett*, 131 S. Ct. at 2828–2829.

121. Ibid., 2835 (Kagan, J., dissenting)

122. Ibid., 2833 (Kagan, J., dissenting).

123. Ibid., 2820.

124. Ibid., 2821. The majority cited some evidence of a decrease in speech by the actors "burdened" by the matching funds, but ultimately empirical data was not the point. All can see that the law subsidized only one type of speech and that it did so in a way that reduced the spending incentives of privately funded candidates and their supporters.

125. *Buckley*, 424 U.S. at 48–49.

126. *Bennett*, 131 S. Ct. at 2826. The Court notes that "in *Buckley*, we held that *limits* on overall campaign expenditures could not be justified by a purported government 'interest in equalizing the financial resources of candidates.'" Ibid. (my italics).

127. *Buckley*, 424 U.S. at 48–49 (internal quotation marks omitted) (quoting New York Times Co. v. Sullivan, 376 U.S. 254, 266, 269 (1964)).

128. Consider the role of Sheldon Adelson and Foster Friess, for example. Thomas Frank, "It's a Rich Man's World: How Billionaire Backers Pick America's Candidates," *Harper's Magazine*, April 2012, 22.

129. *Davis*, 554 U.S. at 741 (my italics). Justice Alito added that precedent "provide[s] no support for the proposition that this is a legitimate government objective." Ibid. This implies that the Court would have had to affirmatively sanction a particular state interest in order for that interest to be viable. This would assign an essentially legislative function to the Court—that of specifying *ex ante* the scope of important and compelling state interests, instead of deciding *ex post* whether a given interest was important or compelling on the facts of a particular case. Alito's legislative posture on this matter is in keeping with the Court's post-*Buckley* function as an ideological gatekeeper and architect of capitalist democracy. Kuhner, "Citizens United as Neoliberal Jurisprudence."

130. *Davis*, 554 U.S. at 742.

131. Ibid., 753–754.

132. Ibid., 742.

133. *Bennett*, 131 S. Ct. at 2811.

134. Ibid., 2824.

135. This appears to be an extension of Justice Brennan's strange dictate in *MCFL*: "Political 'free trade' does not necessarily require that all who participate in the political marketplace do so with exactly equal resources . . . Relative availability of funds is after all a rough barometer of public support." *MCFL*, 479 U.S. at 257. Justices Breyer and Ginsburg, concurring in *Nixon*, suggested something to make this so: "[B]y limiting the size of the largest contributions, such restrictions aim to democratize the influence that money itself may bring to bear upon the electoral process. . . . they seek to build public confidence in that process and broaden the base of a candidate's meaningful financial support, encouraging the public participation and open discussion that the First Amendment itself presupposes." Nixon v. Shrink Missouri Government PAC, 528 U.S. 377, 401 (2000).

136. See, for example, Lamont v. Postmaster General of the United States, 381 U.S. 301, 307 (1965), a case that discusses a chilling effect in terms of a "deterrent effect." The facts, however, concerned a postal regulation that required the Postmaster General to detain communist propaganda arriving by mail and to deliver such mail only if the addressee so requested. The need to make such a request and the fear of possible government reprisals therefrom constitutes a chilling effect in the traditional sense. The Court noted that the "addressee carries an affirmative obligation . . . almost certain to have a deterrent effect, especially as respects those who have sensitive positions . . . Public officials like schoolteachers who have no tenure, might think they would invite disaster if they read what the Federal Government says contains the seeds of treason."

137. *McConnell*, 540 U.S. at 227–229.

138. Ibid., 227.

139. Ibid., 228.

140. The group's website describes the organization as "seek[ing]to reassert the traditional American values of limited government, freedom of enterprise, strong families, and

national sovereignty and security." Its other goals include "complete U.S. withdrawal from the United Nations, [and the] defeat of the treaty to establish a permanent U.N.-controlled International Criminal Court." Citizens United, "About Citizens United," http://www.citi zensunited.org/about.aspx.

141. Tillman Act of 1907, Pub. L. No. 36, ch. 420, 34 Stat. 864–865 (1907). Its title, "An Act to prohibit corporations from making money contributions in connection with political elections," conveys the Tillman Act's limited coverage. Citizens United, 130 S. Ct. at 900.

142. § 203, 2 U.S.C.A. § 441b(b)(2) (West 2006); 540 U.S. 93, 203–209 (2003). The Court discusses how limits on corporate and union independent expenditures had a long history. Citizens, 130 S. Ct. at 900.

143. Such ads do not support or attack any particular candidate but rather, as their name suggests, present a point of view on a political issue. McConnell, 540 U.S. at 207.

144. Citizens United, 130 S. Ct. at 887–888.

145. 2 U.S.C.A. § 434(f)(3)(A) (West 2011).

146. 11 C.F.R. §§ 100.29(a)(2), 100.29(b)(3)(ii) (2009) (including in the definition of an electioneering communication the condition of public distribution, itself defined as being capable of being "received by 50,000 or more persons in a State where a primary election . . . is being held within 30 days" or by the same number of people "anywhere in the United States within the period between 30 days before the first day of the national nominating convention and the conclusion of the convention").

147. The appeal to the Supreme Court presented an as-applied challenge to campaign finance laws. See Citizens, 130 S. Ct. at 888–896 (discussing why the claim cannot be resolved on grounds narrower than a facial challenge); ibid., 892–894 (discussing the facial challenge and its relationship to the original claim presented).

148. It is for this reason that Justice Stevens writes that "the question [of § 203's, Austin's and McConnell's constitutionality] was not properly brought before us. . . . Our colleagues' suggestion that 'we are asked to reconsider Austin and, in effect, McConnell' would be more accurate if rephrased to state that 'we have asked ourselves' to reconsider those cases." Ibid., 931 (Stevens, J., dissenting).

149. Justice Stevens noted, and the majority could not pretend otherwise, that "the record [in the case] is not simply incomplete or unsatisfactory; it is nonexistent." Ibid., 933 (Stevens, J., dissenting).

150. The two Nixon appointees that remained on the bench in 1990 had in fact sided with the Austin majority. This was no surprise in the case of Rehnquist, who had dissented in Bellotti. But Blackmun, who had joined the Bellotti plurality, recanted his laissez-faire view by joining the majority opinion in Austin.

151. Citizens United, 130 S. Ct. at 886.

152. Ibid., 908.

153. Ibid., 895–896.

154. Ibid., 896.

155. Indeed, the Court's attitude toward precedent is exposed by its view that Austin does not withstand Buckley. But Buckley did not address corporate political expenditures, and both Austin and McConnell garnered more votes than Citizens United, Davis, or Bennett. Moreover, Austin specifically notes that it does not challenge Buckley's stance on equalizing resources.

156. These facts are, as is to be expected, downplayed by the majority and emphasized by the dissent. Compare Citizens United, 130 S. Ct. at 929, 942–945 (Stevens, J., dissenting) with 897–898 (majority opinion).

157. Ibid., 897. "PACs must file detailed monthly reports with the FEC, which are due at different times depending on the type of election that is about to occur . . . [They] have to comply with these regulations just to speak." Ibid. "Under BCRA § 311, televised election-eering communications funded by anyone other than a candidate must include a disclaimer that '_____ is responsible for the content of this advertising.' The required statement must be made in a 'clearly spoken manner,' and displayed on the screen in a 'clearly readable man-ner' for at least four seconds." Ibid., 913–914.

158. Ibid., 897. "Even if a PAC could somehow allow a corporation to speak—and it does not—the option to form PACs does not alleviate the First Amendment problems. . . . PACs are burdensome alternatives[,] . . . expensive to administer and subject to extensive regulations." Ibid.

159. Ibid., 889.

160. Ibid., 900 (quoting Pacific Gas & Elec. Co. v. Pub. Util. Comm'n of Cal., 475 U.S. 1, 8 (1986) (plurality opinion) (quoting *Bellotti*, 435 U.S. at 783)).

161. Ibid., 907 (quoting *McConnell*, 540 U.S. at 257–258 (Scalia, J., concurring in part and dissenting in part)) (alteration in original).

162. Ibid., 912.

163. Ibid., 929 (Scalia, J., concurring).

164. Ibid.

165. Ibid., 917 (Roberts, C.J., concurring). Chief Justice Roberts concludes that the government's theory of the First Amendment would allow censorship of media corporations. He focuses on this possibility even though the law at issue exempts media corporations from its reach and the First Amendment itself mentions "the freedom of the press" by name.

166. FEC v. National Conservative Political Action Committee, 470 U.S. 480, 511 (1985) (White, J., dissenting).

167. Ibid.

168. Ibid., 517.

169. Ibid., 517n12.

170. *Citizens United*, 130 S. Ct. at 912.

171. Ibid.

172. Ibid.

173. Ibid., 913.

174. Ibid.

175. Ibid., 898–899.

176. Ibid., 899.

177. Ibid., 905 (quoting *Austin*, 494 U.S. at 610, 707 (Kennedy, J., dissenting)) (inter-nal quotations removed).

178. Ibid. (quoting *Austin*, 494 U.S. at 658–659).

179. Ibid. (quoting *Austin*, 494 U.S. at 680 (Scalia, J., dissenting)). In his *Austin* dissent, Justice Scalia also labels this position "rudimentary." 494 U.S. at 690 (Scalia, J., dissenting). He notes that "it would make no difference if the law *were* narrowly tailored to serve its goal, since that goal is not compelling." Ibid., 688–690.

180. The majority offers the "dangerous[] and unacceptable[] consequence that Con-gress could ban political speech of media corporations" as the rationale for striking down *Austin*'s antidistortion rationale. *Citizens United*, 130 S. Ct. at 905.

181. Ibid., 906 (citation omitted).

182. Ibid. (internal quotation marks omitted).

183. Ibid., 907 (quoting United States v. Cong. of Indus. Orgs., 335 U.S. 106, 144 (1948) (Rutledge, J., concurring)).

184. Wilcox, "Contributing as Political Participation," as discussed in note 109 above.

185. *Citizens United*, 130 S. Ct. at 908.

186. Ibid., 910.

187. Ibid. (quoting McConnell v. FEC, 540 U.S. 93, 297 (opinion of Kennedy, J.) (alteration in original)).

188. Ibid.

189. Robert Barnes, "In Wis., Feingold Feels Impact of Court Ruling," *Washington Post*, November 1, 2010, A8, http://www.washingtonpost.com/wp-dyn/content/article /2010/10/31/AR2010103104314_pf.html. Wisconsin Election Results 2010, *Washington Post*, November 2, 2010, http://www.washingtonpost.com/wp-dyn/content/article/2010/11/02/ AR2010110207859.html.

190. *NCPAC*, 470 U.S. at 512.

191. *McConnell*, 540 U.S. at 258.

192. Ibid.

193. Ibid., 323.

194. *Nixon*, 528 U.S. at 418.

195. *Bennett*, 131 S. Ct. at 2837.

196. This is the case in that "social interactions that do not involve actually handing over money for goods are talked about as if they did." Radin, *Contested Commodities*, 1.

197. *Bennett*, 131 S. Ct. at 2837.

198. *Citizens United*, 130 S. Ct. at 955 (my italics).

199. *MCFL*, 479 U.S. at 257. In *MCFL*, Brennan considered that for-profit corporations could be obligated to establish a separate political committee for campaign spending in order to ensure that the political money available "in fact reflect[s] popular support for the political positions of [its] committee." Ibid., 258.

200. Red Lion Broadcasting Co. v. FCC, 395 U.S. 367 (1969).

201. Paul Krugman, "How Did Economists Get It So Wrong?" *New York Times Magazine*, September 6, 2009, http://www.nytimes.com/2009/09/06/magazine/06Economic-t.html.

CHAPTER 5

1. Winter, *a clearing in the forest*, 266.

2. Brian Naylor, "2012 Political TV: Ads, Lies, and Videotape," *National Public Radio*, February 24, 2012, http://www.npr.org/2012/02/24/147291667/2012-political-tv-ads-lies-and-videotape?sc=17&f=1003.

3. Saia v. New York, 334 U.S. 558, 565 (1948) (Frankfurter, J., dissenting).

4. Lessig, *Republic Lost*, 141.

5. Heilbroner, *21st Century Capitalism*, 105.

6. Ibid.

7. Certainly a parallel exists between some advocates of regulation during the Industrial Revolution period and those who advocate regulation of working conditions today. And some parallels exist between those who advocated for market freedoms in the past and in the present. But on the whole, the free market rallying call serves very different purposes in times of robust competition than in times of market failure, whether that failure results from imperfect competition, under-production of public goods, or externalities.

8. Sunstein, *Democracy and the Problem of Free Speech*, Kindle Location 119.

9. Ibid.

10. Youngstown Sheet & Tube Co. v. Sawyer, 343 U.S. 579, 634–635 & n1 (1952) (Jackson, J., concurring).

11. We must, after all, bear in mind the social conditions out of which the Framers came. Consider, for example, the restraint on suffrage in "colony elections to those who were free, white, twenty-one, native-born Protestant males who were the owners of property, especially real property." Williamson, *American Suffrage*, 19.

12. Powell, "The Original Understanding of Original Intent."

13. Samples, *The Fallacy of Campaign Finance Reform*, Kindle Location 433–438.

14. U.S. Const., art. I, § 8.

15. Story, *Commentaries*, vol. 3, 732–733.

16. Ibid.

17. U.S. Const., art. IV, § 4.

18. U.S. Const., art. XIV, § 1 and amend. XIV § 1.

19. U.S. Const., amend. IX.

20. As Owen Fiss and Alexander Meiklejohn put it, "[F]reedom of speech implies an organized and structured understanding of freedom, one that recognizes certain limits as to what should be included and excluded." Fiss, *Irony of Free Speech*, 19. This is just one of countless statements pointing toward the fact that "the freedom of speech" is not the same as "all possible speech by all possible entities."

21. U.S. Const., art. I, § 9.

22. Lessig, *Republic Lost*, 19.

23. The lack of evidence in key cases, such as *Citizens United*, *Davis*, and *Bennett*, is discussed in various parts of Chapter 4.

24. Issacharoff and Pildes, "Politics as Markets," 713.

25. These remarks addressed the question of executive power, but they apply fairly to the work of judges generally speaking. Youngstown Sheet & Tube Co. v. Sawyer, 343 U.S. 579, 634–635 & n1 (1952) (Jackson, J., concurring).

26. *Lochner*, 198 U.S. at 76 (Holmes, J., dissenting). What does decide cases, Holmes said, is a "judgment or intuition more subtle than any articulate major premise." Ibid.

27. *Bennett*, 131 S. Ct. at 2817 (quoting *Citizens United*).

28. Bybee, *All Judges Are Political*, 4.

29. Ibid. (quoting Holmes).

30. Hutchinson, *Whizzer White*, 399.

31. Powell, "Reasoning about the Irrational," 238, quoting Marshall, *Life of George Washington*, 4:243 (reprint ed. 1983) (1805).

32. Ibid.

33. Ibid.

34. Ibid.

35. On Hughes and his well-known remark, see Powell, *Constitutional Conscience*, 42.

36. Abrams v. United States, 250 U.S. 616, 630 (1919) (Holmes, J., dissenting).

37. Ibid.

38. Ibid.

39. *Lochner*, 198 U.S. at 75–76 (Holmes, J., dissenting). Although the change in Holmes between 1905 and 1919 can be understood in terms of his shifting attitude toward majority power, it is beyond question that his ideas about truth and the market varied from those of the Framers. Winter offers guidance on the market metaphor, the differing functions of the First Amendment, and the changing attitudes toward truth between the founding and the time of Holmes's remarks. Winter, *A Clearing in the Forest*, 266–273.

40. Schauer, "The Political Incidence of the Free Speech Principle," 936.

41. Ibid., 946.

42. Ibid., 945–946.

43. Macpherson, *The Life and Times of Liberal Democracy*, 1.

44. Ibid. Within his concept of the democracy of a capitalist market society, Macpherson included democracies that were "modified . . . by the rise of the welfare state." Ibid.

45. Ibid.

46. Ibid., 2.

47. Ibid.

48. Ibid.

49. Commentators have analyzed the caselaw and policy debate through a series of oppositions between political theories. The most common juxtapositions are pluralism versus republicanism, and libertarianism versus egalitarianism. This vast literature goes well beyond our inquiry, but select parts of these oppositions between self-interest and the common good, competition and good-faith dialogue, and freedom and equality do help to explain the Court's capitalist public philosophy. On republicanism and deliberative democracy, consider: John Rawls, "The Idea of Public Reason Revisited" (discussing the requirements of deliberative democracy); Sunstein, "Beyond the Republican Revival"; Lori Ringhand, "Defining Democracy"; Edward Foley, "Philosophy, the Constitution, and Campaign Finance," 23; Hasen, "Clipping Coupons for Democracy," 6 ("I replace normative public choice theory's efficiency criterion with the normative goal of promoting an egalitarian pluralist political market").

50. Lowi, *The End of Liberalism*, 34–36. "Pluralism became a potent American ideology . . . [,] reducing the essential conception of government to nothing more than another set of mere interest groups . . . [I]t is the principal intellectual member in a neocapitalist public philosophy, interest-group liberalism."

51. Held, *Models of Democracy*, 159.

52. "The pluralist approach takes the existing distribution of wealth, existing background entitlements, and existing preferences as exogenous variables. All of these form a kind of pre-political backdrop for pluralist struggle." Sunstein, "Beyond the Republican Revival," 1543.

53. Amadae, *Rationalizing Capitalist Democracy*, 4.

54. Key questions raised by this program of research include whether it is possible to produce a rational social ordering through the aggregation of individual preferences and whether any voting system based on individuals' ranked preferences can satisfy basic requirements of fairness and stability. Arrow, *Social Choice*, 1–21, 46–60.

55. Schumpeter, *Capitalism, Socialism, and Democracy*, 250–251.

56. Ibid.

57. Ibid., 252.

58. Amadae, *Rationalizing Capitalist Democracy*, 5.

59. Downs, *An Economic Theory of Democracy*, 5–6.

60. Lippmann, *Public Opinion*, 112.

61. Ibid.

62. Ibid. Pildes and Anderson criticize public choice's "conception of rationality" as ignoring the "plurality and incommensurability of the values at stake in collective decision making" and "invit[ing] complacency or antidemocratic responses." Pildes and Anderson, "Slinging Arrows at Democracy," 2127–2128.

63. Amadae, *Rationalizing Capitalist Democracy*, 114. Rational choice scholarship in the 1950s made it seem as though democracy's collective and public principles "violat[ed]

citizens' sovereignty" by: "transcend[ing] individual desires to achieve a consensual agreement," "restrict[ing] the expression of individual preferences to achieve a societal consensus on ends," and "replac[ing] individuals' unfiltered preferences with 'objective needs' . . . determined by a source external to subjective desire." Ibid., 113. Amadae notes that Rousseau's general will, Marx's use of need as the principle of decision for who gets what, and Kant's categorical imperative all began to appear coercive.

64. *Austin*, 494 U.S. at 680 (Scalia, J., dissenting).

65. Macpherson, *Life and Times of Liberal Democracy*, 79.

66. Amadae, *Rationalizing Capitalist Democracy*, 114.

67. Lowi, *The End of Liberalism*, 4.

68. Smith, "The Wealth of Nations," in Wagner, *Social Reformers*, 18.

69. Held, *Models of Democracy*, 160.

70. Ibid.

71. Ibid.

72. Ibid. Although sometimes conceived of as a self-interested actor competing within the process, government was often construed as a passive register upon which the results of these struggles were recorded. In related accounts, the government mediated between vested interests, but the interests themselves were sacrosanct.

73. Ibid., 159.

74. Lowi, *The End of Liberalism*, 44.

75. Ibid., 51.

76. Even Arrow's work, questioning democracy's quest for a rational and justifiable set of policies aimed at the common good, has been described as aimed at "ensur[ing] one or another aspect of procedural equality[—]conditions of anonymity and neutrality [that] accord equal protection to voters and alternatives respectively." Knight and Johnson, "What Sort of Political Equality Does Deliberative Democracy Require?" in Bohman and Rehg, *Deliberative Democracy*, 282 and 287.

77. Smith, *The Wealth of Nations*, bk. 1, 87–88, 231–232.

78. James Madison, "The Federalist No. 10," in *The Federalist Papers* (Cook ed.), 58–59.

79. Ibid., 59.

80. Ibid. We must ask again, therefore, how the implications of interest-group pluralism change if the facts reveal competition only between various moneyed interests.

81. Ibid., 57.

82. Held, *Models of Democracy*, 163 (quoting Dahl, 1956).

83. Ibid.

84. Ibid.

85. Dahl's description provides one of the few attractive alternatives to popular sovereignty, especially given common concerns over majority tyranny by such heavyweights as Madison, Tocqueville, and Mill.

86. Radin, *Contested Commodities*, 208.

87. Issacharoff and Pildes, "Politics as Markets," 650.

88. Olsen, *The Logic of Collective Action*. Olsen shows that incentives for collective action are strongest when private goods are generated for group members (as compared to public goods for the general public) and helps to explain why concentrated interests can defeat diffuse social interests.

89. Held, *Models of Democracy*, 163 (quoting Dahl, *Preface to Democratic Theory*, 3).

90. Rehnquist's unanimous opinion in *National Right to Work Committee* warned of "[s]ubstantial aggregations of wealth . . . [being] converted into political 'war chests' which

could be used to incur political debts from legislators." FEC v. National Right to Work Committee, 459 U.S. 197, 207–208 (1982).

91. Held, *Models of Democracy*, 170 (quoting Dahl, *On Economic Democracy*, 50).

92. Ibid. (quoting Dahl, *On Economic Democracy*, 55).

93. Ibid., 163–170.

94. Ibid., 171.

95. Miliband, *The State in Capitalist Society*, 6.

96. Lowi, *The End of Liberalism*, 51 (describing interest-group liberalism's "vulgarized version of the pluralist model of modern political science").

97. Held, *Models of Democracy*, 170 (quoting Dahl, *On Economic Democracy*, 50).

98. Farber and Frickey, *Law and Public Choice*, 14–15.

99. Ibid., 19.

100. Landes and Posner, "The Independent Judiciary in an Interest-Group Perspective," 877.

101. Jessup, *Capitalist State*, 12.

102. Ibid.

103. Ibid.

104. Posner, *Law, Pragmatism, and Democracy*, 153.

105. Ibid.

106. Schumpeter, *Capitalism, Socialism, and Democracy*, 263.

107. Ibid., 257.

108. Ibid., 257–258.

109. Ibid., 263.

110. Ibid.

111. As quoted by Ronald Steel in his foreword to Lippmann, *Public Opinion*, xv.

112. Lippmann, *Public Opinion*, 146.

113. Ibid., 229 (1922 ed., New York: Harcourt, Brace and Company).

114. Ibid., 116 (page number refers to the default edition of the book, the 1997 edition cited in the Bibliography).

115. As Lowi put it, we are left to "explain how this model was elevated from a hypothesis about political behavior to an ideology about how our democratic polity ought to work." Lowi, *The End of Liberalism*, 52.

116. Habermas, "Popular Sovereignty as Procedure," 40.

117. Ibid.

118. Ibid.

119. Ibid., 41.

120. Habermas, *The Inclusion of the Other*, 241.

121. Macpherson, *Democratic Theory*, 4.

122. "The Court did not hold that the effort to promote deliberation among political equals was insufficiently weighty, or inadequately promoted by the legislation at issue; the Court held . . . that that effort was illegitimate under the First Amendment." Sunstein, "Republican Revival," 1577.

123. Fiss, *The Irony of Free Speech*, 17.

124. Ibid., 18.

125. Ibid.

126. Posner, *Law, Pragmatism, and Democracy*, 131.

127. Sunstein, *Democracy and the Problem of Free Speech*, Kindle Location 1459–1473.

128. Dworkin, *Freedom's Law*, 25.

129. Sunstein, *Democracy and the Problem of Free Speech*, Kindle Location 1459–1473.

Beitz writes that "democratic politics creates an environment in which persons confront each other not only to manipulate but to persuade and so all must take seriously each other's nature as a rational being." Beitz, *Political Equality*, 93.

130. Posner, *Law, Pragmatism, and Democracy*, 131.

131. Rawls, "The Idea of Public Reason Revisited," 772–773.

132. Frank I. Michelman, "How Can the People Ever Make the Laws?" in Bowman and Rehq, *Deliberative Democracy*, 163.

133. Macpherson, *Democratic Theory*, 9.

134. Ibid.

135. As to reciprocity, consider Beitz's view: "[P]ublic recognition of rights of participation provides grounds for the belief that one is regarded by others as a person whose opinions and choices deserve respect." Beitz, *Political Equality*, 93.

136. Fiss, *The Irony of Free Speech*, 11.

137. Schauer notes that the "arguments for a 'level playing field' do not come from those occupying the high side of a tilted field." Schauer, "The Political Incidence of the Free Speech Principle," 949.

138. Posner, *Law, Pragmatism, and Democracy*, 132.

139. Ibid., 123.

140. Ibid.

141. Ibid., 135.

142. Ibid., 132.

143. *Citizens United*, 130 S. Ct. at 907.

144. Ibid.

145. *Bellotti*, 435 U.S. at 777.

146. Ibid., 790.

147. Smith, *Unfree Speech*, 214.

148. *McConnell*, 540 U.S. at 358–359.

149. Ibid.

150. Ibid., 908.

151. *Citizens United*, 130 S. Ct. at 907.

152. Ibid., 912.

153. Ibid.

154. Ibid., 913.

155. Ibid.

156. Ibid., 896.

157. Smith, "The Sirens' Song," 40.

158. Foley, "Philosophy, the Constitution, and Campaign Finance," 23.

159. Smith, *Unfree Speech*, 204.

160. Ibid., 202.

161. Ibid., 217.

162. Ibid., 207.

163. Ibid., 208.

164. Redish, *Money Talks*, 74–75.

165. Ibid., 75.

166. Ibid., 80.

167. Ibid., 77.

168. Ibid.

169. *Citizens United*, 130 S. Ct. at 899.

170. Redish, *Money Talks*, 78.

171. Ibid.

172. Ibid., 74–75.

173. Ibid.,78 and n. 139.

174. Ibid., 79.

175. Ibid.

176. This is precisely what republicanism and egalitarianism deplore. In Foley's words, "egalitarians consider campaign finance just as much part of the public domain of democratic politics as the ballot box itself." Translation: public financing, corporate exclusion, and strict limitations on contributions and expenditures; not a political-economic system, but two systems, one political, governed by the state, and another economic, governed by the market, and within the former, the mechanisms by which a government is produced. Much more could be said about the juxtaposition between republicanism and its critics, but the quotations already given ought to be sufficient to show that these competing political theories are a wellspring for the Supreme Court minority and majority. Foley, "Philosophy, the Constitution, and Campaign Finance," 29.

177. Samples, *The Fallacy of Campaign Finance Reform*, Kindle Location 1748–1754.

178. *Austin*, 494 U.S. at 712 (Kennedy, J., dissenting).

179. Ibid., 713.

180. *McConnell*, 540 U.S. at 248.

181. Sandel, *Liberalism and the Limits of Justice*, 2.

182. Stanley Fish, "What Is the First Amendment For?" *New York Times*, February 1, 2010.

183. Ibid.

184. Ibid.

185. Sandel, *Liberalism and the Limits of Justice*, 2

186. *Bennett*, 131 S. Ct. at 2823 (describing *Davis* as "requiring no evidence of a burden whatsoever").

17. Fish, "What Is the First Amendment For?"

188. Ibid.

189. Sandell, *Liberalism and the Limits of Justice*, 1–7.

190. Ibid., 1.

191. Consider the rest of Schauer's view: "And as long as we can imagine that there are winners and losers [in those processes] then it should come as no surprise that those who would expect to win . . . would be quite comfortable with keeping government out, while those who would expect to lose . . . might expect that intervention would do them more good than harm." Schauer, "The Political Incidence of the Free Speech Principle," 950.

192. On the difficulty of ensuring that the new unlimited spending environment retains a degree of accuracy and fairness, see Naylor, "2012 Political TV: Ads, Lies, and Videotape."

193. Caperton v. Massey Coal, 129 S. Ct. 2252, 2257 (2009).

194. *Citizens United*, 130 S. Ct. at 910.

195. For a politicized example of this politicization, see Reverend Al Sharpton, "The Supreme Court Cannot Have Its Own Conflict of Interest—Justices Thomas and Scalia Must Recuse Themselves," *Huffingtonpost.com*, November 15, 2011, http://www.huffingtonpost.com/rev-al-sharpton/supreme-court-health-care_b_1094867.html.

196. Walzer, *Spheres of Justice*, 319.

197. Ibid., 120.

198. Ibid.

CHAPTER 6

1. Rawls, *A Theory of Justice*, 224–225.

2. Rawls, *Political Liberalism*, 327.

3. Winter describes Holmes's formulation: "ideas are metaphorical commodities that are bought, sold and traded" and that "the struggle for recognition in the domain of public opinion is like competition in the market." Winter, *A Clearing in the Forest*, 18, 272.

4. I borrow this phrase from Fulcher, *Capitalism*, Kindle Location 219–220. Fulcher writes, "Capitalism is essentially the investment of money in the expectation of making a profit." Ibid.

5. Heilbroner, *Behind the Veil of Economics*, 37.

6. Fulcher, *Capitalism*, Kindle Location 377–379.

7. Mike McIntire and Michael Luo, "The Man Behind Gingrich's Money," *New York Times*, January 28, 2012.

8. Smith, *Unfree Speech*, 202.

9. Ibid.

10. Barrow, *Critical Theories of the State*, 15.

11. Ibid.

12. United Nations, "New Global Treaty to Combat 'Sex Slavery' of Women and Girls," http://www.un.org/events/10thcongress/2098.htm.

13. *Buckley*, 424 U.S. at 54. FECA limited individual contributions to candidates to $1,000, a figure that was later increased to $2,400 by the Bipartisan Campaign Reform Act of 2002. Contribution limits are still good law and their present-day amounts are published online by the Federal Election Commission—http://www.fec.gov/pages/brochures/contrib limits.shtml. In terms of FECA's spending limits, presidential candidates could not use more than $50,000 of their own money; the same limit in the case of congressional candidates varied between $25,000 and $35,000; candidates for nomination for election to the presidency could not spend more than $10 million; and candidates for election to the office of the president could not spend more than $20 million. These limits were struck down. Buckley v. Valeo, 424 U.S. 1, 187–199 (1976).

14. Ibid., 57.

15. Ibid.

16. Fulcher, *Capitalism*, Kindle Location 219–220.

17. Robert Pear, "House Passes Bill Banning Insider Trades by Officials," *New York Times*, February 10, 2012, A12. In lawmakers' words, this practice gave "this body an unfair advantage over Americans who sent us here to represent them"—after all, the "risk of government self-dealing is heightened by the huge growth in recent years of the federal government and its increasing entanglement with the private economy." Lamar Smith called the Stock Act an effort "to reassure the public that decision makers are not enriching themselves by investing based on insider knowledge of government policies." Ibid.

18. Michael Beckel, "Congressional Millionaires to Weigh Obama's Proposed 'Buffett Rule,'" September 20, 2011, *OpenSecretsblog*, http://www.opensecrets.org/news/2011/09/congressional-millionaires-buffett-rule.html.

19. Lessig, *Republic Lost*, 123.

20. House Democrats became lobbyists at a lower rate—32 percent, or 22 of 68 retirees. Jeffrey H. Birnbaum, "Hill a Steppingstone to K Street for Some," *Washington Post*, July 27, 2005, A19. The revolving door also takes people to and from a variety of public and private places. Dick Cheney is a remarkable example: secretary of defense for President George H. W. Bush, then CEO of Halliburton, and finally George W. Bush's vice

president. Or consider Howard Cohen, president of a health care lobbying firm and former chief counsel to the House Energy and Commerce Committee, who returned to the committee once the Republicans gained control of the House in 2010. National Public Radio reported that he is a "registered lobbyist for groups that will have interests before the committee [including] America's Health Insurance Plans, Amgen, Federation of American Hospitals, Genzyme, Group Health Cooperative, Health Net and PhRMA." Bara Vaida, "GOP Lobbyists to Take Key Health Spots on Hill," *National Public Radio*, December 17, 2010, http://www.*National Public Radio*.org/blogs/health/2010/12/17/132145106/gop-lobbyists-to-take-key-health-spots-on-capitol-hill?sc=17&f=1001.

21. Lessig, *Republic Lost*, 123.

22. Ibid.

23. The sums listed for Senate and House fundraising are the average amounts raised by candidates who win elections. Andrea Seabrook, "Who's Weighing Tax on Rich? Congress' Millionaires," *National Public Radio*, September 20, 2011, http://www.npr.org/2011/09/20/140627334/millionaires-in-congress-weigh-new-tax-on-wealthy?sc=17&f=1001.

24. Figures from the Center for Responsive Politics, cited in Alex Blumberg, "Senator by Day, Telemarketer by Night," *National Public Radio*, March 30, 2012.

25. Hasen, "Entrenching the Duopoly," 331.

26. Alex Blumberg, "Senator by Day, Telemarketer by Night," *National Public Radio*, March 30, 2012. Studies show that it is common for members to spend between "30 and 70 percent of their time raising money." Lessig, *Republic Lost*, 138.

27. Blumberg, "Senator by Day."

28. Andrea Seabrook, "On Tour with Nancy Pelosi, Fundraising Rock Star," *National Public Radio*, March 30, 2012.

29. Bradford Plumer, "Purchasing Power," *New Republic*, January 30, 2007, http://www.tnr.com/doc.mhtml?i=w070129&s=plumer013007.

30. Makinson, *Speaking Freely*, 37.

31. Smith, *Unfree Speech*, 46.

32. Quoted in Makinson, *Speaking Freely*, 74.

33. Jeff Zeleny, "$350,000 Goal Is Set for Re-election Donors," *New York Times*, March 18, 2011, A20.

34. Nicholas Confessore and Derek Willis, "2012 Election Ended with Deluge of Donations and Spending," *New York Times*, December 7, 2012, http://thecaucus.blogs.nytimes.com/2012/12/07/2012-election-ended-with-deluge-of-donations-and-spending/?ref=nicholasconfessore.

35. Ezra Klein, "The DISCLOSE Act Won't Fix Campaign Finance," *Washington Post*, July 27, 2012, http://www.washingtonpost.com/blogs/wonkblog/wp/2012/07/27/the-disclose-act-wont-fix-campaign-finance/.

36. Bill Burton, "White House and SuperPAC: How Close Is Too Close?" *National Public Radio*, February 17, 2012, http://www.npr.org/2012/02/17/147010524/white-house-and-superpac-how-close-is-too-close.

37. Mike McIntire and Michael Luo, "Fine Line Between 'Super PACs' and Campaigns," *New York Times*, February 26, 2012, A1.

38. This much has been demonstrated to comic effect by Steven Colbert's remarkable series on PACs in the fall of 2011 and winter of 2012, made possible by campaign finance lawyer Trevor Potter.

39. McIntire and Luo, "Fine Line Between 'Super PACs' and Campaigns."

40. Nicholas Confessore, "Outside Groups Eclipsing G.O.P. as Hub of Campaigns," *New York Times*, October 30, 2011, A1, New York Edition.

41. For a revealing analysis of this trend, see Matt Bai, "How Much Has Citizens United Changed the Political Game?" *New York Times*, July 17, 2012, http://www.nytimes .com/2012/07/22/magazine/how-much-has-citizens-united-changed-the-political-game .html?emc=eta1&pagewanted=all.

42. Macpherson, *Democratic Theory*, 187.

43. Of course, many different outcomes are possible in such a situation. If officehold- ers were elected under conditions of extreme reliance on donors and spenders, but then did not have to run for reelection in the foreseeable future, they might gain a great deal of independence. On the other hand, if the same conditions applied and donors and spenders backed a candidate with sincere ideological interests that favored their own material inter- ests, then the absence of term limits would only cement the power of donors and spenders and remove accountability to the general public. Only one thing is certain: a short election cycle under a system of privatized campaigns constitutes a sort of donor/spender referendum on the performance of each officeholder. The contrast to frequent elections in a plutocratic system would be frequent elections under conditions of substantive political debate and greater political equality.

44. The Center for Responsive Politics explains how influential advocacy groups fit into these various classifications. "The Major Players—Active Advocacy Groups in the 2004 Election Cycle," http://www.opensecrets.org/527s/527grps.php

45. Peter Overby, "Powerful GOP-Linked SuperPAC Has Clear Agenda," *National Pub- lic Radio*, February 9, 2012.

46. Peter Overby, "Who Bankrolls Romney? Big Donors, Not Small Ones," *National Public Radio*, February 21, 2012.

47. Editorial, "Sunlight on Secret Donations," *New York Times*, February 12, 2012, http://www.nytimes.com/2012/02/13/opinion/sunlight-on-secret-donations.html.

48. Eric Lipton, Mike McIntire, and Don Van Natta, Jr., "Top Corporations Aid U.S. Chamber of Commerce Campaign," *New York Times*, October 21, 2010.

49. Overby, "Powerful GOP-Linked SuperPAC Has Clear Agenda."

50. Eric Lipton and Eric Lichtblau, "Rules for Congress Curb but Don't End Junkets," *New York Times*, December 6, 2009, http://www.nytimes.com/2009/12/07/us/politics/07trips .html?pagewanted=2&emc=eta1.

51. Ibid.

52. "Jack Abramoff: The Lobbyist's Playbook," *60 Minutes*, http://www.cbsnews.com /8301-18560_162-57319075/jack-abramoff-the-lobbyists-playbook/?tag=currentVideoInfo; videoMetaInfo. Some skepticism is due, as Abramoff's campaign against the likes of himself does help sell his book, earning him more . . . well . . . more money.

53. Fredreka Schouten, "Corporate Sponsors Pay for Inauguration Parties," *USA Today*, December 24, 2008, http://www.usatoday.com/news/politics/2008-12-23-obamamoney_N .htm?csp=34&POE=click-refer.

54. Sheryl Gay Stolberg, "For Corporate Donors, Inauguration Details," *New York Times*, December 12, 2012, A30, http://www.nytimes.com/2012/12/09/us/politics/obama -team-outlines-four-corporate-donor-packages-for-inauguration.html?ref=politics.

55. Editorial, "The Big Money Behind State Laws," *New York Times*, February 12, 2012, discussing ALEC's political agenda. The killing of Trayvon Martin has recently brought ALEC's model legislation on deadly force to light. That legislation was adopted al- most word for word in Florida. Paul Krugman, "Lobbyists, Guns, and Money," *New York Times*, March 26, 2012, http://www.nytimes.com/2012/03/26/opinion/krugman-lobbyists -guns-and-money.html?partner=rssnyt&emc=rss.

56. Joseph E. Stiglitz, "Of the 1%, by the 1%, for the 1%," *Vanity Fair*, May 2011.

57. Editorial, "The Big Money Behind State Laws," *New York Times*, February 12, 2012, discussing ALEC's political agenda.

58. John M. Broder, "Carmakers and White House Haggling Over Mileage Rules," *New York Times*, July 3, 2011, http://www.*New York Times*.com/2011/07/04/business/energy-environment/04mileage.html?_r=1.

59. Eric Lipton, Mike McIntire, and Don Van Natta Jr., "Top Corporations Aid U.S. Chamber of Commerce Campaign," *New York Times*, October 21, 2010, http://www.nytimes.com/2010/10/22/us/politics/22chamber.html.

60. Eric Lichtblau, "Lobbyists Line Up to Sway the Special Committee," *New York Times*, September 22, 2011, A21.

61. Ibid.

62. Ibid.

63. Ibid.

64. Ibid.

65. Lessig, *Republic Lost*, 117.

66. Ibid.

67. Fredreka Schouten, "Lobbying Spending Tops $3 Billion in '08," *USA Today*, January 26, 2009, http://www.usatoday.com/news/washington/2009-01-26-lobbying_N.htm?csp=34&POE=click-refer.

68. Ibid.

69. Ibid.

70. Eric Lichtblau, "Lobbyists Line Up to Sway the Special Committee," *New York Times*, September 22, 2011, A21.

71. Barrow, *Critical Theories of the State*, 30–31.

72. Lessig, *Republic Lost*, 150. Lessig notes that the "prevention of governmental action . . . is the aim of many lobbies" and that the "opportunity for invisible influence is great." Ibid.

73. Political intelligence consultants collect information "from political insiders for the use of hedge funds, mutual funds and other investors." This industry has only recently come within the regulatory agenda. Republicans in the House eliminated a piece of pending legislation that imposed registration and disclosure requirements on these consultants. Robert Pear, "G.O.P. Leaders in House Excise Part of Ethics Bill," *New York Times*, February 9, 2012, A17.

74. For example, Rose-Ackerman notes that "[c]ontributions seem to be viewed by many donors as long-term investments in developing relationships of mutual trust." Rose-Ackerman, *Corruption and Government*, 134, describing findings by Snyder's 1992 study.

75. Makinson, *Speaking Freely*, 59.

76. *McConnell*, 540 U.S. at 297 (Kennedy, J., dissenting). Markets, not democracy, are premised on that kind of responsiveness. It is telling that Kennedy, who would soon author the *Citizens United* opinion, conflated the two.

77. Fredreka Schouten, Ken Dillanian, and Matt Kelley, "Lobbyists in 'Feeding Frenzy,'" *USA Today*, September 24, 2008, http://www.usatoday.com/news/politics/election2008/2008-09-24-lobbying_N.htm?csp=34&POE=click-refer#senate.

78. For a contrasting view, see Smith, *Unfree Speech*, 50.

79. Muller, *The Mind and the Market*, Kindle Location 253–257.

80. Furubotn and Richter, *Institutions and Economic Theory*, 420 (quoting Demsetz).

81. Candidates do not have proof of who voted for them, and even if they did, no supporter voted for them more than others, and so there can be no variation in shares. The dis-

tinction would be between a region of the country that voted for the candidate and a region that voted against her. The latter would hold no shares in the company and could indeed be rationally excluded from receiving legislative dividends. Another possible exception comes in the case of grassroots organizers who motivate many people to cast their votes on one side or another. The gratitude that candidates feel toward organizers could be great indeed, but it stands to reason that it would have a civic quality. The organizer inspired others to exercise their own political power. A big donor-spender-bundler lends a different sort of service and earns a different sort of gratitude.

82. Ogus, *Regulation*, 65.

83. Michael Cooper, "New State Rules Raising Hurdles at Voting Booth," *New York Times*, October 3, 2011, A1 N.Y. Edition; Michael Cooper and Jo Craven McGinty, "Florida's New Election Law Blunts Voter Drives," *New York Times*, March 28, 2012. The Brennan Center for Justice has estimated that 19 laws and 2 executive orders from 2011 "could make it significantly harder for more than five million eligible voters to cast ballots in 2012." Quoted in Cooper, "New State Rules."

84. Lippmann, *Public Opinion*, 149.

85. Pasquale, "Reclaiming Egalitarianism," 601.

86. Lessig, *Republic Lost*, 162.

87. Rahm Emanuel, quoted in Lessig, *Republic Lost*, 162.

88. Compare this assessment to Demsetz: "Competition subjects politicians and political parties to *the filter* of the polling place, much as competition subjects managers to the filter of the market place." Demsetz, quoted in Furubotn and Richter, *Institutions and Economic Theory*, 420.

89. Pasquale, "Reclaiming Egalitarianism," 644.

90. Wright, "Money and the Pollution of Politics," 640–641.

91. Reportedly, 63 million votes were cast during the 2006 season finale of American Idol. The Guardian reported that this surpassed the amount of votes Reagan achieved in the 1984 election (54.5 million), which the *Guardian* reported as the most votes cast for any presidential candidate at the time. Mark Sweney, "American Idol Outvotes the President," *Guardian*, May 26, 2006, http://www.guardian.co.uk/media/2006/may/26/realitytv.usnews. This appears to be correct, although total voter turnout is much higher than the number of people who vote for any single candidate, ranging from roughly 92 million to 132 million between 1984 and 2008. "The American Presidency Project, Voter Turnout in Presidential Elections, 1828–2008," http://www.presidency.ucsb.edu/data/turnout.php.

92. Muller, *The Mind and the Market*, Kindle Location 259–260.

93. Although he flips the terminology on its head in order to describe the demand for suitable policy and the supply of policymakers, Robert Reich helps explain a relevant dynamic in the supply of money in politics: "The supply of senators, representatives, cabinet members, and senior White House staffers has not substantially increased over this period of time. But the demands of corporations seeking to influence the policy process have grown as competition among them has intensified. It has been like an arms race: The more one competitor pays for access, the more its rivals must pay in order to counter its influence." Reich, *Supercapitalism*, 143.

94. Muller, *The Mind and the Market*, Kindle Location 258–259.

95. Marian Wang, "FEC Deadlocks (Again) on Guidance for Big-Money Super PACs," *ProPublica*, December 2, 2011, http://www.propublica.org/article/deadlocks-again-on-guidance-for-big-money-super-pacs.

96. Andy Fixmer, "Political TV Ads on CBS Will Increase Profit by $180 Million, Moonves

Says," *Bloomberg.com*, March 10, 2012, http://www.bloomberg.com/news/2012-03-10/
political-tv-ads-on-cbs-will-increase-profit-by-180-million-moonves-says.html.

97. Muller, *The Mind and the Market*, Kindle Location 253–257.

98. There are many types of political capitalism, but, ironically, none permits a complete lack of regulation. The survival of the fittest in the state of nature does not constitute a market, certainly not one in which capitalists, with their need to make initial investments in reasonable expectation of reaping a profit, would feel safe. Recall that the state must protect private property, enforce contracts, maintain its monopoly on the legitimate use of force, and maintain a military to prevent foreign powers (and lower classes) from pillaging. The state also establishes and backs a currency.

99. Ewing and Issacharoff, *Party Funding and Campaign Financing in International Perspective*; Gunlicks, *Campaign Finance and Party Finance*.

100. Barrow, *Critical Theories of the State*.

101. Macpherson, *Democratic Theory*, 188.

102. Ogus, *Regulation*, 60. "Transactions in conventional markets usually relate to *specific* products. The institutional mechanisms for making collective decisions on policy and law . . . typically involve voting on a *package* of proposals." Ibid.

103. Heilbroner credits capitalism with "a highly adaptive method of matching supplies against demands without the necessity of political intervention . . . free contractual relations as the means for social coordination; the establishment of a social realm of production and distribution from which government intervention is largely excluded; the legitimation of acquisitive behavior as the social norm; and activating the whole, the imperious search for the enlargement of exchange value as the active principle of the historical formation itself." *Behind the Veil*, 53.

104. Heilbroner, *21st Century Capitalism*, 96.

105. Walzer, *Spheres of Justice*, 15.

106. Ogus, *Regulation*, 58.

107. Rand, *Capitalism*, 13 and introduction (Kindle location 144–156).

108. Fulcher, *Capitalism*, Kindle location 392–395; Consider Heilbroner's description: "In exchange for a wage payment, the worker surrenders all claims to this output, even though it would appear—and many conventional economists claim—that labor and capital as 'factors of production' exist on an entirely equal conceptual footing . . . The capacity of the market to secure acquiescence in a provisioning process in which the surplus automatically accrues to the property of only one class obviously makes the market mechanism an executive instrument for a particular social order, precisely as the dispositions of command or reciprocity make these systems the instruments for the reproduction of their respective social orders." *Behind the Veil*, 30–31.

109. Lessig, *Republic Lost*, 17.

110. Ross Douthat, "The Virtues of the Super PAC," *New York Times*, April 3, 2012, http://campaignstops.blogs.nytimes.com/2012/04/03/the-virtues-of-the-super-pac/.

111. Richard Cohen, "A Defense of Big Money in Politics," Washington Post, January 17, 2012, http://www.washingtonpost.com/opinions/how-political-donations-changed-his tory/2012/01/16/gIQA60H63P_story.html.

112. Rose-Ackerman, *Corruption and Government*, 134.

113. Lessig, *Republic Lost*, 152.

114. Ibid.

115. Ibid., 143.

116. Ibid., 145.

117. Ibid., 147.

118. Ibid., 123.

119. Ibid., 138–141.

120. *McConnell*, 540 U.S. at 259 (Scalia, J., dissenting).

121. Ibid., 297 (Kennedy, J., dissenting).

122. Jennifer Epstein, "Obama: 'Not Going to Just Unilaterally Disarm' on Super PACs," *Politico.com*, February 14, 2012, http://www.politico.com/news/stories/0212/72882 .html#ixzz1tvINz6Wi.

123. A recent news report questions whether negative advertising is genuinely effective, but concludes that the issue is not effectiveness per se but the persuasiveness of firms who help to produce the ads. Because campaign managers cannot afford to cede any ground to the opposition, even an inkling of effectiveness may prove sufficient to make the sale. A lobbying firm that adds a powerful former congressman to its staff is like any other firm with a tremendous new product in its lineup—eager to publicize and sell. Once a new line of chemical fertilizers comes to market, each farm ignores it at the peril of being overtaken by their competitors.

124. This dynamic is thoroughly discussed in Schweizer, *Extortion*.

125. Samples, *The Fallacy of Campaign Finance Reform*, Kindle Location 3500–3503.

126. Ibid.

127. Garrett Hardin, "The Tragedy of the Commons," *Science* 162 (1968): 1243, at http://www.constitution.org/cmt/tragcomm.htm.

128. Ibid.

129. Federal Election Commission v. Wisconsin Right to Life, Inc., 127 S. Ct. 2652 (2007) (Souter, J., joined by Stevens, J., Ginsburg, J., and Breyer, J., dissenting).

130. *Citizens United*, 130 S. Ct. at 910. The quote continues: "By definition, an independent expenditure is political speech presented to the electorate that is not coordinated with a candidate . . . The fact that a corporation, or any other speaker, is willing to spend money to try to persuade voters presupposes that the people have the ultimate influence over elected officials. This is inconsistent with any suggestion that the electorate will refuse 'to take part in democratic governance' because of additional political speech made by a corporation or any other speaker."

131. Dan Eggen, "Poll: Large Majority Opposes Supreme Court's Decision on Campaign Financing," *Washington Post*, February 17, 2010, http://www.washingtonpost.com/wp-dyn/content/article/2010/02/17/AR2010021701151_pf.html.

132. Clyde Wilcox, "Contributing as Political Participation," in Lubinow, *User's Guide*, 169 and 48–51.

133. David Welna, "Even Lawmakers Ask: Does Anyone Like Congress?" *National Public Radio*, November 25, 2011, http://www.npr.org/2011/11/25/142705292/even-lawmakers-ask-does-anyone-like-congress?sc=17&f=1014

134. Ibid.

135. Williamson, *American Suffrage*, 3.

136. Ibid.

137. Ibid.

138. Bogle, *The Battle for the Soul of Capitalism*.

139. Williamson, *American Suffrage*, 6.

140. Ibid.

141. Warren E. Buffett, "Stop Coddling the Super-Rich," *New York Times*, August 13, 2011, http://www.nytimes.com/2011/08/15/opinion/stop-coddling-the-super-rich.html.

142. Williamson, *American Suffrage*, 5.

143. Ibid., 10n20.

144. Ibid., 11.

145. Williamson describes the maintenance of a property tax as a test for voter quali-fication in Pennsylvania on the books until 1931. Ibid., 136.

146. Barrow, *Critical Theories of the State*, 22.

147. Paul Krugman, "Oligarchy, American Style," *New York Times*, November 4, 2011.

148. Joseph E. Stiglitz, "Of the 1%, by the 1%, for the 1%," *Vanity Fair*, May 2011.

149. Ibid.

150. Krugman, "Oligarchy."

151. Ibid.

152. Stiglitz, "Of the 1%, by the 1%, for the 1%."

153. Barrow, *Critical Theories of the State*, 23. Accordingly, it is not absurd to use the phrase "the fluidity of wealth in American society." Smith, *Unfree Speech*, 209.

154. Smith celebrates the plausible truth that the wealthy are "less homogenous than other political elites . . . represent[ing] a greater cross section than do, say, network news anchors, political consultants, or professional activists." Smith, *Unfree Speech*, 209.

155. Mills, *The Power Elite*, 97.

156. Macpherson, *Democratic Theory*, 193.

157. For an anecdotal report on the question of salary versus value, see Hannah Selig-son, "No Six-Figure Pay, but Making a Difference," *New York Times*, July 13, 2013, http://www.nytimes.com/2013/07/14/business/no-six-figure-pay-but-making-a-difference.html?_r=0.

158. Stiglitz, "Of the 1%, by the 1%, for the 1%."

159. Macpherson, *Democratic Theory*, 173.

160. Ibid., 174

161. Heilbroner, *Behind the Veil*, 52.

162. Williamson, *American Suffrage*, 11.

163. Samples, *The Fallacy of Campaign Finance Reform*, Kindle location 3523–3524.

164. Ibid.

165. Redish, *Money Talks*, 86.

166. Ibid., 85.

167. Ibid., 86.

168. Samples, *The Fallacy of Campaign Finance Reform*, Kindle location 3518–3520.

169. Rand, *Capitalism*, 42.

170. Ibid., 188.

171. Ibid.

172. I discuss Rand's view of lobbyists in Chapter 7.

173. Ibid., conclusion, Kindle location 5784–5792.

174. Bakan, *The Corporation*, 113.

175. Lindblom, *Politics and Markets*, 172.

176. Ibid.

177. Barrow, *Critical Theories of the State*, 59.

178. Ibid., 60.

179. Stiglitz, "Of the 1%, by the 1%, for the 1%."

180. Jessup, *The Capitalist State*, 22, describing "the veto power of business confidence entailed in the institutional separation of the economic and political—a power that is inde-pendent of interpersonal connections."

181. Lindblom, *Politics and Markets*, 173.

182. Barrow, *Critical Theories of the State*, 101.

183. Ogus, *Regulation*, 58.

184. Held, *Models of Democracy*, 170.

185. Barrow, *Critical Theories of the State*, 62.

186. Ibid., 31.

187. Radin, *Contested Commodities*, 208.

CHAPTER 7

1. Arthur C. Brooks, "America's New Culture War: Free Enterprise vs. Government Control," *Washington Post*, May 23, 2010, http://www.washingtonpost.com/wp-dyn/con tent/article/2010/05/21/AR2010052101854.html.

2. Ibid.

3. Dan Eggen, "Poll: Large Majority Opposes Supreme Court's Decision on Campaign Financing," *Washington Post*, February 17, 2010, http://www.washingtonpost.com/wp-dyn/content/article/2010/02/17/AR2010021701151_pf.html.

4. Americans are critical of money in politics: 77% say that "elected officials in Washington are mostly influenced by the pressure they receive on issues from major campaign contributors"; 60% believe that "public officials don't care much what people like me think"; and only 24% of Americans believe that Congress is not owned by special-interest groups. Wilcox, "Contributing as Political Participation," in Lubenow, *A User's Guide*, 169 and 48–51.

5. Smith, "The Wealth of Nations," in Wagner, *Social Reformers*, 18.

6. Quotation in Richard C. Levin, "Democracy and the Market," in Purdy, *Democratic Vistas*, 155.

7. Friedman, *Capitalism and Freedom*, 166.

8. Ibid.

9. Smith, *The Wealth of Nations* (Canaan ed., Modern Library Series, Random House, 1937), 508.

10. Consider Heilbroner's parallel between property in one's self and in one's labor power and property in one's land and machines: The "right of the working person to deny the capitalist access to labor power [arose from] exactly the same legal basis as that which enables the capitalist to deny the worker access to property." *Behind the Veil*, 45.

11. Rand, *Capitalism*, 10.

12. Smith, "The Wealth of Nations," in Wagner, *Social Reformers*, 14.

13. Ibid., 25.

14. Ibid.

15. Macpherson, *Democratic Theory*, 181.

16. Smith, "The Wealth of Nations," in Wagner, *Social Reformers*, 20. Consider Macpherson's view as well: "With a liberal state guaranteeing a free market, everyone's natural desire to maximize his own utility, or at least not to starve, would bring everyone into productive relations which would maximize the aggregate utility of the society." *Democratic Theory*, 173. "The value judgment it finds in modified neo-classical economic theory, that the best society is the market society because it maximizes utilities and distributes them according to each man's deserts." Ibid., 177.

17. Levin, "Democracy and the Market," in Purdy, *Democratic Vistas*, 157.

18. Rand, *Capitalism*, 16.

19. Ibid.

20. Ibid., 44.

21. Ibid., 46.

22. Ibid.

23. Ibid.

24. Alan Greenspan, "Antitrust," in Rand, *Capitalism*, 65.

25. Rand, *Capitalism*, 188.

26. Ibid.

27. Ibid., 206 and 188, respectively.

28. Ibid., 189.

29. Ibid.

30. Nathaniel Branden, "Common Fallacies about Capitalism," in Rand, *Capitalism*, 74.

31. Ibid., 77.

32. Rand, *Capitalism*, 18.

33. Galbraith, *American Capitalism*, 13.

34. Lessig, *Republic Lost*, 155.

35. Thomas B. Edsall, "Happy Lobbyists, Unhappy Citizens," *New York Times*, January 8, 2012, http://campaignstops.blogs.nytimes.com/2012/01/08/happy-lobbyists-unhappy-citizens/?emc=eta1.

36. Lekachman, "Capitalism or Democracy," in Goldwin and Schambra, *How Capitalistic Is the Constitution?*, 137.

37. Lessig, *Republic Lost*, 46.

38. Ibid., 48.

39. Ibid., 45–46.

40. Ibid., 46.

41. Ibid., 47.

42. Ibid., 51.

43. With a government doling out subsidies to some domestic producers and heaping tariffs onto some foreign ones, it is natural that individual firms would be drawn into the political market. If the producers of corn sweetener keep their subsidies, but the sugar producers do not, logically the former could offer lower prices and capture a greater share of the sweetener market. The sugar companies cannot afford for this to happen, and so they cannot be blamed for continuing to spend money on politics. Absent mandatory public funding, officeholders are vulnerable to whatever demands private companies can dream up in order to get a competitive advantage over their rivals. And as if that was not incentive enough for political spending, cash-hungry officeholders and parties will be hard at work finding ways to get private interests to spend money on politics. Again, actors on both sides of the political market are locked into a collective action problem. Whoever abstains from the money game is likely to be overtaken by those who keep playing.

44. "House Democratic leaders on Wednesday banned budget earmarks to private industry, ending a practice that has steered billions of dollars in no-bid contracts to companies and set off corruption scandals. . . . Had the ban on for-profit earmarks been in place last year, it would have meant the elimination of about 1,000 awards worth a total of about $1.7 billion." Eric Lichtblau, "Leaders in House Block Earmarks to Corporations," *New York Times*, March 11, 2010, http://www.nytimes.com/2010/03/11/us/politics/11earmark.html?emc=eta1. A more basic earmark ban has been in effect for three years. Nathan Hurst, "House Earmarks Ban May Be Tested in Writing Water Bill," *Roll Call*, June 6, 2013, http://www.roll call.com/news/house_earmarks_ban_may_be_tested_in_writing_water_bill-225372-1.html.

45. Patrick Bernhagen, "Democracy, Business, and the Economy," in Grugel, *Democratization*, 115.

46. Of course the 2008–2009 bailouts were motivated by more than just political favoritism and an interest in preserving the life of particular companies. For example, the goal of

ensuring the stability of the economy itself loomed large in pro-bailout arguments. Gretchen Morgenson, "Seeing the Bailout through Rose-Colored Glasses," *New York Times*, May 19, 2012, http://www.nytimes.com/2012/05/20/business/a-bailout-analysis-thats-incomplete -fair-game.html.

47. Gary Becker, "Public Policies, Pressure Groups, and Dead Weight Cost," *Center for the Study of the Economy and the State*, Working Paper No. 35, November, 1984, http://research.chicagobooth.edu/economy/research/articles/35.pdf, p. 26. This was Becker's response to what he called "the almost universal condemnation of special interest pressure groups" focusing on "the many redistributions to special interest groups that clearly reduce social output because of deadweight costs of taxes and subsidies." Becker saw a positive role for interest groups in light of the fact that "actual political systems do not have social welfare functions . . . or other political procedures that automatically choose the optimal production of public goods . . . and other policies that raise output and efficiency." Ibid.

48. Ibid.

49. Farber and Frickey, *Law and Public Choice*, 19. Surveying the literature in the field, Farber and Frickey noted the "basic assumption . . . that taxes, subsidies, regulations, and other political instruments are used to raise the welfare of more influential pressure groups."

50. Quoted in Nicholas D. Kristof, "Crony Capitalism Comes Home," *New York Times*, October 27, 2011.

51. Francis Fukuyama, "The Future of History: Can Liberal Democracy Survive the Decline of the Middle Class," *Foreign Affairs*, January/February, 2012, http://www.foreignaffairs .com/articles/136782/francis-fukuyama/the-future-of-history.

52. Kristof, "Crony Capitalism Comes Home."

53. Heilbroner, *21st Century Capitalism*, 162.

54. Ibid., 163.

55. Quoted in Thomas B. Edsall, "Is This the End of Market Democracy?" *New York Times*, February 19, 2012.

56. Ibid.

57. Jessop, *The Capitalist State*, 32.

58. Ibid.

59. Ibid., 52.

60. Ibid., 58.

61. Ibid.

62. Barrow, *Critical Theories*, 18.

63. Ibid.

64. Those advantages take familiar forms, including tariffs on foreign competitors, selective tax benefits, price controls, no-bid contracts, and simple subsidies. These government favors enable firms to charge higher prices or provide them additional revenue directly so that they can compete against other, more-talented firms.

65. Gethin Chamberlain, "Apple's Chinese Workers Treated 'Inhumanely, like Machines,'" *The Guardian*, April 30, 2011, http://www.guardian.co.uk/technology/2011/apr/30/ apple-chinese-workers-treated-inhumanely.

66. I would also posit that Company A respects its employees' civil rights at home and their human rights abroad, but human rights observance is still not commonly considered a collective good. This is the case even though poor labor conditions impose many costs on society, including injuries, death, the weakening of the family unit (as occurs when one or both parents are exhausted when at home or never at home given an obscenely long workday), and so on.

67. A *New York Times* editorial reports interest from the business world in "setting and enforcing tough standards to ensure that companies with cheap, dirty standards don't have a competitive advantage over those businesses protecting the environment." Jared Diamond, "Will Big Business Save the Earth?" *New York Times*, December 5, 2009, http://www.nytimes.com/2009/12/06/opinion/06diamond.html?emc=eta1.

68. Heilbroner, *21st Century Capitalism*, 110–111.

69. Quoted in Rosanvallon, *Democracy Past and Future*, 151–152.

70. The superior power of wealthy groups operating within political markets makes it incredibly costly and time-consuming to persuade the government to force industries to internalize their externalities. What a reasonably independent and accountable government might do naturally, on its own, becomes an uphill battle to be waged by comparatively weak and disorganized elements within society.

71. John M. Broder, "Carmakers and White House Haggling Over Mileage Rules," *New York Times*, July 4, 2011.

72. Justin Gillis, "In Poll, Many American Link Weather Extremes to Climate Change," *New York Times*, April 17, 2012, http://www.nytimes.com/2012/04/18/science/earth/americans-link-global-warming-to-extreme-weather-poll-says.html.

73. Leslie Kaufman, "G.O.P. Push in States to Deregulate Environment," *New York Times*, April 16, 2011.

74. Sunstein, *Democracy and the Problem of Free Speech*, Kindle location 1402–1405.

75. Macpherson, *Democratic Theory*, 187.

76. Epstein, *Modern Republicanism*, 1641.

77. Elster, "The Market and the Forum," in Bohman and Rehg, *Deliberative Democracy*, 4.

78. Ibid.

79. Consider for example, that between 1978 and 2003, Philip Morris was the Republican Party's top overall donor. Surely this prolonged the company's ability to profit despite widespread public health concerns. The Republican Party makes "tort reform" part of its political platform, which includes making it more difficult for people, such as smokers, to sue tobacco companies. Freddie Mac was the sixth-highest donor, and Enron made the top 25. Again, there is little doubt that these two companies were able to fend off the regulations we now know were necessary to avoid an economic crisis—regulations aimed at protecting the economy as a whole. Top donors in Lewis, *The Buying of the President 2004*, 119–128; Lindblom, *Politics and Markets*, 195.

80. Macpherson, *Democratic Theory*, 181–182. "What the state does thereby is to alter the terms of the equations which each man makes when he is calculating his most profitable course of action . . . As long as prices still move in response to these calculated decisions, and as long as prices still elicit the production of goods and determine their allocation, we may say that the essential [capitalist] nature of the system has not changed."

81. Macpherson has described the government's role similarly: "to alter the terms of the equation which each man makes when he is calculating his most profitable course of action." Ibid., 182.

82. Heilbroner, *Behind the Veil of Economics*, 43–44.

83. Heilbroner, *21st Century Capitalism*, 69.

84. Ibid.

85. Quoted by Noam Chomsky in "Consent without Consent," 415.

86. Jefferson, "Letter from Thomas Jefferson to Tom Logan" (November 12, 1816), in Ford, ed., *The Writings of Thomas Jefferson*, 10:69.

87. Jefferson, "Autobiography," in *Writings*, 5–22.

88. Tribe, *American Constitutional Law*, 1158–1159.

89. Ibid., 1159.

90. Walzer, *Thinking Politically*, 60.

91. Radin, *Contested Commodities*, 206–207. For a complementary articulation, see Winter, *A Clearing in the Forest*, 272. Winter articulates marketplace thinking with similar clarity: "[I[deas are commodities; persuasion is selling; speakers are vendors; members of the audience are potential purchasers; acceptance is buying; intellectual value is monetary value; and the struggle for recognition in the domain of public opinion is like competition in the market."

92. Redish, *Money Talks*, 236.

93. James Madison, "The Federalist No. 51," in *The Federalist Papers* (Clinton Rossiter ed.), 321.

94. Ibid., 322.

95. I owe this conception of the issue to Walzer, as the next note and its associated text make clear.

96. Walzer, *Spheres of Justice*, 316.

97. Ibid., citing "the bureaucracy and the courts, in markets and factories, in parties and unions, in schools and churches, among friends and lovers, kinfolk and fellow citizens," as places where the tyrant's power could extend.

98. Smith, *Unfree Speech*, 204.

99. Ibid., 210.

100. *Davis*, 554 U.S. at 742.

101. Samples, *The Fallacy of Campaign Finance Reform*, Kindle location 1769.

102. Ibid.

103. Ibid.

104. Smith, *Unfree Speech*, 205.

105. Walzer, *Spheres of Justice*, xii.

106. Ibid., xiii.

107. Smith, *Unfree Speech*, 203.

108. Ibid.

109. Walzer, *Spheres of Justice*, 22.

110. Smith attempts to save his recipe for economic power within politics by equating the wealthy with the majority of citizens. Conceding that political donors are disproportionately wealthy, male, white, and conservative, Smith nonetheless maintains that donors are more representative of the citizenry than other people who exercise political power. Smith claims that the wealthy are a more varied group than the rest of the political class, noting that they are "less likely to work for government, less likely to be college professors, more likely to have business management experience, more likely to live outside political capitals, and less likely to be Democrats." Smith, *Unfree Speech*, 209. Citing the "fluidity of wealth in American society," Smith portrays the wealthy as an ever-changing group with diverse life experiences. Ibid. Having already conceded wealthy donors to be mostly male, white, conservative, and more business-oriented, however, and having just described the wealthy as less oriented toward government and education, Smith has merely restated the previous question: Should we insist on the business elite using their money to check the political power of those who work in journalism, education, and government, and who, as a group, have a greater mix of genders and races? If Smith's real concern were the overrepresentation of urban, democratic, professorial, and journalistic actors in political debate, increased political power for the wealthy would be a strange remedy. A better way to increase the political

power of rural, less-educated, and less journalistically inclined citizens would be to expand the deliberative forum itself. John Samples also concedes that the donors are not representative of the overall population. As Samples notes, "80 percent or more of such 'significant donors' reported an annual family income of more than $100,000. The donors are also well-educated, with more than one-half holding postgraduate degrees, often JDs or MBAs. They also tended to be older than the general population, male, and white. Because about 18 percent of all U.S. households earn more than $100,000 annually and about 9 percent of Americans hold an advanced degree, it follows that contributors are not an accurate sample of the U.S. population as a whole. Of course, the same might be said of Congress." Samples, *The Fallacy*, Kindle location 1858–1862.

111. Wealthy candidates who use their economic capital to buy their way into political races are the counterparts of powerful politicians who use their political capital to acquire economic power.

112. For instance, single men and women are led to increase revenue for matchmaking companies, clothing retailers, perfume vendors, nightclub proprietors, and purveyors of all manner of status symbols, en route to bringing about an overall state of affairs in dating behavior and human companionship that was no part of their intention. Because this behavior unfolds in the intimate and mostly law-free zone of human relationships, there is little role for (or justice in) laws tampering with the design or its outcomes. Exceptions are made at the margins in order to control extreme behaviors—violence, rape, and the like. And once commodification figures into the equation, as in the case of clothing manufacturers, nightclubs and brothels, additional exceptions are made—the banning of hazardous materials, liquor licenses, fire safety codes, maximum occupancy regulations, and certain outright prohibitions. Otherwise the invisible hand operating in this overall setting could lead to greater male domination or lesser public safety.

113. Individual rights are included among those goals and values, but because there is no omnipotent provider or unchanging natural law to implement such rights, they flow from positive law—that is, from the judgment of the political community acting through legitimate channels.

114. Smith, "The Wealth of Nations," in Wagner, *Social Reformers*, 20.

115. *Rent Control*, 454 U.S. at 295.

116. *NCPAC*, 470 U.S. at 493 (repeating the same quotations that were featured in *Buckley*).

117. Ibid., 508.

118. Ibid., 509.

119. Ibid., 512.

120. Ibid., 513.

121. Nixon v. Shrink Miss. Government PAC, 528 U.S. 377, 398 (2000) (Stevens, J., concurring).

122. Ibid.

123. Ibid. "Our Constitution and our heritage properly protect the individual's interest in making decisions about the use of his or her own property." Consider Stevens's *Davis* dissent as well: "[C]ampaign expenditures are not themselves core political speech," adding that "it is simply not the case that the First Amendment provides the same measure of protection to the use of money to enable speech as it does to speech itself."

124. Ibid., 400. Contributions are a matter of First Amendment concern "not because money is speech (it is not); but because it enables speech. . . . contributor associates himself with the candidate's cause, helps the candidate communicate a political message

..., and helps the candidate win by attracting the votes of similarly minded voters. Both political association and political communication are at stake. On the other hand, restrictions [on contributions] seek to protect the integrity of the electoral process—the means through which a free society democratically translates political speech into concrete governmental action."

125. *Randall*, 548 U.S. at 278.

126. Ibid.

127. Ibid., 230.

128. *Davis*, 128 S. Ct. at 2781.

129. *Wisconsin Right to Life (WRTL)*, 551 U.S. 449 (2007).

130. Ibid., 507.

131. As discussed at the close of Chapter 2. *Buckley*, 424 U.S. at 266 (White, J., dissenting).

132. *NRWC* 459 U.S. at 207–208.

133. Ibid.

134. *Citizens United*, 130 S. Ct. at 59.

135. *NCPAC*, 470 U.S. at 480; *NRWC*, 459 U.S. at 208.

136. Ibid., 511 (White, J., dissenting).

137. Ibid., 517.

138. Ibid., 517n12.

139. Ibid., 517–518.

140. Citizens Against Rent Control v. City of Berkeley, 454 U.S. 290, 307 (1981) (White, J., dissenting).

141. Ibid., 308.

142. Ibid.

143. FEC v. Colorado Republican Federal Campaign Committee (Colorado II), 533 U.S. 431 (2001).

144. Ibid., 452.

145. Ibid., 456.

146. Ibid., 450.

147. Ibid.

148. Ibid., 450–451.

149. Ibid., 451.

150. Ibid., 451–452. Souter cited former senator Paul Simon for the proposition that "people contribute to party committees on both sides of the aisle for the same reason that Federal Express does, because they want favors [and believe] that giving to party committees helps you legislatively." Ibid., 452n12.

151. *NCPAC*, 470 U.S. 480, 521 (1985) (Marshall, J., dissenting).

152. Ibid., 519.

153. Colorado Republican Federal Campaign Committee v. Federal Election Commission (Colorado I), 518 U.S. 604, 649 (1996).

154. Ibid., 649–650.

155. As discussed in Chapters 4 and 6.

156. *Colorado II*, 533 U.S. at 442.

157. McConnell v. FEC, 540 U.S. 93, 150 (2003). Given *Austin* and *McConnell*'s recent fate, it is not worth discussing whether the Court will assert an enhanced version of *Austin* anytime soon.

158. Ibid., 124–125, 149–151, 270.

159. *Bellotti*, 435 U.S. at 821.

160. *Citizens United*, 130 S. Ct. at 80.

161. Ibid., 60.

162. *MCFL*, 479 U.S. at 268 (Rehnquist, C.J., dissenting).

163. Ibid.

164. Ibid., 269.

165. Ibid., 241, 270.

166. This would respond to the danger cited again by Justices Souter, Stevens, Ginsburg, and Breyer in a 2007 dissent: "[T]he same characteristics that have made them engines of the Nation's extraordinary prosperity have given them the financial muscle to gain 'advantage in the political marketplace' when they turn from core corporate activity to electioneering." *Wisconsin Right to Life*, 551 U.S. at 449.

167. *Citizens United*, 130 S. Ct. at 947 (Stevens, J., dissenting).

168. Ibid., 972.

169. Ibid.

170. Ibid.

171. This is not a small thing, however. The right to choose one's profession and apply one's energies and talents without restraint is a remarkable civilizational achievement. But ultimately, such projects can be sustained in the market only to the extent that supply and demand permit. And those with greater financial power can acquire more goods, services, and opportunities for the realization of their own projects, however profound or narrow.

172. *Davis*, 128 S. Ct. at 2788 (Stevens, J., dissenting) (quoting Cass Sunstein).

173. *Bennett*, 131 S. Ct. at 2845–2846 (Kagan, J., dissenting).

174. Ibid., 2846.

175. Ibid., 2830.

176. Ibid., 2846.

177. Ibid., 2833.

178. As Martin Redish put it ten years before *Bennett*, "[T]he power to selectively subsidize private speech enables the government to undermine First Amendment interests by distorting the expressive marketplace." Redish, *Money Talks*, 12.

179. *Bellotti*, 435 U.S. at 826.

180. Ibid., 821.

181. This is the case assuming that individual rights are never interpreted as positive rights.

182. U.S. Const., art. V. ("The Congress, whenever two thirds of both Houses shall deem it necessary, shall propose Amendments to this Constitution, or, on the Application of the Legislatures of two thirds of the several States, shall call a Convention for proposing Amendments, which, in either Case, shall be valid to all Intents and Purposes, as part of this Constitution, when ratified by the Legislatures of three fourths of the several States, or by Conventions in three fourths thereof, as the one or the other Mode of Ratification may be proposed by the Congress.")

183. Levinson, *Our Undemocratic Constitution*, 21.

184. On the problems associated with its age, consider Law and Versteeg, "The Declining Influence of the United States Constitution."

185. Rawls, "The Idea of Public Reason Revisited," 795–797.

186. Ibid., 797.

187. Center for Responsive Politics, "2012 Overview: Donor Demographics," *OpenSecrets.org*, http://www.opensecrets.org/overview/donordemographics.php.

188. Macpherson, *Democratic Theory*, 79.

189. Gray v. Sanders, 372 U.S. 368, 377 (1963).

190. Jackson describes this chain of amendments in terms of the Constitution's "deepening commitments to a basic norm of equality of citizenship." Jackson, "Fiss's Way," 271–274.

191. Macpherson, *Democratic Theory*, 79.

192. Gary Gutting, "Liberty, Equality, Hostility," *New York Times*, February 1, 2012, http://opinionator.blogs.nytimes.com/2012/02/01/liberty-equality-hostility/.

193. Lowi, *The End of Liberalism*, 31.

194. Heilbroner, *The Nature and Logic of Capitalism*, 107.

195. Ibid.

Bibliography

Akerlof, George A., and Robert J. Shiller. *Animal Spirits: How Human Psychology Drives the Economy and Why It Matters for Global Capitalism*. Princeton, N.J.: Princeton University Press, 2009.

Alexander, Herbert E. *Financing Politics: Money, Elections, and Political Reform*. 4th ed. Washington, D.C.: Congressional Quarterly, Inc., 1992.

Allen, Davis S. *Democracy, Inc.* Urbana and Chicago: University of Illinois Press, 2005.

Amadae, S. M. *Rationalizing Capitalist Democracy*. Chicago: University of Chicago Press, 2003.

Amar, Akhil Reed. "The Consent of the Governed: Constitutional Amendment Outside Article V." *Columbia Law Review* 94 (1994): 457.

Arrow, Kenneth J. *Social Choice and Individual Values*. 2d ed. New York: John Wiley and Sons, 1963.

Bakan, Joel. *The Corporation: The Pathological Pursuit of Profit and Power*. New York: Free Press, 2004.

Barrow, Clyde W. *Critical Theories of the State: Marxist, Neo-Marxist, Post-Marxist*. Madison: University of Wisconsin Press, 1993.

Bartels, Larry M. *Unequal Democracy*. Princeton, N.J.: Princeton University Press, 2008.

Bebchuk, Lucian A., and Robert J. Jackson, Jr. "Corporate Political Speech: Who Decides?" *Harvard Law Review* 124 (2010): 83.

Beitz, Charles R. *Political Equality: An Essay in Democratic Theory*. Princeton, N.J.: Princeton University Press, 1989.

Bennett, W. Lance. *The Governing Crisis: Media, Money, and Marketing in American Elections*. New York: St. Martin's Press, 1992.

Berg, Larry L., Harlan Han, and John R. Schmidhauser. *Corruption in the American Political System*. Morristown, N.J.: General Learning Press, 1976.

Blasi, Vincent. "Free Speech and the Widening Gyre of Fund-Raising," *Columbia Law Review* 94 (1994): 1281.

Blocher, Joseph. "Institutions in the Marketplace of Ideas." *Duke Law Journal* 57 (2008): 821.

Bogle, John C. *The Battle for the Soul of Capitalism*. New Haven, Conn.: Yale University Press, 2005. Kindle edition.

Bohman, James, and William Rehg, eds. *Deliberative Democracy: Essays on Reason and Politics*. Cambridge, Mass.: MIT Press, 1997.

Bowman, Scott R. *The Modern Corporation and American Political Thought: Law, Power, and Ideology*. University Park: Pennsylvania State University Press, 1996.

Bybee, Keith J. *All Judges Are Political Except When They Are Not*. Palo Alto: Stanford University Press, 2010.

Cafaggi, Fabrizio, Colin Scott, and Linda Senden, eds. *The Challenge of Transnational Private Regulation: Conceptual and Constitutional Debates*. Hoboken, N.J.: Wiley-Blackwell, 2011.

Calhoun, Craig, ed. *Habermas and the Public Sphere*. Cambridge, Mass.: MIT Press, 1992.

Chester, Lewis. *Watergate: The Full Inside Story*. New York: Ballantine Books, 1973.

Chomsky, Noam. "Consent without Consent: Reflections on the Theory and Practice of Democracy." *Cleveland State Law Review* 44 (1996): 415.

Chomsky, Noam, and Edward S. Herman. *Manufacturing Consent: The Political Economy of the Mass Media*. New York: Pantheon Books, 1988.

Cohen, Jerry S., and Morton Mintz. *America, Inc.: Who Owns and Operates the United States*. New York: Dial Press, 1971. Original copyright 1949.

Congressional Quarterly, Inc. *The Washington Lobby*, 5th ed. Washington, D.C.: Editorial Research Service, 1987.

Cooke, Jacob E., ed. *The Federalist Papers*. Middletown, Conn.: Wesleyan University Press, 1961.

Cooper, John W., and Michael Novak. *The Corporation: A Theological Inquiry*. Washington and London: American Enterprise Institute for Public Policy Research, 1981.

Corrado, Anthony, Thomas E. Mann, Daniel R. Ortiz, Trevor Potter, and Frank J. Sorauf, eds. *Campaign Finance Reform: A Sourcebook*. Washington, D.C.: Brookings Institution, 1997.

Corrado, Anthony, Thomas E. Mann, and Trevor Potter, eds. *Inside the Campaign Finance Battle: Court Testimony on the New Reforms*. Washington, D.C.: Brooking Institution, 2003.

Corrado, Anthony, Thomas E. Mann, Daniel R. Ortiz, and Trevor Potter. *The New Campaign Finance Sourcebook*. Washington, D.C.: Brookings Institution, 2005.

Cox, James D., and Thomas Lee Hazen. *Corporations*. 2d ed. New York: Aspen Publishers, 2002.

Cray, Charlie, and Lee Drutman. *The People's Business: Controlling Corporations and Restoring Democracy*. San Francisco: Berrett-Koehler Publishers, 2004.

Croteau, David, and William Hoynes. *The Business of Media: Corporate Media and the Public Interest*. Thousand Oaks, Calif.: Pine Forge Press, 2001.

Dahl, Robert A. *Dilemmas of Pluralist Democracy: Autonomy vs. Control*. New Haven, Conn.: Yale University Press, 1983.

———. *On Democracy*. New Haven, Conn.: Yale University Press, 1998.

———. *On Political Equality*. New Haven, Conn.: Yale University Press, 2006.

———. *A Preface to Democratic Theory*. Chicago: University of Chicago Press, 1956.

Davidson, Roger H., and Walter J. Oleszek. *Congress and Its Members*. Washington, D.C.: Congressional Quarterly Press, 2002.

Davis, Joseph Stancliffe. *Essays in the Earlier History of American Corporations*, Vol. 1. Cambridge, Mass.: Harvard University Press, 1917.

———. *Essays in the Earlier History of American Corporations*, Vol 2. Cambridge, Mass.: Harvard University Press, 1917.

Deane, Phyllis. *The State and the Economic System*. Oxford: Oxford University Press, 1989.

Demaris, Ovid. *Dirty Business: The Corporate-Political Money-Power Game*. New York: Harpers Magazine Press, 1974.

Derber, Charles. *Corporation Nation: How Corporations Are Taking over Our Lives and What We Can Do about It*. New York: St. Martin's Griffin, 1998.

Dewey, John. *The Middle Works: 1899–1924*. Edited by Jo Ann Boydston. Carbondale: Southern Illinois University Press, 1980.

———. *The Public and Its Problems*. Athens: Swallow Press/Ohio University Press, 1927.

Donnelly, David, Janice Fine, and Ellen S. Miller. *Money and Politics: Financing Our Elections Democratically*. Boston: Beacon Press, 1999.

Downs, Anthony. *An Economic Theory of Democracy*. New York: Harper and Row, 1985. Originally published in 1957.

Duncan, Graeme, ed. *Democracy and the Capitalist State*. Cambridge: Cambridge University Press, 1989.

Dunn, John. *Democracy: A History*. New York: Atlantic Monthly Press, 2005.

Dworkin, Ronald. *Freedom's Law*. Oxford: Oxford University Press, 1996.

———. *Is Democracy Possible Here?* Princeton, N.J.: Princeton University Press, 2006.

Ellul, Jacques. *Propaganda: The Formation of Men's Attitudes*. New York: Vintage Books, 1965.

Emerson, Ralph Waldo. *The American Scholar: Self-reliance, Compensation*. New York: American Book Company, 1911.

Emerson, Thomas Irwin. *The System of Freedom of Expression*. New York: Vintage Books, 1971.

Epstein, Richard. "Modern Republicanism—or the Flight from Substance." *Yale Law Journal* 97 (1988): 1633.

Ewen, Stuart. *PR!: A Social History of Spin*. New York: Basic Books, 1996.

Ewing, K. D. *The Cost of Democracy: Party Funding in Modern British Politics*. Oxford, UK: Hart Publishing, 2007.

Ewing, Keith, and Samuel Issacharoff, eds. *Party Funding and Campaign Financing in International Perspective*. Oxford, UK: Hart Publishing, 2006.

Fairfax, Lisa M. "Making the Corporation Safe for Shareholder Democracy." *Ohio State Law Journal* 69 (2008): 53.

Farber, Daniel, and Phillip Frickey. *Law and Public Choice*. Chicago: University of Chicago Press, 1991.

Fiss, Owen M. "Free Speech and Social Structure." *Iowa Law Review* 71 (1986): 1405.

———. *The Irony of Free Speech*. Cambridge, Mass.: Harvard University Press, 1996.

———. *Liberalism Divided*. Boulder, Col.: Westview Press, 1996.

Fleishman, Joel L. "The 1974 Federal Election Campaign Act Amendments: The Shortcomings of Good Intentions." *Duke Law Journal* 4 (1975): 851.

Foley, Edward. "Philosophy, the Constitution, and Campaign Finance." *Stanford Law and Policy Review* 10 (1998): 23.

Follesdal, Andreas, Michele Micheletti, and Dietlind Stolle, eds. *Politics, Products, and Markets: Exploring Political Consumerism Past and Present*. New Brunswick, N.J.: Transaction Publishers, 2007.

Ford, Paul L., ed. *The Writings of Thomas Jefferson*. New York: G. P. Putnam's Sons, 1892–1899.

Forer, Lois G. *Money and Justice: Who Owns the Courts?* New York: W. W. Norton, 1984.

Fox, Gregory H., and Brad R. Roth. *Democratic Governance and International Law*. Cambridge: Cambridge University Press, 2000.

Frank, Thomas. *What's the Matter with Kansas?: How Conservatives Won the Heart of America*. New York: Henry Holt, 2004.

Frederick, William C. *Corporation Be Good! The Story of Corporate Social Responsibility*. Indianapolis: Dog Ear Publishing, 2006.

Freedman, Adam. *The Naked Constitution*. New York: Broadside Books, 2012.

Friedman, Milton. *Capitalism and Freedom*. Chicago: University of Chicago Press, 1982

Fulcher, James. *Capitalism: A Very Short Introduction*. New York: Oxford University Press, 2004. Kindle edition.

Furubotn, Eirik G., and Rudolf Richter. *Institutions and Economic Theory*. Ann Arbor: University of Michigan Press, 1997.

Galbraith, John Kenneth. *American Capitalism: The Concept of Countervailing Power*. New Brunswick, N.J.: Transaction Publishers, 1993. Originally published in 1952.

Goldwin, Robert A., and William A. Schambra, eds. *How Capitalistic Is the Constitution?* Washington, D.C.: AEI Press, 1982.

Gore, Al. *The Assault on Reason.* New York: Penguin, 2007.

Greider, William. *Who Will Tell the People: The Betrayal of American Democracy.* New York: Simon and Schuster, 1992.

Grugel, Jean. *Democratization: A Critical Introduction.* New York: Palgrave Macmillan, 2002.

Gunlicks, Arthur, ed. *Campaign Finance and Party Finance in North America and Western Europe.* Boulder, Col.: Westview Press, 1991; now iUniverse.com, 2000.

Habermas, Jürgen. *The Inclusion of the Other.* Edited by C. Cronin and P. De Greiff. Cambridge, Mass.: MIT Press, 1998.

———. "Popular Sovereignty as Procedure." In Bohman and Rehg, *Deliberative Democracy.*

———. *The Structural Transformation of the Public Sphere: An Inquiry into a Category of Bourgeois Society.* Translated by Thomas Burger. Cambridge, Mass.: MIT Press, 1991.

Haerpfer, Christian W., Patrick Bernhagen, Ronald F. Inglehart and Christian Welzel, eds. *Democratization.* Oxford: Oxford University Press, 2009.

Haley, Usha C. V. *Multinational Corporations in Political Environments: Ethics, Values, and Strategies.* River Edge: World Scientific Publishing, 2001.

Harris, Richard Jackson. *A Cognitive Psychology of Mass Communication.* Mahwah and London: Lawrence Erlbaum Associates, 2004.

Hasen, Richard L. "Beyond Incoherence: The Roberts Court's Deregulatory Turn in *FEC v. Wisconsin Right to Life.*" *Minnesota Law Review* 92 (2008): 1064.

———. "Clipping Coupons for Democracy." *California Law Review* 84 (1996): 1.

———. "Entrenching the Duopoly: Why the Supreme Court Should Not Allow the States to Protect the Democrats and Republicans from Political Competition." *Supreme Court Review* 1997 (1997): 331.

———. "The Political Market Metaphor and Election Law. *Stanford Law Review* 50 (1998): 719.

Heilbroner, Robert L. *Behind the Veil of Economics.* New York: W. W. Norton, 1988.

———. *The Nature and Logic of Capitalism.* New York: W. W. Norton, 1985.

———. *21st Century Capitalism.* New York: W. W. Norton, 1993.

Held, David. *Introduction to Critical Theory: Horkheimer to Habermas.* Berkeley and Los Angeles: University of California Press, 1980.

———. *Models of Democracy.* 3rd ed. Palo Alto: Stanford University Press, 2006.

Herman, Edward S., and Noam Chomsky. *Manufacturing Consent: The Political Economy of the Mass Media.* New York: Pantheon Books, 1988.

Hertz, Emanuel. *Abraham Lincoln: A New Portrait.* New York: Horace Liveright, 1931.

Hohenstein, Kurt. *Coining Corruption: The Making of the American Campaign Finance System.* DeKalb: Northern Illinois University Press, 2007.

Holmes, Oliver Wendell. *The Common Law.* Cambridge: Harvard University Press, 1963. Originally published in 1881.

Horowitz, David. *The Art of Political War and Other Radical Pursuits.* Dallas: Spence Publishing Company, 2000.

Houck, Oliver A. "With Charity for All." *Yale Law Journal* 93 (1984): 1415.

Hurst, James Willard. *Law and Markets in United States History: Different Modes of Bargaining among Interests.* Madison: University of Wisconsin Press, 1982.

Hutchinson, Dennis J. *The Man Who Once Was Whizzer White.* New York: Free Press, 1998.

Issacharoff, Samuel, and Pamela S. Karlan. "The Hydraulics of Campaign Finance Reform." *Texas Law Review* 77 (1999): 1705.

Issacharoff, Samuel, and Richard H. Pildes. "Politics as Markets: Partisan Lockups of the Democratic Process." *Stanford Law Review* 50 (1998): 643.

Jackson, Vicki C. "Fiss's Way: Holistic Interpretation, Comparative Constitutionalism, and Fiss-ian Freedoms." *University of Miami Law Review* 58 (2003): 265.

Jefferson, Thomas. *Writings*. New York: Library of America, 1984.

Jessup, Bob. *The Capitalist State*. New York: New York University Press, 1982.

Kara, Siddharth. *Sex Trafficking: Inside the Business of Modern Slavery*. New York: Columbia University Press, 2008.

Karlan, Pamela S. "Politics by Other Means." *Virginia Law Review* 85 (1999): 1697.

Kelly, Marjorie. *The Divine Right of Capital: Dethroning the Corporate Aristocracy*. San Francisco: Berrett-Koehler Publishers, 2001.

Kelman, Steven. *Making Public Policy: A Hopeful View of American Government*. New York: Basic Books, 1987.

Klein, Joe. *From RFK to W: How Politicians Have Become Less Courageous and More Interested in Keeping Power Than in Doing What's Right for America*. New York: Broadway Publishing Group, 2006.

Kramnick, Isaac, ed. *The Federalist Papers*. New York: Penguin, 1987.

Kuhner, Timothy K. "*Citizens United* as Neoliberal Jurisprudence: The Resurgence of Economic Theory." *Virginia Journal of Social Policy and the Law* 18 (2011): 395.

———. "Consumer Sovereignty Trumps Popular Sovereignty: The Economic Explanation for Arizona Free Enterprise v. Bennett." *Indiana Law Review* 46 (2013): 603.

———. "The Separation of Business and State." *California Law Review* 95 (2007): 2353.

Kutler, Stanley I. *The Wars of Watergate: The Last Crisis of Richard Nixon*. New York: Knopf, 1990.

Landes, William M., and Richard A. Posner. "The Independent Judiciary in an Interest-Group Perspective." *Journal of Law and Economics* 18 (1975): 875.

Law, David S., and Mila Versteeg. "The Declining Influence of the United States Constitution." *New York University Law Review* 87 (2012): 762.

Lessig, Lawrence. *Republic Lost: How Money Corrupts Congress—and a Plan to Stop It*. New York: Twelve, 2011.

Levinson, Sanford. *Our Undemocratic Constitution: Where the Constitution Goes Wrong*. New York: Oxford University Press, 2006.

Levinson, Sanford, ed. *Responding to Imperfection: The Theory and Practice of Constitutional Amendment*. Princeton, N.J.: Princeton University Press, 1995.

Lewis, Charles, and the Center for Public Integrity. *The Buying of the President 2004: Who's Really Bankrolling Bush and His Democratic Challengers—and What They Expect in Return*. New York: HarperCollins Publishers, 2004.

Lindblom, Charles E. *Politics and Markets*. New York: Basic Books, 1977.

Lippmann, Walter. *Public Opinion*. New York: Free Press, 1997. Originally published in 1922.

Lowi, Theodore J. *The End of Liberalism: The Second Republic of the United States*. New York: W. W. Norton, 1979. Originally published in 1969.

Lubenow, Gerald C., ed. *A User's Guide to Campaign Finance Reform*. Berkeley, Calif.: Berkeley Public Policy Press and Rowman and Littlefield Publishers, 2001.

Luger, Stan. *Corporate Power, American Democracy, and the Automobile Industry*. Cambridge: Cambridge University Press, 2000.

Macpherson, C. B. *Democratic Theory: Essays in Retrieval*. Oxford: Oxford University Press, 1973.

———. *The Life and Times of Liberal Democracy*. Oxford: Oxford University Press, 1977.

————. *The Real World of Democracy*. Concord, Ontario: Anansi Press, 1965 and 1992.

Makinson, Larry, and the Staff of the Center for Responsive Politics. *The Big Picture: The Money behind the 2000 Elections*. Washington, D.C.: Center for Responsive Politics, 2001.

————. *Speaking Freely: Washington Insiders Talk about Money in Politics*. 2nd ed. Washington, D.C.: Center for Responsive Politics, 2003.

Malbin, Michael J., and Thomas L. Gais. *The Day After Reform: Sobering Campaign Finance Lessons from the American States*. New York: Rockefeller Institute Press, 1998.

Manheim, Jarol B. *The Death of a Thousand Cuts: Corporate Campaigns and the Attack on the Corporation*. Mahwah, N.J., and London: Lawrence Erlbaum Associates, 2001.

Marchand, Roland. *Creating the Corporate Soul: The Rise of Public Relations and Corporate Imagery in American Big Business*. Berkeley: University of California Press, 1998.

Marx, Axel, Miet Maertens, Johan Swinnen, and Jan Wouters, eds. *Private Standards and Global Governance: Legal and Economic Perspectives*. Northampton, Mass.: Edward Elgar Publishing, 2012.

Mason, Edward S. *The Corporation in Modern Society*. Cambridge, Mass.: Harvard University Press, 1959.

Means, Howard. *Money and Power: The History of Business*. New York: John Wiley and Sons, 2001.

Meiklejohn, Alexander. *Free Speech and Its Relationship to Self-Government*. 1948.

Micklethwait, John, and Adrian Woolridge. *The Company: A Short History of a Revolutionary Idea*. New York: Modern Library, Random House, 2005.

Miliband, Ralph. *The State in Capitalist Society*. London: Quartet Books, 1969.

Mill, John Stuart. *Principles of Political Economy*. Edited by W. Ashley. New York, Bombay, and Calcutta: Longmans, Green, 1909.

Millder, James C. III. *Monopoly Politics*. Stanford, Calif.: Hoover Institution Press, 1999.

Mills, C. Wright. *The Power Elite*. New York: Oxford University Press, 1959.

Mirowski, Philip, and Dieter Plehwe, eds. *The Road from Mont Pelerin: The Making of the Neoliberal Thought Collective*. Cambridge, Mass.: Harvard University Press, 2009.

Muller, Jerry Z. *The Mind and the Market: Capitalism in Western Thought*. New York: Anchor Books, Random House, 2002. Kindle edition.

Mutch, Robert E. *Campaigns, Congress, and the Courts: The Making of Federal Campaign Finance Law*. Westport, Conn.: Praeger, 1988.

Ogus, Anthony I. *Regulation: Legal Form and Economic Theory*. Oxford: Hart Publishing, 1994, 2004.

Olsen, Mancur. *The Logic of Collective Action: Public Goods and the Theory of Groups*. Cambridge, Mass.: Harvard University Press, 1971.

Ortiz, Daniel R. "The Democratic Paradox of Campaign Finance Reform." *Stanford Law Review* 50 (1998): 893.

Overton, Spencer. "The Donor Class: Campaign Finance, Democracy, and Participation." *University of Pennsylvania Law Review* 153 (2004): 73.

Palast, Greg. *The Best Democracy Money Can Buy: The Truth about Corporate Cons, Globalization, and High-Finance Fraudsters*. New York: Penguin Group, 2003.

Pasquale, Frank. "Reclaiming Egalitarianism in the Political Theory of Campaign Finance Reform." *University of Illinois Law Review* 2008 (2008): 599.

Phillips, Kevin. *Bad Money: Reckless Finance, Failed Politics, and the Global Crisis of American Capitalism*. New York: Penguin Group, 2008.

————. *Wealth and Democracy: A Political History of the American Rich*. New York: Broadway Books, 2002.

Pildes, Richard H., and Elizabeth S. Anderson. "Slinging Arrows at Democracy: Social Choice Theory, Value Pluralism, and Democratic Politics." *Columbia Law Review* 90 (1990): 2121.

Polanyi, Karl. *The Great Transformation: The Political and Economic Origins of Our Time*. Boston: Beacon Press, 2001. Originally published in 1941.

Posner, Richard A. *Law, Pragmatism, and Democracy*. Cambridge, Mass.: Harvard University Press, 2003.

Powell, H. Jefferson. *Constitutional Conscience: The Moral Dimension of Judicial Decision*. Chicago: University of Chicago Press, 2008.

———. "The Original Understanding of Original Intent." *Harvard Law Review* 98 (1985): 885.

———. "Reasoning about the Irrational: The Roberts Court and the Future of Constitutional Law." *Washington Law Review* 86 (2011): 217.

Prindle, David F. *The Paradox of Democratic Capitalism: Politics and Economics in American Thought*. Baltimore: Johns Hopkins University Press, 2006.

Purdy, Jedediah, ed. *Democratic Vistas*. New Haven, Conn.: Yale University Press, 2004.

Quinn, T. K. *Giant Business: Threat to Democracy*. New York: Exposition Press, 1953.

Radin, Margaret Jane. *Contested Commodities: The Trouble with Trade in Sex, Children, Body Parts, and Other Things*. Cambridge, Mass.: Harvard University Press, First Harvard Paperback ed. 2001. Originally published in 1996.

Rampton, Sheldon, and John Stauber. *Toxic Sludge Is Good for You!: Lies, Damn Lies, and the Public Relations Industry*. Monroe, Maine: Common Courage Press, 1995.

Rand, Ayn. *Capitalism: The Unknown Ideal (with additional articles by Nathaniel Branden, Alan Greenspan, and Robert Hessen)*. New York: New American Library, Penguin, 1946. Kindle edition.

Rawls, John. "The Idea of Public Reason Revisited." *University of Chicago Law Review* 64 (1997): 765.

———. *Political Liberalism*. Rev. ed. New York: Columbia University Press, 1996. Originally published in 1993.

———. *A Theory of Justice*. Rev. ed. Cambridge, Mass.: Belknap Press of Harvard University Press, 1999. Originally published in 1971.

Redish, Martin H. *Money Talks: Speech, Economic Power, and the Values of Democracy*. New York: New York University Press, 2001.

Reich, Robert. *Supercapitalism*. New York: Alfred A. Knopf, 2007.

Rejai, M. *Democracy: The Contemporary Theories*. New York: Atherton Press, 1967.

Ribstein, Larry E. "The First Amendment and Corporate Governance." *Georgia State University Law Review* 27 (2011): 1019.

Ringhand, Lori. "Defining Democracy." *Hastings Law Journal* 56 (2004–2005): 77.

Rosanvallon, Pierre. *Democracy Past and Future*. New York: Columbia University Press, 2006.

Rose-Ackerman, Susan. *Corruption and Government: Causes, Consequences, and Reform*. Cambridge: Cambridge University Press, 1999.

Rousseau, Jean-Jacques. *Discourse on the Origin of Inequality*. Translated and edited by Donald A. Cress. Indianapolis: Hackett Publishing, 1983. Originally published in 1754.

Roy, William G. *Socializing Capital: The Rise of the Large Industrial Corporation in America*. Princeton, N.J.: Princeton University Press, 1997.

Samples, John. *The Fallacy of Campaign Finance Reform*. Chicago and London: University of Chicago Press, 2006. Kindle edition.

Sandel, Michael J. *Democracy's Discontent*. Cambridge, Mass.: Belknap Press of Harvard University Press, 1996.

————. *Liberalism and the Limits of Justice.* Cambridge: Cambridge University Press, 1982.

Schauer, Frederick. "The Political Incidence of the Free Speech Principle." *University of Colorado Law Review* 64 (1993): 935.

Schultz, David A., ed. *Money, Politics, and Campaign Finance Reform Law in the States.* Durham: Carolina Academic Press, 2002.

Schumpeter, Joseph A. *Capitalism, Socialism, and Democracy.* 3rd ed. New York: Harper and Brothers, 1950.

Schwartz, Donald E. "Defining the Corporate Objective: Section 2.01 of the ALI's Principles." *George Washington Law Review* 52 (1984): 511.

Schweizer, Peter. *Extortion: How Politicians Extract Your Money, Buy Votes, and Line Their Own Pockets.* Boston and New York: Houghton Mifflin Harcourt, 2013.

Shapiro, Ian. *The State of Democratic Theory.* Princeton, N.J.: Princeton University Press, 2003.

Siebecker, Michael R. "A New Discourse Theory of the Firm after Citizens United." *George Washington Law Review* 79 (2010): 161.

Smith, Adam. *The Wealth of Nations.* Everyman's Library, 1910; repr. London: Random Century Group, 1991.

Smith, Bradley A. "The Sirens' Song: Campaign Finance Regulation and the First Amendment." *Journal of Law and Policy* 6 (1997): 1.

————. *Unfree Speech: The Folly of Campaign Finance Reform.* Princeton, N.J.: Princeton University Press, 2001. Kindle edition.

Smith, Rodney A. *Money, Power, and Elections: How Campaign Finance Reform Subverts American Democracy.* Baton Rouge: Louisiana State University Press, 2006.

Story, Joseph. *Commentaries on the Constitution of the United States.* Boston, 1833.

Stout, Lynn A. "Bad and Not-So-Bad Arguments for Shareholder Primacy." *Southern California Law Review* 75 (2002): 1189.

Streb, Matthew. *Rethinking American Electoral Democracy.* New York: Routledge, 2008.

Sullivan, Kathleen M. "Discrimination, Distribution and Free Speech." *Arizona Law Review* 37 (1995): 439.

Sunstein, Cass R. "Beyond the Republican Revival." *Yale Law Journal* 97 (1988): 1539.

————. *Democracy and the Problem of Free Speech.* New York: Free Press, Kindle edition, 1993.

————. *Free Markets and Social Justice.* New York: Oxford University Press, 1997.

————. "Political Equality and Unintended Consequences." *Columbia Law Review* 94 (1994): 1390.

Teachout, Zephyr. "The Anti-Corruption Principle." *Cornell Law Review* 94 (2009): 341.

Tocqueville, Alexis de. *Democracy in America.* New York: Alfred A. Knopf, 1945.

Tribe, Laurence H. *American Constitutional Law.* 2nd ed. Mineola, NY: Foundation Press, 1988.

Tucker, Anne. "Rational Coercion and a Modern-Day Prisoner's Dilemma." *Georgia State University Law Review* 27 (2011): 1105.

Tye, Larry. *The Father of Spin: Edward L. Bernays and the Birth of Public Relations.* New York: Henry Holt and Company, 1998.

Unger, Roberto Mangabeira. *Democracy Realized.* New York: Verso, 2001.

Urofsky, Melvin I. *Money and Free Speech: Campaign Finance Reform and the Courts.* Lawrence: University Press of Kansas, 2005.

U.S. Chamber of Commerce. "The Powell Memorandum." *Washington Report*, Supp. No. 2900, 1971.

Vogel, David. *The Market for Virtue: The Potential and Limits of Corporate Social Responsibility.* Washington, D.C.: Brookings Institution Press, 2006.

Wagner, Donald O., ed. *Social Reformers: Adam Smith to John Dewey*. New York: Macmillan, 1934.

Walzer, Michael. *Spheres of Justice: A Defense of Pluralism and Equality*. New York: Basic Books, 1983.

———. *Thinking Politically: Essays in Political Theory*. Edited by David Miller. New Haven, Conn.: Yale University Press, 2007.

Whitman, Walt. *Complete Poetry and Prose*. New York: Library of America, 1982.

Williamson, Chilton. *American Suffrage: From Property to Democracy, 1760–1860*. Princeton, N.J.: Princeton University Press, 1960.

Winkler, Adam. "Beyond Bellotti." *Loyola of Los Angeles Law Review* 32 (1998): 133.

———. "'Other People's Money': Corporations, Agency Costs, and Campaign Finance Law." *Georgetown Law Journal* 92 (2004): 871.

Winter, Ralph K. *Watergate and the Law*. Washington, D.C.: AEI Press, 1974.

Winter, Steven L. *A Clearing in the Forest: Law, Life, and Mind*. Chicago: University of Chicago Press, 2001.

Woodruff, Paul. *First Democracy: The Challenge of an Ancient Idea*. New York: Oxford University Press, 2005.

Wright, J. Skelly. "Money and the Pollution of Politics: Is the First Amendment an Obstacle to Political Equality?" *Columbia Law Review* 82 (1982): 609.

Zunz, Olivier. *Making America Corporate: 1870–1920*. Chicago and London: University of Chicago Press, 1990.

Index

Abramoff, Jack, 1, 205
Abrams v. United States (1919), 151
Adams plaintiffs, in McConnell, 124–26, 222
Adelson, Sheldon, 1–2, 27, 193, 219
Advertising: corporate spending on political, 91–92; issue-oriented, 113; politics conducted using principles of, 58, 165, 302n113; restrictions on, 127–29; superPAC-sponsored, 201–2; 30-second television ads, 132, 174, 273
Akerlof, George, 89, 289n3, 309n118
ALEC, 2, 8, 185, 205, 326n55
Alito, Samuel, 10–11, 90, 93, 94, 112, 114–16, 121–22, 128, 130, 186, 262, 265, 268
Alliance for Democracy, 21
Amadae, S. M., 157, 158
American Airlines, 205
American Anti-Corruption Act, 19, 295n97, 98
American Crossroads, 202, 204
American Jobs Creation Act (2004), 206
American Legislative Exchange Council (ALEC), 205
Antagonistic viewpoints. See Diverse and antagonistic viewpoints
Anuzis, Saul, 203
Archer Daniels Midlands, 246
Aristocracy, 8, 24, 28–29, 226, 228–29, 257–59, 260, 285
Aristotle, 258
Arizona, 11, 113–14, 116–17, 119–20, 125, 278,
Arizona Free Enterprise v. Bennett (2011), xii, 113–26, 129, 136, 146, 168–69, 170, 178, 181, 190, 197, 230, 269, 278–79
Arrow, Kenneth, 156, 308n91, 319n54, 320n76
Asymmetrical regulatory scheme, 114
AT&T, 2, 137
Austin v. Michigan Chamber of Commerce (1990), 95–106, 113, 128, 131, 134, 148–49, 153, 162–63, 180, 190, 220, 268, 274, 278–79, 310n21

Auto Workers. See United States v. UAW-CIO (Auto Workers, 1957)

Bakan, Joel, 84, 308n94
Bartels, Larry, 60–61
Becker, Gary, 247, 334n47
Bellotti. See First National Bank of Boston v. Bellotti (1978)
Benjamin, Brent, 307n78
Bennet, Michael, 225
Bennett. See Arizona Free Enterprise v. Bennett (2011)
Bentham, Jeremy, 168, 230, 231
Bernhagen, Patrick, 246
Bipartisan Campaign Reform Act (2002). See McCain-Feingold Act (2002)
Black markets, 197
Blackmun, Harry, 65, 276, 304n1, 310n15, 315n150
Blackstone, William, 227–28
Blasi, Vincent, 60–61, 111–12
Blocher, Joseph, 54
Bopp, James, 13
Borski, Robert, 200
Brandeis, Louis, 54
Branden, Nathaniel, 244
Brennan, William, 79, 103, 139, 314n135, 317n199
Breyer, Stephen, 225, 269–72, 314n135, 339n166
Bribery, 1, 3, 7, 163, 197, 212, 214, 218, 270, 287. See also Corruption
Brooks, Arthur, 237
Buckley v. Valeo (1976), 34–65, 71–72, 92–94, 96, 101, 103, 106, 111–12, 114–15, 117, 120, 126, 127, 136, 150, 153, 162, 163, 168, 197–98, 230, 268, 271, 273, 275, 293n65, 298n10, 299n27, 303n119, 310n21, 312n89, 315n155
Buffett, Warren, 227
Bundling of contributions, 2, 5, 20, 203
Burdens: on corporations, 130–31; on free speech, 38–39, 97, 115, 117, 149–50; used in court tests, 120, 149–50
Burger, Warren, 62, 63, 65, 69, 94, 268

Burger Court: and *Buckley*, 94; conservatism of, 94, 101; and the First Amendment, 150; jurisprudence of, 149; market principles underlying decisions of, 154, 160; on money in politics, 92; Roberts Court in relation to, 94, 136; and state as mirror of society, 162
Burton, Harold, 103
Bush, George W., 3, 90, 112
Buttenwieser, Peter, 42

Campaign finance: expenditures on, 2–4, 51, 57, 109–10, 199; as First Amendment issue, 13, 14, 22, 26; impact of, on election outcomes, 199; limits on, 3, 6, 10, 12–13, 35, 38–39 (*see also* Contribution limits; Expenditures, political: limits on); market principles applied to, 50–51; media's effect on, 42, 57–58, 302n109; public, 20; soft money in, 106–9; sources of, 203; supply and demand view of, 58. *See also* Expenditures, political; Money in politics
Campaign finance law: *Buckley* and, 34–64; capitalism supported by, 250; democracy supported by, 267; freedom of speech and, 152; ineffectiveness of, 212; influence of, ix–x. *See also* Contribution limits; Expenditures, political: limits on
Campaign finance reform: corporate reform and, 14–17; economic arguments against, 10; government interests in, 40; ineffectiveness of, x; instances of, 9; of 1970s, 34–35; opposition to, 10, 12–14; partial, 17–20; proposed solutions concerning, 11–23; public opinion on, x, 92, 116, 134, 225, 237, 250; rationale for, 3; Supreme Court weakening of, 9–14; topics of, 9. *See also* Federal Election Campaign Act
Campaign rallies, 4
Canada, expenditure limits in, 46
Candidates. *See* Lawmakers and candidates
Caperton v. Massey Coal (West Virginia, 2009), 186, 307n78
Capitalism: capitalist threats to, 240–57, 283; challenges to, 28; crony capitalism, 248–50, 254, 256, 266; democracy interdependent with, 274; democracy vs., for political control, x, 17, 24–29, 31–32, 35–62, 141–88,

239, 248–49; entrepreneurial, 249–50; excesses of, 239; forms of, 89; and freedom, 243; government intervention in aid of, 250–54, 257; logic of, 192–93; and origins of United States, 23–24; private, not public, good the concern of, 8; Smith's basic conception of, 240–42; and social stratification, 229; societal benefits of, 230–31, 241–42, 256–57; state monopoly capitalism, 248–49. *See also* Market
Capitol Hill Club, 1
Carnegie, Andrew, 243
Caselaw: ambiguity in, 151; as basis of exercise of law, 148–49; *Buckley* and, 48; on money in politics, 92, 128, 131; overturning of, 128; Roberts Court and, 148; separatist principles in, 102–03, 268
Cato, 226
Caution, in jurisprudence, 148
Censorship, 26, 36, 38, 48, 58, 69, 128–30, 134, 180–81, 183, 186
Center for Competitive Politics, 13, 301n69
Central Pacific Railroad, 243
Chilling effect, on campaigns, 123–24
Chomsky, Noam, 165
Church-state separation, 259–60
Cicero, 226
Citizens: confidence/cynicism of, 224–25, 274–75; corporations as, 275–77; manipulation of, 164–65; political participation of, 44, 46–47, 73–74, 87–88, 102, 109, 162–63, 172, 190, 230; public opinion on campaign finance reform, x, 92, 116, 134, 225, 237, 250; republican theory and, 169–70, 172; responsibility of, for evaluating political speech, 72, 76–77, 105, 121–22, 173–74; voter abstention and apathy of, 186
Citizens United v. FEC (2010), 10–11, 14, 21, 90–92, 126–36, 139, 148–49, 153, 173–74, 178, 181, 182, 186, 190, 202, 221, 222, 225, 237, 269, 271, 274–76, 292n54
Clark, Tom, 103
Classical economic theory, 61–62
Cohen, Roger, 219
Cold War, 154, 157–58, 160
Collective action, 209
Collective action problems, 110, 224
Collective interests, 156–57
Commodification: in political market, 196–97; of speech, 59

Common good, 156–57, 255
Commons, tragedy of, 224
Communal conceptions, 56
Communism, 29, 261
Competition: as economic principle, 24, 28, 52, 61–62, 244–45; First Amendment applied to, 123; ideal of free, 30, 70; obstacles to, 249–50; perfect vs. imperfect, 61–62, 75–76, 139–40; as political principle, 53–54, 62
Conflicts of interest, 2
Congress. *See* U.S. Congress
Consequentialism, 181–82, 186
Constitutional avoidance, 149
Consumer sovereignty: *Buckley* and, 50–52; for corporations, 126–36; and legislative capture, 107–8; politics harmed by, 283–84; resulting from economic approach to politics, 156
Contractual freedoms, 55–56, 231
Contribution limits, 12–13, 19, 34, 38–39, 50, 62, 138. *See also* Expenditures, political: limits on
Corporate social responsibility, 84, 252
Corporations: advertising restrictions on, 127–29; as check on government, 232–36; as citizens, 275–77; consolidation of, 75; consumer sovereignty for, 126–36; and corruption, 135; domination of politics by, 21–22, 76, 83, 85–88, 93–94, 100–101, 133, 137, 151–52, 164, 173, 249, 272, 275–76; economic power of, 83, 86; First Amendment applied to, 11, 21, 130; free speech rights for, 11, 21, 26, 65, 67–73, 81, 90–91, 149, 174, 177; government-conferred benefits for, 82, 97–98, 101–2, 133–34, 234, 244–49, 276; meaning of expenditures of, 79–80; Michigan legislation on, 95–103; nature of, 82–85, 97; as persons, 149; political action committees of, 127, 129–31, 182; political advertising expenditures of, 91–92; political expenditures of, 67, 95–103; political power of, 21–22, 65–89, 92, 131; political role of, 177; profit maximization as purpose of, 178–79; reform of, 14–17; rights of, 10–11, 21, 296n108; rules on contributions of, 10–11, 14, 292n54, 293n65; Supreme Court on, 17
Corruption: appearance of, guarding against, 40–41, 57, 97, 138, 141, 270, 275; corporations and, 135; narrow

definition of, 40–41, 186; quid pro quo, 40, 57; relative insignificance of, as threat to democracy, 1; systematic, 7, 41; wealth as source of, 8, 9, 101, 103. *See also* Bribery
Corrupt Practices Act, 106
Countervailing power, 87–88
Court tests, 149–50
Crony capitalism, 248–50, 254, 256, 266
Crossroads GPS, 5, 204
Cunningham, Randy, 1

Dahl, Robert, 161–63
Dark money groups, 4–6, 18, 291n26
Davis v. FEC (2008), 114–26, 129, 168, 170, 178, 190, 262, 269, 270, 277
Dean, John, 66
Deck stacking, 166, 219–20, 254
Declaration of Independence, 7, 24
Deliberative democracy, 168–69, 172, 185
Democracy: capitalism interdependent with, 274; capitalism vs., for political control, x, 17, 24–29, 31–32, 35–62, 141–88, 239, 248–49; checks on full, 231; economic theory applied to, 154–60; emotion as component of, 154–56; erosion of confidence in, 224–25; inequalities in, 264; invisible hand of, 263–66; justice in relation to, 180–84; laissez-faire approach to, 52–57, 118–24, 137, 237–38; liberal, 153, 257–67; as a market, 50–64; minority interests in, 161; representative, 209; republicanism and, 169; and self-realization, 81–82, 84, 307n82; Supreme Court on, 23, 39; threats and challenges to, 1, 8–9, 28, 31. *See also* Democratic integrity
Democratic integrity: candidate expenditures as factor in, 41; constitutional obstacles to, xi–xii; corruption as threat to, 40–41, 103–4; limits on power and influence as component of, 89; market principles as threat to, 63; political process as source of, 73; as state interest, 270–74; wealth detrimental to, 6
Democratic Party, fundraising by, 110
Democratic perfectionism, 168
Deontological liberalism, 180–86
Dewey, John, 81, 157, 165, 307n82
DISCLOSE Act, 17–19
Disclosure requirements, 5, 17–19, 54, 76, 204
Diverse and antagonistic viewpoints, 45–48, 68, 71, 73, 79, 120, 124, 181

Division of labor, 242
Dodd, Christopher, 208
Dow Chemical, 5
Downs, Anthony, 156–57
Durbin, Dick, 200

Eagleton, Thomas, 131
Economic power: of corporations, 83, 86;
inequalities in, 42, 86; political power
attained by, 8–10, 23–24, 31, 38, 42,
83, 87, 160–61, 187, 191, 247–48,
261–63, 265–66, 284. *See also* Wealth
Economic rights, 233, 273
Economic theory: classical, 61–62; democ-
racy-friendly, 85–89; democracy from
perspective of, 154–60; misapplication
of, 61, 79; neoclassical, 33, 47, 50,
56. *See also* Free market ideology
Economy: crisis in (2008), 30; domination
of politics by, 258–59, 284–86; equality for citizens in, 179; government
intervention in, 33–34; origins of U.S.
and, 28–29; origins of U.S. political
system and, 23–24; political sphere
in relation to, 98–99, 102–3, 105,
189–90, 244–45, 247–48, 258–59,
264–65, 267–79; privatization in,
233–35; public opinion on, 237. *See
also* Capitalism; Economic power;
Economic theory; Market
Edsall, Thomas, 245
Effectiveness principle, 57–58, 74, 117–20,
122–26, 136–38, 178
Efficient-market hypothesis, 33, 35, 63
Electoral College, 209
Elster, Jon, 255
Emerson, Ralph Waldo, 81
Empirical democratic theory, 154
Empowering Citizens Act, 19
Entrepreneurial capitalism, 250
Entry, into markets, 69–70, 74, 137, 277
Environmental Protection Agency, 205
Environmental regulations, 251–57
Epstein, Richard, 255
Equality: in economic sphere, 179; free-
dom and, 46–49, 59–60, 175; and
freedom from domination, 262; mar-
ket view of, 59–60; opposing voices
concerning, 45–50, 172–75, 230, 262;
republicanism and, 167–71; as valued
concept, 43–45; wealth and, 262–63.
See also Inequality
Espionage Act (1917), 151
Exclusiveness, of political access, 6, 58,
79, 144
Exelon, 205

Expenditures, political: amount of, 191–
92; corporate, 67, 95–103; as filtering
device, 210; by foreign governments/
nationals, 69–70; as freedom of
speech, 10–11, 18, 26, 36–38, 41–42,
45–48, 63, 65, 268–70; impact of,
on election outcomes, 199; limits on,
11, 34–40, 46, 51, 63, 65, 128, 146
(*see also* Contribution limits). *See also*
Campaign finance; Money in politics
Externalities, 253–54
Exxon Mobil, 205

Factions, 160, 173–74
Fairfax, Lisa, 15
Farber, Daniel, 163
FECA. *See* Federal Election Campaign Act
*FEC v. National Right to Work
Committee* (*NRWC*, 1982), 93–95,
102, 271
FEC v. NCPAC (1985), 271, 273
Federal Election Campaign Act (FECA),
34–35, 43–47, 49, 53–54, 62, 65,
120, 298n17
Federal Election Commission (FEC), 91,
128–29, 212
*Federal Election Commission v. Wisconsin
Right to Life* (2007), 113
Feingold, Russ, 136
Financial products, oversight of, 25
First Amendment: applied to competition, 123; *Austin* and, 96–97, 99–100;
Bellotti and, 70; *Bennett* and *Davis*
and, 115–24; *Buckley* and, 36–38,
45–48, 51, 62; and campaign finance,
13, 14, 22; church-state separation
in, 259; corporations as object of, 11,
21, 130, 276–77; and effective speech,
57–58, 74, 117–19, 122–26, 136–38;
and interchange of ideas, 268; interpretation of, 144–48, 183; market
view of, 54, 115–26, 130–32; political context of, 260; Roberts Court
and, 137, 145, 173–74, 273; Supreme
Court's interpretation of, 147–48,
278. *See also* Freedom of speech
First National Bank of Boston v. Bellotti
(1978), 65, 67–73, 78–88, 90–91, 93,
94, 96–100, 126, 130, 136, 162, 169,
173, 177, 268, 272, 275, 276
Fish, Stanley, 181–82
Fiss, Owen, 31, 42, 168–69, 171
Foley, Edward, 175
Foreign governments/nationals, political
involvement of, 69–70
Fourteenth Amendment, 47, 55, 99

Fox, Justin, 33
Framers of the Constitution, 141–48, 261, 281
Frankfurter, Felix, 103–6
Freedom: capitalism and, 243; and equality, 46–49, 59–60, 175; free market ideology and, 75, 241
Freedom of speech: abridgement of, 47, 68, 115, 129, 146; for corporations, 21, 26, 65, 67–73, 81, 90–91, 149, 174, 177; Framers and, 141–48; historical conditions for, 143–44; interchange of ideas as issue in, 45–48, 54, 68, 73, 79–81, 99–100, 119–20, 130–32, 138–39, 151, 174, 181, 268; market ideology applied to, 59, 142; meaning of, 145–46; as negative right, 48; rights-based rationale for, 71; rights in conflict with, 147; and speaker's sovereignty, 116; spending money as form of, 10–11, 18, 26, 36–38, 41–42, 45–48, 63, 65, 268–70; state interests and, 38, 68–70, 95, 97, 99–102, 134. See also First Amendment
Freeholders, 226–27
Freeman, Richard, 248
Free market ideology: *Buckley* and, 63–64; capitalism harmed and endangered by, 240–57; equality understood through, 45–50; and financial crisis of 2008, 30–31; and ideal vs. real economies, 58–59; political applications of, 31, 93, 122–26, 134–40, 183, 260, 287; public opinion on, 237; simplistic, 72; speech understood through, 68; utilitarian justification of, 70. See also Economic theory
Free rider problems, 255, 257
Frickey, Phillip, 163
Friedman, Milton, 33–34, 63, 240
Friess, Foster, 27, 219
Fukuyama, Francis, 247
Fundraising: electability of candidates premised on, 210; escalations in, 109–10; lawmakers' representative function impeded by, 111–12; misuses of office in, 109; and political influence, 60–61, 108; pressures of, 109–12, 200–203, 222–23, 266, 270; private vs. public events, 4; strategies in, 4; time devoted to, 199–200, 221, 270

Galbraith, John Kenneth, 61, 75–76, 86–88, 244–45
General Motors (GM), 206
Gingrich, Newt, 1–2, 193, 219

Ginsburg, Ruth Bader, 224, 269–73
Good, conception of, 182–84
Gore, Al, 3
Government interests. *See* State interests
Government intervention: capitalism aided by, 250–54, 257; as censorship, 128–30, 134; Cold-War suspicions of, 157; corporate benefits conferred by, 82, 97–98, 101–2, 133–34, 234, 244–49, 276; and countervailing power, 88; in the economy, 30–31, 33–34, 52, 54, 56, 69, 249–51; in individual freedoms, 48; money in politics as check on, 232–36; opposition to, 48, 54–55, 62, 68–69, 120, 132, 157–58, 232–36, 241, 243–51, 256; and politics as a market, 215–18, 256; purpose of, 255
Government offices, in political markets, 197–202
Graduated income tax, 67–68
Great Depression, 33
Greenfield, Kent, 14–17, 293n70
Greenspan, Alan, 30–31, 243

Habermas, Jürgen, 167
Hardin, Garrett, 224
Harlan, John, 103
Hasen, Richard, 31, 199
Health care reform, 25
Heilbroner, Robert, 248, 253, 258, 286–87
Held, David, 162
Herman, Edward, 165
Hillary: The Movie (documentary), 127–28
Hobbes, Thomas, 229
Holmes, Oliver Wendell, 54, 61, 148, 150–52
Hughes, Charles Evans, 151
Human nature, 82, 84, 157, 168, 221
Hurst, James, 179

Inaugurations, 5
Income tax, graduated, 67–68
Inequality: democratic, 264; economic, 42, 86; political, 27, 42–50, 57, 73–74, 86, 102, 162–64, 285–86; in wealth, 27, 42–44, 228. *See also* Equality
Informative speech, corporate political speech portrayed as, 36, 41, 71, 134, 173, 178–79
Insider trading, 198–99
Interest-group liberalism, 154, 157, 159
Interest-group pluralism, 154, 159–64, 166, 178

Interest groups and lobbyists: for competitive economic advantages, 245–47; dependency of lawmakers and candidates on, 219–21, 223, 271; economic emphasis of, 163, 247; emergence of, 243–44; former lawmakers as, 199, 206; fundraising pressure on, 109–10; gifts from, 147, 204–5; indirect action of, 213; influence of, 58, 91, 107–11, 205–8, 221; in mid-twentieth century, 159; political benefits of, 27; political expenditures of, 109; politicians' manipulation of, 109, 223. *See also* Interest-group liberalism; Interest-group pluralism; Wealthy donors
Invisible hand theory: applied to democracy, 263–66; in economics, 52, 241–42, 253, 256–57
Issacharoff, Samuel, 29, 161
Issue ads, 113

Jackson, Robert, 144, 148
Jefferson, Thomas, 7, 63, 259
Jefferson, William, 1
Jessup, Bob, 235, 248–49
Johnson, Lyndon, 219
Judicial restraint, 105, 128
Judicial review, xi, 9, 150, 289*n*3(Preface). *See also* U.S. Supreme Court: Constitution interpreted by
Judiciary branch, xi, 289*n*3(Preface). *See also* U.S. Supreme Court
Jurisprudence. *See* Law and jurisprudence
Justice, democracy in relation to, 180–84

Kagan, Elena, 11, 116, 119, 138, 140, 278
Katz, Lawrence, 247
Kennedy, Anthony, 10–11, 91, 114, 126–27, 128, 130, 135, 207–8, 221–22, 268, 276
Kerry, John, 3
Keynes, John Maynard, 33, 139–40
Koch brothers, 2, 27
Koch Industries, 205
Krugman, Paul, 33, 139–40

Labor Management Relations Act (1947), 127
Labor restrictions, 55–56, 84–85
Laissez-faire democracy, 52–57, 118–24, 137, 237–38
Landes, William, 58, 163
Law and jurisprudence: caution in interpretation and exercise of, 148; in political market, 216; politics in, 150; role of interpretation in, 148–50

Lawmakers and candidates: attributes of, 121–22, 195–96; campaign strategies of, 4; conduct of government by, 142, 266–67; contributions to, 2; donations refused by, 222; electability of, 210; and government office, 197–202; improper fundraising behavior by, 3, 109, 223; insecurity of, 3, 219–20; as lobbyists, 199, 206; net worth of, 199; pressures on decision-making of, 219–21, 271; and public policy, 202–8; special interests influencing, 107–9; superPACs' relations with, 201–2; wealth as necessity for, 200, 210, 266–67. *See also* Fundraising
Legal realism, 150
Legislative capture, 107–9, 161
Lekachman, Robert, 49, 51–52, 245–46
Lessig, Lawrence, 19, 219, 245–46
Liberal democracy, 153, 257–67
Liberalism. *See* Deontological liberalism
Libertarianism, 175
Limits, monetary. *See* Contribution limits; Expenditures, political: limits on
Lincoln, Abraham, 8
Lindblom, Charles, 29–30, 78, 234–35
Lippmann, Walter, 156–57, 164–65, 210
Listeners' rights, 169, 173, 177, 178
Lobbyists. *See* Interest groups and lobbyists
Lochner v. New York (1905), 55–56, 84–85, 152
Lowi, Theodore, 158, 159, 286

Macpherson, C. B., 153–54, 158, 215
Madison, James, 21, 160, 260–61
Market: central principle of, 240; convictions signaled in, 79–81; democracy as, 50–64; efficiency of, 33, 35; faith/trust in, 33–34, 63–64; historical conditions of, 61–62, 142, 152; perfect vs. imperfect, 139–40, 212; political role of, 25–26, 28–31, 138–40, 187–88; principles of, applied in other fields, 25–26, 35, 45–63, 72–73, 89, 93, 122–26, 134–40, 152–53, 183, 237–39, 259–60; rights in, 241; shortcomings and drawbacks of, 58–59; societal benefits of, 230–31. *See also* Capitalism; Free market ideology; Money in politics; Politics as a market
Marketplace of ideas, 79–81, 100, 139, 151, 174, 181. *See also* Freedom of speech: interchange of ideas as issue in
Marshall, Thurgood, 43, 79, 94, 96–101, 119, 140, 150, 273

Marx, Karl, 192–93
Marxism, 163–64, 248, 249
Massachusetts, 67–68, 71, 73, 83
Matching funds, 113–24, 129, 146, 151–52
McCain, John, 3
McCain-Feingold Act (2002), 106, 110, 114, 116, 124, 127, 128
McCarthy, Eugene, 219
McConnell, Mitch, 106
McConnell v. Federal Election Commission (2003), 106–13, 124–28, 135, 137, 149, 153, 162–63, 173, 180, 190, 222, 268, 274, 275
McCutcheon v. FEC (2013), 12
Media: access to, 37, 81; influence of, on money in politics, 42, 57–58, 91, 302*n*109; market entry requirements of, 74
Meiklejohn, Alexander, 177
Mercantilism, 68–69, 240, 247–48, 257–58
Michelman, Frank, 170
Michigan Campaign Finance Act (1976), 95–96, 101, 180
Michigan Chamber of Commerce, 96
Microsoft, 137
Miliband, Ralph, 162
Milk Producers' Association, 34
Mill, John Stuart, 39, 153, 168
Millionaires' Amendment, 114, 115
Mills, C. Wright, 229
Minnesota Citizens Concerned for Life v. Swanson (8th Cir. 2012), 293*n*65
Money in politics: advocates of, 175–78; in campaigns and elections, 210; as check on government, 232–36; conflicts over, 28; as constitutional issue, 22–28, 35, 145, 280–81; corporate role in, 14–17; impact of, ix, 1–9, 26–27; media's effect on, 42, 57–58, 302*n*109; proposed solutions concerning, 11–23; pros and cons of, 27; Supreme Court on, 9–14, 20, 22–23, 29, 31–32, 35–64, 92–93, 237–38. *See also entries beginning with* Campaign finance; Expenditures, political; Market: political role of; Politics as a market; Wealthy donors
Monopoly, 137, 248–49
Montesquieu, Charles-Louis de Secondat, Baron de La Brède et de, 227
Moonves, Les, 213
Move to Amend, 21–22

Nader, Ralph, 77–78
Natural order, 118–19, 121, 155

Neoclassical economic theory, 33, 47, 50, 56
Neo-Keynesianism, 123, 140, 277
Neoliberalism, 140
Neo-pluralism, 162
New York Times (newspaper), 204
Nixon, Richard, 34, 65–67
Noble, Lawrence, 91
NRWC. See FEC v. National Right to Work Committee (NRWC, 1982)

Obama, Barack: campaign finance of, 3, 4, 222; criticisms of, 25; donations to inauguration of, 5, 205; Supreme Court criticized by, 90–92
O'Connor, Sandra Day, 93, 94, 106
Oligopoly, 75–76, 81, 88, 137
Olson, Mancur, 161, 308*n*91
Orwell, George, 133, 135
Overton, Spencer, 60

Pelosi, Nancy, 200
Pfizer, 2
Pildes, Richard, 29, 161
Pliny, 226
Pluralism. *See* Interest-group pluralism; Neo-pluralism
Pluralist elitist equilibrium model, 154
Plutocracy, 189, 260–64, 268, 279, 281, 287
Political action committees (PACs): of corporations, 127, 129–31, 182; influence of, 147, 201, 271; personnel of, 201; undue influence of, 131. *See also* SuperPACs
Political participation: citizens', 44, 46–47, 73–74, 87–88, 102, 109, 162–63, 172, 190, 230; by corporations, 76, 132, 177; spending money as form of, 175–77
Political parties, and campaign spending, ix, 2, 4–6, 10–13, 18–20, 35, 57, 62, 67, 103–104, 106–109, 114, 187, 210, 272
Political power: of corporations, xi, 7, 21–22, 65–89, 92, 131; economic power as means to, 8–10, 23–24, 31, 38, 42, 83, 87, 160–61, 187, 191, 247–48, 261–63, 265–66, 284; inequalities in, 27, 42–50, 57, 73–74, 102, 162–64, 285–86; interest groups and, 159; wealth as necessity for, ix, x, 2–3, 5–6, 22, 38, 42–46, 59–60, 91–92, 103–5
Political talents, 176–77, 179, 261–65
Politics: advertising principles employed in, 58, 165, 302*n*113; constitutional interpretation and, 29; economic

sphere in relation to, 98–99, 102–3, 105, 189–90, 244–45, 247–48, 258–59, 264–65, 267–79; in judicial decisions, 150; the market's role in, 25–26, 28–31, 138–40, 187–88; religion in relation to, 259–60, 282–83. *See also* Money in politics; Political power; Politics as a market; U.S. political system

Politics as a market, 57–62, 191–218, 263; capitalists and consumers in, 193; commodification in, 196–97; critique of, 284; dominance of money in, 195–96; effects of, 219–25; forms of, 214–15; function of elites in, 231; goods and services in, 194–95, 217–18, 285; government held in check by, 232–36, 256; government offices in, 197–202; justifications of, 225–36; legal construction of, 197; legal portion of, 213; as a meta market, 215–18; private control of means of decision in, 216–18; public policy in, 202–8; Rand's criticism of, 244; regulation of, 211–15; supply and demand in, 202–3; voting in, 208–11. *See also* Money in politics

Polyarchy, 161

Poor, bias against, 227–29

Popular sovereignty, 105–12, 278

Posner, Richard, 53, 58, 163–64, 172–73, 178

Potter, Trevor, 19

Powell, H. Jefferson, 29, 151

Powell, Lewis, 65–73, 76–78, 90–91, 96, 126, 130, 173, 276

Power. *See* Economic power; Political power

Preferences, 154–60, 165, 172, 243

Presidential Funding Act, 19

Price system, 33–34, 252–53

Privatization, economic and industrial, 233–35

Profit maximization, 80–81, 178–79

Property, 38–39, 269

Protectionism, 249

Prudential Financial, 5

Public, the. *See* Citizens

Public campaign financing, 20, 62, 113–14

Public choice theory, 154–68, 176

Public Citizen, 21

Public good. *See* Common good

Public goods, 255–56

Public matching funds, 19–20

Public policy, in political markets, 202–8, 220

Pull peddlers, 243, 251, 254

Quid pro quo corruption, 40, 57

Radin, Margaret Jane, 55–56, 161, 260

Rand, Ayn, 216, 232–33, 241, 243–44, 251

Randall v. Sorrell (2006), 112, 168, 270

Rational choice theory, 154

Rationality, of political and economic actors, 155–56

Rawls, John, 43–44, 55, 170, 190, 282

Reagan, Ronald, 1

Redish, Martin, 175, 177–79, 185, 232, 260

Reed, Stanley, 103

Rehnquist, William, 10, 65, 82–87, 93–94, 98–100, 103, 119, 140, 268, 271, 276, 279

Rehnquist Court: on money in politics, 92, 94–103, 106–13, 136, 149; and popular sovereignty, 106–12; progressive evolution of, 94–103, 106–13, 136; on undue influence, 94–103, 150, 160, 162–63, 278–79

Religion, politics in relation to, 259–60, 282–83

Representative democracy, 209

Represent Us, 19

Republicanism, 167–74, 179, 185

Republican Party: and campaign finance, 12, 18, 92; disclosure requirements opposed by, 204; and funding of 2012 presidential primaries, 120

Revolving door, 199, 324n20

Reynolds American, 2

Ribstein, Larry, 14

Rights: deontology and, 180–82; economic, 233; in the free market, 241; fundamental nature of, 180; negative vs. positive, 48

Roberts, John, 10–11, 90, 93, 112, 114, 116–17, 128, 130, 150, 181, 186, 268

Roberts Court: and *Buckley*, 35; Burger Court in relation to, 94, 136; on campaign finance law, 270; conservatism of, 10–11, 93, 233; Constitution interpreted by, 255–56; critical trends ignored by, 160–67; distrust shown toward the government by, 157; and the First Amendment, 137, 145, 173–74, 273; jurisprudence of, 149; market principles underlying decisions of, 112–40, 154, 159–60, 187, 237–38; minority views on, 138; Obama's criticism of, 90; on politics-economics

relationship, 189–90; principles favored by, rather than evidence, 117, 128–29, 132, 147, 148–49, 181, 184–85; republicanism anathema to, 167–71; separatism anathema to, 268; on undue influence, 278–79
Roemer, Tim, 200
Romney, Mitt, 4, 204, 219
Roosevelt, Franklin, 233
Rose-Ackerman, Susan, 219
Ros-Lehtinen, Ileana, 204
Rousseau, Jean-Jacques, 84
Rove, Karl, 5, 204
Rudman, Warren, 107

Samples, John, 172–73, 175, 180, 223, 232, 262
Sandel, Michael, 181
Sanders, Bernie, 21
Santorum, Rick, 219
Scalia, Antonin, 10–11, 94, 114, 128, 130, 137–38, 157, 173–74, 180, 183, 186, 221, 268
Schauer, Frederick, 152
Schumpeter, Joseph, 38, 58, 72, 156, 164–65
Seavoy, Ronald, 179
Securities and Exchange Commission, 15
Self-interest, 52, 70, 84, 155–57, 165, 240–41, 253
Self-realization: corporations as vehicles for, 177–78; democracy as vehicle for, 81–82, 84, 307n82
Sensenbrenner, F. James, Jr., 204
Separation of powers, 260–61, 281–82
Separation of spheres: American tradition of, 281; citizen confidence dependent on, 274–75; citizen-corporation distinction and, 276; democratic integrity and, 270–74; money-speech distinction and, 268–70; as principle of liberal democracy, 257–67; principles underlying, 267–79
Shareholder Protection Act, 15
Shelley, Mary, 84
Shiller, Robert, 89
Siebecker, Michael, 16, 293n70
Simon, Paul, 42
Simpson, Alan, 108
Smith, Adam, 8, 34, 52, 68–69, 75, 158, 160, 167, 178, 240–42, 247; The Wealth of Nations, 8, 24
Smith, Bradley, 48, 173, 175–77, 196, 200, 261–63, 336n110
Societal interests. See State interests
Soft money, 106–9

Soros, George, 27
Sotomayor, Sonia, 11
Sound bites, 131, 174
Souter, David, 11, 224, 270–72, 275
Special interests. See Interest groups and lobbyists
Speech: as commodity, 59; effective, 57–58, 74, 117–19, 122–26, 136–38, 178; free market view of, 68; historical conditions for, 143–44; monetary influence on, 210–11; nature of, 142; social purpose of, 143. See also Freedom of speech
SpeechNow.org v. FEC (D.C. Court of Appeals, 2010), 91–92
Stakeholders, in corporations, 15–16
State interests: corruption and, 138; in democratic integrity, 270–74; freedom of speech and, 38, 68–70, 95, 97, 99–102, 134, 149–50; used in court tests, 149–50
State monopoly capitalism, 248–49
Stevens, John Paul, 11, 15, 106, 121, 129, 139, 140, 224, 268–73, 275–78, 310n15
Stewart, Potter, 38
Stiglitz, Joseph, 228–30
Story, Joseph, 146–47
Subsidies, for campaigns, 114–24
Sunstein, Cass, 31, 56, 144, 255, 277
SuperPACs: advertising by, 201–2; contributions of, 4–5, 13; disclosure rules governing, 5, 18, 204; emergence of, 92; influence of, 201–2, 222
Supreme Court. See U.S. Supreme Court
Supreme Court of Canada, 46

Taxation, 67–68
Thomas, Clarence, 10–11, 94, 114, 128, 130, 138, 186, 268
Tillman Act (1907), 127
Time-protection rationale, 111–13
Tocqueville, Alexis de, 43
Tragedy of the commons, 224
Tribe, Lawrence, 259
Trigger mechanisms, 113–24
Tucker, Anne, 14, 293n69
Twenty-Fourth Amendment, 285
Twenty-Sixth Amendment, 285
Twenty-Third Amendment, 285
Two-party system, 53
Tyranny, 261

Undue influence, 73, 95–106, 131, 136, 150, 160, 162–63, 274, 275, 278
Union expenditures, 103–6

United States v. Danielczyk (4th Cir. 2012), 293*n*65
United States v. UAW-CIO (*Auto Workers,* 1957), 103–7, 127, 274
U.S. Chamber of Commerce, 5, 65–66, 77, 204, 206
U.S. Congress: campaign regulations instituted by, 9, 19, 56; foreign political contributions prohibited by, 69–70; insider trading banned by, 198–99; and money in politics, 145; Supreme Court deferral to, 95; Supreme Court opposed to, 14, 35, 39, 45, 53–54, 56, 65, 89, 121–22
U.S. Constitution, 23–28; ambiguity in, 151; amendments to, 21, 280–81; campaign regulations instituted by, 39; democratic corruption embodied in, xi; foundational status of, 289*n*2(Preface); interpretation of, 144–48; market view of, 255; and money in politics, 22–28, 35, 145, 280–81; reform of, 20–23; Roberts Court's interpretation of, 255–56; Supreme Court's interpretation of, xi, 23, 29, 47, 148–52. *See also* Framers of the Constitution, and freedom of speech
U.S. political system: corruption of, by wealth, 7–9; design of, 23–28, 267; dual nature of, 28; origins of, 23–24, 28; proposed solutions to problems in, 11–23; two-party, 53
U.S. Supreme Court: beneficiaries of decisions by, 148; Congress opposed by, 14, 35, 39, 45, 53–54, 56, 65, 89, 121–22; Constitution interpreted by, xi, 23, 29, 47, 148–52, 255–56; on corporations, 17; deferral to Congress by, 95; democratic theory underlying decisions and opinions by, 23, 39, 134, 141; and disclosure rules, 18; on expenditure limits, 128; First Amendment interpreted by, 147–48, 278; ideologies and theories of, 31, 150–52, 166, 181, 184–88, 225–26, 279, 281, 286–88; jurisprudence of, 148–49; on the market, 34; on money in politics, 9–14, 20, 22–23, 29, 31–32, 35–64, 92–93, 237–38; power of, 29; societal/political role of, 150;

written opinions of, 31. *See also individual cases*
Utilitarianism, 168
Utility maximization, 155

Vanderbilt, Cornelius, 243
Vermont, 112
Voting: as consumption, 211; fear of universal and private, 231; impact of, 210; in political markets, 208–11; psychology of, 209; restrictions on, 209–10

Walzer, Michael, 42, 55–56, 87, 187–88, 215, 259, 261–63
Warren Court, 101
Washington, George, 7, 21
Watergate scandal, 34, 65–66
Wealth: accounting for distribution of, 184; aggregations of, 8, 94–95, 100–101, 103–5, 107, 160; corruption grounded in, 8, 9, 101, 103; and equality, 262–63; inequalities in, 27, 42–44, 228; as measure of accomplishment, 229; as part of natural order, 118–19, 121, 155; as threat to democratic integrity, 103–5; virtues attendant on, 226–31. *See also* Economic power
Wealthy donors: administrative posts secured by, 5; attitudes toward, 27–28; campaign roles of, 203–4; characteristics of, 60, 200, 303*n*117, 336*n*110; dependency of lawmakers and candidates on, 219–21, 223, 271; desires and demands of, 205–8; gifts from, 204–5; identities of, 5, 204; influence of, ix, 1–9, 22, 45–46, 59–60, 92, 103–5, 200, 221, 247, 263; insecurity of, 3; limits on expenditures of, 98; as percentage of population, 6, 60; politicians' manipulation of, 3, 109, 223; virtues of, 226–31. *See also* Interest groups and lobbyists; Money in politics
White, Byron, 62–63, 79–87, 97–100, 103, 111, 119, 131, 137, 140, 150, 268–69, 271–72, 275–76, 279
Whitman, Walt, 81
Wilkes, Brent, 1
Williamson, Chilton, 226–27
Winkler, Adam, 15